Claude Debussy and the Poets

Claude Debussy and the Poets

ARTHUR B. WENK

UNIVERSITY OF CALIFORNIA PRESS
Berkeley / Los Angeles / London

University of California Press
Berkeley and Los Angeles, California

University of California Press, Ltd.
London, England

ISBN 0–520–02827–9
Library of Congress Catalog Card Number: 74–82854

Printed in the United States of America
Designed by Jim Mennick

For E. M. and W. A.

Contents

Preface

The musician writing about poetry, perhaps even more than the poet writing about music, faces a problem in deciding just what his audience shall be. Many of his insights will seem naive to those with more literary experience, while the musical generalizations which could be of real use to literary people may seem so familiar that the musician overlooks them. This book is addressed to that ideal creature, the intelligent common reader. My goal has been, in the words of Donald Grout, to write about the subject in a way capable of enlisting the interest of any educated person. The subject, admittedly, is not an easy one. Writing about poetry in a foreign language, like writing about music in any verbal language, puts one several steps away from the object of study. An essay written in English about the interrelationships between music and French poetry makes considerable demands of the reader.

In the interest of clarity I have endeavored to explain basic principles in musical and literary analysis as I go along, and beg the indulgence of scholars in either field to whom such material may seem abecedarian. At the same time I have not avoided technical discussion when the occasion demands it, and hope that the flow of the narrative will permit anyone who wishes, to skip lightly over the analyses.

Translations of the poems may be found in Appendix D. I am indebted to Edward Morris for translations of Verlaine, Baudelaire, and

Mallarmé's *Soupir* and *Placet futile*, and to Robert Greer Cohn for Mallarmé's *Eventail* and *L'Après-midi d'un faune.* I have not attempted to translate Debussy's witty prose, but have summarized the sense of a passage as it occurs. I should like to thank Edward Morris for the patience with which he guided my efforts in writing the original dissertation and for his encouragement in making it into a book; I also wish to thank William Austin for his tireless efforts to extend my breadth of vision. Thanks are also due to Robert Greer Cohn and Charles C. Cushing for their kind suggestions for revising this manuscript. Finally I should like to thank Bruce Archibald for continually guiding me toward greater rigor in analysis.

1

INTRODUCTION

Paul Dukas wrote about Debussy: "La plus forte influence qu'ait subie Debussy est celle des littérateurs. Non pas celle des musiciens." [1] As far back as Debussy's early years at the Conservatoire in the 1870s he was discontented with music as it was then being taught, and preferred the company of literary men to that of musicians. Dukas writes: "Dès le début de sa vie d'artiste, il s'était ardemment mêlé au mouvement littéraire d'alors." [2]

In the early 1880s Debussy accompanied singers at the newly opened cabaret *Le Chat Noir,* which became a favorite gathering place for different literary personalities. Here Debussy met, among others,[3] Maurice Vaucaire, for whose adaptation of *As You Like It* Debussy agreed to write music; the playwright Maurice Donnay, who described an

[1] Robert Brussel, "Claude Debussy et Paul Dukas," *Revue Musicale* 7 (1926):101.

[2] *Ibid.*

[3] Alphonse Allais, the writer; Raoul Ponchon, the humorist; Edmond Haraucourt, author of the scandalous *Poèmes hystériques*, later one of the Parnassians; Maurice Rollinat, one of the founders of *Le Chat Noir*, whom Lockspeiser describes as "a sort of local Heine" (*Debussy: His Life and Mind* [New York: Macmillan, 1962], vol. 1, p. 144); and Marie Krysinska, the Polish poetess and song writer, one of the originators of *vers libre.*

occasion at *Le Chat Noir* with "the joyous Debussy conducting our wild chorus throughout the evening";[4] Adolphe Willette, who illustrated the first edition of Debussy's *Mandoline*; Charles Cros, inventor and poet, whose *L'Archet* Debussy tried to set to music; and Paul Bourget, literary critic, novelist, and author of *Les Aveux*, a collection of poems of which Debussy set seven to music.

From this circle Debussy was introduced to Comte Robert de Montesquieu, a wealthy poet and patron whom Debussy later approached for a private performance of *Pelléas et Mélisande*; Gabriel Vicaire, the satirical poet; Jules Bois, for whose play *Les Noces de Sathan* Debussy was commissioned to compose incidental music; and Gabriel Mourey, poet, playwright, critic, with whom Debussy planned several operas including *La Légende de Tristan* and *L'Embarquement pour ailleurs.*

During his "exile" from Paris in 1885 to 1887, as winner of the *Prix de Rome* Debussy was sent works of Verlaine, Shelley, Moréas, Vignier, Huysmans, Morice, and Henry Becque. He also read Shakespeare, Baudelaire, Laforgue, and Goncourt, and the literary journals—*La Revue Indépendante*, *La Vogue*, *La Vie Moderne*, and *La Nouvelle Revue.* He found his fellow musicians an uninspiring lot, and accomplished little of musical importance himself, although his long struggle to write a cantata on a text of Banville brought him face to face with critical questions of aesthetics.

Returning to Paris in 1887 Debussy found an atmosphere of literary ferment, as Dukas recounts:

> Verlaine, Mallarmé, Laforgue nous apportaient des tons nouveaux, des sonorités nouvelles. Ils projetaient sur les mots des lueurs qu'on n'avait encore jamais vues; ils usaient de procédés inconnus des poètes leurs devanciers; ils faisaient rendre à la matière verbale des effets dont on ne soupçonnait pas, avant eux, la subtilité ou la force; par-dessus tout, ils concevaient les vers ou la prose comme des musiciens; ils leur connaient des soins de musiciens et, comme des musiciens encore, combinaient les images et leur correspondance encore.[5]

It was a period during which artists in all fields were reaching out in new directions, seeking guidance from the other arts.

[4] Quoted by Lockspeiser, *Debussy*, p. 145.

[5] Dukas, quoted in Brussel, "Claude Debussy," p. 101.

> Impressionnisme, symbolisme, réalisme poétique se confondaient dans un grand concours d'enthousiasme, de curiosité, de passion intellectuelle. Tous, peintres, poètes, sculpteurs décomposaient la matière, se penchaient vers elle, l'interrogeaient, la déformaient, la reformaient à leur gré, appliqués à faire rendre aux mots, aux sons, aux couleurs, au dessin, des nuances, des sentiments nouveaux.[6]

Assuredly this was a time of musical flowering as well, with works of Franck, Saint-Saëns, Fauré, and d'Indy making their appearance. "Mais ce mouvement musical, si important qu'il ait été dans ses conséquences, demeura, je le crois, sans effet sur le développement de Debussy." [7] While the musicians sought to recover the spirit and style of the great symphonic works that formed the summit of music, Debussy pursued a different line, based on his conception of music and word.

> Je conçois une force dramatique autre: la musique qui commence là où la parole est impuissante à exprimer; la musique est faite pour l'inexprimable; je voudrais qu'elle eût l'air de sortir de l'ombre et que, par instants, elle y rentrât; que toujours elle fût discrète personne.[8]

Debussy became involved in a number of literary circles. At the *Librairie de l'Art Indépendant* he encountered Villiers de l'Isle-Adam, author of the play *Axël*, for which Debussy composed incidental music in 1889; Henri de Régnier, the poet whose *Scènes au crépuscule* inspired Debussy's *Nocturnes* and influenced his *Proses Lyriques*; and Maurice Denis, the artist and critic who illustrated *La Damoiselle élue.* Also frequenting the *Librairie* at this time were Pierre Louÿs, Paul Verlaine, Stéphane Mallarmé, and André Gide.

At the *Taverne Weber* Debussy met his close friends Pierre Louÿs, the novelist Jean de Tinan, Paul-Jean Toulet, who later planned a collaboration with Debussy on *As You Like It*, and René Peter, who undertook a number of projects with Debussy including three comedies, and for whose play *Tragédie de la mort* Debussy composed a *Berceuse.* These friends in turn introduced Debussy to the pamphleteer Léon Daudet; the journalist André Tardieu; Henri Gauthier-Villars, the witty music critic and first husband of Colette; and Marcel Proust.

[6] *Ibid.,* p. 102. [7] *Ibid.,* p. 103.

[8] Quoted by Pasteur Valléry-Radot in *Lettres de Claude Debussy à sa femme Emma* (Paris: Flammarion, 1957), p. 44.

Perhaps the richest opportunities for literary acquaintanceship came at the *mardis chez Mallarmé,* where one might meet Catulle Mendès, poet, journalist, and librettist who collaborated unsuccessfully with Debussy on an opera, *Rodrigue et Chimène*; Jules Laforgue, whose poetry Debussy admired and quoted; Jean Moréas, with whom Debussy discussed Schopenhauer and Goethe; Francis Vielé-Griffin, who published two of Debussy's poems; Paul Valéry, whose Monsieur Teste became the model for Debussy's Monsieur Croche; and Charles Morice, who attempted a collaboration with Debussy based on poems of Verlaine.[9]

When Debussy entered the Conservatoire at the age of ten he had not attended a day of school. Although his mother had tutored him at home during his early years, in subjects outside of music he was largely self-taught. The importance of his literary associations, therefore, can scarcely be overestimated. The influence on his choice of musical genres is evident. The catalogue of Debussy's works shows a paucity of traditional forms—symphonies, sonatas, concertos, chamber music—and a predominance of works with text: songs, cantatas, choruses, and dramatic works.[10] This preponderance of works with text becomes even more notable when we include works which Debussy left unfinished, most of them collaborations intended for the stage.

The influence of the poets can also be observed in the large number of pieces with descriptive titles. Some are names of poems—*La Fille aux cheveux de lin* (Leconte de Lisle) and *Clair de lune* (Verlaine)—or lines from poems—"Les sons et les parfums tournent dans l'air du soir" (Baudelaire). Many others sound like names of poems—*La Cathédrale engloutie*; *Reflets dans l'eau*—or lines from poems—*Et la lune descend sur le temple qui fut.*

[9] Also to be found here were Octave Mirbeau, the proponent of Maeterlinck; Emile Verhaeren, the Belgian Symbolist and *vers libre* poet; José-Marie de Hérédia, one of the first of the Parnassians; Edouard Dujardin, editor of *La Revue Wagnérienne*; Théodore de Wyzewa, essayist and critic; Gustave Kahn, Symbolist poet and essayist; René Ghil, author of the *Traité du Verbe,* which attempted to associate phonetic sounds with colors; Arthur Symons, the English authority on Symbolist literature; Georges Rodenbach, the Belgian Symbolist poet; Marcel Schwob, essayist and critic; Joris Karl Huysmans, the art critic; Félix Fénéon, the avant-garde critic; Maurice Maeterlinck; Oscar Wilde; and Paul Claudel.

[10] See Appendix A.

Other titles contain literary references: *La Danse de Puck* (William Shakespeare); *Hommage à S. Pickwick, Esq., P.P.M.P.C.* (Charles Dickens); *Les Fées sont d'exquises danseuses* (James Matthew Barrie); *Ondine* (La Motte-Fouqué).[11] So deeply engrained did literary habits become that Debussy changed the title of one of his piano pieces to *Et la lune descend sur le temple qui fut*, explaining to his publisher, "J'ai un peu modifié le titre de la 2e *Image*, ce qui nous donne un alexandrin sans défaut (Vive Alexandre I!)." [12]

Not surprisingly, Debussy did a substantial amount of writing on his own. His song cycle *Proses Lyriques* (1892–1893) reflects the influence of the different literary movements with which he was involved at the time. Debussy started, but never completed, another cycle on his own texts, *Nuits blanches.* He also wrote the text for one of his last works, the *Noël des enfants qui n'ont plus de maison*, composed at the end of 1915. Although his notion of starting a literary journal came to naught, beginning in 1901 Debussy wrote regularly for *La Revue Blanche*, and served as critic for *Gil Blas* and *La Revue S.I.M.* Other articles appeared in the *Mercure de France*, *Musica*, *La Plume*, *Le Figaro*, *Le Matin*, *Les Annales Politiques et Littéraires*, and *L'Intransigeant.* Many of these articles were gathered into his book, *Monsieur Croche Antidilettante.*

Debussy's correspondence is full of literary allusions and parodistic references to poetry that he set to music. His letters to Pierre Louÿs, in particular, contain frequent bits of doggerel in the form of dedications or simply as pleasantries. Debussy often employed a kind of literary detachment to alleviate the burdens of his personal life, and could appreciate the melodramatic aspects of his confrontation with Gaby when she discovered a compromising letter in his pocket. He writes to Pierre Louÿs in February 1897:

> Là-dessus! . . . drame . . . pleurs . . . vrai revolver et le *Petit Journal* comme historien . . . Ah! mon vieux loup, j'aurais eu besoin que tu sois là pour m'aider à me reconnaître dans cette mauvaise littérature.[13]

[11] Paul Hooreman, "Les fées sont d'exquises danseuses," Special Issue, *Revue de Musicologie* (1962):104–107.

[12] *Lettres de Claude Debussy à son éditeur* (Paris: A. Durand et fils, 1927), p. 46.

[13] *Correspondance de Claude Debussy et Pierre Louÿs*, ed. Henri Borgeaud (Paris, Librairie José Corti, 1945), p. 87.

It is enough to know Debussy's habits, observe his titles, listen to his prose, to know how literary he really is. Dukas' assertion receives additional support from the literary character of French music in general. One thinks of Machaut, Jannequin, Couperin, Rameau, Rousseau, Berlioz, Boulez—composers who wrote their own texts, employed descriptive titles, or wrote extensively about music. Indeed, veneration of the word is an essential element of French culture. "Any educated Frenchman can make up a poem, just as any American can improvise a new 'popular' tune. The French language is heavy with old literature, as the American air is loaded with ta tá, ta ta tá." [14]

This general literariness of French music invites us to inquire further into the particular case of Debussy. What was the effect of these literary associations on Debussy's music? Did it go any deeper than the title page? Did the poets influence Debussy's ideas on music—what it is, what it can do? How did these ideas affect his music? While the Dukas question may seem to answer itself, it soon leads to other questions that have no definite answer at all.

It is evident from Debussy's letters that he was not content with a music which would merely complement the mood of a text, or illustrate certain of its words. Describing his difficulties in dealing with the first draft of Segalen's *Siddharta* Debussy remarks

> C'est un prodigieux rêve! Seulement dans sa forme actuelle, je ne connais pas de musique capable de pénétrer cet abîme! elle ne pourrait guère servir qu'à souligner certains gestes ou préciser certains décors. En somme, une illustration, beaucoup plus qu'une parfaite union avec le texte et l'effarante immobilité du personnage principal.[15]

The ultimately unresolvable question of the relationship between poetry and music with which Debussy struggled throughout his career challenges us to study his music from a new perspective.

We might expect that the clearest examples of literary influence on Debussy's music are to be found in the works associated with a text. To keep the subject manageable, this book will be limited to those poets

[14] Rosenberg, introducing Marcel Raymond, *From Baudelaire to Surrealism* (New York: Wittenborn, Schultz, 1950).

[15] *Segalen et Debussy*, ed. Annie Joly-Segalen and André Schaeffner (Monaco: Editions du Rocher, 1961), p. 66.

whom Debussy set to music most frequently and whose influence on him was the greatest: Banville, Baudelaire, Verlaine, Mallarmé, and Louÿs. This means excluding several poets who deserve further consideration, the most prominent of whom is Maeterlinck, who wrote the play which became Debussy's *Pelléas et Mélisande.* The association of word and music in that work is of sufficient complexity to merit a full-length investigation of its own. Other poets also invite study—François Villon, Charles d'Orléans, Gabriele d'Annunzio—but for practical reasons must be put off for the present. Still another name whose absence from these pages may seem conspicuous is that of the composer of *Parsifal* and *Tristan.* Old Klingsor, as Debussy liked to call the German music-dramatist, exerted an extraordinary influence on the French poets in addition to a musical influence which Debussy spent much of his adult life trying to escape.[16]

The poets whom we shall consider span the nineteenth century in three generations: Baudelaire and Banville, born about 1820; Mallarmé and Verlaine, born about 1843; Debussy himself, born in 1862, and his younger friend Louÿs, born in 1870. The interrelations between these men make it hazardous to talk about them separately. It would be misleading to suggest that they can be placed on a single line of development; rather, they were the most important figures in interacting literary movements.

The order of narrative in this book generally follows the order in which Debussy composed his music, from *Nuit d'étoiles* on a text of Banville, dating from Debussy's early years at the Conservatoire, to the Mallarmé songs, composed five years before Debussy's death. Into this historical warp we shall endeavor to introduce an analytical woof of rather a different pattern from previous studies of Debussy's music.

The music associated with Banville's poetry anticipates many elements of Debussy's later style and raises some of the most basic questions concerning poetry and music. The first of the chapters devoted to Verlaine illustrates techniques for relating poetry to music by comparing six poems as set to music by both Debussy and Fauré. Chapter 4 shows the substantial influence of Charles Baudelaire on Debussy's aesthetic thought and the musical devices with which he

[16] Lockspeiser, *Debussy,* discusses Wagner's influence on French poetry; Laurence Berman investigates the influence on Debussy's music in his dissertation, "The Evolution of Tonal Thinking in the Works of Claude Debussy," Harvard University, 1965.

interpreted Baudelaire's poetry. Two chapters on Verlaine continue the study of Debussy's musical language, the first considering his use of harmony, the second, his indebtedness to the author of the *Art Poétique* in forming a consistent musical aesthetic.

Building on this groundwork, the chapter on Debussy's *Prélude à l'après-midi d'un faune* deals with a musical composition which is related to a text without being a setting of that text. The chapter on Louÿs illustrates the preeminence of melody in Debussy's musical thought. A chapter on the *Proses Lyriques* examines the direct expression of literary thought which occurs when the composer acts as his own poet. A fourth chapter on Verlaine studies the development of Debussy's style over the two decades during which he set Verlaine's poetry to music. Finally, Debussy's *Trois Poèmes de Stéphane Mallarmé* offer themselves as a culmination in the development of several musical procedures which pervade Debussy's music.

In this work our discussion centers more on Debussy's music as a whole than on the evolution of his musical personality, and more on music and its connection to literature than on music as an independent art. For such a literary composer a purely musical discussion would be inadequate. This book may be regarded as one response to Dukas' dictum on the study of Debussy: "Il faut le poétiser."

2

BANVILLE:
A Prelude to Analysis

Théodore de Banville (1823–1891) was the first poet to exert a substantial influence on Debussy. Raymond Bonheur recalls seeing Debussy at the Conservatoire at the age of sixteen, carrying a book of Banville poems under his arm. Debussy sustained an active interest in Banville for nearly a decade, continuing to set his poetry to music even after he had begun to compose music on texts of Verlaine and Mallarmé. Years later, when Debussy had ceased to set Banville's poetry to music, he continued to quote the poet in conversation.[1]

Some of the music inspired by Banville is lost, much of it is unpublished, and what remains is uneven in quality. Yet we continue to be interested in the relationship between Debussy and Banville, since in many respects it foreshadows Debussy's association with later poets. Debussy's decided preference for poets with an ear to the musicality of

[1] Raymond Bonheur, "Souvenirs et impressions d'un compagnon de jeunesse," *Revue Musicale* 7 (1926):3. My principal source of information on Banville is the set of articles by Eileen-Margaret Souffrin listed in the bibliography.

their verse, his ability to express the inspiration of a poem in purely musical terms, his general lack of success in applying his genius to the theater, as well as the musical elements which appeared in his later style are all to be found here, in his association with Banville.[2]

To begin with, Banville was a rather musical poet. As a journalist he often attended concerts; he enjoyed the music of Berlioz and was personally acquainted with Gounod. He once wrote an article entitled "La Fugue" in which he defended contrapuntal technique. Banville also had an affection for popular music, for the *chansons* which became the titles for several of his poems. Banville announced his intention of writing a volume of poems called *Chansons sur des airs connus*, to be based on popular melodies. Although he later abandoned the project, Banville did write at least one poem in this genre, *Nous n'irons plus au bois*, based on the children's round.

Banville's interest in the relationship between music and poetry is evident in his *Petit traité de poésie française* of 1872: "Le vers est la parole humaine rythmée de façon à pouvoir être chantée, et, à proprement parler, il n'y a pas de poésie et de vers en dehors du Chant. Tous les vers sont destinés à être chantés et n'existent qu'à cette condition."[3] It was Banville who encouraged Verlaine and Mallarmé to "musicalize" their verse, and one can find premonitions of Mallarmé's poetic philosophy in the following passage:

> [La Poésie] est à la fois Musique, Statuaire, Peinture, Eloquence, elle doit charmer l'oreille, enchanter l'esprit, représenter les sons, imiter les couleurs, rendre les objets visibles, et exciter en nous les mouvements qu'il lui plaît d'y produire; aussi est elle le seul art complet, nécessaire, et qui contienne tous les autres, comme elle préexiste à tous les autres.[4]

The musicality of Banville's poetry can be seen in his careful use of rhythm. Banville frequently employs lines of varying lengths for a particular rhythmic effect, and continually modulates the patterns of

[2] We should not be misled by the success of the isolated masterpieces, *Pelléas et Mélisande* and *Jeux*, and the rather uneven *Le Martyre de Saint-Sebastien* and *Khamma*. Debussy's career was strewn with abandoned theater projects, as Appendix A illustrates, and his last years were consumed in a futile search for a successor to his unique opera.

[3] Théodore de Banville, *Petit Traité de Poésie Française* (Paris: G. Charpentier, 1888), p. 3.

[4] *Ibid.*, p. 9.

accented and unaccented syllables within the line. Yet all this must be accomplished without straying too far from the cadences of ordinary speech. The treatment of the mute *e* illustrates both the difference between poetry and speech and Banville's sensitivity in handling the conventions of poetry. Banville concludes the second stanza of *Aimons-nous et dormons* with the lines

Tant que tu cacheras
Ta tête entre mes bras!

In ordinary speech the mute *e* in *cacheras* and at the end of *entre* are swallowed up:

Tant qu' tu cach'ras
Ta tête entr' mes bras!

In reciting these lines, conscious of the pattern of six syllables to a line, one lengthens the mute *e* ever so slightly, and makes an imperceptible pause after *cacheras.* Within this constant pattern of six syllables Banville varies the rhythm by placing the mute *e*'s at syllable two and five in the first line, then at syllable four in the second line.

Of greater magnitude is the rhythmic change which takes place when poetry is set to music. When Debussy imposes a pattern of strictly measured time on these lines, for example, some important decisions must be made. Although a careful performer will minimize the effect, there is usually an accent on the downbeat of a musical measure. The composer has to decide on which words of text these primary accents will fall, as well as consider the position of secondary accents within the measure. He may insert a rest or a tie at the beginning of the measure to avoid the downbeat accent altogether. Debussy sets these lines in triple meter, which means that there will be a primary accent on the first beat and secondary accents on the second and third beats (Example 1). The effect of this setting on the mute *e*'s is to exaggerate the differences between poetry and ordinary speech. The mute *e* in *cacheras* sounds for just as long as the first syllable of that word. The rest at the beginning of

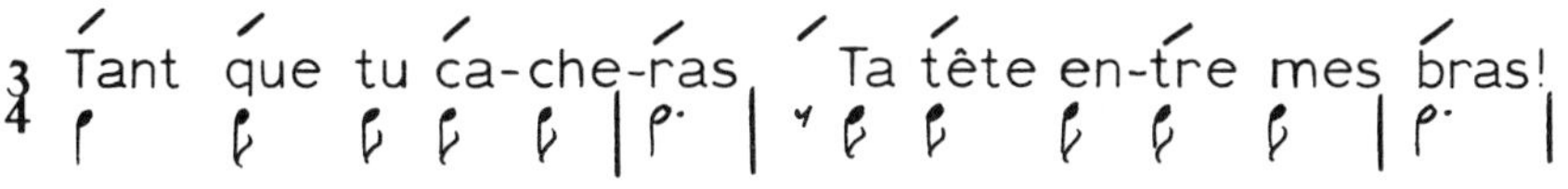

Example 1

the second line, which displaces the primary accent, gives more emphasis to the secondary accent on *tête.* The separation between the two lines is underlined by the lengthening of the last syllable of *cacheras.* Still another rhythmic alteration is introduced by the performer, who will very likely extend the value of the word *tête* just a shade and pass lightly over the second syllable of *entre.*

This ability of music to enlarge upon poetic effects can be seen again later in the poem in Debussy's setting of "Alors, comme deux fleurs/ Joignons nos lèvres amoureuses" (Example 2). The word *Alors* is set off from the rest of the text by a comma, which would be translated into a

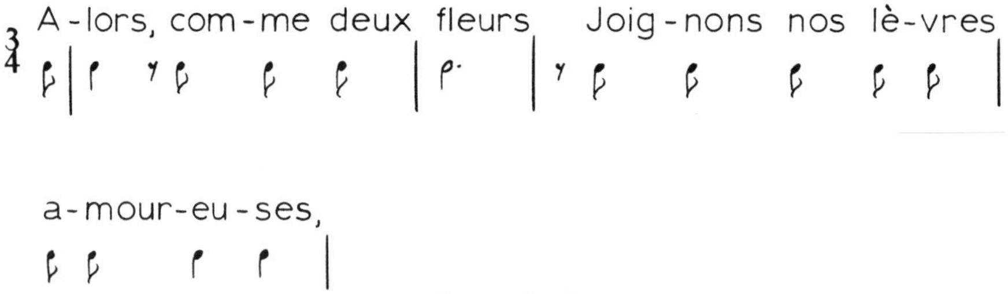

Example 2

slight pause in a recitation. The musical setting provides a rather larger pause, so that the temporal separation between the two syllables of *Alors* is only one-third the separation between *Alors* and *comme.* At the end of this phrase the lengthening of the last two syllables of *amoureuses* forms a graceful *rallentando* which helps to emphasize the word.

A song which may be more familiar to singers than the one we have been discussing is *Nuit d'étoiles*, Debussy's first published work. The story behind this song offers an amusing example of the interplay between poetry and music. The text, Banville's *La Dernière Pensée de Weber*, was inspired by a familiar waltz, purportedly the last complete piece composed by Carl Maria von Weber (1786–1826). The popularity of the waltz is attested by the number of songs based on its melody. The incipit appears in the thematic index to Weber's works[5] (Example 3). As it

[5] Friedrich Wilhelm Jähns, *Carl Maria von Weber in seinen Werken, Chronologisch-thematisches Verzeichniss seiner sämmtlichen Compositionen* (Berlin: Verlag der Schlesinger-'schen Buch- und Musikhandlung, 1871).

Example 3

happens, the waltz was not the last thought of Weber, after all, but rather the work of C. G. Reissiger, Weber's successor as Kapellmeister at Dresden; it appears as the fifth of his *Danses brillantes pour le pianoforte*, Op. 26.

The specific points of correspondence, if any, between the waltz and Banville's poem remain unknown. One may look upon the recurring refrain as a particularly musical device. Banville also may have regarded the alternation of a heterometric refrain in three and seven syllables with isometric octosyllabic quatrains as somehow capturing the rhythm of a waltz. The ease with which one falls into triple meter in reciting the refrain, with an upbeat as in the Reissiger waltz, suggests that the poet knew what he was about in constructing the poem (Example 4).

In setting Banville's poem to music, Debussy brought the affair full circle, from music to poetry to music. There is no evidence that Debussy knew the music which originally inspired Banville's poem, however, and

3/4
Nuit d'é - toi - les,
Sous tes voi - les,
Sous ta bri - se et tes par - fums

Example 4

we find no discernible trace of the Reissiger waltz in his song. Debussy's choice of rhythm in setting the refrain seems closer to a *siciliano* than to a waltz (Example 5). Debussy omitted the second stanza of the poem and

Nuit d'é-toi-les,
Sous tes voi - les,
Sous ta bri-se et tes par-fums

Example 5

changed the title to *Nuit d'étoiles*, inviting possible confusion with another Banville poem of that title. The setting, published in 1882, was apparently composed four or six years before. If the earlier date is accepted, Debussy was a boy of fourteen, having just entered the harmony class of Emile Durand at the Conservatoire.

The song anticipates several elements of Debussy's later style. The opening chords of the accompaniment, like the opening of *Zéphyr*, outline an incomplete pentatonic scale (Example 6). Later in the song the melody also has a pentatonic arabesque (Example 7). There are also

Allegro
pp una corda

Example 6

Example 7

frequent chords of the ninth, not only on the dominant degree but also on the supertonic. Before the final chorus there is a six-measure dominant pedal in a distant key.

Two important features of Debussy's mature style are absent from this song. The first is the whole-tone scale, which does not appear in Debussy's music until later. But if Jacques Chailley's argument prevails, that Debussy's discovery of the whole-tone scale evolved from his use of the chord of the eleventh, one sees the practice foreshadowed here in the free use of ninth chords.[6] The second feature is Debussy's use of parallelism, which appeared rather early in his development. Several examples occur in his *Triomphe de Bacchus* of 1882, based on Banville's *Le Triomphe de Bacchos* [sic] *à son retour des Indes*, the poem which immediately precedes *La Dernière pensée de Weber* in the *Stalactites.*

Banville's idea for the poem came from a painting by Bouchardon. Drawing on his thorough knowledge of the different versions of the Bacchus legend, Banville attempted to translate the painted images into poetic ones. His use of thirteen-syllable lines is one of the notable innovations of the *Stalactites* and anticipates the practice of Verlaine. Debussy originally intended to compose an orchestral interlude on the poem but completed only the four-hand piano version.

Debussy's free use of parallel chords and his unorthodox harmonic procedures were the bane of his instructors at the Conservatoire. On one

[6] Jacques Chailley, "Apparences et Réalités dans le langage musical de Debussy," in Edith Weber, ed., *Debussy et l'évolution de la musique au XXe siècle* (Paris: Editions du Centre National de la Recherche Scientifique, 1965), p. 60.

occasion Debussy was challenged by the registrar: "What rule do you follow?" Debussy is said to have replied: "Mon plaisir!" (The words, taken from Banville's play *Hymnis*, were spoken with an emphasis which apparently differed from Banville's intention. In the reconciliation scene, in which Hymnis and Anacreon exchange salutations, Hymnis exclaims excitedly, "Le Plaisir est ma loi!") Debussy's attempt to set *Hymnis* to music ended in failure. Of the other two stage works of Banville that attracted Debussy's attention, *Florise* has evidently disappeared. The composer had only little more success with *Diane au bois.*

Debussy's first attempt to set this play to music came in 1884, at the Conservatoire, when it provoked Guiraud's oft-quoted remark: "C'est très intéressant, tout ça, mais il faudra la réserver pour plus tard; ou bien vous n'aurez jamais le Prix de Rome!" The young composer put the score aside, but turned to it again in Rome in 1885–1886, once he had won the coveted award. Debussy even sought the necessary authorization for the work from Banville's godson, who was evidently acting as the poet's literary agent at the time.

Debussy's letters from Rome provide an unusual insight into the close relationship between text and compositional process in the young musician. At the Conservatoire Debussy had been compelled to work with texts which had little appeal to his literary sensibilities: *Printemps* (1882) by the Comte de Ségur; *La Gladiateur* (1883) by Emile Moreau; *Invocation* (1883) by Lamartine; *Printemps* (1884) by Jules Barbier. Largely for political reasons Debussy composed for these texts music which would satisfy the academic tastes of his professors, and in 1884 he won the Prix de Rome with his cantata *L'Enfant Prodigue* on a text by Edouard Guinand.

Now, in Rome, Debussy was finally free to choose his own text. His first selection, *Zuleima*, based on Heine's *Almansor*, turned out not to be conducive to the kind of music he wanted to compose, as he explains to Vasnier:

> J'ai changé d'avis pour mon premier envoi, et ne le ferai pas comme j'en avais l'intention, avec *Zuleima*, qui décidément ne me satisfait pas. C'est trop vieux et sent trop la vieille ficelle. Ces grands imbéciles de vers qui ne sont grands que par la longueur, m'assomment, et ma musique serait dans le cas de tomber sous le poids—puis autre chose de plus sérieux, c'est que je crois que jamais je ne pourrais

> enfermer ma musique dans un moule trop correct. Je me dépêche de vous dire que je ne parle pas de la forme musicale, c'est simplement à un point de vue littéraire.

Perhaps a libretto in which action is subservient to inner feelings would provide a more suitable vehicle for Debussy's music:

> J'aimerai toujours mieux une chose où, en quelque sorte, l'action sera sacrifiée à l'expression longuement poursuivie des sentiments de l'âme. Il me semble que là, la musique peut se faire plus humaine, plus vécue, que l'on peut creuser et raffiner les moyens d'expression.

Diane au bois recommended itself, if only because it departed from the familiar cantata texts that Prix de Rome composers were expected to choose for their *envois.*

> Je ne sais si je vous avais déjà parlé de *Diane au bois*, par Th. de Banville, je crois que oui! eh bien, c'est cela qui va me servir d'essai et de premier envoi, il y a encore un raison qui me fait faire *Diane.* C'est que cela ne rappelle en rien les poèmes dont on se sert dans les envois, qui ne sont, au fond, que des cantates perfectionnées.[7]

A few months later Debussy recounts his difficulties in working with Banville's text, difficulties due in part to the nature of the task he has set for himself: that of writing music which will accurately convey the changes in a character's feelings while maintaining the character's individual identity.

> *Diane* me donne beaucoup de mal, je ne peux arriver à trouver une phrase qui m'en donne la physionomie comme je le voudrais, et de fait, c'est assez difficile car il faut une phrase d'une belle froideur, n'éveillant aucune idée de passion; l'amour chez Diane ne vient que beaucoup plus tard, et, n'est au fond qu'un accident, et il y aurait un effet à produire dans les transformations que subirait cette phrase à mesure que Diane perdrait de ses forces contre l'amour, tout en lui gardant le même contour.[8]

[7] Published in Henry Prunières, "A la Villa Médicis," *Revue Musicale* 7 (1926):125. A description and a few examples of the existing music may be found in Eileen-Margaret Souffrin, "Debussy Lecteur de Banville," *Revue de Musicologie* 46 (1960):200–222. Further information on this period of Debussy's life may be found in Francis Ambrière, "La Vie Romaine de Claude Debussy," *Revue Musicale* 15 (1934):20–26; Raymond Bonheur, "Souvenirs et impressions," and Henri Busser, "Les envois de Rome de Claude Debussy," *Revue des deux mondes* 17 (1962):70–75.

[8] Prunières, "A la Villa Médicis," p. 129.

At the end of January 1886 Debussy writes again of his discouragement with *Diane* and his inability to prolong a particular mood for an extended scene while finding musical nuances to match different shades of emotion.

> Vous me demandez des nouvelles de mon envoi. C'est beaucoup lui qui m'a fait tant retarder ma réponse. Il m'occupe et me préoccupe beaucoup. Un jour je crois avoir trouvé, le lendemain j'ai peur de m'être trompé, jamais je n'ai tant éprouvé ce sentiment d'inquiétude en face d'une oeuvre. Puis, si vous saviez la difficulté qu'il y a à conserver dans une forme aussi claire que possible, les mille sensations d'un personnage, et dans *Diane*, où les scènes nullement faites au point de vue de la musique, peuvent paraître longues, c'est le diable pour que l'intérêt ne faiblisse pas, afin qu'on ne bâille pas d'ennui.
>
> Mais je ne peux me plaindre de mon livret, c'est moi qui l'ai choisi et je dois en porter toute la responsabilité; je ne vous en parle que pour vous prouver combien je suis occupé et ennuyé.[9]

By October Debussy had abandoned an over-ambitious project for which he had no precedents to guide him.

> Pour *Diane* il y a une scène de faite, bien qu'elle ne me satisfasse que très peu, n'étant pas du tout au point; j'ai du reste entrepris un travail peut-être au-dessus de mes forces, cela n'ayant pas de précédent, je me trouve dans l'obligation d'inventer de nouvelles formes.[10]

Debussy may have felt some sense of fulfillment a decade later in completing an orchestral prelude on Mallarmé's *L'Après-midi d'un faune*, whose indebtedness to *Diane au bois* Mallarmé himself acknowledged.

Mallarmé was not alone in recognizing the influence of Banville. Verlaine, in his *Confessions*, referred to "ce magicien de Banville" with whom he had so much in common. Both Banville and Verlaine were interested in the theory of poetry, and while they differed as to the importance of rhyme and fixed forms, they were both preoccupied with *vers impair,* or poetic lines containing an uneven number of syllables.

Banville's preface to the *Stalactites* collection contains a number of

[9] *Ibid.,* p. 130.
[10] *Ibid.,* p. 135.

phrases which anticipate Verlaine's *Art poétique*, which we shall consider in greater detail in chapter 6. Banville suggests that readers who may have found his previous volume of poems a bit too strict ("taillé à angles trop droits et trop polis") may discover in the *Stalactites* "une certaine mollesse." One thinks of the second and third lines of the *Art poétique* where Verlaine counsels poets to "préfère l'Impair / Plus vague et plus soluble dans l'air."

Banville continues: "En effet, il ne serait pas plus sensé d'exclure le demijour de la poésie, qu'il ne serait raisonnable de le souhaiter absent de la nature." Banville's "demijour" anticipates Verlaine's lines "Rien de plus cher que la chanson grise / Où l'Indécis au Précis se joint." Banville concludes his paragraph, ". . . et il est nécessaire, pour laisser certains objets poétiques dans le crépuscule qui les enveloppe et dans l'atmosphère qui les baigne, de recourir aux artifices de la négligence. C'est le métier qui enseigne à mépriser le métier; ce sont les règles de l'art qui apprennent à sortir des règles." Verlaine translates Banville's prose into verse: "Il faut aussi que tu n'ailles point / Choisir tes mots sans quelque méprise."

Banville then explains the aesthetic idea underlying such poems as *La Dernière Pensée de Weber*: "C'est surtout quand il s'agit d'appliquer des vers à de la musique qu'on sent vivement cette bizarre et délicate nécessité, et surtout encore lorsqu'il faut exprimer en poésie certain ordre de sensations, de sentiments qu'on pourrait appeler musicaux." [11]

Banville was one of the first poets to discover Watteau, and like Verlaine, was attracted to the *commedia dell'arte* tradition portrayed in his paintings. Eileen Souffrin has observed that of Banville's works Debussy usually selected "des poèmes en avance verlainiennes." [12] Those who know Verlaine's *Fêtes galantes* will recognize familiar characters in Debussy's Banville songs: Phyllis and Aminte, Colombine, Pierrot, and Arlequin.

At about the same time that Debussy was making his first settings of poems from Verlaine's *Fêtes galantes* he composed *Pierrot*, based on a text by Banville which might itself have come from the Verlaine collection:

[11] Eileen-Margaret Souffrin, *Les Stalactites de Théodore de Banville* (Paris: H. Didier, 1942), pp. 101–102.

[12] Souffrin, "Debussy Lecteur de Banville," p. 203.

Pierrot

Le bon pierrot que la foule contemple,
Ayant fini les noces d'Arlequin,
Suit en songeant le boulevard du temple
Une fillette au souple casaquin
En vain l'agace de son oeil coquin;
Et cependant mystérieuse et lisse
Faisant de lui sa plus chère délice,
La blanche lune aux cornes de taureau
Jette un regard de son oeil en coulisse
A son ami Jean Gaspard de bureau.
[For translation, see p. 295]

Debussy employs the piquant dissonance of the major seventh (or its inversion, the minor second) to offset the blandness of the popular tune, *Au clair de la lune*, on which the music of the song is based. He characteristically chooses a musical quotation which will be familiar to any of his listeners. A fragment suffices to suggest the tune, which Debussy then transposes to various pitch levels.[13] The extreme tessitura of the song, which ends in the wordless melisma which appears in so many of Debussy's early works, matched the unusually high voice of Madame Vasnier, "qui seule peut chanter cette musique inchantable." [14]

Banville also shared with Verlaine an attention to lighting and to the physical setting of his poems. Banville's *Aimons-nous et dormons* seems to anticipate Verlaine's *L'Ombre des arbres* or *En sourdine*, in its withdrawal into nature. The rich sound effects of *Aimons-nous* foreshadow Verlaine's familiar poem, *Il pleure dans mon coeur.*

Aimons-nous et dormons
Sans songer au reste du monde!
Ni le flot de la mer, ni l'ouragan des monts,
Tant que nous nous aimons
Ne courbera ta tête blonde,

[13] Another tune which recurs in quotation is "Nous n'irons plus au bois," the basis for one of Banville's best-known poems. For a discussion of Debussy's quotations see Virginia Raad, "Musical quotations in Claude Debussy," *American Music Teacher* 17 (1968):22–23, 34.

[14] Charles Koechlin, "Quelques anciennes mélodies inédites de Claude Debussy," *Revue Musicale* 7 (1926):117.

Car l'amour est plus fort
Que les Dieux et la Mort!

[Banville]

Il pleure dans mon coeur
Comme il pleut sur la ville;
Quelle est cette langueur
Qui pénètre mon coeur?

[Verlaine]

Banville balances two closely related nasal vowel sounds: "an"—"s*a*ns," "t*a*nt,"—and "on"—"aim*o*ns," "s*o*nger," "m*o*nts," "bl*o*nde." Both these nasal sounds are played off against unnasalized "o" sounds: "fl*o*t," "f*o*rt," "m*o*rt." The sound shift even appears in a single word, "d*o*rm*o*ns."

Verlaine similary exploits the apophony between "pleure" and "pleut." At the same time, he contrasts the "oe" sound—"coeur," "pleure," "langueur"—with the "i" sound: "il," "ville," and later in the poem, "bruit," "pluie," "s'ennui."

Raymond Bonheur has remarked on "une sorte de mystérieux instinct" which led Debussy from the start to the two poets "dont la fantaisie et la sensibilité avaient le plus d'affinité avec la sienne," first to Banville, then to Verlaine.[15] The affinity between the two poets should become even more apparent as we study Debussy's settings of Verlaine.

[15] Bonheur, "Souvenirs et impressions," p. 8.

3

VERLAINE I: Six Poems

The earliest point of connection between Debussy and Paul Verlaine (1844–1896) was Madame Antoinette-Flore Mauté de Fleurville, the mother-in-law of Verlaine and one of Debussy's first piano teachers. It was she who urged that Debussy pursue a career in music and she who trained the ten-year-old boy for his entrance examinations to the Conservatoire. Since at this time Verlaine and his wife were living with Madame Mauté, it seems not unlikely that Debussy saw Verlaine at one time or another. The paths of Debussy and Verlaine almost surely crossed later in their lives, yet we possess no record of their meeting, nor even evidence of any correspondence between the two men. This is surprising since they had numerous friends in common, and since for the large amount of Verlaine's poetry that Debussy put to music, the composer must have sought publication rights as he did in the case of Banville, Maeterlinck, and others, and as Fauré did in the case of Verlaine.

Debussy composed nineteen songs—nearly one-third of his total output—based on texts of Paul Verlaine: several early pieces drawn from the *Fêtes galantes* and published in 1882–1884; the *Ariettes oubliées* of 1888; *Trois mélodies* in 1891; and two sets of three songs each, titled *Fêtes galantes* series one and two, published in 1892 and 1904 respectively.

The direct influence of Verlaine appears in several other works as well. The first two movements of the *Petite Suite* (1889) bear the names of Verlaine poems: *En bateau* and *Cortège.* Likewise the third movement of the *Suite Bergamasque* (1905), the familiar *Clair de lune*, takes its title from a poem of Verlaine. In 1909 Debussy wrote the scenario for a one-act ballet for Diaghilev; the libretto was peopled with characters already encountered in the *Fêtes galantes*—Scaramouche, Harlequin, the Bolognese doctor—and was appropriately titled *Masques et Bergamasques.* Debussy attempted a collaboration with Laloy in 1913, an opera-ballet on Verlaine's *Fêtes galantes*, also referred to as *Crimen Amoris.*

We shall study the influence of Verlaine's poetry on Debussy's musical style further in chapter 6. The present chapter will deal with the more general questions of song-setting which logically precede considerations of individual musical style.

When a composer sets a poem to music he creates an independent work of art bearing a complex, ultimately unresolvable relationship with the original poem. A poem resists translation into another medium as vigorously as it resists translation into another language. Music can no more embody the uniqueness of a poem than a verbal exegesis can, but the composer, like the literary critic, may be able to increase our understanding of the poem by illuminating some of its various facets. If we compare a poem to a single word, then the musical setting of a poem may be thought of as the use of that word in a line of poetry. While the word retains the reverberations of all its various associations and connotations, its confinement within the syntax emphasizes some meanings while suppressing others. A musical setting subdues the richness of multiple suggestions contained in a poem while heightening certain of the poem's images, connections, and structural relationships. Let us push the analogy a bit further: just as the poet may use a word precisely and yet not necessarily produce with it a great line of poetry, so a composer may slavishly follow the intentions of the poet and still write a poor piece of music. Similarly, a composer may create a glorious piece of music with only the most general comprehension of his text.[1]

Just as we can better understand the meaning of a word if we see it illustrated in more than one sentence, so we can better understand the process of setting a poem to music if we can see the same poem in more than one setting. Among the songs published by Gabriel Fauré in 1889–1890 are six on poems of Verlaine which Debussy also set to music at roughly the same time. Two of the poems, *En sourdine* and *Clair de lune*, Debussy set to music twice. A study of how the two composers differ in their treatment of these texts will illustrate how accompaniment, melody, and harmony function in interpreting a text, and will serve to introduce a method of analysis based on both music and poetry.

Clair de lune

Votre âme est un paysage choisi
Que vont charmant masques et bergamasques
Jouant du luth et dansant et quasi
Tristes sous leurs déguisements fantasques.

Tout en chantant sur le mode mineur
L'amour vainqueur et la vie opportune,
Ils n'ont pas l'air de croire à leur bonheur
Et leur chanson se mêle au clair de lune,

Au calme clair de lune triste et beau,
Qui fait rêver les oiseaux dans les arbres
Et sangloter d'extase les jets d'eau,
Les grands jets d'eau sveltes parmi les marbres.

[For translation, see p. 295]

"Votre âme est un paysage choisi"; Verlaine has selected it as the stage upon which the troupe of *commedia dell'arte* players shall present their art, charming you into suspending disbelief, into accepting their illusion as reality. Moreover, your soul is the best choice of a landscape for this purpose, since Verlaine can create in your soul a scene which

[1] For a somewhat different approach to this question see Edward T. Cone, "Words into Music: The Composer's Approach to the Text," in *Sound and Poetry*, ed. Northrop Frye (New York: Columbia University Press, 1956), pp. 3–15. Also see the bibliographical entries under "Poetry and Music," particularly the writings of Burnshaw and Langer.

could not occur in nature. This poem, which opens the *Fêtes galantes*, sets the stage for the drama to follow.

Verlaine has yet to name the players of the troupe, identifying only the characteristic masks, "leurs déguisements fantasques," behind which the actors hide their true feelings. But the phrase "masques et bergamasques" suggests that the cast will include the two *zanni* Brighella and Arlequin, who originate from Bergamo, just as the Doctor comes from Bologna and Pantalon from Venice.[2]

This improvisational theater follows no definite script, though Verlaine provided careful stage directions in *Pantomime* and *Fantoches* which come next. Although there may be certain conventional themes, much of the action takes place on the spur of the moment. One does not even know when the masquers will appear. The construction "Que vont charmant masques . . ." implies no continuity or regularity. Rather, "Your soul is a landscape which the masquers are always charming." You can never tell when they may turn up. The theme of unpredictability and caprice suggested by the word *fantasques* recurs in the word *bonheur*, or "good fortune." These actors have no control over their destiny but must accept whatever fortune brings, enjoying the propitious "vie opportune" whenever it happens to come. They sing of "L'amour vainqueur"—one of the traditional themes of pastoral poetry—without believing in it. Their disbelief is revealed in the manner of their singing: such positive, affirmative subjects as "L'amour vainqueur et la vie opportune" ought to be sung in the major mode, which composers have conventionally associated with happiness and well-being. Instead, these strange masquers sing "sur le mode mineur," conventionally associated with melancholy and regret.

The moonlight, "triste et beau," preserves the ambivalence of the players' mood. The still moonlight, which sets the birds to dreaming and makes the fountains sob with ecstasy, leaves the marble statues unchanged. One may perhaps regard them as the audience for this moonlit performance, like the "marbres" in Watteau's *Le Mezzetin.* The ninth line of the text originally read "Au calme clair de lune de Watteau." Verlaine changed it when Anatole France pointed out that Watteau was

[2] Jacques-Henry Bornecque, *Lumières sur les "Fêtes galantes" de Paul Verlaine* (Paris: Librairie Nizet, 1959), p. 151.

"le peintre ensoleillé" and that Verlaine could not likely have seen "des clairs de lune de Watteau." But Verlaine later maintained, in his lecture at Anvers, that the *Fêtes galantes* deal with "sentiments costumés en personnages de la comédie italienne et de féeries à la Watteau." [3] Even though the reference to Watteau did not appear in the final version of the poem, the eighteenth-century setting is clear, both in the reference to the *masques* and the *luth*, and also in the decasyllabic writing, a poetic atavism by nineteenth-century standards.

The repetition in the last two lines, ". . . les jets d'eau, / Les grands jets d'eau . . ." and especially their association with *extase* reminds us that the entire last stanza is a description of the "paysage choisi" of the first line. The external world is but a mask which reflects, sometimes clearly, sometimes deceptively, the internal universe of "votre âme." Verlaine returns to this theme in *En sourdine, C'est l' extase*, and *Il pleure dans mon coeur.* In *Clair de lune*, having once established the striking metaphor of the opening line, the poet declines to make too clear a statement, maintaining an equivocal air to match his moonlit landscape.

Debussy made two settings of *Clair de lune*, the first around 1882, the second in 1892. Although the latter piece was supposedly a revision of the first, it is in fact a completely new song, with a new interpretation of the poem. Debussy's earlier setting exhibits a generally optimistic, luminous atmosphere, established by cascading triads and the predominating major mode of the piano accompaniment. Although there is a brief descent to "le mode mineur" in measures 31–34, the song is only "quasi triste" and more concerned with soaring climaxes on "la vie opportune" and "au calme clair de lune" than with any doubting of "leur bonheur." Two distinct accompanimental motives—one rising, the other falling—are associated with "les grands jets d'eau" which the moonlight causes to sigh. But these motives have individual associations as well: the descending triads belong to the light of the moon, while the ascending chords are strummed to suggest the lute which accompanies the masquers' song. Thus "leur chanson *se mêle* au clair de lune . . . qui fait . . . sangloter d'extase les jets d'eau."

Lest there be any doubt about the importance of the line "Et leur

[3] Paul Verlaine, *Selected Poems*, ed. R. C. D. Perman (London, Oxford University Press, 1965), p. 167.

chanson se mêle au clair de lune," Debussy sets it twice, to harmonies whose exotic flavor is appropriate to the "masques et bergamasques" from the Italian and Spanish theater. After a melismatic "ah" following the last line of Verlaine's text, Debussy repeats the line "au calme clair de lune triste et beau," and ends his song as it began with an accompaniment of affirmative major triads.

The atmosphere of Debussy's later setting is darker than before; there is more emphasis on "le mode mineur," less on "la vie opportune." The accompaniment includes a number of "minor modes." It opens in the d♯ minor pentatonic scale, introducing a motive which appears throughout the piece: (Example 1). The song of the masquers, *très doux et très expressif,* is in the G♯ Aeolian mode (Example 2). The piece ends in the G♯ Dorian mode (Example 3). All three of these scales can be described as "modes mineurs" for they all contain a minor triad constructed on the tonic degree.

The point of correspondence among these accompanimental scales—the minor triad—occurs repeatedly in the vocal line, and its presence

Example 1

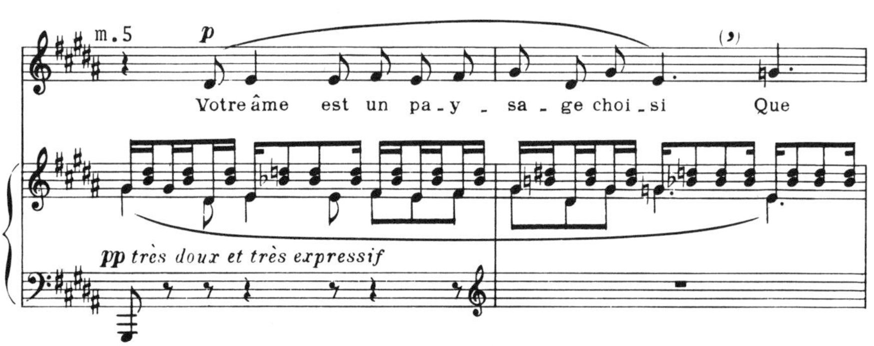

Example 2

Example 3

at the climax of the song—"Ils n'ont pas l'air de croire à leur bonheur"—suggests that this feeling of doubt is the reason why the masquers go about "Tout en chantant sur le mode mineur" (Example 4). The chords at the end of the song affirm the minor mode as strongly as

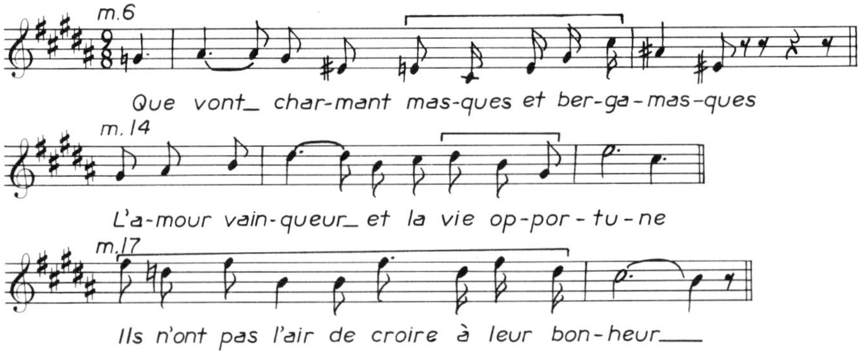

Example 4

the conclusion of the earlier version expresses the major mode. The whole-tone harmonization of the word *tristes* conveys a desolation which goes beyond the "quasi" of the text[4] (Example 5).

Example 5

Fauré's setting is dominated by the music of the masquers, "jouant du luth et dansant . . . tout en chantant sur le mode mineur." Their song appears not in the vocal line but in the accompaniment. In fact, in Fauré's *Clair de lune* the vocal line is no longer of primary interest, but serves as an expressive accompaniment to the song of the piano, written in the form of a *menuet.* For it is this *chanson* which begins and ends the piece, and when the voice enters it does not displace this prior melody but blends with it, just as "leur chanson se mêle au clair de lune."

This manner of setting the poem, with the piano as an almost independent part which the voice accompanies, suggests a slightly different reading of the word *choisi:* the past participial "pris de préférence" in place of the familiar adjective form "ce qu'il y a de mieux" (Littré). It is as if the singing and dancing never ceased, but simply moved from one place to another, and on this occasion had selected "votre âme" as the stage for their performance. In Fauré's setting the masquers are only "quasi tristes," as the piano part moves back and forth between minor and major. Fauré captures the whimsy of this capricious company by setting the words "sur le mode mineur" in the *major* mode. The moonlight furnishes a propitious moment for the masquers' play. Then it is over and they depart.

[4] For a detailed comparison of Debussy's settings see Roger Nichols, "Debussy's Two Settings of 'Clair de Lune,'" *Music and Letters* 48 (1967):229–235.

The association of accompanimental motives with moonlight and fountains in Debussy's earlier setting of *Clair de lune* brings to mind an idea which applies even more strongly in some of the other Verlaine songs. This is Debussy's habit of letting the piano accompaniment represent "nature." This notion may be understood more easily if we consider the circumstances of a performance: one person sings the words of a poem while a second person plays the piano. In poems dealing with man's relation to nature, we tend to identify the singer with the poet, since it is his words that are being sung. From there it is but a step to identify the wordless accompaniment with nature's response. Debussy deliberately encourages these associations through his treatment of the piano accompaniment. In *En sourdine* the motive of a nightingale—the representation of nature's response—appears only in the piano accompaniment, not in the vocal line. In *C'est l'extase* the interplay of motives between voice and piano represents the ecstatic unity of man and nature. In *Il pleure dans mon coeur* the accompaniment depicts the rain which provides the source of the poet's reflections. Like Debussy's other expressive devices, this one does not occur everywhere. One cannot simply equate accompaniment and nature in all instances. Still, the correspondence appears with sufficient frequency to bear keeping in mind.

Mandoline

Les donneurs de sérénades
Et les belles écouteuses
Echangent des propos fades
Sous les ramures chanteuses.

C'est Tircis et c'est Aminte,
Et c'est l'éternel Clitandre,
Et c'est Damis qui pour mainte
Cruelle fait maint vers tendre.

Leurs courtes vestes de soie,
Leurs longues robes à queues,
Leur élégance, leur joie
Et leurs molles ombres bleues

Tourbillonnent dans l'extase
D'une lune rose et grise,
Et la mandoline jase
Parmi les frissons de brise.

[For translation, see p. 296]

The poetic vision expressed in *Mandoline* comes to us in a succession of images, each one glimpsed from a slightly different perspective. The first image presents serenaders offering flattering remarks to their ladies under singing boughs. In the second stanza we draw a bit closer, so that individual identities can be distinguished: Tircis, Aminta, Clitander, Damis. These names recall familiar personages from the pastoral tradition. The identification of this literary antecedent makes us look at the first stanza a bit differently. In the phrase "Les belles écouteuses," for example, we recognize a conventional term of description: in *précieux* poetry ladies are always "belles." Likewise, in the phrase "donneurs de sérénades" we hear an echo of the periphrastic construction of which the *précieux* poets were so fond.

While we appear to have drawn nearer to this pastoral scene, however, the language of the second stanza suggests that Verlaine has pulled back from it to a more detached point of view. The appearance of the archaism *mainte* in place of *beaucoup de* in the seventh line is consistent with the language of the first stanza. But to place the word *mainte* at the end of a run-on line, and to repeat the word in the line following—this goes beyond the evocation of a literary tradition and becomes a gentle parody of it.

Verlaine gives further evidence of his detachment from the scene in his description of these characters. These are not persons, or even personages, but types. It is not the Clitander from any particular poem but "l'*éternel* Clitandre," the archetype of all Clitanders. Damis has been making verses for many a *cruelle*, the conventional word for a lady, for a long time. This sense of timelessness, of carefully posed archetypes, continues into the next stanza, where the description of the costumes—"leurs courtes vestes de soie" and "leurs longues robes à queue"—suggests a scene from Watteau.

The image changes again. The sight of these characters becomes confused with their shadows, just as their idle *galanterie* blends with the sounds of the branches. It is truly an extraordinary evening, a mixture of blue and rose and gray. The *extase* produced by this whirling of sight and sound is a more attenuated version of the "Valse mélancolique et langoureux vertige" of Baudelaire's *Harmonie du soir*, where "Les sons et les parfums tournent dans l'air du soir." In this confusion of sensations, the abstract qualities of "leur élégance" and "leur joie" have become so real that they can serve as subjects of the same verb as articles of apparel.

As if to suggest his basic sympathy for the serenaders and for the tradition which they represent, Verlaine hints in the last stanza that his air of detachment is partly a façade, that the poet is really present after all. The first clue is the word *extase*—whose ecstasy is it? Then the phrase "Et la mandoline jase"—who is playing the instrument? Finally, "Les frissons de brise"—*frissons* is a word which usually applies to a person; the breezes themselves do not shiver. The suggestion is that Verlaine himself is transported to an unnatural vantage point by this vision; it is he who trembles in the breeze, this sympathetic breeze that makes the branches sing and brings to mind the expression "souffle de l'inspiration." We have the impression that if only we could get close enough to make out the musician's face, we would find that it was Verlaine himself who was playing the mandolin. For Verlaine here offers us a serenade: he has succeeded in reworking the conventions of an archaic tradition into a song of his own. "C'est Tircis et c'est Aminte"—the line describes Verlaine's poem itself as well as the scene within the poem. The pastoral characters are all here, in a poem which only pretends to be a parody.

In making a musical setting of a poem a composer commonly seizes upon a musical reference in the text—often he has chosen the text with this in mind—and makes it the foundation of his accompaniment. In the poem at hand the image of the mandolin is an obvious choice. The musical depiction of the mandolin exerts a considerable influence over our understanding of the composer's interpretation, since in this case the instrument appears not just as an incidental detail but as the basic figure of the poem.

The nuances of attitude in this poem are subtle, perhaps too subtle for music to capture. Both Fauré and Debussy adopt a single attitude in place of the changing perspectives expressed in the language of the poem. Furthermore, both composers alter the text to fit their needs. Fauré adopts an attitude of sympathy to the pastoral tradition. His setting is a song of joy whose vocal melody is a sweet serenade. The accompaniment imitates closely the adroit maneuverings of a skilled mandolin player (Example 6). One recalls that the mandolin was the favorite popular

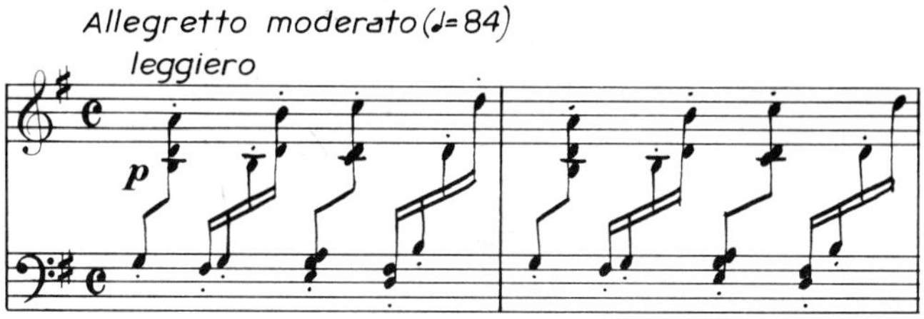

Example 6

instrument of the seventeenth and eighteenth centuries, and that Mozart employed the mandolin to accompany the serenade *Deh vieni* in *Don Giovanni.* Melodic repetition makes it clear that the singing branches are in concord with the song. For the second half of the poem the strumming alternates with arpeggios, while the *tourbillonnement* represented by sinuous quarter-notes in the left hand of the piano part interrupts the serenade with its dizzying whirl. This ecstatic dance, however, is only an interruption. Fauré repeats the first stanza in its entirety at the end of the song so that the music ends as it began with the sounds of serenaders under the singing boughs. There is no conclusion; rather Fauré turns the poem into an endless circle.

Debussy's setting casts a rather different light on the poem. The accompaniment begins with a tentative pluck of the mandolin followed not by real music but by the idle strumming of open fifths by an insincere serenader faking it (Example 7).

This ingenious mockery in the accompaniment, this tone of mild asteism, influences our understanding of the poem. We may think of the game of *propos interrompus* in which several speakers "ne se comprenant pas, parlent de choses différentes" (Littré). We give more weight to the pointlessness, the insipidity expressed by the word *fades.* The character of the key figure of the poem, "la mandoline jase," also changes. In place of *babiller*, which the accompaniment of Fauré's song might suggest, we are more likely to associate the sound of the mandolin with the *fadeurs* of the serenaders. Truly "la mandoline jase" in the open fifths C–G–D–A at the

Example 7

end of the song and in E–B–F♯–C♯–G♯ in measures 28–29. The "propos fades" of the serenaders are made literal in the wordless coda which Debussy draws from measures 35–37 of the melody. Instead of ending with *brise,* the last word of Verlaine's text, the singer continues for another twenty measures singing "la, la, la." The accompaniment ends with the same plucked note which opens the song. This repetition, along with Debussy's directions for the end of the piece—*toujours en allant se perdant*—suggest that Debussy intends something of the same effect that Fauré produces by repeating the first stanza—we hear the serenaders at a distance, draw nearer to learn more about them, then depart, with the sounds of their music dying away in the distance.

Debussy's interpretation focuses on the relationship between man and nature. It dwells on the contrast between the idle chattering of the serenaders and the purposefulness of nature. In the poem it is not the men that sing, but the branches, moved by a trembling of the breeze. From this point of view the words like *extase* and *frissons*—which we cited earlier as evidence of the poet's presence in the scene—can be taken as a personification of nature, in contrast to the depersonalization of the serenaders. It is really "l'extase d'une lune"; there are literally "les frissons de brise." As for the mandolin—it just plays.

As we shall see in our discussion of *Le Son du cor* in chapter 6, to mention the name of a musical instrument in a poem is to evoke many different associations. How a composer chooses to represent that instrument in his song setting influences our understanding of the poem.

En sourdine

Melody is the point at which speech and music most nearly coincide. Of all the elements that make up a song, melody is the one most influenced by the patterns of speaking. Opera recitative has often been described as "heightened speech." As one moves from ordinary speech to recitation to recitative to song, melody departs further and further from speech inflections. Purely musical considerations begin to take precedence, and sometimes the cadences of speech are lost entirely and the words are simply fitted to a preexisting tune. It is part of the tradition of opera, for example, that the text of an aria can be repeated indefinitely, and that a composer may dwell on a single syllable for a dozen measures if he so desires. Debussy's earliest songs often seem to have but a casual regard for the text, and the young composer felt free to repeat lines or add textless melismas on "la" or "ah," but before long he developed a scrupulous concern for the poet's words which continued throughout his life.[5]

Even for a composer who is attentive to the proper accentuation and inflection of his chosen text, melody is influenced by musical as well as poetic considerations. Although two passages might not be spoken alike, a composer may set them to the same melody, both to connect two poetic ideas and to fulfill the requirements of musical form. A skillful composer will be able to satisfy both poetic and musical obligations with a minimum of conflict between the two.

A comparison of several melodic settings of *En sourdine*, detached from their accompaniments and transposed to the same key for ease of comparison, demonstrates both the wide latitude of declamation permissible within French prosody and the number of ways that declamation can be expressed in music. Before investigating the variations among these settings, let us examine the poem in detail.

[5] Klara Magdics, "From the Melody of Speech to the Melody of Music," *Studia Musicologica* 4 (1963):325–346; Nicholas Ruwet, "Fonction de la parole dans la musique vocale," *Revue Belge de Musicologie* 15 (1961):8–28; George P. Springer, "Language and Music: Parallels and Divergencies," *For Roman Jakobson* (The Hague: Mouton & Company, 1956), pp. 504–513.

En sourdine

Calmes dans le demi-jour
Que les branches hautes font,
Pénétrons bien notre amour
De ce silence profond.

Fondons nos âmes, nos coeurs
Et nos sens extasiés,
Parmi les vagues langueurs
Des pins et des arbousiers.

Ferme tes yeux à demi,
Croise tes bras sur ton sein,
Et de ton coeur endormi
Chasse à jamais tout dessein.

Laissons-nous persuader
Au souffle berceur et doux
Qui vient à tes pieds rider
Les ondes de gazon roux.

Et quand, solennel, le soir
Des chênes noirs tombera,
Voix de notre désespoir,
Le rossignol chantera.
[For translation, see p. 296]

The desire to return to nature as a relief from human suffering is often accompanied by the conviction that nature somehow answers, somehow responds to this desire.[6] Verlaine develops both themes in this poem of muted sensation. The attempt to become one with nature is expressed in six imperative verbs:

Pénétrons bien notre amour
De ce silence profond.

Let us imbue our love with silence—the profound silence which one seldom encounters in the turmoil of human affairs but which one can experience in communion with nature.

[6] *En sourdine,* like *C'est l'extase,* illustrates what John Ruskin termed the "pathetic fallacy," an infelicitous phrase too often used as a convenient pigeonhole to dismiss a philosophical question that Verlaine, among others, found worthy of serious consideration.

Fondons nos âmes, nos coeurs
Et nos sens extrasiés.

Let us dissolve, let us blend our souls, our hearts, and our senses, which had been stimulated to ecstasy.

Ferme tes yeux à demi.

Shut out sensation by half-closing your eyes, just as the arching of the high branches forms a half-light of the afternoon sun.

Croise tes bras sur ton sein.

Cross your arms in the attitude of sleep, or the position of burial.

Chasse à jamais tout dessein.

Eliminate all intention, and thereby all time. Live suspended in the eternal moment of the present without memory, without thought, without purpose.[7]

Laissons-nous persuader
Au souffle berceur et doux.

Let us be convinced by the cradling wind; let us surrender to its invitation to sleep.

Running parallel to this theme of deliberate languor is the theme of nature's response. The poem contains six expressions in which nature seems to exhibit the very purposefulness which the lovers have abdicated.

Calmes dans le demi-jour
Que *les branches hautes font.*

The verb *faire* does not always imply deliberate intention, to be sure—"deux fois deux font quatre" is an obvious example—but in light of what follows, the muting of sunlight by the branches seems to be an indication of design.

Parmi *les vagues langueurs*
Des pins et des arbousiers.

Trees do not ordinarily feel languor, and the personification here may seem a little strong, but it is muted by the word *vagues* and by the use of

[7] Bornecque, *Lumières sur les "Fêtes galantes,"* p. 176.

the plural. The word *langueur* usually occurs in the singular; the plural *langueurs* suggests the absence of any specific cause.

> Laissons-nous *persuader*
> Au souffle *berceur* et doux.

The implication of purpose in the word *persuader* is strengthened by the notion of intention conveyed by *berceur.* Likewise, the word *souffle* is a more personal word than the usual *vent.*

> Qui *vient à tes pieds rider*
> Les ondes de gazon roux.

The use of *venir* plus the infinitive implies a sense of purpose; in poetry, the expression appears commonly without connoting personification, but in company with other expressions in this poem it strengthens the feeling of intention.

> Et quand, solennel, *le soir*
> *Des chênes noirs tombera.*

In the expression "night falls" it makes no sense to ask, Where does it fall from? By telling us that it falls from the black oaks, Verlaine makes the evening more like a tangible presence.

> *Voix* de notre désespoir
> Le rossignol chantera.

The last two lines of the poem are the culmination of a progression from "silence profond" to "souffle berceur et doux" to a purposive "voix." The couple has deliberately surrendered all purposefulness to nature. Having rejected "à jamais tout dessein," they commit to nature the expression of their despair.

Let us see how the words of this poem are treated in the melodies of five different settings: A, Claude Debussy (1882); B, Gabriel Fauré (1891); C, Claude Debussy (1892); D, Reynaldo Hahn (1892); E, Raoul Laparra (1927). We shall not essay a full-scale melodic analysis of the five settings but shall attempt to illustrate some of the musical possibilities open to a composer by comparing points of significant difference among the settings.

In setting the first two lines of the text, our composers have chosen either a descending melodic line or the repetition of a single note. The former suggests a relaxing of tension suitable to the overall idea of the poem; the latter has an incantatory, hypnotic effect. The difference between the melodic line of Fauré, which descends a perfect fifth, and that of Laparra, which descends a full octave, corresponds to the difference between a word spoken casually in a living room and the same word declaimed by an actor in a large theater: the inflection is the same in both cases but the amplitude varies (Example 8).

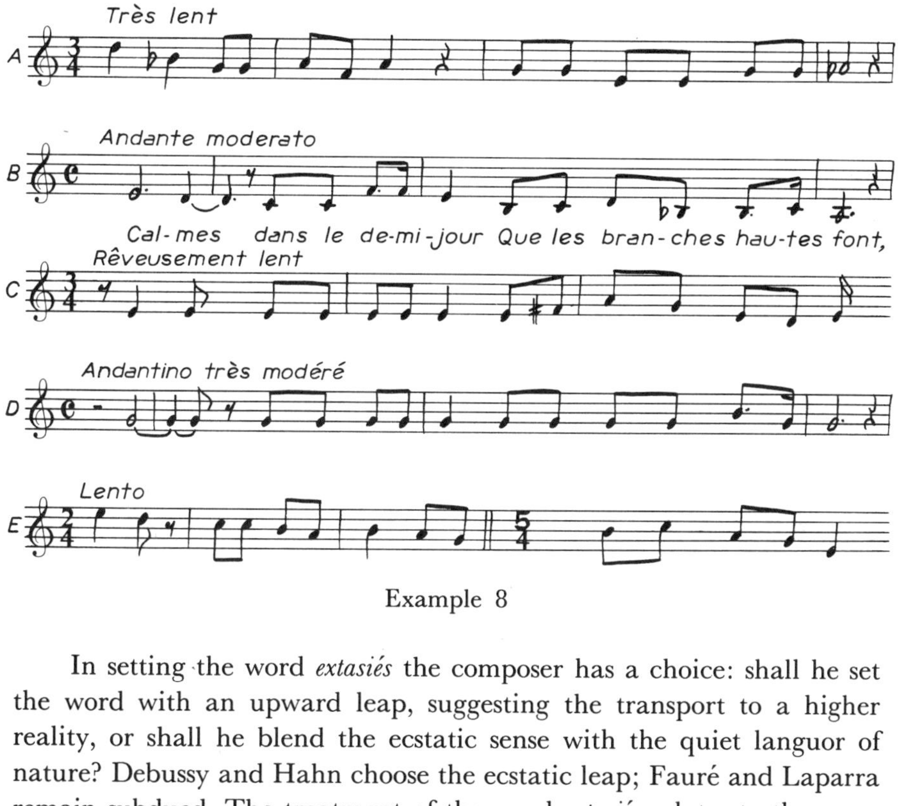

Example 8

In setting the word *extasiés* the composer has a choice: shall he set the word with an upward leap, suggesting the transport to a higher reality, or shall he blend the ecstatic sense with the quiet languor of nature? Debussy and Hahn choose the ecstatic leap; Fauré and Laparra remain subdued. The treatment of the word *extasiés* relates to the more general question of the musical treatment of a negative expression. In setting a text such as "the rain no longer falls," a composer may be unable to resist the tendency to set the word *falls* to a falling melodic motive, even though strictly speaking this violates the sense of the phrase as a whole (Example 9).[8]

Example 9

In the fourth stanza a similar problem arises, for the text contains both the expression "Laissons-nous persuader," which continues the theme of surrender to nature, and the word *souffle*, which is an important element of the other theme of the poem, the response of nature. Fauré sets the stanza to a succession of descending melodic lines whose narrow compass recalls the melodic descent at the beginning of the song. Debussy, on the other hand, begins with a low repeated note on

[8] Burnshaw includes such evocation by negation among the ways in which poems speak, writing of Keats's lines, "The sedge is withered from the lake, / And no birds sing." The reader experiences a presence not only in the first of these lines but also in the second, for the "no" cannot stop him from feeling and knowing what the negation tries to remove. "No birds sing," however, is not the same presence as that embodied by "And birds sing." The "no" casts a darkening veil which, as it were, causes the presence to recede—to recede in brightness, not to disappear; for it remains there, fully visible, its veiled significance bodied forth by the negative naming. Such strangely affecting presence cannot be evoked except in a poem and by the poem's power to place it there while saying it is not there. Stanley Burnshaw, *The Seamless Web* (New York: George Braziller, 1970), p. 103.

"Laissons-nous persuader," then rises an octave and a half to a climactic *roux.* Laparra, whose melody has proceeded in quarter notes and eighth notes up to this point, employs a flurry of sixteenth notes to depict the rippling of the waves of grass by the wind (Example 10).

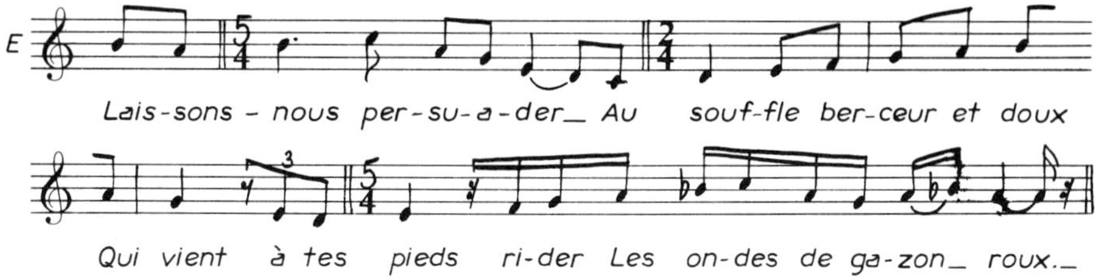

Example 10

Most musical settings exhibit some variant of the form A B A′. In most cases this means that the composer must seek two points in the text that he can reasonably set to the same melody. This may present a problem in the case of a poem which does not follow an A B A′ pattern. Still, many poems do have an element of rounding-off which relates the end to the beginning. In *En sourdine* the element of time connects the first and last stanzas, the *demi-jour* produced by the high branches and the *soir* which falls from these same branches. Fauré, Debussy, and Hahn link the beginning of the outer stanzas through melodic repetition. It need not be a literal repetition since the trained ear makes the connection between two similar melodies the same way that a careful reader makes the connection between the first and last stanzas of this poem. The repetition in Debussy's setting of 1882 occurs somewhat later in the stanza, beginning with "voix de notre désespoir." Since this melody originally sets four lines of text, the last two lines of the poem must be repeated in order to make the song come out right.

While the element of time connects the beginning of the outer stanzas, the end of these stanzas is rather different. The first stanza is about *silence,* the last about a *voix.* The image of the nightingale evokes a variety of responses. Debussy's melodies give no particular attention to the word, although the accompaniment of the later setting imitates the nightingale's song. Hahn's melody contains a dramatic upward leap for a melisma on the last syllable of *chantera.* Perhaps the setting which reflects the clearest understanding of the text at this point is that of Fauré. The first syllable of *chantera* is set to the highest note of the vocal melody, a note which has been implied all through the song and which, when it finally arrives, seems like an inevitable conclusion (Example 11).

B
Voix de not-re dé-ses-poir, Le ros-si-gnol chan-te-ra.

Example 11

The rhythmic variety in these five settings of the poem is remarkable. As we noted in the previous chapter, a major transformation takes place when a poem without beat accents is forced into a musical meter which has an implicit accent on the first beat of every measure. Laparra, and to a lesser extent Debussy and Hahn, try to relieve the difficulty by occasionally changing meters, but the question still remains—which words go on which beats? At the very opening of the song, for example, Debussy (1882), Fauré, and Laparra place the first word on a downbeat, Hahn places it on the secondary accent of a 4/4 measure, while Debussy (1892) begins the piece with a syncopation. There are only four points in the poem where all five composers agree on a downbeat accent: the last syllable of *extasiés*, the first syllable of *ferme*, and the last syllables of *dessein* and *chantera.* These points of uniformity are probably without significance; of greater interest than the uniformity is the amount of variety permissible within the rules of prosody. This freedom seems to be due to the basically unstressed character of the French language. A more detailed study of musical accents in the five settings of *En sourdine* might well reveal further evidence of the effect of melody on the interpretation of a song.

C'est l'extase

C'est l'extase langoureuse,
C'est la fatigue amoureuse,
C'est tous les frissons des bois
Parmi l'étreinte des brises,
C'est, vers les ramures grises,
Le choeur des petites voix.

O le frêle et frais murmure!
Cela gazouille et susurre,
Cela ressemble au cri doux
Que l'herbe agitée expire . . .
Tu dirais, sous l'eau qui vire,
Le roulis sourd des cailloux.

Cette âme qui se lamente
En cette plainte dormante
C'est la nôtre, n'est-ce pas?
La mienne, dis, et la tienne,
Dont s'exhale l'humble antienne
Par ce tiède soir, tout bas?

[For translation, see p. 297]

"C'est l'extase langoureuse": the combination of these words seems somewhat surprising at first sight. Ordinarily we associate ecstasy with rapturous exaltation, with the fireworks and surging fountain of Baudelaire's *Le Jet d'eau,* or with the flash of light in his *La Mort des amants.* But ecstasy, literally a "standing apart," is a mental transport which does not necessarily depend on the metaphor of elevation. There can be an ecstatic experience in "la fatigue amoureuse" for which the usual language of ascent is inappropriate.

"L'extase langoureuse" is best described in muted tones: *grises, petites, doux, frêle, sourd, dormante, humble, tiède.* Unity with nature, frequently part of the ecstatic experience, no longer expresses itself in the sobbing fountains of *Clair de lune.* Nature's response is "en sourdine": "C'est . . . le choeur des *petites* voix." Verlaine suggests a state of languorous ecstasy through both his choice of words of subdued overtones and a loose syntax which borders on discontinuity. The sounds of the woods are weak murmurs, mere whispers, soft cries, sleeping moans. The poem itself is a suggestion rather than a statement. In the first stanza, for example, there are no logical connecting words joining one line to the next. The reader must recognize for himself that emotions or sensations have been juxtaposed with physical motion or natural sounds:

C'est l'extase . . .
C'est la fatigue . . .
C'est . . . les frissons . . .
C'est . . . le choeur. . . .

Yet the unity of the soul with nature appears as strongly as if there were fountains of melancholy tears or some other striking image. The suggestion that our soul has become one with the wind, stated most clearly in "Cette âme . . . c'est la nôtre," runs through the poem in images of the woods embraced by the breeze, in the soft cry of a plant, troubled, presumably, by the wind, in the humble antiphon passed off into the evening air, and of course, in the etymological kinship between the breath and the soul.

An apt setting of such a poem will not likely have an assertive, self-contained melody. The sounds of the woods are better evoked through music which verges on melody without becoming melody. The choir of little voices is best expressed through melodic motives, the premelodic fragments from which melody may emerge, and rhythmic patterns, which can appear and reappear throughout a song without dominating it. In the settings of *C'est l'extase* by Debussy and Fauré, we find sections connected not by the literal repetition of melody but by the recurrence of melodic motives and rhythmic patterns. A certain amount of melodic repetition does occur in Fauré's setting, but it follows the rhyme scheme within the stanza rather than making connections between stanzas. In Verlaine's poem the pattern of rhymes in each stanza is a a b c c b. In Fauré's setting of the poem the melody of the first line of each stanza is similar to the second line of that stanza.

Fauré underlines connections between stanzas through the use of prevailing rhythms in the accompaniment and melodic motives in both voice and accompaniment. The syncopation in the prevailing rhythm of the first stanza and a half suggests both the state of ecstasy—the standing apart from normal relationships—and the inability to produce any more than fragmentary sounds. Of course there must be some downbeat accents in the music—otherwise we would not recognize the syncopation —but the principal rhythm is that of a beat displacement (Example 12).

In setting the second half of the second stanza, Fauré fills in the offbeat sixteenth notes with eighth notes to accompany the soft cry "que l'herbe agitée expire . . ." (Example 13). In the first half of the third

Rhythm I

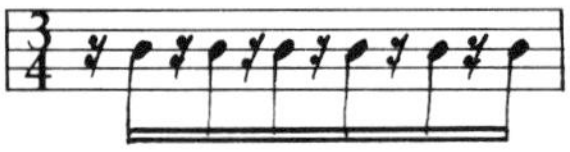

Example 12

Rhythm 2

Example 13

Rhythm 3

Example 14

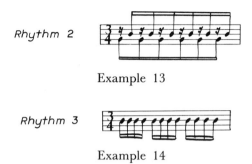

stanza the sixteenth notes and eighth notes blend into a continuous line of sixteenth notes, a "plainte dormante" which combines the murmuring in the trees with the rustling of the grass (Example 14).

The conclusion of the song has the same basic rhythm as the opening, perhaps in order to connect "le choeur des petites vois" with "l'humble antienne." Both *choeur* and *antienne* are formal words for singing, implying that the sounds of nature are not individual but concerted, joined in a common expression.

Two melodic motives complement this rhythmic scheme. Motive *a* first appears after the words "Le choeur des petites voix" and then reappears after "O le frêle et frais murmure," and after "Cela gazouille et susurre," as if to identify individual voices within the choir. The motive appears twice more in the last stanza, after the words "C'est la nôtre, n'est-ce pas?" and after "le mienne, dis, et la tienne," as if to give

Motive a

Example 15

an affirmative answer to that question (Example 15). Motive *b* appears only in the third stanza at the lines

> Cette âme qui se lamente
> Et cette plainte dormante.

(Fauré uses *Et* in place of *En.*) Although the motive makes no connections within this poem, it is the same as a motive which occurs in Fauré's setting of *En sourdine* at the words

Ferme tes yeux à demi;
Croise tes bras sur ton sein,
Et de ton coeur endormi
Chasse à jamais tout dessein.
Laissons-nous persuader
Au souffle berceur et doux.

This rather unusual bit of self-borrowing apparently serves here to underline the points which the two poems have in common—the unity of man with nature, the wind as an expression of the soul, the mood of languor. It also functions as a unifying element within Fauré's song cycle (Example 16).[9]

Example 16

Debussy's treatment of rhythms and motives is somewhat more tightly organized than Fauré's. Like Fauré, Debussy compensates for the absence of any large-scale melodic repetitions with the immediate repetition of one- or two-measure groups. Again, connections between stanzas appear in the form of recurring motives rather than overall repetitions.

The song opens with motive *a*, a low dominant chord followed by a leap of several octaves and a cascade of dominant ninth chords of gradually increasing speed. Closely related to the melody to which, later in the song, Debussy sets "Dont s'exhale l'humble antienne," motive *a* is a musical representation of a sigh, both of the wind and of the soul (Example 17). Motive *a* appears at the beginning and end of section I, measures 1–10, in which Debussy has set off the first two lines of the poem with the indication *lent et caressant.*

[9] Debussy's only use of this device in his songs seems to be the quotation of a motive from *En sourdine* in *Colloque sentimental.* See chapter 10.

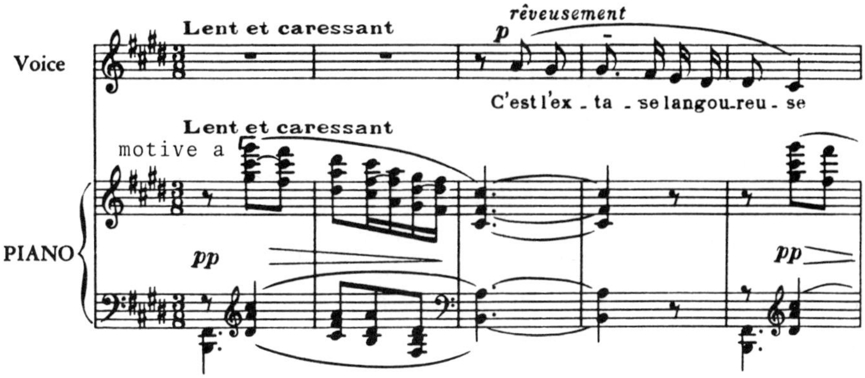

Example 17

Section II, measures 11–19, marked *Un poco mosso,* sets the remainder of the first stanza. The accompaniment in this section is dominated by rhythm 1 (Example 18). Motive *a,* associated with "l'humble antienne,"

Example 18

Example 19

appears in the accompaniment directly after "le choeur des petites voix," and serves to connect these two lines of text.

A new rhythmic figure appears in the third section of the song, measures 20–33, corresponding to the second stanza of text (Example 19). The connection between the murmuring and warbling of small voices, the "cri doux / Que l'herbe agitée expire," and the muted rolling of pebbles is further strengthened by the presence of motive *b* throughout this section (Example 20).

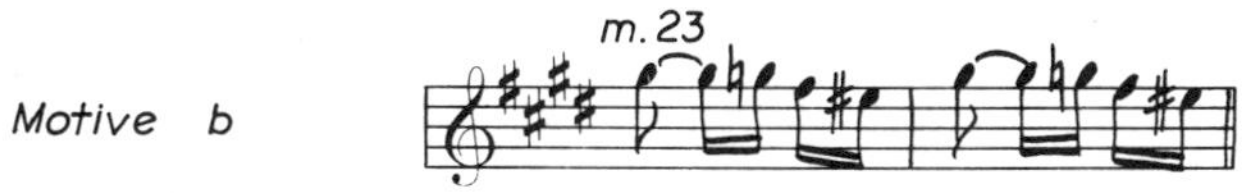

Example 20

The rhythm of the final section, measures 34–52, corresponding to the third stanza of the poem, may be seen as a synthesis of the two preceding rhythms, an extension of rhythm 1 by rhythm 2 (Example 21). Motive *c*, derived from the beginning of motive *a*, accompanies the lines

> Cette âme qui se lamente
> En cette plainte dormante
> C'est la nôtre, n'est-ce pas?
> La mienne, dis, et la tienne.

This descent of a major second, with the second note softer than the first, is a traditional musical representation of a sigh, of which motive *a* may be considered an extension (Example 22).

Example 21

Example 22

The music of measures 43–48 summarizes the poem: first the voice sings the melody from which motive *a* is taken; then the accompaniment states an altered form of motive *b*. In its original presentation, motive *b* began with a half-step. Now the first interval is increased to a whole-step, like motive *c* and the beginning of motive *a*. Thus the final appearance of motive *c* in measures 48–49, representing a joining together of all three motives, unites "notre âme" with "tous les frissons" and "L'humble antienne" with "le choeur des petites voix," (Example 23). This argument may be summarized as follows:

Line	*Section*	*Measure*	*Rhythm*	*Motive*	*Approximate Train of Thought*
1–2	I	1–10		*a*	the state of ecstasy
3–6	II	11–19	1	concludes with *a*	the sounds of nature
7–12	III	20–33	2	*b*	the essential unity of nature
13–18	IV	34–52	3	*c, a, b*	the inclusion of our soul in nature

The notion of motive, as it applies to musical representation, is not

Example 23

an easy one. For the purpose of connecting two points within a song-setting, a composer could imaginably use any motive at all. The only requirement is that it be sufficiently distinctive to be recognized when repeated. In practice, however, a composer will usually adopt a musical motive, either melodic or rhythmic, which somehow represents the text. Such a representation, of course, covers a rather wide range. Certain poetic ideas have natural musical counterparts which have been exploited by composers for centuries. The idea of ascent, for example, can be conveyed by an ascending melodic line. The sixteenth-century madrigalists, in particular, went to great lengths in devising musical equivalents for poetic ideas. Some of these correspondences have become part of the conventional language of music, such as a two-note descending motive to convey the idea of a sigh. The text must be relied upon to indicate whether it be a sigh of longing, of anguish, or of some other kind.

Although these conventional representations occur in Debussy's music with some frequency, one is more likely to encounter the motive which is simply appropriate to its text. Hearing the motive alone, one would be unable to say just what it was meant to represent, but given its association with a text, the motive seems somehow right. It does not require a great deal of imagination to see that a jagged melodic motive or a highly syncopated rhythmic figure will not do to represent the idea of tenderness, but this hardly places much of a restriction upon the composer's inventiveness. Of the three melodic motives in Debussy's setting of *C'est l'extase*, motive *c* is a well-established form for a sigh, motive *a* is Debussy's own depiction of a sigh, and motive *b* seems right for the setting of a "cri doux." In the following chapters we shall pay particular attention to musical devices such as motive *a* which comprise Debussy's expressive vocabulary.

Green

Voici des fruits, des fleurs, des feuilles et des branches
Et puis voici mon coeur qui ne bat que pour vous.
Ne le déchirez pas avec vos deux mains blanches
Et qu'à vos yeux si beaux l'humble présent soit doux.

J'arrive tout couvert encore de rosée
Que le vent du matin vient glacer à mon front.
Souffrez que ma fatigue à vos pieds reposée
Rêve des chers instants qui la délasseront.

Sur votre jeune sein laissez rouler ma tête
Toute sonore encor de vos dernier baisers;
Laissez-là s'apaiser de la bonne tempête,
Et que je dorme un peu puisque vous reposez.

[For translation, see p. 297]

In *Green* Verlaine expresses the confusion of feelings attending a new love, the ambivalent sensations of eagerness and diffidence, of intimacy and detachment. From the first line, where the natural order of growth from branch to leaf to flower to fruit has been compressed into a single poetic instant, Verlaine plays with the relation between literature and life. Writing in a tone which stands "à mi-chemin de l'ironie et du sentiment" the poet draws on and mixes together elements of several literary traditions.[10]

The literature of *amour courtois* centers on the beautiful, virtuous woman, a woman beyond reach whom the lover wins through braving some ordeal or bringing back some inaccessible trophy (in *Green* the triumph over the usual succession of seasons). The lover presents his heart, the seat of emotions, to the lady, often with the complaint that she will not accept the body as well. The tradition of *amour courtois* is further reflected in the conventional "mains blanches" (the woman's hands are always white); in the elevated, archaic language of the petition "Souffrez que ma fatigue," where the personification increases the distance between convention and actual feeling; and in the opening line, which suggests the metaphor of a love which grows, blossoms, and bears fruit.

Green also resounds with reverberations of *préciosité.* In the third quatrain the phrase "jeune sein" has the sound of a conventional description, like "mains blanches" or "beaux yeux." The word *derniers*, used in a simple temporal sense in the second line, was one of the favorite adjectives of *précieux* poets of the seventeenth century, who liked to express their emotions in adjectives of extremes, such as *effroyable, furieuse.* They delighted in periphrasis, referring to "les yeux" as "les miroirs de l'âme," to "le miroir" as "le cristal d'amour," and to "les femmes" as "les divinités visibles." These abstract expressions were part of a codified language characterized by elegance and playfulness.

Literary *préciosité* has been characterized as "un certain abus des ressources de la rhétorique."[11] With Verlaine the "abus" consists of turning metaphors back into reality. The knight of *amour courtois* does not really give his heart, but the cliché "qui ne bat que pour vous" as it appears in *Green* makes a figure of speech become a physical, palpitating organ. The *précieux* description of a lady as "cruelle" (cf. *Mandoline*) turns into a frightening potentiality in the line "ne le déchirez pas."

Verlaine undercuts the rhetorical force of these metaphors by slipping into casual speech. The catalogue of gifts rolls along majestically on the impetus of the opening *voici*, while the gift of the heart, rather than climaxing this recital, follows an everyday idiom like an after-

[10] René Bray, *La Préciosité et les Précieux* (Paris: A. G. Nizet, 1945), p. 324.
[11] *Ibid.*, p. 12.

thought. The woman's white hands are removed from convention and pulled back into physical reality by the specific "vos deux." The final stanza recaptures the intimacy of the lover's passion, but the last phrase, "puisque vous reposez," almost a remark of courtesy, ends the poem on an unemphatic, casual note.

Debussy and Fauré, in their respective settings of this text, employ the resources of harmony to suggest the ambivalence of intimacy and detachment, of effusiveness and diffidence, which Verlaine conveys through shades of literary styles. The word *harmony* refers to the chordal (or vertical) structure of a musical composition, in contrast to the melodic (or horizontal) structure. The choice of a chord to support a given note of the melody colors that note and hence our understanding of the word it sets. Consonant chords may represent normality or repose, while dissonant chords tend to suggest disturbance or tension.[12] A chord normally appears not as an isolated phenomenon but as an element of a series, or harmonic progression. The most common harmonic progressions take on the aspect of formulas—they fulfill our musical expectations and lead to a sense of well-being, sturdiness, and in the extreme, banality.[13] Avoidance of common progressions—the frustration of our musical expectations—piques our interest but in the extreme leads to incoherence. The overall scheme of harmonies in a composition helps to define its structure. Let us see how these principles operate in the two settings of *Green.*

Debussy expresses the youthful fervor of the lover with strong harmonic progressions moving by perfect fifth. The direct fulfillment of our expectations, at least on the chord-to-chord level, helps to convey the effusiveness, perhaps even the naiveté, of the young lover. The slow harmonic rhythm (the speed with which the harmony changes) also contributes to this feeling of earnestness (Example 24).

The first interruption of these strong progressions occurs at the text "Ne le déchirez pas," where a chord which sounds at first like a

[12] Willi Apel, *Harvard Dictionary of Music,* 2d. ed. (Cambridge, Mass.: Harvard University Press, 1969); see articles on "Consonance, dissonance," "Harmony," and "Harmonic analysis."

[13] Leonard Meyer generates a theory of meaning from the notion of musical expectation and its fulfillment or frustration in *Emotion and Meaning in Music* (Chicago: University of Chicago Press, 1956).

Example 24

dominant seventh is resolved not V^7–I but $\sharp IV^{\sharp 6}_{\flat 5}$–V, the so-called German sixth chord. This progression, less common than V^7–I, is further complicated by the appearance of V/V before the chord of resolution.

This unexpected bit of chromatic harmony, after the directness of the opening, helps to express the diffidence which the lover feels in presenting his heart (Example 25).

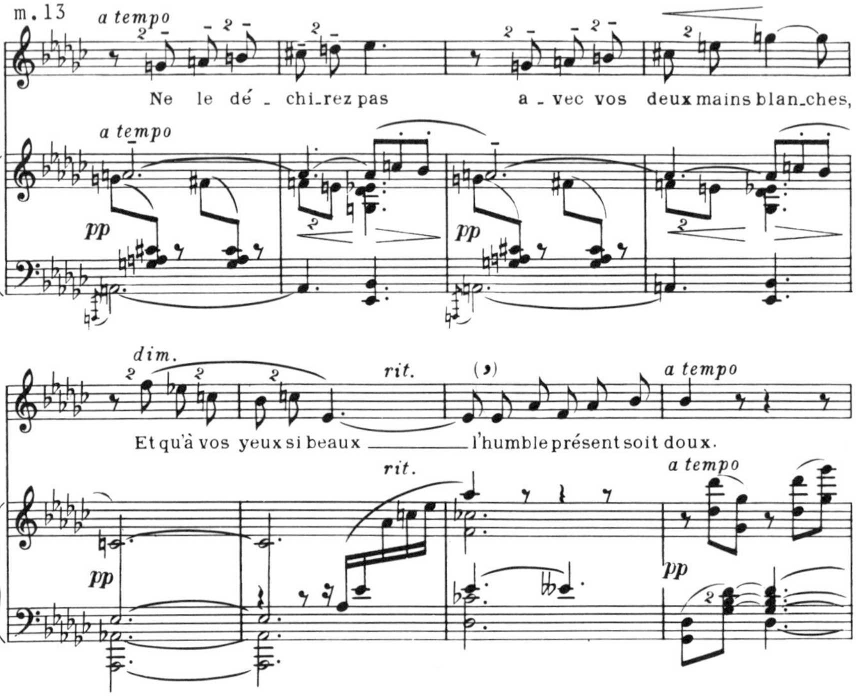

Example 25

A similar bit of chromatic harmony accompanies the recollection of recent ecstasies—"rêve des chers instants qui la délasseront" (Example 26).

These exceptions aside, the harmony of the song is remarkably stable, particularly the musical expression of the repose which concludes the poem (Example 27).

The individual chords of Debussy's setting are mostly consonant; the chord-to-chord progressions are mostly strong. How do these details relate to the overall harmonic scheme (Example 28)?

The song opens not in G♭ major, the key of the piece, but in an extended prolongation of a♭ minor. In fact, the entire first stanza,

Example 26

Example 27

marked A in our example, may be regarded as an elaboration of the familiar II–V–I cadential formula. The effect of this progression is to stress the point of arrival on the word *doux* in measure 20, and to show that everything previous, although it sounds like a perfectly respectable way to begin a song, is only leading up to this point. The presentation of fruit, flowers, leaves, and branches is only the preparation for the gift of the heart, which itself stands for the true desire of the lover, "qu'à vos yeux si beaux l'humble présent soit doux."

The accompaniment bears out this interpretation. Debussy sets the line "Voici des fruits . . ." to the offbeat rhythms of the introduction. The accompaniment changes completely—becoming less involved rhythmically—at the words "Et puis voici mon coeur," which is quite a different kind of gift. The accompaniment becomes still further simplified at the end of the stanza—"Et qu'à vos yeux si beaux l'humble présent soit doux." The young lover so fervently desires his lady's acceptance that he turns almost timid in addressing her, an ambivalence reflected in the language of the poem.

Fauré also employs the principles of harmony to suggest both the fervor and the fearfulness of the young lover. The rapid harmonic changes, up to half a dozen chords in a single measure, suggest exuberance and confusion. Unlike the youth in Debussy's setting, the speaker here tosses off his heart in a flurry of sixteenth notes as if it were scarcely more important than the fruit and flowers, a gesture as casual as the "et puis" of Verlaine's text.

If we divert this torrent of changing harmonies into two levels—one depicting the chord-by-chord movement as in Example 28, the other

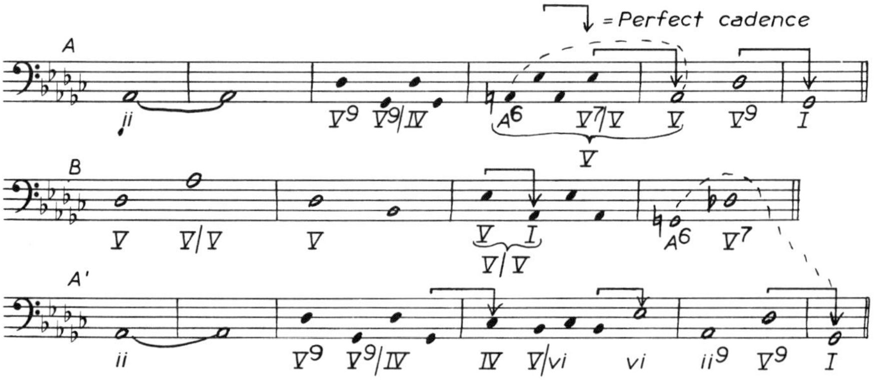

Example 28

sifting out the most important harmonies—we observe that unlike the strong, direct movement of Debussy's song, the harmony in Fauré's setting keeps returning to the tonic (Example 29). For all the apparent

Example 29

activity, the harmony never strays far nor remains long away from home base. Moreover, the chords move predominantly by thirds, a weaker progression than the movement by fifths which we observe in Debussy's setting.

Both composers, then, use harmony to convey the ambivalent feelings of Verlaine's poem. Debussy, through the use of straightforward, standard progressions and slow-moving harmonies suggests the directness and earnestness of the speaker, while the striking postponement of the tonic emphasizes a carefully prepared act of presentation. Fauré, through the use of rapidly changing, often deceptive, harmonies, suggests the confused eagerness of the speaker, while the relatively weak progressions and continual return to the tonic betray his underlying timidity.

Il pleure dans mon coeur

Il pleut doucement sur la ville.
[Arthur Rimbaud]

Il pleure dans mon coeur
Comme il pleut sur la ville;
Quelle est cette langueur
Qui pénètre mon coeur?

O bruit doux de la pluie
Par terre et sur les toits!
Pour un coeur qui s'ennui
O le chant de la pluie!

Il pleure sans raison
Dans ce coeur qui s'écoeure.
Quoi! nulle trahison? . . .
Ce deuil est sans raison.

C'est bien la pire peine
De ne savoir pourquoi
Sans amour et sans haine
Mon coeur a tant de peine!
[For translation, see p. 298]

The grammatical parallel between "Il pleure" and "Il pleut" makes us wonder who is crying. The conjunction *comme* is the key: "Il pleure dans mon coeur / *Comme* il pleut sur la ville." Verlaine asks us to understand the *il* of "il pleure" the same way as we understand the *il* of "il pleut." Can the *il* of either expression be so easily dismissed as "impersonal"? Is there not possibly some real, yet indescribable, antecedent for the pronoun in the expression "il pleut"? Is it not perhaps "le grand neutre de la nature"? [14] The poet must know the source of this languor, since "de ne savoir" "c'est bien la pire peine."

[14] Gerald Hilty, " 'Il' impersonnel; Syntaxe historique et interprétation littéraire," *Française Moderne* 27 (1959):241–251; the quotation may be found on p. 242.

In the second stanza the poet considers the rain, for if only he can comprehend "il pleut" then perhaps he will be able to fathom "il pleure." In the second stanza, in fact, there does seem to be a suggestion of purpose. The rain is a song for him, "pour un coeur qui s'ennuie." But no; even the overeagerness of the exclamation points suggests that he is deceiving himself. This weeping has no reason, any more than the rain has a reason. He has been betrayed by neither lover nor friend. "Ce deuil est sans raison." This is indeed the worst pain, "De ne savoir pourquoi / Sans amour et sans haine / Mon coeur a tant de peine!"

To provide an accompaniment in sound for this feeling of ennui Verlaine makes use of a device called apophony, the modification of timbres for expressive purposes. In the first two lines the variation in vowel sound from *œ* to ϕ is underlined by the parallelism of the consonant *pl.* We observe that the poet has not chosen just any vowel. An apophony e—δ would have badly served his design. The similarity of the dark vowel sounds emphasizes the kinship between the weeping and the rain while the insistence on the timbre *œ,* as in

Il pl*eu*re sans raison
Dans ce c*oe*ur qui s'écoeure

becomes nearly an onomatopoeic figure for nausea.[15]

As poetry and music differentiate themselves from a common prelinguistic parentage, the role played by tone color in poetry is assumed in music by timbre and by harmony.[16] The affective properties of harmony are among the most difficult characteristics of music to describe in words. Even the most carefully chosen language really makes sense only to those who have heard the musical phenomenon that is being described. Although for centuries the major mode has been associated with "happy" music and the minor mode with "sad," one can easily think of examples for which these too-simple generalizations do not

[15] Henri Morier, *Dictionnaire de Poétique et de Rhétorique* (Paris: Presses Universitaires de France, 1961), p. 35.

[16] See articles on "Tone Color" and "Sound in Poetry" in *Encyclopedia of Poetry and Poetics*, ed. Alex Preminger (Princeton: Princeton University Press, 1965); also "Affections, doctrine of" and "Aesthetics of Music" in Apel, *Harvard Dictionary*, both for an introduction to the subject and for bibliographical references.

apply. And yet one does feel a difference between the modes, and a particular quality to "le mode mineur" which is as appropriate to *Il pleure dans mon coeur* as to *Clair de lune.*

The so-called Neapolitan sixth heightens those elements that give the minor mode its particular flavor. The effect can be heard most readily by comparing the sound of the familiar cadential progression ii_6–V–I first in major, then in minor, then in minor with the Neapolitan sixth (Example 30). In *Il pleure dans mon coeur* Debussy seems to go one

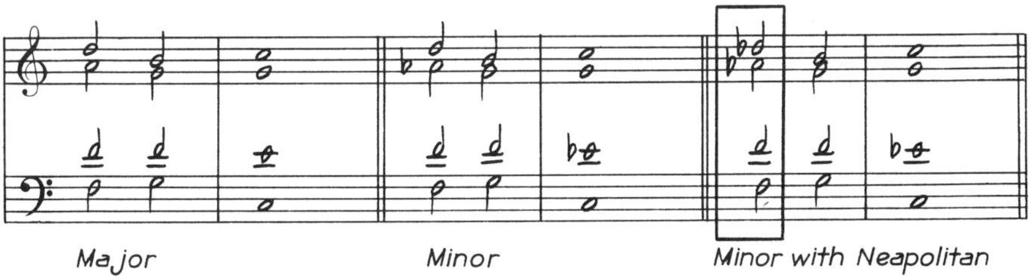

Example 30

step further by using not the Neapolitan sixth but a chord in root position which functions in much the same way as the Neapolitan sixth. Debussy repeatedly prolongs this Neapolitan chord for several measures to form a tonal area in which he can isolate certain ideas in the text. The first section of the song (measures 1–22) is primarily in g♯ minor, and is primarily concerned with the sound of rain, represented graphically by the muted sixteenth notes and symbolically by a melody which returns later at the words "O bruit doux de la pluie" (Example 31). The harmony of the first eight measures. is essentially no more than a stretched-out g♯ minor triad. Debussy sets the lines "Quelle est cette langueur / Qui pénètre mon coeur?" which first raises the question of agency, to a long A major chord, the Neapolitan of g♯ minor. The accompaniment, which as we have seen in Debussy's music frequently represents nature, merely echoes the question without giving any consolation and the harmony returns to g♯ minor.

Debussy sets the second stanza and the first half of the third to a succession of harmonies which moves around the circle of fifths: G♯–C♯–F♯–B–E, then an interruption, and C–F–B♭. Composers have often used the circle of fifths either to get from one key center to another or to establish one key center firmly. The poetic parallel is the speaker's attempt to reason his way through to an answer. But such reasoning is futile; there seems to be no answer, as the "illogical" harmonic progression of "sans raison" in measures 40–41 suggests.

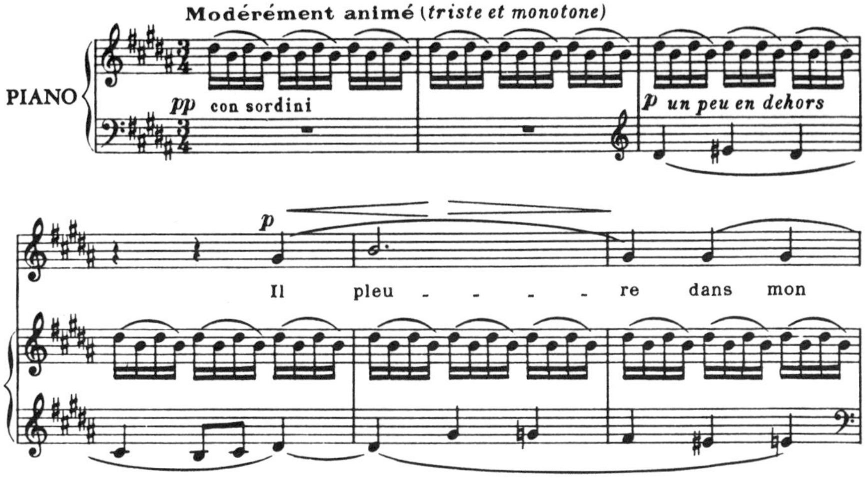

Example 31

But wait! No reason? If, in fact, there is no answer, then there is no point in pursuing the questioning any further, as Debussy suggests by the cessation of the rain in the accompaniment. The words "Quoi! nulle trahison?" are set to a chord which changes from B♭ major to b♭ minor, the musical equivalent of apophony, as it were. The final stanza of the song strongly resembles the first: g♯ minor, with an elevation of the words "Mon coeur a tant de peine" to the Neapolitan A major, set to the melody of "Quelle est cette langueur?" Thus the plaintive query of the first stanza is joined to the resignation of the last. Debussy singles out the word *peine* for special treatement. The pain is compounded by the discovery that the question "Quelle est cette langueur?" has no answer. The speaker begins with the unexplained suffering of ennui; he ends with the greater suffering of unexplained ennui. Nature answers only with the dying of the rain, *a tempo e morendo.*

Fauré's setting of the text illustrates the degree to which harmony and melody intermingle, a subject to which we shall return in chapter 8. The melody of the first two lines descends from the tonic to the dominant in the minor mode, a gesture associated in Western music with the expression of painful emotions.[17] As the melody comes to rest temporarily on the dominant, so the harmony moves to this new plateau, but unlike Debussy's intermittent use of the Neapolitan, Fauré dwells on the dominant for nearly the entire remainder of the song. At the text "Pour un coeur qui s'ennuie" the harmonic line begins to ascend the e minor scale, but alternates between the sixth and seventh degrees without ever regaining the tonic (measures 20–26) then diverges to remote harmonies at "sans raison." "Quoi! nulle trahison?" repeats the musical material of "Quelle est cette langueur" (measures 31–37). The harmony surrounds the dominant on both sides without stating it in measures 45–46 and 49–50, then returns to the tonic as the vocal melody falls from dominant to tonic, a conventional expression of resignation well suited to the final line of the poem, "Mon coeur a tant de peine!" [18] So Fauré completes the descending scale which he had begun at the opening of the song (Example 32).

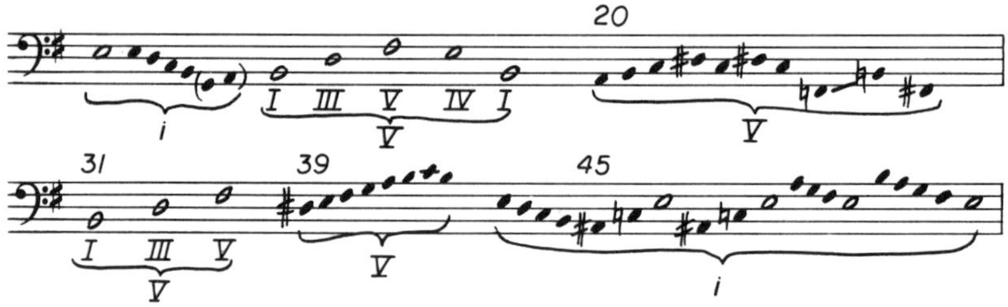

Example 32

Both Debussy and Fauré employ the affective characteristics of the minor mode to express the feelings of languor and ennui in Verlaine's text. Both make use of the melodic descent from tonic to dominant, Debussy further increasing the chromatic tension by filling in the semitones of that descent (see Example 31). Both prefer great prolongations of harmony in order to convey the monotony of a pain without

[17] See Deryck Cooke, *The Language of Music* (London: Oxford University Press, 1959), pp. 162–165, for numerous examples.

[18] See Cooke, *ibid.*, pp. 133–137 for examples.

cause and to set off sections of text without interrupting the accompaniment of the rain.

In studying these settings of six poems by Verlaine we have seen how two composers use the established conventions of music to relate their accompaniment, melody, and harmony to the text. In the two chapters that follow we shall explore the elements of Debussy's style in greater detail.

4

BAUDELAIRE: *Cinq Poems*

Voici venir le temps où, vibrant sur sa tige
Chaque musique militaire s'évapore ainsi qu'un
encensoir!

Et que Baudelaire veuille bien m'excuser.[1]

So Debussy begins a rather unusual essay on an imaginary "musique de plein air." The essay itself, which we shall consider presently, draws so heavily on Debussy's assimilated understanding of Baudelaire, that we might best consider the affinities between the two men before proceeding further.

Debussy first became acquainted with Baudelaire's writings during his sojourn at the Villa de Médicis in Rome. The extent of the poet's influence on the young composer can be seen in a letter to Vasnier dated

[1] Claude Debussy, *Monsieur Croche et autres écrits*, ed. François Lesure (Paris: Gallimard, 1971), p. 45.

19 October 1886 in which Debussy describes the kind of music he would like to compose:

> le genre de musique que je veux faire, j'en veux une qui soit assez souple, assez heurtée pour s'adapter aux mouvements lyriques de l'âme, aux caprices de la rêverie.[2]

The phrases come directly from Baudelaire's letter to Arsène Houssaye introducing *Le Spleen de Paris*:

> Quel est celui de nous qui n'a pas, dans ses jours d'ambition, rêvé le miracle d'une prose poétique, musicale sans rhythme et sans rime, assez souple et assez heurtée pour s'adapter aux mouvement lyriques de l'âme, aux ondulations de la rêveries, aux soubresauts de la conscience? [3]

Debussy describes the act of composition as a receptivity to the inner self, expressed as *caprice* or *rêve,* a theme manifested some years later in a letter to Chausson:

> Il faut bien se dire que nous ne sommes rien du tout vis-à-vis de l'art, nous ne sommes que l'instrument d'une destinée, faut-il donc encore la laisser s'accomplir! [4]

In his later writings as a music critic Debussy again disavows the notion of composition as the active pursuit of a craft, following certain well-established principles, in favor of a detached attentiveness to the subconscious, here referred to as an inner landscape from which a musical dream may emerge.

> J'abomine les doctrines et leurs impertinences. C'est pourquoi je veux écrire mon songe musical avec le plus complet détachement de moi-même. Je veux chanter mon paysage intérieur avec la candeur naïve de l'enfance.[5]

Baudelaire also esteems the detached perceptions of dream, describing too well-defined art as a blasphemy. In *Le Spleen de Paris* he imagines

[2] Quoted in Henry Prunières, "A la Villa Médicis," *Revue Musicale* 7 (1926):135.

[3] Charles Baudelaire, *Oeuvres complètes*, ed. Y.-C. le Dantec and Claude Pichois (Paris: Bibliothèque de la Pléiade, 1961), p. 229. All subsequent quotations of Baudelaire come from this source.

[4] "Correspondance inédite de Claude Debussy et Ernest Chausson," *Revue Musicale* 7 (1926):126.

[5] Debussy, *Monsieur Croche*, p. 303.

a room which resembles a daydream, in which the soul bathes in idleness:

> Sur les murs nulle abomination artistique. Relativement au rêve pur, à l'impression non analysée, l'art défini, l'art positif est un blasphème. Ici, tout a la suffisante clarté et la délicieuse obscurité de l'harmonie.[6]

Instead of the counsels of an obsolete tradition, Debussy suggests nature as a source of learning:

> Il faut chercher la discipline dans la liberté et non dans les formules d'une philosophie devenue caduque et bonne pour les faibles. N'écouter les conseils de personne, sinon du vent qui passe et nous raconte l'histoire du monde.[7]

Musical composition should be a collaboration with nature resulting from an attentiveness to sensation. Debussy has no patience with the "chanson spéculative":

> J'aime mieux les quelques notes de la flûte d'un berger égyptien, il collabore au paysage et entend des harmonies ignorées de vos traités. Les musiciens n'écoutent que la musique écrite par des mains adroites; jamais celle qui est inscrite dans la nature.[8]

If one can receive sense impressions openly, with a certain innocence, memory and imagination mysteriously transform experience into musical thought:

> Qui connaîtra le secret de la composition musicale? Le bruit de la mer, la courbe d'un horizon, le vent dans les feuilles, le cri d'un oiseau déposent en nous de multiples impressions. Et, tout à coup, sans que l'on y consent le moins du monde, l'un de ces souvenirs se répand hors de nous et s'exprime en langage musicale. Il porte en lui-même son harmonie. Quelque effort que l'on fasse, on n'en pourra trouver de plus juste, ni de plus sincère. Seulement ainsi, un coeur destiné à la musique fait les plus belles découvertes.[9]

Baudelaire expresses nearly the same idea in his Salon of 1859:

[6] Baudelaire, *Oeuvres complètes*, p. 234.
[7] Debussy, *Monsieur Croche*, p. 52.
[8] *Ibid.*, p. 51.
[9] *Ibid.*, p. 303.

> Tout l'univers visible n'est qu'un magasin d'images et de signes auxquels l'imagination donnera une place et une valeur relative; c'est une espèce de pâture que l'imagination doit digérer et transformer.[10]

This metamorphosis of perceptions into the patterns of a work of art occurs as an act of the subconscious:

> C'est l'imagination qui a enseigné à l'homme le sens moral de la couleur, du contour, du son et du parfum. Elle a crée, au commencement du monde, l'analogie et la métaphore. Elle décompose toute la création, et, avec les matériaux amassés et disposés suivant des règles dont on ne peut trouver l'origine que dans le plus profond de l'âme, elle crée un monde nouveau, elle produit la sensation du neuf.[11]

To become at one with nature demands a certain submergence of the personality, a development of objectivity which Debussy describes as "le plus complet détachement de moi-même" and "la candeur naïve de l'enfance." Such a childlike state may be natural for "un berger égyptien" or for those of a poetic sensibility. Baudelaire suggests that the metaphor as a means of expression may be supplanted by metaphor as an actual perception. In *Le Poëme du Haschisch* he recounts the sensations of a narcotic dream-state:

> Votre oeil se fixe sur un arbre harmonieux courbé par le vent; dans quelques secondes, ce qui ne serait dans le cerveau d'un poëte qu'une comparaison fort naturelle deviendra dans le vôtre un réalité. Vous prêtez d'abord à l'arbre vos passions, votre désir ou votre mélancolie; ses gémissements et ses oscillations deviennent les vôtres, et bientôt vous êtes l'arbre.[12]

Debussy describes this assimilation of experience as a form of listening, the attentive perception of sounds by an "oreille fine":

> Tous les bruits qui se font entendre autour de vous peuvent être rendus. On peut représenter musicalement tout ce qu'une oreille fine perçoit dans le rythme du monde environnant. Certaines personnes veulent tout d'abord se conformer aux règles; je veux, moi, ne rendre que ce j'entends.[13]

[10] Baudelaire, *Oeuvres complètes*, p. 1044.
[11] *Ibid.*, p. 1038.
[12] *Ibid.*, p. 365.
[13] Debussy, *Monsieur Croche*, p. 289.

The composer must not attempt to imitate the sounds of nature directly, but rather let them penetrate the depths of his imagination, there to be translated into the language of music. Debussy admired this ability in Beethoven; writing about the Pastoral Symphony he says:

> Combien certaines pages du vieux maître contiennent d'expression plus profonde de la beauté d'un paysage, cela simplement parce qu'il n'y a plus imitation directe mais transposition sentimentale de ce qui est "invisible" dans la nature.[14]

In nature the composer may find not only a source of musical expression but also the key to its development—the sense of line defined by natural growth, the trajectories of natural objects in wind and water. In this context Debussy's oft-quoted remark, that nothing is more musical than a sunset, reveals its true significance:

> La musique est une mathématique mystérieuse dont les éléments participent de l'Infini. Elle est responsable du mouvement des eaux, du jeu de courbes que décrivent les brises changeantes; rien n'est plus musical qu'un coucher de soleil! Pour qui sait regarder avec émotion c'est la plus belle leçon de développement écrite dans ce livre, pas assez fréquenté par les musiciens, je veux dire: la Nature. Ils regardent dans les livres, à travers les maîtres, remuant pieusement cette vieille poussière sonore; c'est bien, mais l'art est peut-être plus loin.[15]

Debussy's language in these excerpts from his writings seems to come almost directly from Baudelaire—the "profondeur insondable," the participation in Infinity. The metaphor of a "mathématique mystérieuse," which Debussy states without pursuing, is developed further in Baudelaire's *Le Poëme du Haschisch*, where he describes the effect of listening to music while under the influence of opium:

> Les notes musicales deviennent des nombres, et si votre esprit est doué de quelque aptitude mathématique, la mélodie, l'harmonie écoutée, tout en gardant son caractère voluptueux et sensuel, se transforme en une vaste opération arithmétique, où les nombres engendrent les nombres et dont vous suivez les phrases et la génération avec une facilité inexplicable et une agilité ëgale à celle de l'exécutant.[16]

[14] *Ibid.*, p. 94.
[15] *Ibid.*, p. 171.
[16] Baudelaire, *Oeuvres complètes*, p. 365.

Debussy's ideal of artistic freedom through embracing nature as a source of musical thought may be summarized in a remark written fifteen years after the composition of the *Cinq Poèmes*:

> Je voulais à la musique une liberté qu'elle contient peut-être plus que n'importe quel art, n'étant pas bornée à une reproduction plus ou moins exacte de la nature, mais aux correspondances mystérieuses entre la Nature et l'Imagination.[17]

Baudelaire deals with these mysterious correspondences among nature, imagination, and sensation in his poem *Correspondances*:

La Nature est un temple où de vivants piliers
Laissent parfois sortir de confuses paroles;
L'homme y passe à travers des forêts de symboles
Qui l'observent avec des regards familiers.

Comme de longs échos qui de loin se confondent
Dans une ténébreuse et profonde unité,
Vaste comme la nuit et comme la clarté,
Les parfums, les couleurs et les sons se répondent.

Il est des parfums frais comme des chairs d'enfants,
Doux comme les hautbois, verts comme les prairies,
—Et d'autres, corrompus, riches et triomphants,

Ayant l'expansion des choses infinies,
Comme l'ambre, le musc, le benjoin et l'encens
Qui chantent les transports de l'esprit et des sens.

[For translation, see p. 298]

The multiple meanings of the word *correspondances* which intersect in this poem radiate outward among the other *Fleurs du Mal* and invite us to follow them at least until we meet the poems that Debussy chose to set to music:

1. "La nature est *un* temple"—a singularity composed of many experiences. The sensations of scents, colors, and sounds echo together at a distance in a profound unity. The phrase "de loin" reverberates later in "des choses infinies," recalling Debussy's description of music as "une mathématique mystérieuse dont les éléments participent de l'Infini." The union of sensations at the limit—described here as a "ténébreuse et

[17] Debussy, *Monsieur Croche*, p. 61.

profonde unité, vaste comme la nuit"—finds expression elsewhere as "le gouffre," a word which carries with it both the notion of vastness and of darkness.

> Ces serments, ces parfums, ces baisers infinis,
> Renaîtront-ils d'un gouffre interdit à nos sondes,
> Comme montent au ciel les soleils rajeunis
> Après s'être lavés au fond des mers profondes?
> *[Le Balcon]*

The "gouffre" is "interdit à nos sondes," and yet we desire to plunge into it in search of truth.

> Nous voulons, tant ce feu nous brûle le cerveau,
> Plonger au fond du gouffre, Enfer ou Ciel, qu'importe
> Au fond de l'Inconnu pour trouver du *nouveau!*
> *[Le Voyage]*

We find here a possible source of Debussy's "profondeur insondable qui déclenche l'imagination."

All experience is one. Correspondence = agreement.

2. "De la vaporisation et de la centralisation du *Moi.* Tout est là," Baudelaire writes at the head of *Mon Coeur mis à nu.* This principle of polarity, which runs throughout Baudelaire's poetry, appears in *Correspondances* both in "l'expansion des choses infinies" and in a number of pairs of opposites: the "profond unité" is vast "comme la nuit" on the one hand, and "comme la clarté" on the other. There are "des parfums frais . . . doux . . . verts," all suggesting a certain innocence, and others "corrompus, riches et triomphants." The final tercet includes both amber and musk, scents associated with depravity and "des sens," and benzoin and incense, associated with triumphs of "l'esprit." [18]

A striking example of polarity may be found in the central stanza of *Le Jet d'eau*:

> Ainsi ton âme qu'incendie
> L'éclair brûlant des voluptés
> S'élance, rapide et hardie,

[18] Charles F. Roedig, "Baudelaire and Synesthesia," *Kentucky Foreign Language Quarterly* 5 (1958):128–135. See also Jean Pellegrin, "Baudelaire et les 'Correspondances,'" *Revue des Sciences Humaines* 121 (January–March 1966):105–120; Ihab H. Hassan, "Baudelaire's *Correspondances*: The Dialectic of a Poetic Affinity," *French Review* 27 (1954):437–445.

Vers les vastes cieux enchantés.
Puis, elle s'épanche, mourante,
En un flot de triste langueur,
Qui par une invisible pente
Descend jusqu'au fond de mon coeur.

Similarly in *Recueillement* night falls "Aux uns portant la paix, aux autres le souci." Correspondence = reciprocity.

3. "Les parfums, les couleurs et les sons se répondent." Sensations and experiences blend together like "confuses paroles." In the second half of the sonnet different kinds of sensations—tactile ("frais comme des chairs d'enfants"), auditory ("doux comme les hautbois"), and visual ("verts comme les prairies") all become olfactory ("Il est des parfums . . ."). The echoes form a music "qui chantent les transports de l'esprit et des sens." Baudelaire develops the same theme in *Tout entière*:

O métamorphose mystique
De tous mes sens fondus en un!
Son haleine fait la musique,
Comme sa voix fait le parfum!

The correspondence of sensory impressions invites the poet to join two sensations into a single metaphor:

Je croyais respirer ton sang. *[Le Balcon]*

Les sons et les parfums tournent dans l'air du soir.
[Harmonie du soir]

Correspondence = harmony.

4. As man passes through the forests of symbols, it is they who watch him "avec des regards familiers" and not the other way around. Nature becomes an extension of man's sensibility, singing his raptures and speaking in "confuses paroles." Natural fragrances take on personal characteristics—"corrompus, riches, et triomphants." Debussy makes playful use of this manner of viewing nature in his poem *De soir*:

Dimanche les trains vont vite,
Dévorés par d'insatiable tunnels;
Et les bons signaux des routes
Echangent d'un oeil unique,
Des impressions toutes mécaniques.

In *Le Jet d'eau* Baudelaire suggests that nature or the outer world not only observes man but also acts as a projection of his personality:

Dans la cour le jet d'eau qui jase
Et ne se tait ni nuit ni jour,
Entretient doucement l'extase
Où ce soir m'a plongé l'amour.

The fountain, which never ceases its constant flow, prolongs the fleeting ecstasy of love. Correspondence = sympathetic response.

5. "La nature et un *temple*"—a place of worship, a place where truth is revealed. Behind the forest of symbols, behind the living pillars of our experiences, "de confuses paroles" emanate from, reflect, stand for a True Word. Poetry reaffirms the correspondence of our sensations to this underlying unity. Poetry approximates Nature's language by elevating our ordinary *mots* to the level of *paroles.*

Entends, ma chère, entends la douce Nuit qui marche.
[Recueillement]

Through the capitalization of certain words in the text Baudelaire suggests that a familiar experience—the coming of night—is something more than it seems.

Baudelaire shows a preference for sensations with the expansion of infinite things, sensations "qui chantent les transports de l'esprit et des sens," for at the limit of experience is a profound unity in which the physical corresponds to the spiritual, and where the present may somehow correspond to the future.

This transcendental quality in Baudelaire's poetry reflects a desire to discover in death a revelation of the Beyond. In *La Mort des amants* Baudelaire speculates on the possibility of a resurrection in which "un Ange, entr'ouvrant les portes / Viendra ranimer . . . / Les miroirs ternis et les flammes mortes." In other poems Baudelaire is less specific about the nature of this spiritual beyond, but reasserts his determination to discover it. In *La Mort des pauvres* he describes death this way:

C'est la gloire des Dieux, c'est le grenier mystique,
C'est la bourse du pauvre et sa patrie antique,
C'est le portique ouvert sur les Cieux inconnus!

Correspondence = symbolic reference.

Debussy, having discovered in nature a source of musical expression, employs the ideas of Baudelaire's *Correspondances* to describe a "musique de plein air" appropriate to a natural setting:

> On peut entrevoir un orchestre nombreux s'augmentant encore du concours de la voix humaine (pas l'orphéon! je vous remercie). Par cela même, la possibilité d'une musique construite spécialement pour "le plein air," toutes en grandes lignes, en hardiesse vocales et instrumentales qui joueraient et planeraient sur le cime des arbres dans la lumière de l'air libre.[19]

Debussy's music might enjoy a better reception in the freedom of such a setting than in the too sharply defined limits of the concert hall, where critics are quick to fault liberties of form and tonality. Debussy would accept the possible loss of detail in the open air for the sake of the "grande ligne."

> Telle succession harmonique paraissant anormale dans le renfermé d'une salle de concert prendrait certainement sa juste valeur en plein air; peut-être trouverait-on là le moyen de faire disparaître ces petites manies de forme et de tonalité trop précises qui encombrent si maladroitement la musique? Celle-ci pourrait s'y renouveler et y prendre la belle leçon de liberté contenue dans l'épanouissement des arbres; ce qu'elle perdrait en charme minutieux ne la regagnerait-elle pas en grandeur? [20]

The power of such music would lie not in sheer volume but in a spaciousness of conception in which "de longs échos qui de loin confondent" would prolong the composer's musical dream in the imagination of the audience. "Les parfums, les couleurs et les sons se répondent" in a mysterious collaboration, reunited by music into a "correspondance."

> Il faut comprendre qu'il ne s'agit pas de travailler dans "le gros," mais dans "le grand"; il ne s'agit pas non plus d'ennuyer les échos à répéter d'excessives sonneries, mais d'en profiter pour prolonger le rêve harmonique dans l'âme de la foule. La collaboration mystérieuse des courbes de l'air, du mouvement des feuilles et due parfum des fleurs s'accomplirait, la musique pouvant réunir tous ces éléments dans une entente si parfaitement naturelle qu'elle semblerait participer de chacun d'eux.[21]

In the spaciousness of an open-air setting music might find its own equivalent to the "gouffre" of Baudelaire's poetry. Music denied the

[19] Debussy, *Monsieur Croche*, p. 75.
[20] *Ibid.*, p. 45.
[21] *Ibid.*, p. 75.

movement of space will always smell a little stuffy, in obvious contrast to the olfactory feast of nature:

> Puis, enfin, on pourrait vérifier décidément que la musique et la poésie sont les deux seuls arts qui se meuvent dans l'espace. Je puis me tromper, mais il me semble qu'il y a, dans cette idée, du rêve pour des générations futures. Pour nous autres pauvres contemporains, j'ai bien peur que la musique continue à sentir un peu le renfermé.[22]

From the poems of Baudelaire "qui se meuvent dans l'espace" Debussy chose to begin his *Cinq Poèmes* with *Le Balcon.*

Le Balcon

Mère des souvenirs, maîtresse des maîtresses,
O toi, tous mes plaisirs! ô toi, tous mes devoirs!
Tu te rappelleras la beauté des caresses,
La douceur du foyer et le charme des soirs,
Mère des souvenirs, maîtresse des maîtresses!

Les soirs illuminés par l'ardeur du charbon,
Et les soirs au balcon, voilés de vapeurs roses.
Que ton sein m'était doux! que ton coeur m'était bon!
Nous avons dit souvent d'impérissables choses
Les soirs illuminés par l'ardeur du charbon.

Que les soleils sont beaux dans les chaudes soirées!
Que l'espace est profond! que le coeur est puissant!
En me penchant vers toi, reine des adorées,
Je croyais respirer le parfum de ton sang.
Que les soleils sont beaux dans les chaudes soirées!

La nuit s'épaississait ainsi qu'une cloison,
Et mes yeux dans le noir devinaient tes prunelles,
Et je buvais ton souffle, ô douceur! ô poison!
Et tes pieds s'endormaient dans mes mains fraternelles.
La nuit s'épaississait ainsi qu'une cloison.

Je sais l'art d'évoquer les minutes heureuses,
Et revis mon passé blotti dans tes genoux.
Car à quoi bon chercher tes beautés langoureuses
Ailleurs qu'en ton cher corps et qu'en ton coeur si doux?
Je sais l'art d'évoquer les minutes heureuses!

[22] *Ibid.*, p. 46.

Ces serments, ces parfums, ces baisers infinis,
Renaîtront-ils d'un gouffre interdit à nos sondes,
Comme montent au ciel les soleils rajeunis
Après s'être lavés au fond des mers profondes?
—O serments! ô parfums! ô baisers infinis!

[For translation, see p. 299]

The principle of polarity which we saw illustrated in *Correspondances* appears in *Le Balcon* not so much in the separation of opposites as in their union. The balcony itself becomes a symbol of this communion, this coming together, as it extends outward from the apartment into "le charme des soirs," a gesture embodied in the line "en me penchant vers toi."

The balcony leans from "la douceur du foyer" into "l'espace profond," from the intimacy of the apartment into the anonymity of the world, from the warmth of the hearth into the cold of the night. The communion on the balcony stands apart from the passionate love-making which has taken place within the apartment, as Baudelaire savors the moment of repose between ardor and sleep ("tes pieds s'endormaient dans mes mains fraternelles.") The meditation takes place at twilight, just before the disappearance of "les soleils . . . beaux" into "un gouffre interdit à nos sondes." The twilight as union of day and night corresponds to the present as the union of past and future. "Je . . . revis mon passé": the act of meditation which occurs in the present moment recollects deathless things from the past. "Tu te rappelleras": the sensations of the present become the memories of the future. Baudelaire addresses his love as "Mère des souvenirs," the source of memories, the joining of past ("plaisirs") and future ("devoirs").

The form of the poem takes the shape of its basic metaphor: each stanza becomes a "place set apart" through the repetition of lines, but then leans toward the next stanza through connecting words. "Le charme des soirs" of the first stanza leads to "Les soirs illuminés" in the second; the solemn words of the second stanza ("Nous avons dit souvent d'impérissables choses") become explicit in the third ("Que les soleils sont beaux dans les chaudes soirées! / Que l'espace est profond! que le coeur est puissant!"). The supposition of the third stanza ("Je croyais respirer le parfum de ton sang") becomes realized in the fourth ("je buvais ton souffle").

The opening line of the last stanza incorporates all that has preceded: "Ces serments"—the imperishable words that the lovers have exchanged; "ces parfums"—the fragrance of your blood, the sweetness of your breath; "ces baisers infinis"—the beauty of caresses, the tenderness of your heart, the snuggling at your knee. All these experiences: do they return the way the sun returns in the morning, the way sexual desire is renewed? Here again the form of the poem shares in its content, for the first line of each strophe is "reborn" at the end of the strophe, and in the last strophe is cleansed, as kisses are washed at the bottom of deep seas, so that "Ces serments, ces parfums, ces baisers infinis" becomes "O serments! ô parfums! ô baisers infinis!" Thus Baudelaire suggests an affirmative answer to his question; he is able to perpetuate experience through poetry: "Je sais l'art d'évoquer les minutes heureuses"—the meditation on the balcony, the recalling of things past.

Debussy recognized the role of memory as a means of meditating on past experience without being overwhelmed by the immediacy of the moment:

> Je n'ai jamais pu faire quoi que ce soit, toutes les fois qu'il s'est passé quelque chose dans ma vie; c'est je crois ce qui fait la supériorité du souvenir: de cela on peut retirer des émotions valables, mais les gens qui pleurent en écrivant des chefs-d'oeuvre sont d'implacables blagueurs.[23]

Debussy follows the form of the poem in setting the first and last lines of each stanza to the same melodies. He further emphasizes the integrity of the individual stanzas by relating each one to a different tonal center. Each stanza thus becomes a "place set apart" which leans toward the next stanza in a sequence of tonal centers, C-G-B-F-A- . . . , which breaks off at the final stanza, the one that differs from the others in that its first and last lines are not the same. The final stanza begins on D and ends—"rajeunis"—in C, the original key of the piece, "après s'être lavés" in such remote tonal centers as F♯ and B.

The individual stanzas are further connected by the presence of a basic melodic motive which recurs throughout the song and which serves as the source of the melodies which appear at the beginning and end of each stanza (Example 1).

[23] *Correspondance de Claude Debussy et Pierre Louÿs*, ed. Henri Borgeaud (Paris: Librairie José Corti, 1945), pp. 109–110.

Example 1

The major third, whose importance is readily apparent in the example, appears in the first stanza both as a limit to the chromatic movement of the bassline and as the distance separating the first section of the stanza (centering on C) from the second (centering on E) (Example 2).

The tonality of the second stanza seems deliberately less forthright than the others to suggest evenings "voilés de vapeurs roses." This is the only stanza in which Debussy does not indicate the change of tonal center by a change in key signature. The first two lines of text are set to long chromatic descents in the bass extending over a tritone: the first

C–F♯, the second E♭–A. Only in the third line does the convergence of F♯ and A on the center G become apparent (Example 3).

The principle of the sequence, which Debussy uses to organize the overall tonal structure of the song, appears in smaller scale in the third stanza, beginning with the text "en me penchant vers toi," the words which embody the basic gesture of the poem (Example 4).

In the fifth stanza Debussy departs from the center on A at the point where the text describes "chercher tes beautés langoureuses / Ailleurs," returning to center on A at "ton coeur si doux." Once again the device of the sequence appears, not, as in the third stanza, as "penchant vers" (C♯–E♭–F–G leading back to B) but "chercher ailleurs" (D–F♯–B♭).

The final stanza, which opens on D, shows no definite signs of C major until the third line, "Comme montent au ciel les soleils rajeunis," set to a bassline which mounts to the dominant G, sustains a long dominant pedal, then finally arrives, "reborn," at C major.

Example 2

Example 3

Le Balcon is one of the earliest songs to contain extensive examples of the whole-tone scale. As yet Debussy uses only five notes of the hexachord at a time, but the pattern of the scale's appearances anticipates Debussy's later practice of associating it with elements of darkness, obscurity, sleep: "Les soirs au balcons, voilés de vapeurs roses" (see Example 3). The night grows deeper—Debussy uses the whole-tone scale to underline *s'épaississait* and *cloison.* It becomes so dark that the poet can only guess at the pupils of his lover's eyes. In setting "lavés au fond des mers profondes" Debussy depicts the vast depths of the sea in the most extended whole-tone passage in the song.

This use of the whole-tone scale to suggest obscurity eventually becomes an idiom in Debussy's expressive language. In *Le Son du cor* Debussy sets to a whole-tone melody the lines "La neige tombe à longs traits de charpie / A travers le couchant sanguinolent." In *Pelléas et Mélisande* a whole-tone ostinato accompanies Golaud and Pelléas in the darkness of the castle vaults. The piano prelude *Voiles* is set almost entirely in the whole-tone scale. The whole-tone scale is musically appropriate for these uses because it clouds the continuity of harmonic progression. With no intrinsic allegiance to a particular center, the whole-tone scale obscures the musical train of thought like a tonal fog.

By contrast, in *Le Balcon* the chromatic scale supplies melodic

Example 4

segments with which Debussy associates elements of light, intimacy, and evocation of the past:

> The act of recalling the past: (Measure 10)
> The brightness of the evenings: (Example 3)
> The expression of intimacy: (Example 4)
> The act of evoking the past: (Example 5).

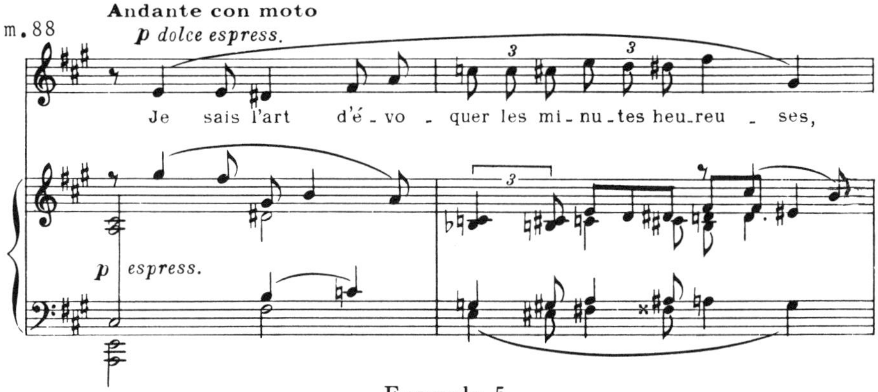

Example 5

The common element here, as in Debussy's other works, appears to be a movement forward, an immediacy, a sense of presence which contrasts with the receding nature of the whole-tone scale. Debussy uses the chromatic scale in *La Mort des amants* to depict images of light in the following lines:

> deux vastes flambeaux
> Qui réfléchiront leurs doubles lumières.
>
> un éclair unique
> Comme un long sanglot, tout chargé d'adieux.

The chromatic scale appears in the melody of *C'est l'extase* to evoke the voices of nature:

> Cela gazouille et susurre
> Cela ressemble au cri doux
> Que l'herbe agitée expire.

Composers have used the descending chromatic scale for centuries to depict pain or anguish. Debussy uses it in this fashion in setting the first line of *Il pleure dans mon coeur.* Again, this scale is musically well suited to that use. The melodic tension produced by introducing semitones in between the regular scale degrees lends a piquancy to the music which is quite the opposite of the obscuring, muting effect of the whole-tone scale.

Harmonie du Soir

Voici venir les temps où vibrant sur sa tige
Chaque fleur s'évapore ainsi qu'un encensoir;
Les sons et les parfums tournent dans l'air du soir;
Valse mélancolique et langoureux vertige!

Chaque fleur s'évapore ainsi qu'un encensoir;
Le violon frémit comme un coeur qu'on afflige;
Valse mélancolique et langoureux vertige!
Le ciel est triste et beau comme un grand reposoir.

Le violon frémit comme un coeur qu'on afflige,
Un coeur tendre, qui hait le néant vaste et noir!
Le ciel est triste et beau comme un grand reposoir;
Le soleil s'est noyé dans son sang qui se fige.

Un coeur tendre, qui hait le néant vaste et noir,
Du passé lumineux recueille tout vestige!
Le soleil s'est noyé dans son sang qui se fige . . .
Ton souvenir en moi luit comme un ostensoir!

[For translation, see p. 300]

Harmonie du soir takes the form of a *pantoum,* a Malayan verse pattern in which the second and fourth lines of each stanza become the first and third lines of the following stanza. The resulting interplay of lines creates a feeling of "vertige" described in the text by the verbs *vibrer, tourner, frémir.* Each line or each pair of lines evokes an image which takes on different shades of meaning depending on its position in the pattern. This playing together of various images in the poem produces the effect of musical harmony.

Les sons et les parfums tournent dans l'air du soir;
Valse mélancolique et langoureux vertige.

The whirling of the sounds and fragrances of the evening produces a vertiginous waltz.

Le violon frémit comme un coeur qu'on afflige,
Valse mélancolique et langoureux vertige.

The new juxtaposition of lines clarifies the phrase "Valse mélancolique," a waltz played by the violin which quivers like an afflicted heart.

Voici venir les temps où vibrant sur sa tige
Chaque fleur s'évapore ainsi qu'un encensoir.

The flowers move back and forth on their stems, spreading their fragrance the way an acolyte swings a censer.

Chaque fleur s'évapore ainsi qu'un encensoir;
Le violon frémit comme un coeur qu'on afflige,

The violin quivers as the bow causes the strings to vibrate; the similar vibration of the flowers calls to our attention the double meaning of *tige:* both the stem of a plant and the wood part of a violin bow.

Le violon frémit comme un coeur qu'on afflige,
Valse mélancolique et langoureux vertige!

Le violon frémit comme un coeur qu'on afflige,
Un coeur tendre, qui hait le néant vaste et noir!

The new line extends the description of "un coeur"—a tender heart, afflicted because it abhors the blackness which signifies the end of day.

Le violon frémit comme un coeur qu'on afflige,
Un coeur tendre, qui hait le néant vaste et noir!

Un coeur tendre, qui hait le néant vaste et noir,
Du passé lumineux recueille tout vestige!

A tender heart, which abhors the black void, piously gathers every vestige of a luminous past. Line by line the image becomes clearer—it is a heart afflicted by the loss of the sun.

Baudelaire's poem differs from the Malayan *pantoum* in one important respect. In the *pantoum* the last line repeats the first so that the poem becomes an endless circle. In *Harmonie du soir*, by contrast, the last line represents a point of arrival, the culmination of two converging trains of thought, represented by the two rhymes "oir" for words of spiritual significance, and "ige" for words of sensual significance.

The revolving sensations illustrate the lines from *Correspondances*:

"Les parfums, les couleurs et les sons se répondent . . . comme de longs échos qui de loin se confondent." The fragrances of the flowers mix with the sound of the violin and "les sons . . . du soir" in a melancholy waltz. The image of a drowning sun and of congealing blood, the sensations of "un coeur qu'on afflige" and the emptiness of "le néant vaste et noir"—produce a giddy languor which corresponds to the movement of the poem itself.

A second train of thought illustrates the opening words of *Correspondances*: "La nature est un temple . . ." as Baudelaire transforms the outdoors into a cathedral. "Voici venir les temps": the poem opens with a biblical incantation, "Ecce venit hora . . ." (John 16:32). Each flower swings back and forth on its stem like a censer. The "langoureux vertige" suggests the dizziness of mystical ecstasy. The sky is like a temporary altar, "triste" because of associations with death, "beau" because of associations with resurrection.

The last line synthesizes these converging trains of thought in a transubstantiation of the sensual into the spiritual. The heart had been sad at the thought of death, symbolized by the rather macabre demise of the sun. But in the celebration of the Mass—"ton souvenir" recalls Christ's words: "Hoc facite in meam commemorationem" (Luke 22:19)—the elevation of the Host reverses the downward movement of drowning. The triumphant upward movement of the "ostensoir," whose very shape embodies the sun, stands for the transfiguration of death into everlasting life.

Debussy preserves the poetic form of the oriental *pantoum* in his song setting, composed in 1889, the year of his encounter with Eastern music at the Paris Exposition. Just as the repeated lines of poetry take on different shades of meaning as different lines surround them, so the musical setting of these lines changes in repetition, either by transposition or by an alteration of the accompaniment. The reiteration of "Chaque fleur s'évapore ainsi qu'un encensoir," for example, has a new accompaniment based on that of the line which precedes it, "Valse mélancolique et langoureux vertige."

Debussy also finds musical expression for the other organizing principle of the poem—the presentation of two trains of thought and their synthesis in the final line. Two motives, *a* and *b*, occur at the beginning of the song, and while they never appear in the voice, they form the basis of the accompaniment. At their first appearance the two motives are juxtaposed harmonically (Example 6). Later they are juxtaposed melodically (Example 7). In the course of the song the two motives are modified (Example 8). At the climactic last line of the song,

Example 6

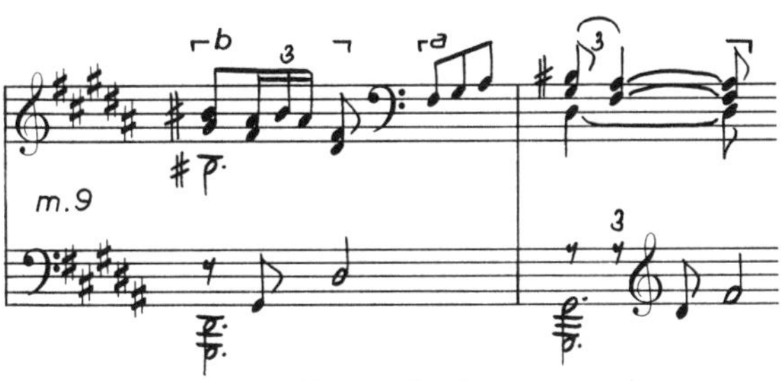

Example 7

Example 8

the two motives become one. This new consummate motive is repeated to accompany the last line, and at its final statement ends in a long tonic triad of resolution and fulfillment (Example 9). Just as the spiritual and the sensual are united in the last line of Baudelaire's poem, so that two

Example 9

melodic motives become one in the musical accompaniment of this final line.

Baudelaire's "vaporisation et centralisation du Moi," which aptly describes the opposing movements in the poem, also epitomizes the tonal scheme of Debussy's song setting. The harmonies for the most part do not follow traditional linear progressions but seem to emanate from the central tonality like perfume from flowers. Chords, largely released from their usual functional bonds, become gradually more distant in a spatial, rather than a tonal, sense. Bass notes become more important than theoretical roots in defining temporary centers (Example 10). The

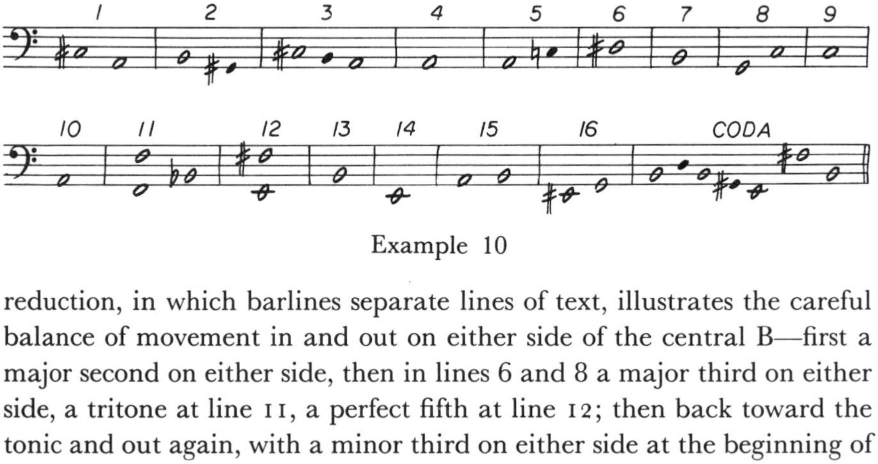

Example 10

reduction, in which barlines separate lines of text, illustrates the careful balance of movement in and out on either side of the central B—first a major second on either side, then in lines 6 and 8 a major third on either side, a tritone at line 11, a perfect fifth at line 12; then back toward the tonic and out again, with a minor third on either side at the beginning of the coda. Even the conclusion of the song, with a bassline which follows the traditional IV-V-I formula, is actually harmonized with the much weaker chords IV^7-iii_6-I to preserve the illusion of harmony "trembling on its stem" of B.

Le Jet d'eau

Tes beaux yeux sont las, pauvre amante!
Reste longtemps, sans les rouvrir,
Dans cette pose nonchalante
Où t'a surprise le plaisir.
Dans le cour le jet d'eau qui jase
Et ne se tait ni nuit ni jour,
Entretient doucement l'extase
Où ce soir m'a plongé l'amour.

La gerbe d'eau qui berce
    Ses mille fleurs
Que la lune traverse
    De ses pâleurs
Tombe comme une averse
    De larges pleurs.

Ainsi ton âme qu'incendie
L'éclair brûlant des voluptés
S'élance, rapide et hardie,
Vers les vastes cieux enchantés.
Puis, elle s'épanche, mourante,
En un flot de triste langueur,
Qui par une invisible pente
Descend jusqu'au fond de mon coeur.

La gerbe d'eau qui berce
    Ses mille fleurs
Que la lune traverse
    De ses pâleurs
Tombe comme une averse
    De larges pleurs.

O toi, que la nuit rend si belle,
Qu'il m'est doux, penché vers tes seins,
D'écouter la plainte éternelle
Qui sanglote dans les bassins!
Lune, eau sonore, nuit bénie,
Arbres qui frissonez autour,
Votre pure mélancolie
Est le miroir de mon amour.

La gerbe d'eau qui berce
Ses mille fleurs
Que la lune traverse
De ses pâleurs
Tombe comme une averse
De larges pleurs.
[For translation, see p. 300]

Le Jet d'eau, like the two preceding poems, displays more repetition than most of Baudelaire's poetry. It may have been this repetition—more typical of music than of poetry—which attracted Debussy to these particular poems. While a word or two may appear several times within a poem, the repetition of whole lines is less common, perhaps because poetry draws its basic vocabulary from ordinary speech. Music, a language which we use for no other purpose than for music itself, must include considerable redundancy to be intelligible. The degree of repetition in these three poems, then, brings them closer than most poems to the state of music.[24]

In *Le Balcon* the repetition of lines symbolizes rebirth. In *Harmonie du soir* the intertwining of repeated lines produces a kind of poetic counterpoint. In *Le Jet d'eau* the repeated refrain serves as a fixed point, a basin out of which Baudelaire's poetry rises and to which it returns. The column of water first rocks its droplets as in a cradle, then falls like a shower of great tears. The erotic symbolism of the erect fountain and the gushing jet of water contrasts with the "triste langueur" which follows the act of love. The passing of the moon across the scene anticipates the narcissistic identification of the poet with nature in the final stanza: "Lune . . . Votre pure mélancolie / Est le miroir de mon amour."

Alternating with the refrain are the three stanzas, each of which moves from the girl back to the poet: from "Tes beaux yeux sont las" to "m'a plongé"; from "ton âme" to "mon coeur"; from "O toi" to "mon amour." This sense of movement from the girl to the poet within each stanza also characterizes the poem as a whole. In the first stanza the poet

[24] Redundancy as an element of communication brings us tangentially to the fascinating subject of information theory. Those interested in pursuing the subject are directed to Colin Cherry, *On Human Communication* (Cambridge, Mass.: M.I.T. Press, 1957, 1966); J. R. Pierce, *Symbols, Signals and Noise: The Nature and Process of Communication* (New York: Harper & Row, 1961); Claude E. Shannon and Warren Weaver, *The Mathematical Theory of Communication* (Urbana: University of Illinois Press, 1964).

sympathizes with the "pauvre amante" whom pleasure has taken by surprise. In the courtyard the poet hears the fountain which he subjectively interprets as perpetuating his ecstasy. The eight lines are divided into two quatrains of *rimes croisés,* balanced by parallel last lines: "Où t'a surprise le plaisir" and "Où ce soir m'a plongé l'amour." The language of the second quatrain abandons the casual, sympathetic tone of "Reste longtemps, sans les rouvrir" for an idealization of the ecstatic experience. The second stanza likewise divides into two quatrains, the first corresponding to upward motion, "rapide et hardie," the second to downward motion, "Mourante, / En un flot de triste langueur." Baudelaire uses essentially masculine words to describe the ecstatic elevation of the girl's soul: "ton âme . . . s'élance, rapide et hardie." The poet appears temporarily to have abdicated his dominant masculine role in order to create this idealized image. He imagines that the girl's soul ascends to "les vastes cieux enchantés" and descends "par une invisible pente." In the final strophe the poet incorporates nature into himself just as he incorporates the girl's soul in the previous strophe. In the first quatrain he addresses the girl once more, but she ceases to have any real existence save as part of the poet's own experience. In the second quatrain he addresses nature—"lune, eau sonore, nuit bénie, arbres"—they, too, exist not as independent entities but only as a mirror of the poet's love.

We recall Baudelaire's remark from *Mon coeur mis à nu:* "De la vaporisation et de la centralisation du *Moi.* Tout est là." The opposing directions in *Le Jet d'eau* establish the dimensions of this centralization and evaporation through which the self encompasses all. The fountain, of course, displays up and down motion in the vertical plane. This direction is reflected in the movement of the girl's soul, in the rays of the moon, and in the upward extension of the trees. Just as in Mallarmé's *Soupir,* which this poem resembles in several respects, a horizontal plane contrasts with the vertical. The court, the basin, the supine "pose nonchalante" of the girl belong to the horizontal plane, reflected above in the passing of the moon and in the vast expanse of the "nuit bénie." All this the poet embodies within himself: the "vaporisation" in which the girl's soul passes out into nature; the "centralisation" in which all of nature is drawn back into the poet. "Tout est là."

The image of the fountain represents both constancy and change. Its outward appearance remains the same even though the individual drops of water which compose it rise and fall. This combination of constancy and change carries over into the form of the poem. The refrain, which describes the fountain, recurs unaltered throughout the poem, while the image of the fountain changes from one stanza to the next. In the first stanza the sound of a fountain prolongs the ecstasy of love. In the second stanza the upward striving of the fountain, like that of the fountain in Mallarmé's *Soupir*, aspires to the ideal. In the third stanza the fountain, along with other elements of nature, is incorporated into the poet himself.

In Baudelaire's poem the literal repetition of the refrain symbolizes the constancy of the fountain. In Debussy's setting of the poem this distinction between stanza and refrain is weakened. While the melody of the refrain is always the same, the accompaniment varies with each repetition, and often continues the accompanimental pattern of the preceding stanza. This influence of the stanzas upon the refrain has its greatest effect at the end of the song. In the second half of the third stanza of Baudelaire's poem, all nature is encompassed by the poet's self:

Lune, eau sonore, nuit bénie,
Arbres qui frissonez autour
Votre pure mélancolie
Est le miroir de mon amour.

At this point Debussy recapitulates a motive from the opening of the song. The figure from measure 2—"Tes beaux yeux sont las"—that is, weary, drooping—appears in the accompaniment at measure 73, then is altered in the vocal melody at "votre pure mélancolie" (Example 11).

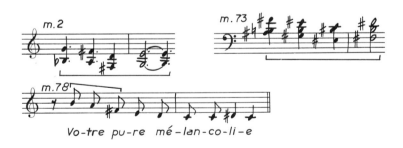

Example 11

This "tear" motive appears repeatedly in the accompaniment of the final refrain, particularly at the words "De larges pleurs." Debussy associates the drooping of the girl's eyes with the tears of the fountain and the melancholy of nature, all of which reflect "mon amour." Debussy has sacrificed the independence of stanza and refrain to express Baudelaire's synthesis of all the elements of the poem into the self of the poet.

Debussy has other ways to express the notion of constancy, which in the poem is represented by the unchanging refrain. For one thing, the melody of the refrain stays the same in each recurrence. The shape of the melodic line tends to imitate the directions expressed in the refrain: the shaft of water, the path traversed by the moon, the sudden shower of tears. A smaller version of the arch appears in the last two lines of the first stanza, with the apex at the middle syllable of the word *extase* (Example 12). A larger, somewhat less well-defined arch characterizes the overall melody of the second stanza.

Example 12

The accompaniment also helps to polarize the melodic activity of the song, with an oscillating motive running almost throughout stanza one and the second half of stanza two, and a large-scale oscillation in the accompaniment of the refrain (Example 13).

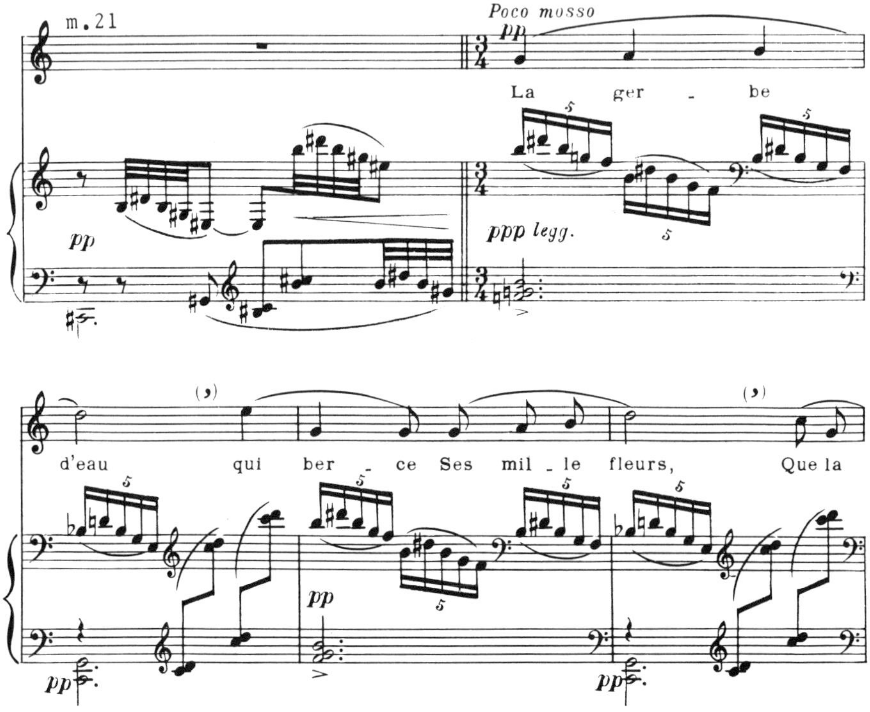

Example 13

The harmony also reflects the imprint of this polarity: the opening of each refrain oscillates between chords on G and chords on C, with a sidewards harmony from f minor to E major at the text "Que la lune traverse / De ses pâleurs," followed again by the descent of a perfect fifth to conclude the refrain.

Throughout *Le Jet d'eau* Debussy emphasizes not the upward flight of the water but the fall. We have seen the prevalence of the descending "tear" motive in the song. A similar downward pull can be felt tonally, beginning with the cascade of perfect fifths ending the first stanza. A more extended cascade occurs at the end of the last stanza: B-E-A-D (Example 14). The final words of the song, "larges pleurs," are

Example 14

accompanied by chords on G♯ minor, F♯ major, and D♯ major before settling into C major.

This emphasis on downward motion contributes to a feeling of repose, sustained by the recurrence of C major in the refrain.

> The predictability of this return has the effect of reducing the degree of tension perhaps otherwise engendered by the intervening

chromatic passages. Repose, therefore, is the guiding principle of this piece, as opposed to a more "tumultuous" conception of harmonic relations in the other . . . songs.[25]

Recueillement

Sois sage, ô ma Douleur, et tiens-toi plus tranquille.
Tu réclamais le Soir; il descend; le voici:
Une atmosphère obscure enveloppe la ville,
Aux uns portant la paix, aux autres le souci.

Pendant que des mortels la multitude vile,
Sous le fouet du Plaisir, ce bourreau sans merci,
Va cueillir des remords dans la fête servile,
Ma Douleur, donne-moi le main; viens par ici,

Loin d'eux. Vois se pencher les défuntes Années,
Sur les balcons du ciel, en robes surannées;
Surgir du fond des eaux le Regret souriant;

Le Soleil moribond s'endormir sous une arche,
Et, comme un long linceul traînant à l'Orient,
Entends, ma chère, entends la douce Nuit qui marche.

[For translation, see p. 301]

"Sois sage, ô ma Douleur, et tiens-toi plus tranquille." The poet addresses his sorrow as one would speak to an unruly child. She has been impatient for evening; now, at last, night is falling. "Il descend; le voici." Darkness envelops the city, "Aux uns portant la paix, aux autres le souci." This separation of "uns" and "autres," the central polarity of the poem, occurs in two other treatments of the same theme. In *Le Crépuscule du soir* from *Le Spleen de Paris* Baudelaire writes: "Le jour tombe. Un grand apaisement se fait dans les pauvres esprits fatigués du labour de la journée. . . . La tombée de la nuit a toujours été pour moi le signal d'un fête intérieure et comme la délivrance d'une angoisse." On the other hand, "Le crépuscule excite les fous. . . . J'ai eu deux amis que le crépuscule rendrait malades. . . . L'ombre qui fait la lumière dans mon esprit fait la nuit dans le leur."

Likewise in *Le Crépuscule du soir* from *Les Fleurs du mal* Baudelaire distinguishes between the peace which comes to the laborer:

[25] Laurence D. Berman, "The Evolution of Tonal Thinking in the Works of Claude Debussy," Dissertation, Harvard University, 1965, p. 83.

O soir, aimable soir, désiré par celui
Dont les bras, sant mentir, peuvent dire: Aujourd'hui
Nous avons travaillé!

and the unpleasant transformation which overtakes the "multitude vile":

Voici le soir charmant, ami du criminel;
Il vient comme un complice, à pas de loup; le ciel
Se ferme lentement comme une grande alcôve,
Et l'homme impatient se change en bête fauve.

In the second quatrain of *Recueillement* Baudelaire describes the fate of the "others," the "multitude vile." They must suffer the whip of Pleasure, that merciless executioner; they store up remorse "dans la fête servile." Baudelaire makes a similar distinction between the base multitude of mankind and the chosen few in *Mon coeur mis à nu*: "Il n'y a de grand parmi les hommes que le poëte, le prêtre et le soldat, l'homme qui chante, l'homme qui bénit, l'homme qui sacrifie et se sacrifie. Le reste est fait pour le fouet." [26]

The poet addresses his sorrow as before: "Ma Douleur, donne-moi la main; viens par ici, / Loin d'eux." A similar drawing apart from the multitude occurs in *Le Crépuscule du soir*, expressed in strikingly similar language:

Recueille-toi, mon âme, en ce grave moment,
Et ferme ton oreille à ce rugissement.
C'est l'heure où des douleurs des malades s'aigrissent!
La sombre Nuit les prend à la gorge; ils finissent
Leur destinée et vont vers le gouffre commun.

The phrase, "Loin d'eux," occupies a pivotal position between the quatrains and the tercets of this sonnet. In an extraordinary enjambment Baudelaire leads his sorrow by the hand, as it were, from "Le souci" of the quatrains to "la paix" of the tercets, across the boundary symbolized, as in *Le Balcon*, by a balcony. Over the clouds, "les balcons du ciel," lean the dead years, garbed in faded dresses. From the depths of the waters—perhaps a river—looms "le Regret souriant." In the west the poet sees the dying sun going to sleep beneath an arch—perhaps a bridge

[26] Baudelaire, *Oeuvres complètes*, p. 1287.

across the Seine—while from the east he hears the approach of "la douce Nuit qui marche." [27]

The capitalization of certain words in the poem—*Douleur, Soir, Plaisir, Années, Regret, Soleil, Orient, Nuit*—suggests that this "nuit" should be understood allegorically. Intimations of mortality pervade the text: *mortels; bourreau; les défuntes Années; en robes surannées; moribond; s'endormir; comme un long linceul.* The particular choice of images, and their relation to expressions of time, connects the cycle of day and night with the longer measure which turns days into years. Thus "le soleil moribond" becomes "les défuntes Années." It is not simply evening which approaches; it is the Evening at the end of Life, an allegory for the death of sorrow.

Night comes for all mortals, but the poet urges his sorrow to accept it with equanimity, to come away from the suffering of "la multitude vile." Debussy, in his setting of this poem, emphasizes the separation between those to whom night brings peace and those to whom it brings anxiety. The pivotal point of the song, as of the poem, occurs at the word "Loin d'eux." In the quatrains the most important structural intervals are the minor third and minor second. Composers have traditionally associated the minor third with sadness, while they have often used the minor second to express pain.[28] The minor third, by extension, produces the minor triad, the tritone, and the diminished seventh chord (Example 15). The minor second, by extension, produces chromatic progressions (Example 16). The introduction of the song contains both extended diminished seventh chords, as in measures 4 and 5, and diminished seventh chords moving chromatically, as in measure 6 (Example 17). The first entrance of the vocal melody is likewise accompanied by elements based on the minor third—diminished triad, tritone—and the chromatic movement of the minor second (Example 18). These elements combine with striking effect at the line "Va cueillir des remords dans la fête servile," where melodic tritones are accompanied by a descending chromatic line.

[27] Madeleine Remacle, "Analyses de poèmes français," *Revue des langues vivantes* 17 (1951):218–227; Bernard Weinberg, *The Limits of Symbolism* (Chicago: University of Chicago Press, 1966), pp. 51–63.

[28] See Deryck Cooke, *The Language of Music* (London: Oxford University Press, 1959) for numerous examples.

Example 15

Example 16

The intervals of minor second and minor third also form the basis of the tonal framework of the piece. In the introduction of the song the roots oscillate between C♯ and E, a minor third apart; this pattern recurs in measures 36–40 and, with interpolations, at the conclusion of the piece. In measures 45–50 the implied root movement is downward by minor third: G♯(= A♭)–F–(D)–B. Root movement by minor second appears in measures 12–14, with an extended chromatic progression in measures 32–34 at the text "Va cueillir des remords dans la fête servile" (Example 19).

The "souci" of the quatrains is set apart from the "paix" of the tercets by the words "Loin d'eux." In the song setting these two words are set to an unexpected *major* second (Example 20). The evocation of propitious night is accompanied by a gradual increase in the number of

Example 17

Example 18

major seconds and major thirds and their extensions, the whole-tone progression and the major triad. Root movement by major second occurs in measures 53–55, supporting a melody in whole steps and an accompaniment of augmented triads (Example 21). The supremacy of major triads and major seconds continues in measures 56–59 (Example 22). The conclusion of the song leads to a final major triad (Example 23).

As we observed in our discussion of Verlaine, composers have for centuries associated the minor triad with feelings of sadness and regret, while associating the major triad with happiness and well-being. Some theorists have speculated that these associations are not completely arbitrary, since the major third, and hence the major triad, occur early in the natural harmonic series.[29] In discussing *Le Balcon* we observed the differences between the chromatic scale—the extension of the minor second—and the whole-tone scale—the extension of the major second. The obscurity and oblivion which accompany the whole-tone scale seem well suited to express resignation toward approaching death, while the piquant quality of the chromatic scale can well be applied to the "fouet du Plaisir." Debussy employs the conventional associations of these

Example 19

Example 20

[29] *Ibid.*

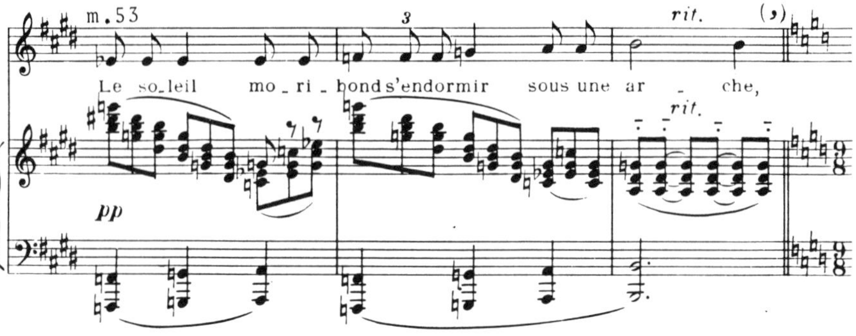

Example 21

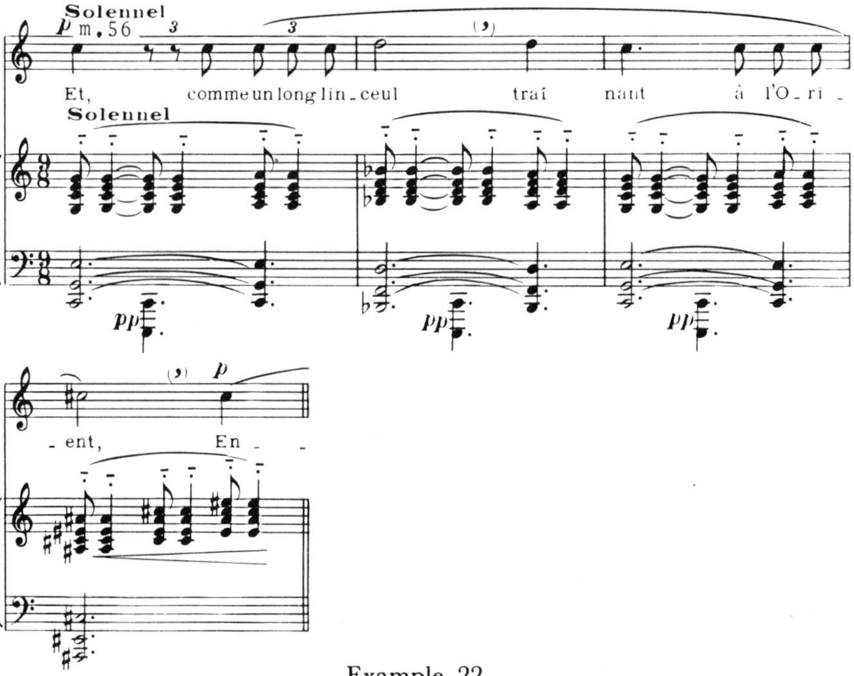

Example 22

intervals to express in musical terms the change of tone between the quatrains and the tercets of Baudelaire's sonnet.

These relationships deserve further consideration, particularly in

Example 23

pieces like *Recueillement* where a consistent vocabulary based on intervals permeates not only the melodic but also the harmonic and tonal structures. The expressive use of intervals has not been paid sufficient attention by music theorists. Deryck Cooke has confronted such questions directly in *The Language of Music.* Most critics of this book refuse to debate Cooke on his own ground and attempt instead to discount the validity of expression in music. The relationship between text and music in *Recueillement* in particular and in Debussy's songs in general attests to the necessity of keeping these questions open if we are to understand Debussy's music.

La Mort des amants

Nous aurons des lits pleins d'odeurs légères,
Des divans profonds comme des tombeaux,
Et d'étranges fleurs sur des étagères,
Ecloses pour nous sous des cieux plus beaux.

Usant à l'envi leurs chaleurs dernières,
Nos deux coeurs seront deux vastes flambeaux,
Qui réfléchiront leurs doubles lumières
Dans nos deux esprits, ces miroirs jumeaux.

Un soir fait de rose et de bleu mystique,
Nous échangerons un éclair unique,
Comme un long sanglot, tout chargé d'adieux;

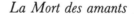

Et plus tard un Ange, entr'ouvrant les portes,
Viendra ranimer, fidèle et joyeux,
Les miroirs ternis et les flammes mortes.

[For translation, see p. 302]

The principle of polarity which we observed in *Correspondances* implies a certain dualism, either of opposites, as in *Le Jet d'eau* or *Recueillement*, or of complements, as in *La Mort des amants.* This dualism appears most forcefully in the second quatrain, where the word *deux* appears three times, accompanied by the cognate *double* and *jumeaux.* These direct expressions of duality are reinforced by the expressions "usant à l'envi," "réfléchiront," and "miroirs," each of which implies a complementary "other."

This idea of dualism in the sense of complementing rather than replicating is reflected both in the form and in the rhythm of the poem. Two matching quatrains precede two matching tercets, a difference in size suggesting the male/female complementarity. Feminine and masculine rhymes alternate in lines of eleven and ten syllables, each line breaking in the middle, so that the eleven-syllable lines fall into two unequal parts. The single *alexandrin* "Et plus tard un Ange/entre'ouvrant les portes" emphasizes the duality of a half-open door, with as much space on one side as on the other, like the balancing of six syllables on either side of the caesura.

The apposition which occurs on a small scale in "des lits/des divans" and the complementarity of "rose" and "bleu" are mirrored on the large scale by the correspondence between the scents of the first quatrain with the colors of the first tercet, and the "flambeaux/miroirs" of the second quatrain with the "miroirs/flammes" of the second tercet, now restored to life, animated for a second time.

Baudelaire exploits the traditional metaphor in which love complements death. The "lits pleins d'odeurs légères" represent both the scene of sensual pleasure and the tombs redolent with mortuary fragrances. "D'étranges fleurs" open voluptuously in the full bloom which immediately precedes their death. The "vastes flambeaux" stand for physical ardor as well as spiritual being. The lovers exchange "un éclair unique" like a sob of passion before entering a deathlike sleep.

Unlike the sixteenth-century madrigalists who commonly employed the language of death to describe sexual passion, Baudelaire enlists the language of sensual pleasure to speculate about death. The words *profonds, dernières,* and *vastes* hint at the *gouffre* which extends beyond the fathoming of ordinary experience. The sensual somehow corresponds to the spiritual, the now to the hereafter. The flowers whose fragrance fills the lovers' beds are described as "étranges," grown "sous les cieux plus beaux." The "rose et bleu" which color an evening of passionate leavetaking are "mystique." The angel of the second tercet, whether a holy messenger or some other supernatural being, comes from beyond the realm of physical experience. In a personal reinterpretation of Roman Catholic theology, Baudelaire suggests that just as the sexual impulse is renewed after the act of love, so the spirit is reanimated after death.

Debussy's setting of *La Mort des amants* incorporates the principle of reflection into every element of the music. The basic motive consists of a minor third repeated at the octave, varied in the second and third measures to minor seconds answered by minor seconds (Example 24).

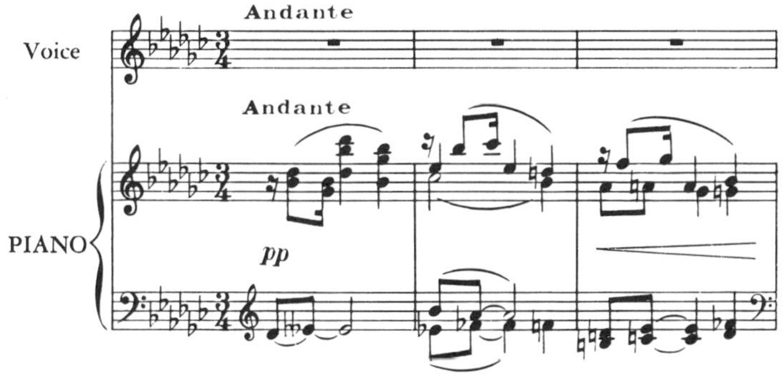

Example 24

Longer phrases correspond to one another, as "un soir fait de rose et de bleu mystique," set entirely on two pitches a minor third apart, reflected in "Et plus tard un Ange" where the same relationship exists. The most dramatic repetition comes toward the end of the piece where "Les miroirs ternis et les flammes mortes" extends the melody first employed for "Nous échangerons un éclair unique." Measure 8 introduces a rhythmic mirror—a rhythm which reads the same forward or backward—which returns in measures 14, 16, 17, 18, and the entire first tercet. In the second quatrain the entire accompaniment takes part in the musical correspondence between the first two lines and the second two lines, while the melody exhibits another reflection in "Qui réfléchiront leurs doubles lumières."

The tonal structure of the song shares in the principle of correspondence. The opening material is reflected a tritone away in the interlude which separates the tercets. Each quatrain moves tonally the distance of an ascending perfect fifth; each tercet descends a major third, with the difference that the second tercet may be regarded as an augmentation of the first. A harmonic motive (bracketed in our example) which runs through the entire structure has the relationship ii–V–I, which may be looked on as the descent of two perfect fifths (Example 25).

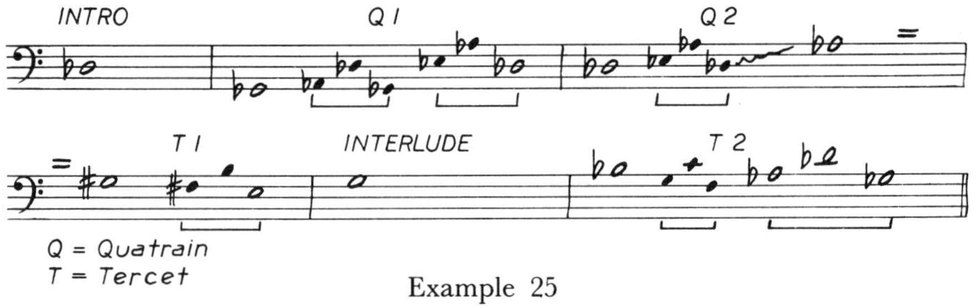

Example 25

In learning the elements of Debussy's expressive vocabulary we have made connections between the text of a song and the musical events which the composer has chosen to fill with meaning. We should not regard these relationships as some kind of strict code. "An artist as ingenious and as rebellious to coercion as Debussy was unable to employ methodically the same means for the same purposes," writes Constantin Brailoiu.[30] Rather we are learning in analyzing Debussy's songs certain idioms which often turn out to be significant. Debussy does not always use melodic motives, or special scales, or structural intervals in a way that seems to have interpretive value, but frequently he does. In the *Cinq poèmes de Charles Baudelaire*, as elsewhere, Debussy displays "a supreme liberty of choice and an unfailing aesthetic judgment, which is commonly called genius." [31]

[30] Constantin Brailoiu, "Pentatony in Debussy's music," in *Studia Memoriae Belae Bartók Sacra* (Budapest: Publishing House of the Hungarian Academy of Sciences, 1959), p. 399.

[31] *Ibid.*, p. 417.

5

VERLAINE II: *Ariettes oubliees* and *Trois Melodies*

In 1888 Debussy gathered some recent songs on texts from Verlaine's collection *Romances sans paroles* into a set called *Ariettes, paysages belges et aquarelles*, a title derived from Verlaine's own division of his poems. The songs remained largely unnoticed by the public, but were reissued in 1903, after *Pelléas* had established Debussy's name, as *Ariettes oubliées*, with a somewhat ironic dedication "A Miss Mary Garden, inoubliable Mélisande, cette musique (déjà un peu vieille) en affectueux et reconnaissant hommage."

We have studied three of the songs in chapter 3: *C'est l'extase, Il pleure dans mon coeur*, and *Green.* The remaining three come under our attention now, along with two of the *Mélodies* of 1891. These songs, including *Le Son du cor*, which we shall consider in the next chapter, are settings of poems from Verlaine's volume *Sagesse.* Around the time they were published

Debussy wrote to his publisher Hamelle, indicating his great admiration for Verlaine's poetry: "Je n'aime plus que ça." Debussy sent Hamelle a volume of Verlaine's poetry, along with some musical manuscripts, and asked that the publisher select those poems he would like set to music. The book remained with the publisher without a selection ever being made.[1]

The five songs to be studied here provide an insight into the way Debussy shapes both moment-to-moment harmonies and the overall harmonic scheme of a song to his expressive purposes.

L'Ombre des Arbres

Le rossignol qui du haut d'une branche se regarde dedans, croit être tombé dans la rivière. Il est au sommet d'un chêne et toutefois il a peur de se noyer. *[Cyrano de Bergerac]*

L'ombre des arbres dans la rivière embrumée
Meurt comme de la fumée,
Tandis qu'en l'air, parmi les ramures réelles,
Se plaignent les tourterelles.

Combien, ô voyageur, ce paysage blême
Te mira blême toi-même,
Et que tristes pleuraient dans les hautes feuillées
Tes espérances noyées!

[For translation, see p. 302]

Taking as point of departure the innocent game of mistaken reflections in the Rostand epigraph, Verlaine constructs an intricate network in which object, image, and symbol are artfully confounded. The first four lines of the poem include several kinds of reflection. The clearest reflection, the guiding image of the poem, appears only by implication: the reflection of trees in the water. The word *comme* coordinates the disappearance of shadows with the disappearance of smoke. An interesting opposition occurs here: when smoke vanishes it leaves clarity whereas the mist, thick as smoke, makes the shadows vanish into obscurity. "Ramures réelles" reflects "l'ombre des arbres," with *tandis que* coordinating the opposition of water images and air

[1] Related in Léon Vallas, *Claude Debussy et son temps* (Paris: Editions Albin Michel, 1958), p. 130.

images. Finally, "se plaindre" is a *reflexive* verb, a *jeu de mots* certainly not lost on Verlaine.

In the second stanza the pallid landscape reflects the pallor of the traveler, and, by extension of the image of the first stanza, the drowned hopes weep in the high foliage. The second stanza thus mirrors the metaphor of the first, with *combien* as the point of reflection: as the water mirrors the trees, so the landscape mirrors the traveler. The lamenting of turtledoves in the first stanza is mirrored in the weeping of the second. Likewise "se plaignent" is mirrored by "te mira," where Verlaine, by grammatical sleight of hand, makes the verb seem reflexive.

The structure of the poem itself displays a mirror image as the two stanzas have the same rhyme scheme and same alternation between *alexandrins* and octosyllabic lines. Verlaine's careful attention to sounds creates an audible counterpart to the reflected images—in the first line the bringing together of words using the relatively uncommon *br* sound:

L'om*br*e des ar*br*es dans la rivière em*br*umée

—in the second stanza the recurrence of rhymes within the line as well as at its end:

Combien, ô voyageur, ce paysage bl*ême*
Te mira bl*ême*, toi-m*ême*,
Et que tristes pleur*aient* dans les hautes feuill*ées*
Tes espérances noy*ées*!

One critic maintains that Verlaine goes a step further in the game of reflections, and joins the end of the poem to the beginning, making a full circle:

> From the river, mirror, one's gaze rises to seek the real in the trees. But one sees there only a reflection, that of the pale traveller, and one hears only a symbol of that which is no longer: the drowned hopes. The second stanza is in the past, a curious *jeu de temps.* The dying reflection of the first stanza thus takes on a greater reality than the object it reflects. The last word of the poem leads us back to the first line where the near non-existence of what has been described—one sees indistinctly in the mist-covered river the reflection, not of the tree but of the shadow of the tree, itself the reflection of the traveller, thus a reality only at the fifth degree—dissolves entirely in terms of

air ("meurt comme de la fumée") just as the "espérances noyées" dissolve in terms of water. The circle is closed.[2]

Debussy's setting of the poem contains fully as many mirrors as Verlaine's text. The second half of the song is a distorted image of the first half, in which the accompaniment of measures 11–16 is almost a literal repetition of the accompaniment of measures 1–6, an effect itself mirrored in miniature in the opening of the piece, where the accompaniment of measures 1–2 is repeated in measures 3–4, and where measures 6–10 can be heard as a distorted reflection of measures 1–5. (Example 1).

The harmony consists largely of unresolved dominant seventh chords, chords which "point to" the chord a fifth below. No cadential resolution of these chords appears anywhere in the first half of the song until a veritable cascade of descending fifths in measures 9–10, each one pointing to the next—F♯ (the sustained note in the right hand of the piano part)-B-E-A-D—finally reaching a resolution at the weeping of the turtledoves, the first "real" object in the poem.

This gesture is reflected in the musical conclusion following the last words of the text, "espérances noyées": E♯ (the sustained note in the right hand of the piano part)—A♯–D♯–G♯–C♯, finally resolving on the actual key of the piece (Example 2).[3]

In this manner Debussy reflects Verlaine's use of the past tense to obscure the distinction between object and image. Here the fifths of the first half, objectifying the weeping of the turtledoves, end on a remote D major triad, while the drowned hopes conclude in the true tonic of the piece.

The elemental building block of the song is the tritone, drawn from the prevalent dominant seventh chords. The opening two measures contain the tritone melodically (B–E♯) and harmonically (root-movement C♯–G). Moreover, the main structural interval for the melody of the opening line is the tritone E♯–B (see Example 1).

Now the tritone is the one interval which reflects into itself when

[2] Eléonore M. Zimmermann, *Magies de Verlaine* (Paris: José Corti, 1967), p. 76.

[3] Bruce Archibald suggests that the whole song is a reflection harmonically, pointing out that the key of C♯ (which is perfectly convincing at the end) is never once supported by its dominant. Instead, the entire song aims at (or suggests) the *subdominant* of C♯—a mirror of tonal practice.

┌┐ = tritone

Example 1

Example 2

inverted, an ideal device to represent the pure essence of reflection, Verlaine's central image. Furthermore, the tritone, an interval which itself stands outside of any key, is the closest interval in size to the perfect fifth, the most stable, key-defining interval. The root movement by tritone at the beginning of each half of the song, then, is an imperfect reflection of the extended movement by perfect fifth at the end of each half.

Finally, a continuation by perfect fifths in either direction from a given note eventually returns to that note by way of the so-called circle of fifths (Example 3). In the chain of fifths at the end of the first half, Debussy moves outward along the circle from C♯ to D. At the end of the piece, he returns to C♯ from the other side, very nearly completing the circle that Zimmermann finds in Verlaine's poem of mirrors. The distance across the circle of fifths at any point is, of course, a tritone.

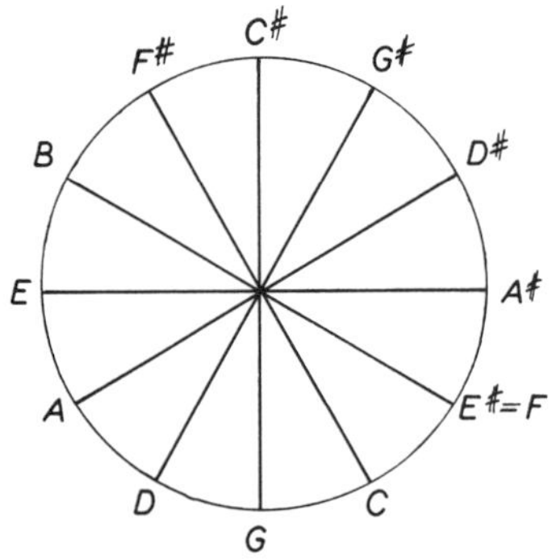

Example 3

Chevaux de bois

Tournez, tournez, bons chevaux de bois,
Tournez cent tours, tournez mille tours,
Tournez souvent et tournez toujours,
Tournez, tournez au sons des hautbois.

L'enfant tout rouge et la mère blanche,
Le gars en noir et la fille en rose,
L'une à la chose et l'autre à la pose,
Chacun se paie un sou de dimanche.

Tournez, tournez, chevaux de leur coeur,
Tandis qu'autour de tous vos tournois
Clignote l'oeil du filou sournois,
Tournez au son du piston vainqueur!

C'est étonnant comme ça vous soûle
D'aller ainsi dans ce cirque bête:
Bien dans le ventre et mal dans la tête,
Du mal en masse et du bien en foule.

Tournez, dadas, sans qu'il soit besoin
D'user jamais de nuls éperons
Pour commander à vos galops ronds:
Tournez, tournez, sans espoir de foin.

Et dépêchez, chevaux de leur âme:
Déjà voici que sonne à la soupe
La nuit qui tombe et chasse la troupe
De gais buveurs que leur soif affame.

Tournez, tournez! Le ciel en velours
D'astres en or se vêt lentement.
L'église tinte un glas tristement.
Tournez au son joyeux des tambours![4]

[For translation, see p. 303]

In *Chevaux de bois* Verlaine creates a popular song as might have been sung by the *chansonniers* of *Le Chat noir*, the celebrated cabaret that Banville and Verlaine both frequented in the 1880s and where Debussy was often the life of the party with his singing and playing. Like the

[4] Debussy omits two stanzas which in the original poem come after the fourth stanza quoted here.

popular *chanson* Verlaine's poem has a refrain, whose unusual lines of nine syllables make an off-balance departure from the rhythms of classical verse. Verlaine gives the impression of making up the poem as he goes along, extemporizing phrases that sound like popular idioms. "Chevaux de leur coeur" means "beloved horses," but "chevaux de leur âme" is a phrase of Verlaine's own devising. Likewise, one is not to question too closely the meaning of phrases like "l'une à la chose et l'autre à la pose" and "bien dans le ventre et mal dans la tête, / Du mal en masse et du bien en foule." Verlaine is improvising his own colloquialisms.

The incantatory repetitions of the word *tournez* produce an effect of *vertige* in the reader-listener. The word occurs seventeen times, eight times in the first stanza alone. Verlaine further reinforces the *ou* sound in other words: *tours, souvent, toujours,* in the first stanza; *autour, tournois, filou, sournois,* in the third. The reiteration of *ou* sounds in the refrains, along with the alliterative *t* which frequently precedes the *ou,* helps to unify the poem as well as underlining its nature as a *chanson.*

In the first stanza Verlaine weaves the sound of the oboe into the whirling of the carrousel. In the course of the poem we hear cornet, bells, and drum (as well as violin and trombone in the stanzas that Debussy omitted).

The people in the poem are all stock characters—"l'enfant tout rouge," "la mère blanche," "le gars en noir," "la fille en rose"—just faces in the crowd. Although a thief catches our eye as we whirl about (the dizziness increases to the point that we think he is moving about us) the circular motion permits us to see people only "en masse," as a "troupe de gais buveurs." The language of the fourth stanza becomes a bit vulgar, and we recall in viewing this "paysage belge" that the French have always regarded the Belgians as somewhat earthy people.

As frequently happens in Verlaine's landscapes, the people are types while the subjects of the active verbs are often inanimate objects or elements of nature. The supper bell is sounded not through human agency but by "la nuit." The sky vests itself with stars while the church tolls the funeral knell. As for the people in the poem, they are governed by their appetites ("gais buveurs que leur soif affame") or caught up in the whirl of colors and sounds like the serenaders in *Mandoline,* where:

Leur élégance, leur joie
Et leurs molles ombres bleues
Tourbillonnent dans l'extase
D'une lune rose et grise.

The tolling of death in the last stanza jars us a little, reminding us that this is not really a song but a poem in the style of a song. One reflects that the people in the poem have no more life than wooden horses, that perhaps their humanity has been lost in the swirling multitude. But Verlaine gives no support for such speculations; rather he quickly brings the circle around again, "au son joyeux des tambours."

Debussy's setting of *Chevaux de bois* comes somewhat earlier than the other songs in the set, dating from around 1885, during the period of Debussy's reluctant sojourn in Italy. Thompson notes that *Chevaux de bois* was admired by Debussy's associates at the Villa Medici. "Arpeggios and series of parallel common chords contribute effects that must have been novel, indeed, for Debussy's fellow laureates in Rome." [5]

Debussy maintains the alternations of refrain and stanza of Verlaine's poem, setting the first three refrains to the same music, but in different keys. The final refrain, of a darker color in the poem, is freely based on the music of the earlier refrains but the tempo becomes *le double plus lent* and the harmonic rhythm slows down as well. The victorious sound of the cornet occurs in various guises through the song, and the endless trills carry associations of excitement (such as drumrolls, or the trills in instrumental cadenzas). We can expect these descriptive devices from any composer. Debussy goes further in employing harmony as well as melody for expressive purposes, and by letting these harmonies color the entire fabric of the song instead of occurring as isolated bits of word-painting.

To convey the feeling of *vertige* that Verlaine captures so well in the poem, Debussy makes use of chords moving upward and downward by half-step. Chords so based on the chromatic scale, moving, so to speak, sideways rather than following conventional linear progressions, carry a certain dizzying quality with them. Mozart used such chromatic movement for the fateful statue scene in *Don Giovanni*, as did Berlioz for the Witches Sabbath in his *Symphonie fantastique*, as have countless lesser

[5] Oscar Thompson, *Debussy, Man and Artist* (New York: Dover Publications, 1937, 1967), p. 290.

and greater Romantic composers to portray tempests. The first occurrence in the song comes at the text "tournez cent tours, tournez mille tours" (Example 4). In addition to the refrains, the vocal melody

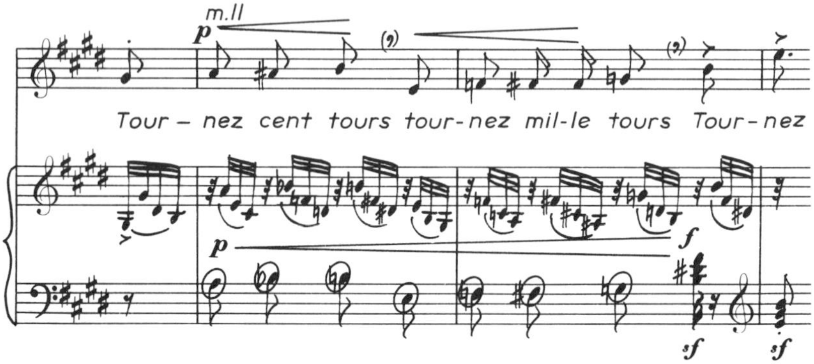

Example 4

employs the chromatic scale to accompany the feeling of intoxication in the fourth stanza: "C'est étonnant comme ça vous soûle / D'aller ainsi dans ce cirque bête" (Example 5).

Finally, chromatic movement occurs in the tonal scheme of the song. The sixth stanza, depicting "la troupe de gais buveurs," stands between a refrain in G major and a refrain in E major. Debussy connects the two keys not with a classical harmonic progression but with a repeated arpeggio pattern in which he changes one note at a time, supported by a chromatic bassline (Example 6).

It was around this time that Debussy remarked to his former harmony teacher,

> Regardez donc l'échelle doublement chromatique. Est-ce que ce n'est pas notre outil?—Ce n'est pas pour des prunes, le contrepoint. En faisant marcher les parties, on attrape des accords chics.[6]

In the final refrain of *Chevaux de bois*, set in the key of E major, the key of the piece, Debussy uses not the usual V–I progression, or even IV–I, but rather an extended section on D♯ followed by a passage on F, finally

[6] Maurice Emmanuel, "Entretiens inédits d'Ernest Guirard et de Claude Debussy," in *Inédits sur Claude Debussy, Collection Comoedia-Charpentier* (Paris: Les Publications Techniques, 1942), p. 32.

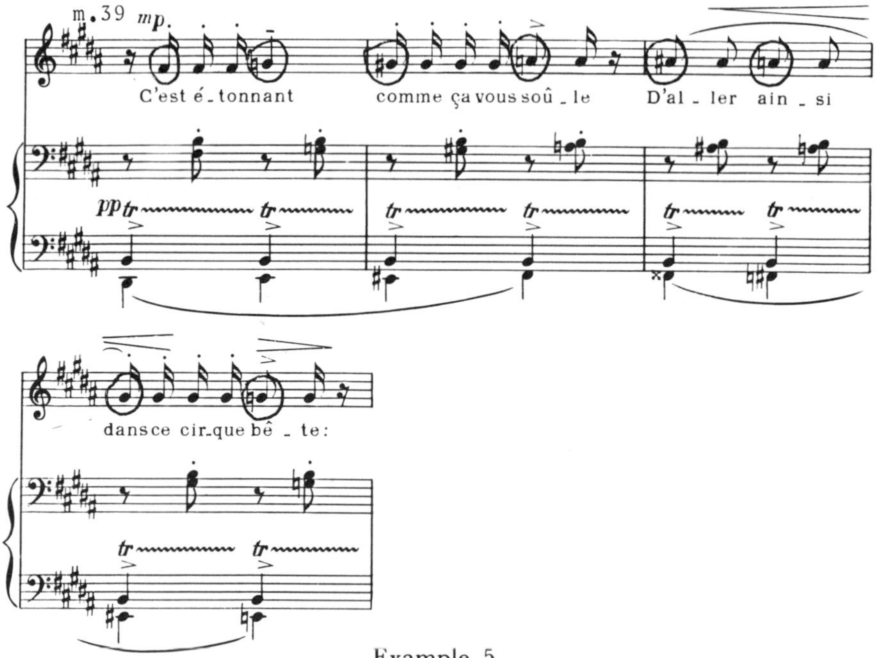

Example 5

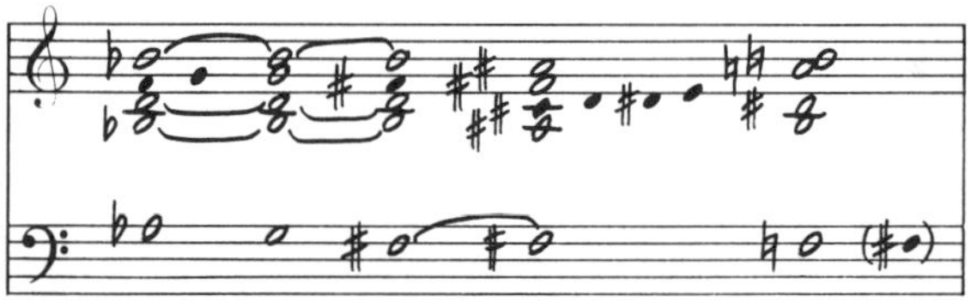

Example 6

concluding with E, sandwiched in, as it were, between "des accords chics" on either side.

While the organization of tonalities in this early song does not yet have the extraordinary consistency displayed in Debussy's more mature music, the use of the chromatic scale melodically, harmonically, and tonally in *Chevaux de bois* foreshadows Debussy's later practice of employing a single musical device to organize all the elements within a piece.

Spleen

Les roses étaient toutes rouges
Et les lierres étaient tout noirs.

Chère, pour peu que tu te bouges,
Renaissent tous mes désespoirs.

Le ciel était trop bleu, trop tendre,
La mer trop verte et l'air trop doux.

Je crains toujours,—ce qu'est d'attendre!—
Quelque fuite atroce de vous.

Du houx à la feuille vernie
Et du luisant buis je suis las,

Et de la campagne infinie
Et de tout, fors de vous, hélas!

[For translation, see p. 303]

The most immediately striking characteristic of Verlaine's poem is its arrangement on the page.[7] Verlaine seldom writes in couplets, and closer inspection reveals that these are not rhymed couplets but segments of four-line stanzas that the poet has chosen to separate in this unconventional manner. Verlaine has further separated the couplets by setting the first and third in *imparfait*, the second and fourth in the present tense.

The first and third couplets are primarily descriptive, identifying roses, ivy, sky, sea, air, but the simple change from *tout* in the first couplet to *trop* in the third begins to suggest a feeling of *ennui*. The two couplets differ in intensity, the first depicting bright, sharply contrasting colors, the third portraying shades of milder hue, even "trop doux."

The second and fourth couplets are primarily subjective, indicating feelings of differing intensity. The second shows occasional anxiety, the fourth constant anguish at the prospect of being abandoned. The intensification and concentration of feeling from the second to the fourth couplet inverts the relaxation of brightness and contrast from the first to the third couplet.

[7] This discussion derives in part from remarks scattered throughout Zimmermann, *Magies de Verlaine*.

The rhythm of this alternation accelerates in the last two couplets so that feeling and description succeed each other line by line until they become inseparable in the last line, the only trimeter in the poem, a rhythm underlined by the assonance between *tout* and *vous*.

The descriptive elements of the poem stand apart both formally and syntactically. The objects have no stronger connections than the verb *être* and the conjunction *et*. One never gets a sense of landscape; the roses and ivy and holly and boxwood simply fade into "la campagne infinie." Unlike the forest breezes in *C'est l'extase* or *En sourdine*, which respond to human feeling, the natural elements in *Spleen* simply exist. The connections among them are all in the mind of the poet. But this very lack of response characterizes *spleen*, the "nom anglais donné quelquefois à une forme de l'hypochondrie, consistant en un ennui sans cause, en un dégout de la vie" (Littré). The elements of nature correspond in their neutrality to the absence of response by the person addressed in the poem. We see no "fuite atroce," only the anguish of its anticipation. In this sense the absence of any other voice, be it a "cri doux que l'herbe agitée expire" or a nightingale, "voix de notre désespoir," constitutes nature's attitude. If, as Zimmermann suggests, the objects in the poem have the value of hermetic signs of unrevealed signification, the poet has successfully kept the metaphor to himself, disclosing only his state of ennui.

Debussy conveys the emptiness of this state of soul in the opening melody of his song, which calls for the singer to repeat a single pitch eleven times with scarcely any variation in rhythm. Both the beginning of the song and certain elements of its structure call to mind Debussy's setting of *L'Ombre des arbres*. Both songs contain a piano motive in which the tritone plays a prominent part, supported by bass notes a tritone apart. In both songs the lower note of the tritone in the piano provides the pitch for a number of repeated notes in the vocal melody. And in both songs the tritone plays an important part in the underlying tonal framework (Example 7).

In discussing Debussy's songs we have mentioned various kinds of root and key movements:[8] strong progressions by fourths and fifths;

[8] Tonality (key movement) may be regarded as harmony (root movement) on the large scale; the fascinating fluctuation and occasional obscuring of the line between harmony and tonality is one of the most interesting aspects of Debussy's music.

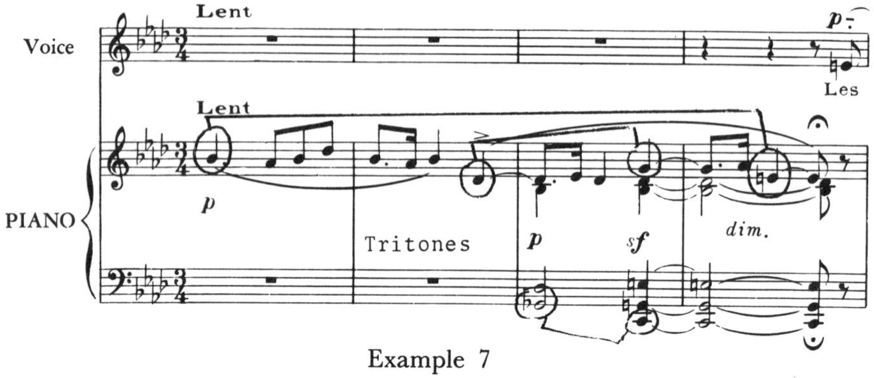

Example 7

somewhat weaker progressions by major and minor thirds; occasional whole-tone or chromatic movement connecting two keys a third or fourth or fifth apart. Movement by tritone has an unsettling quality which composers may employ for affective purposes.

In *L'Ombre des arbres* Debussy offsets the disruptive nature of the tritone movement at the outset of the song with decisive chains of perfect fourths and fifths later on. No such stabilization occurs in *Spleen.* Rather, two chords a tritone apart oscillate back and forth without resolution for the first two thirds of the song, like the unresolved oscillation between descriptive and subjective elements in the poem.

The Neapolitan chord, suggested melodically in the first two measures of the song, appears in root position in the third measure, followed by an unresolved dominant ninth chord, which is prolonged through measure 8. The same progression accompanies the second couplet of the text, but this time Debussy allows the upper four notes of the dominant ninth chord to move upwards as a diminished seventh chord, with chromatic notes increasing the intensity of the dissonance to portray the word *désespoirs.*

To set "trop tendre . . . trop doux" in the third couplet, Debussy uses rich dominant ninth chords which function as a chromatic prolongation of the diminished seventh chord. Again in the fourth couplet, the Neapolitan chord precedes a flurry of diminished seventh chords, this time depicting "Quelque fuite atroce de vous." Up to this point Debussy has effectively employed only two harmonies—a root position Neapolitan chord and a dominant ninth—along with certain chromatic elaborations of those harmonies. Now, in setting the fifth couplet, Debussy momentarily uses triads on B♭ and D, the chords on either side of the dominant C. When the original progression, N–V, returns for the final couplet, Debussy fills in the tritone from G♭ to C in the bassline, resolving the harmony only in the final chord, the ultimate "Hélas!" (Example 8).

Example 8

When asked by Giraud, his former harmony teacher, how he would resolve a particular chord, Debussy replied, "Mais pourquoi voulez-vous absoluement que je le résolve?" According to Debussy the resolution of chords is characteristic of the classical style. He prefers "accords incomplets, flottants." As for the rules of theory, "Il n'y a pas de théorie: suffit d'entendre. Le plaisir est la régle." [9] Nonetheless, the tonal system

[9] Quoted by Ernest Ansermet, "Le langage de Debussy," in *Debussy et l'évolution de la musique*, ed. Edith Weber (Paris: Editions du Centre National de la Recherche Scientifique, 1965), p. 43; Emmanuel, "Entretiens inédits," p. 31.

embodies certain expectations of harmony, the frustration of which produces an affective response in the listener.[10] In *Spleen* Debussy not only postpones the tonic to the end of the piece, as in *L'Ombre des arbres* and elsewhere, but also bases the harmony on an unstable tritone relationship, both procedures that contribute to a feeling of ennui, a musical expression of *spleen.*

La Mer est plus belle

La mer est plus belle
Que les cathédrales,
Nourrice fidèle,
Berceuse de râles,
La mer sur qui prie
La Vierge Marie!

Elle a tous les dons
Terribles et doux.
J'entends ses pardons
Gronder ses courroux . . .
Cette immensité
N'a rien d'entêté.

Oh! si patiente,
Même quand méchante!
Un souffle ami hante
La vague, et nous chante:
"Vous sans espérance,
Mourez sans souffrance!"

Et puis sous les cieux
Qui s'y rient plus clairs,
Elle a des airs bleus,
Roses, gris et verts . . .
Plus belle que tous,
Meilleure que nous!

[For translation, see p. 304]

In *La Mer est plus belle* Verlaine employs the device of oxymoron, frequently encountered in religious poetry, to fuse conflicting elements

[10] See the first chapter of Leonard B. Meyer, *Emotion and Meaning in Music* (Chicago: University of Chicago Press, 1956).

into a unity. Even in the words of forgiveness the rumbling of the sea's wrath can be heard. The lullaby of the first stanza comes in the form of a death-rattle. The musical image returns in the third stanza, where a friendly breeze sings: "Vous sans espérance, / Mourez sans souffrance." The sea is at once terrible and gentle, patient even when malicious. The short lines help to sharpen the dichotomy by bringing the conflicting elements close together.

Verlaine's attention to contrasting sound images emerges from the very structure of the poem. The short five- and six-syllable lines produce a proportionately large number of rhymes. The sounds of the end-rhymes appear frequently within the line as well, where they contrast with other assonant sounds, as in the third stanza, in which the final word combines both opposing sounds:

> Oh! si pati*en*te,
> Même qu*an*d mech*an*te!
> Un souffle ami h*an*te
> La vague, et nous ch*an*te:
> "Vous *sans* espér*an*ce,
> Mourez *sans* souffr*an*ce!"

The shades of sound in the first three stanzas of the poem translate into colors in the closing stanza, where Verlaine's favorite colors—"bleu," "rose," "gris," "vert"—appear together.[11]

Verlaine further exploits the opposition of contrasting planes. In describing the genesis of the poem Verlaine recalls his visit to Bournemouth in 1877:

> The house, built like a *châlet,* looked over the sea, but from a distance, so that we could only see its extreme horizon, the scarcely perceptible "white horses," the shining sails of the fishing-boats, and the red smoke of the steamers as they were on the point of disappearing or were just gone out of sight. . . .
>
> On Sundays we attended the Catholic services in an exquisite little church attached to a picturesque *Jesuitière,* a little to the northern extremity of the town. . . . From this spot, in the top of the high cliffs covered with furze I have seen leagues and leagues of sea in every direction, even as far as the first rocks off the shores of the

[11] See Zimmermann, *Magies de Verlaine*, pp. 191–192, for a full catalog of Verlaine's use of these colors in his poetry.

> Norman Islands, and I composed some verses in this style: "Le mer est plus belle. . . ." [12]

In the first stanza the preposition *sur,* instead of the expected *pour,* suggests the image of heaven above, sea below. The limitless expanse of the plane of the ocean extends itself in "cette immensité." In the fourth stanza, "sous les cieux" suggests the expanse of the plane above, with an association of sky and heaven which comes more naturally in French than in a language which requires an implied metaphor to bridge two different words.

Encompassing all these contrasts of idea, color, sound, and plane is a totality: the unity of the sea, the "nourrice fidèle," the primordial mother of us all, once again an association of *mer* and *mère* which comes as naturally to a French poet as the concern for both *sens* and *son.* Both *mer* and *cathédrale* converge in the person of "La Vierge Marie," the "Mother of God, Queen of Heaven." One recalls the Ave Maris Stella, the evening hymn to the Virgin, whose third stanza reads:

Solve vincla reis
Proffer lumen caesis,
Mala nostra pelle,
Bona cuncta posce.

Loose the bonds of terror,
Lighten blinded error,
All our ills repressing,
Pray for every blessing.

The tonal skeleton of *La Mer est plus belle* resembles the rocking accompaniment of a barcarolle, or of Debussy's own barcarolle, *L'Isle joyeuse* (Example 9). This shape recurs in the rising and falling of the accompaniment (Example 10), as well as in the contour of the vocal melody, which displays rather broader gestures than most of the melodies

Example 9

[12] Verlaine, "Notes on England," in *Oeuvres Posthumes*, volume 3 (Paris: Albert Messein, 1929), pp. 264–266.

Example 10

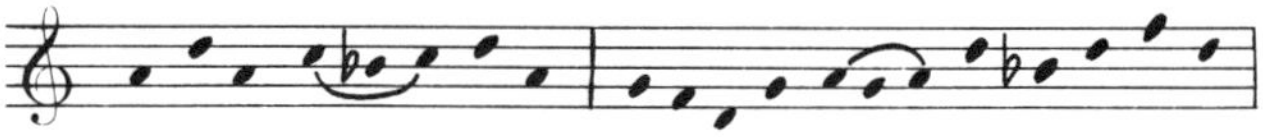

Example 11

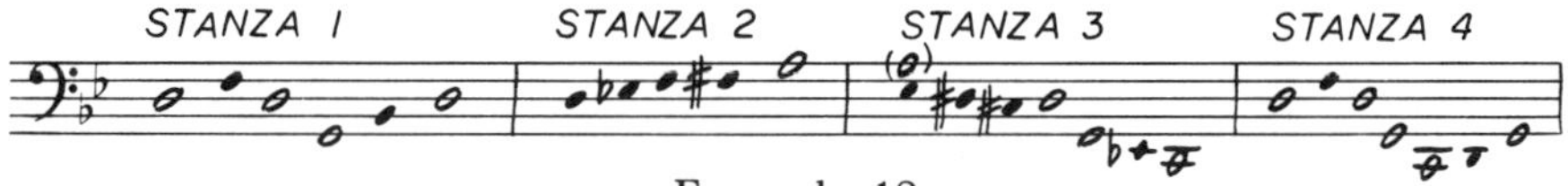

Example 12

we have encountered (Example 11). The complete tonal scheme fills in the open fifths with thirds (Example 12). The harmonic rhythm of the first stanza is slower than usual, consisting of but four chords. In the second stanza the harmonic rhythm increases to the point that the harmony changes with every note of the melody, setting the rumblings of wrath in a crescendo from *piano* to *forte.*

The third stanza returns to the slower harmonic rhythm of the opening, and the dynamic level returns to *piano, calme et doux.* The harmony moves through a series of chords functioning as dominant sevenths first on A then on D. The harmony comes to rest unexpectedly on a dominant ninth chord on E♭, the tempo changes suddenly to *Lent,* the dynamics to *ppp,* for the song of the breeze. The last stanza repeats material from the opening of the song, then sustains a long pedal point on C, the subdominant, to balance the extended harmonies on the dominant side in the rest of the song.

In *La mer est plus belle* the conflicting elements of the text find musical expression not so much in changes of harmony as in changes of harmonic rhythm. By contrasting slow-moving harmonies of the sea at rest with the rapidly changing colors of the sea's wrath, while keeping the harmonic language essentially the same throughout, Debussy represents both the conflict and the unity of Verlaine's text. He dedicated the song to Robert Godet, to whom he also dedicated the Baudelaire songs with these words, reminiscent of Verlaine's poem: "A Robert Godet, pour diminuer un peu des distances que font des mers assurément belles, mais tout de même cruelles, et pour l'assurer d'une amitié gardée avec soin et à jamais."

L'Échelonnement des haies

L'échelonnement des haies
Moutonne à l'infini, mer
Claire dans le brouillard clair
Qui sent bon les jeunes baies.

Des arbres et des moulins
Sont légers sur le vert tendre
Où vient s'ébattre et s'étendre
L'agilité des poulains.

Dans ce vague d'un Dimanche
Voici se jouer aussi
De grandes brebis aussi
Douces que leur laine blanche.

Tout à l'heure déferlait
L'onde, roulée en volutes,
De cloches comme des flûtes
Dans le ciel comme du lait.

[For translation, see p. 304]

Unlike the colors in painting, the shapes in a sculpture, and the sounds in a musical composition, the words that comprise literature cannot leap the barriers of language. A poem in French offers one kind of poetic experience for a Frenchman and other kinds for people who think in other languages. But certain semantic parallels among unrelated languages suggest that "beneath the overwhelming drive toward cultural diversity that has led to a Babel of languages, a contrary force—of human sameness—survives." Consider, for example, the following parallels:

1. *Greek* "aiges" means "goats" and "strong waves"
2. *French* "mouton" means "sheep" and "foamy waves," and "moutonner" means "to cover oneself with small foamy waves."
3. *Spanish* "cordero" means "sheep" and "foamy waves"
4. *Russian* "barashki" means "sheep" and "foamy waves"
5. *Haussa* "rak'umi" means "camel" and "waves"
6. *English* "horses" in "white horses" meaning "horses" as well as the white caps on the surf.
7. *Russian* "volna," though with a difference in the position of the stress accent, means "wool" as well as "wave." [13]

For Verlaine the metaphor came to mind during an excursion in England in 1875.

> Twilight was about to fall on the scenery in front of us. The last rays of daylight were shedding lustre upon a landscape which was exquisite in its rich sweetness of pasture and trees—those English trees with their branches capriciously twisted and "intricated," if I may be allowed the *barbarisme,* which the Bible somewhere says are those that bear the best fruit; both sides of the road, which was flourished with fine quickset hedges, were studded, so to speak, with big sheep and nimble colts roaming free. I made a sketch of the scene in these few verses, which are taken from my book, *Sagesse*: "L'échelonnement des haies. . . ." [14]

Two identities, *haies* and *mer,* fuse into a single unity in the word *moutonne.* The haze of the English countryside permits us to sustain the unresolved metaphoric vision. Verlaine preserves the vagueness of the scene through a *méprise.* The subject of "s'ébattre et s'étendre" is *l'agilité.* We see only the movement of colts. Their playfulness and the mistiness of "ce vague d'un Dimanche" prevents any clearer vision. The use of *clair* in two different senses in the first stanza is reflected in the use of the word *douces* in the third. *Doux* referring to sheep presumably means "gentle" or "mild"; referring to the white fleece it presumably means "soft." A single

[13] Stanley Burnshaw, *The Seamless Web* (New York: George Braziller, 1970), pp. 114–119.

[14] Verlaine, "Notes on England," pp. 233–234.

word does for both, just as the meanings of the word *moutonne* form the central metaphor of the poem.

This intentional vagueness of vision also appears in the description of the trees and windmills in the second stanza. The phrase "sont légers sur le vert tendre" almost suggests that they are floating on the surface of this sealike greensward. A wave of sound breaks into foam. "L'onde . . . de cloches" apparently comes over some distance, since for one to hear bells like flutes one must be too far away to hear the percussive striking of individual notes. Roulades of sound from various corners whirl together like the curliness of lambswool, and fill the milk-white sky. "Du lait," the milk which foams like the sea which stretches out before us, brings the poem full circle as the blankness of the sky merges with the bright ground fog. Verlaine has his own manner of combining all the senses:[15]

Sight: "L'échelonnement des haies," "mer claire," "vert tendre."
Sound: "de cloches comme des flûtes."
Smell and taste: "qui sent bon les jeunes baies," "dans le ciel comme du lait."
Touch: "aussi douces que leur laine blanche."

Lines and colors melt into one another in this impressionistic poem of vibrating light.

Debussy's remarkable setting of *L'Échelonnement des haies* experiments with musical procedures which he develops more fully in the first book of piano preludes more than two decades later.[16] The pentatonic scale, Debussy's favorite scale for pastoral subjects, occurs both in the melody and in the harmonic structure accompanying this eminently pastoral poem of trees, windmills, hedges, fragrant berries, colts, lambs, even the archetypal pastoral sound of the flute.

The piano introduction in the first four measures of the piece is set in the pentatonic scale, using first C♯ as a center, then B (Example 13). Measures 5 and 6, the first entrance of the vocal melody, use a different version of the pentatonic scale. The entire musical fabric comprises only four pitches: B, C♯, E, F♯. This technique of defining harmony through

[15] John Charpentier, *L'évolution de la poésie lyrique de Joseph Delorme à Paul Claudel* (Paris: Les Oeuvres Représentatives, 1931), pp. 167–168.

[16] See the discussion of *Des pas sur la neige* in Arthur Wenk, "An Analysis of Debussy's Piano Preludes, Book I," thesis, Cornell University, 1967.

the use of pedal points, which single out one note of a mode or special scale to serve as a temporary center, belongs to the vocabulary of Debussy's twentieth-century music, which this song anticipates.

If we continue through the piece, tracing the appearance of different scales, each associated in the song with a temporary center, the following pattern emerges:

Measures	*Pitches*	*Scale or Mode*	*Tonal Center*
1–4	C♯–D♯ ( ) F♯–G♯ ( ) B–C♯	Pentatonic	C♯, then B
5–6	B–C♯ ( ) E–F♯ ( ) B	Pentatonic	B
7–8	B–C♯–D–E–F♯–G♯ ( ) B	Dorian	B
9–11	B–C♯–D♯ ( ) F♯–G♯ ( ) B	Pentatonic	B
12–13	C♯–D♯–E–F♯–G♯–A♯ ( ) C♯	Dorian	C♯
14	G–A–B–C♯–D–E ( ) G	Lydian	G
15	C–E–G	Triad	C
16–17	F–G–A♭–B♭–C–D ( ) F	Dorian	F
18	E♭–G–B♭/B♭–D–F♯	Major triad / Augmented triad	E♭/B♭
19–20	A♭–B♭–C–D–E–F♯–G♯	Whole-tone	A♭
21–24	G♯ ( ) B–C♯–D♯ melody	Pentatonic	C♯/F♯
	F♯–G♯–A–B–C♯–D♯–E♯–F♯ accompaniment	Major scale	
25–28	B–C♯–D♯–E♯–F♯–G♯–A–B	Overtone scale[17]	B
29–35	C♯–D♯–E–F♯–G♯–A–B–C♯	Aeolian	E, then F♯–G♯–C♯
36	C♯–E♯–G♯	Major triad	C♯

[17] Françoise Gervais discusses this and other special scales in *Etude parallèle des languages harmoniques de Fauré et de Debussy*, Special Issue, *Revue Musicale* 272 (1971).

Debussy gives the different modes a pentatonic flavor by omitting the seventh scale degree, producing one of the characteristic gaps of the pentatonic scale. A pentatonic scale drawn from the respective mode appears in the vocal melody in measures 5–6, 12–13, 17–18, and 23–24. Debussy employs the whole-tone scale to set off the central image of the song: "De grandes brebis aussi / Douces que leur laine blanche." Debussy felt no need to remain in a particular mode for any length of

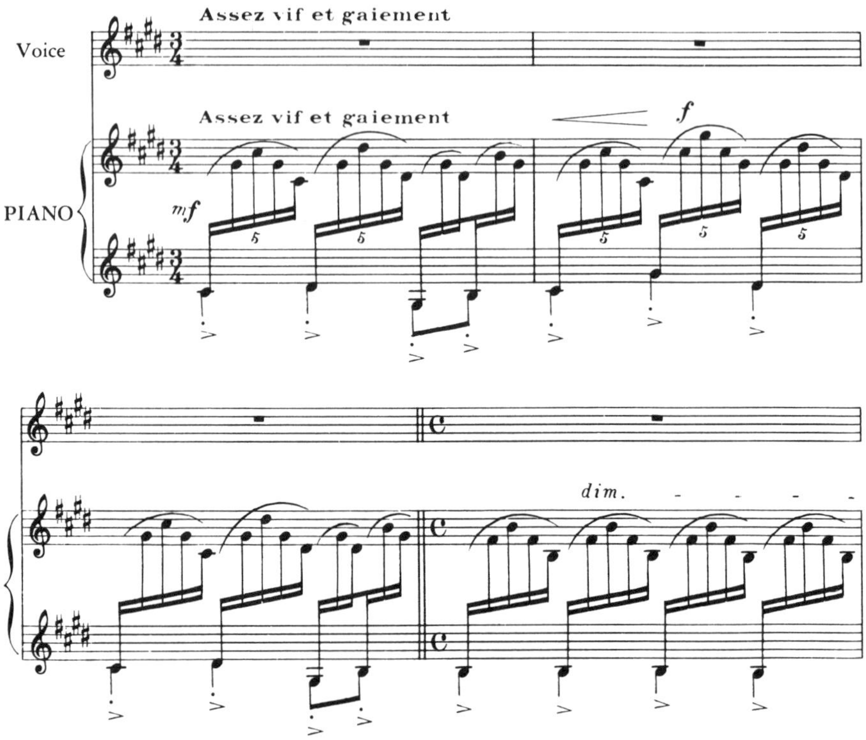

Example 13

time. Modes occur in Debussy's music as devices of color. "Le mode est celui auquel pense le musicien. Instable." [18]

As striking as Debussy's use of scales is the way that he arranges the tonal centers to produce an *échelonnement* of keys. After an introductory section which alternates between C♯ and B in setting the first stanza of text, Debussy leaps a tritone to the opposite side of the circle of fifths, then proceeds by perfect fifths through ten of the twelve degrees of the circle, a brilliant musical expression of both the disposition of "des haies" and also their extension "À l'infini." A lesser composer might have found a satisfactory depiction at the instant where the image appears in the text; few can have been more successful at shaping the entire structure of a song around a poetic idea.

[18] Emmanuel, "Entretiens inédits," p. 30.

In these songs of 1888 to 1891 Debussy is experimenting with chromatic harmony, sometimes conservatively, as in *Chevaux de bois* and *La Mer est plus belle*, sometimes more boldly, as in *L'ombre des arbres* and *Spleen*, sometimes in a manner so characteristically Debussyan that we would describe the music as thoroughly original. In each case Debussy finds a musical expression for the poetic metaphors of Verlaine's texts. The influence of Verlaine's poetry on Debussy's musical aesthetic extends beyond his harmonic practice, which ultimately may not be regarded as the most innovative aspect of Debussy's art. In the following chapter we shall examine this influence as it applies to other areas of Debussy's style.

6

VERLAINE III: *Art poetique* and *Le Son du cor*

Debussy's relationship with Paul Verlaine never included the personal intimacy of his friendship with Louÿs or the immediate contact with the philosophy of Symbolism that he encountered in the *mardis chez Mallarmé.* Yet the poetry of Verlaine had a more profound influence on Debussy's music than that of his closest literary acquaintances. Even in works that have no direct connection with Verlaine's poetry one often detects a tone of voice that somehow sounds like a musical translation of Verlaine's poetic style. Pierre Fortassier finds such a musical translation in the flute solo at the beginning of the *Prélude à l'après-midi d'un faune.* Wilfred Mellers discovers the Harlequin from the *Fêtes galantes* in the last movement of the Cello Sonata. Charles Koechlin goes so far as to say that it was Verlaine who put Debussy on the road to his own personality.[1]

[1] Pierre Fortassier, "Verlaine, la Musique et les Musiciens," *Cahiers de l'Association Internationale des Etudes Françaises* 12 (1960):158; Wilfred Mellers, "The Later Work of

In seeking specific examples of Verlaine's influence we shall take as a focal point his *Art poétique.* Written in 1874, while Verlaine was in prison, the poem both illustrates and explains the precepts which guided Verlaine's early poetry. It was Verlaine's early poetry in particular which attracted Debussy. Of the seventeen poems of Verlaine which he set to music, eight are taken from the *Fêtes galantes* (1869) and six from the *Romances sans paroles* (1874). The remaining three poems were all written before 1877.

Verlaine's ideas on poetry, and their parallels in Debussy's music, can be best understood against the background of literary and musical thought in nineteenth-century France. The beginning of the century saw a reaction against the conventions of classical literature. The chief proponents of *Romantisme*—Hugo, Vigny, Lamartine, and later Musset—took as their motto *liberté dans l'art*, and sought greater freedom of language and of versification, a broader choice of subject matter, and a new emphasis on sensation and emotion, a characteristic of the Romantic movement in all the arts.

By mid-century a counterreaction against the excesses of literary freedom found expression in a group of poets who called themselves *Parnassiens.* Gautier, Banville, Leconte de Lisle, and others, under the banner of *l'art pour l'art*, rejected technical liberties and undertook to preserve the art of versification through objectivity, clarity, and impeccable form.

Symbolism, the synthesis of these opposing movements, had its precursor in Baudelaire, who combined perfection of classical prosody with an exploration of the musical possibilities of the French language.[2] His sonnet *Correspondances* stands beside Verlaine's *Art poétique* and Mallarmé's *Toute l'âme résumée* in embodying the artistic credos of the new movement, which included Rimbaud, Laforgue, and others.

The history of French music in the nineteenth century might be described as an attempt to recover a national idiom—which had been its

Claude Debussy or Pierrot Faché avec la Lune," *Studies in Contemporary Music* (London: Denis Dobson, 1947), p. 53; Charles Koechlin, "Quelques Anciennes Mélodies Inédites de Claude Debussy," *Revue Musicale* 7 (1926):119.

[2] Paraphrased from Sir Paul Harvey and J. E. Heseltine, *The Oxford Companion to French Literature* (Oxford: At the Clarendon Press, 1959, 1969), see articles on "Romantisme," "Les Parnassiens," "Symbolisme."

glory until the death of Rameau—first from Italian and then from German influence. A French composer in the first half of the century had little choice of expression between the pomposity of grand opera on the one hand, as represented by Rossini and Meyerbeer, and the fluffiness of operetta on the other, as typified by Offenbach. The development of lyric opera around mid-century by Gounod, Thomas, and later Massenet, helped to restore eminently French qualities of moderation, elegance, and clarity to a genre which had long been dominated by Italian influence.

The *Société Nationale de Musique*, founded in 1871, brought together Saint-Saëns, Massenet, Fauré, Duparc, and others to the common purpose of an *Ars Gallica.* Yet the music of César Franck, who served as president of the *Société*, displays characteristic features of German romanticism: unrestrained emotionalism, dramatic conflict of contrasting elements, and a conception of music as "primarily an expression of soul, a philosophy of life, in his case half-Christian and half-romantic but wholly emotional." [3]

Hector Berlioz, like Debussy, stood apart from the mainstream of his time in "splendid isolation." The striking originality of Berlioz's harmony and the unconventional forms of his dramatic works had no immediate successors, though his inventiveness in orchestration makes him the "true founder of the 'modern' orchestra." Debussy, for his part, employed the typical forms of German romanticism—the character piece for piano, the art song for voice and piano, and the symphonic poem for orchestra—in creating a new musical aesthetic which embodied the musical genius of France: "quelque chose comme la fantaisie dans la sensibilité." The inspiration for this new musical language came not from French opera, nor from German music drama, nor even from the ideals of the *Société Nationale de Musique.* Rather it emerged from Debussy's understanding of literary symbolism, and in particular the poetry of Paul Verlaine.[4]

[3] Martin Cooper, *French Music from the Death of Berlioz to the Death of Fauré* (London: Oxford University Press, 1951), p. 47.

[4] Rey M. Longyear, *Nineteenth-Century Romanticism in Music* (Englewood Cliffs, N.J.: Prentice-Hall, Inc., 1969), pp. 97, 100; Claude Debussy, *Monsieur Croche et Autres Écrits*, ed. François Lesure (Paris: Gallimard, 1971), p. 272; see also Willi Apel, *Harvard Dictionary of Music*, 2d ed. (Cambridge, Mass.: Harvard University Press, 1969), articles on "Romanticism" and "France."

Art poétique

De la musique avant toute chose,
Et pour cela préfère l'Impair
Plus vague et plus soluble dans l'air,
Sans rien en lui qui pèse ou qui pose.

Il faut aussi que tu n'ailles point
Choisir tes mots sans quelque méprise:
Rien de plus cher que la chanson grise
Où l'Indécis au Précis se joint.

C'est des beaux yeux derrière des voiles,
C'est le grand jour tremblant de midi,
C'est, par un ciel d'automne attiédi,
Le bleu fouillis des claires étoiles!

Car nous voulons la Nuance encor,
Pas la Couleur, rien que la nuance!
Oh! la nuance seule fiance
Le rêve au rêve et la flûte au cor!

Fuis du plus loin la Pointe assassine,
L'Esprit cruel et le Rire impur,
Qui font pleurer les yeux de l'Azur,
Et tout cet ail de basse cuisine!

Prends l'éloquence et tords-lui son cou!
Tu feras bien en train d'énergie,
De rendre un peu la Rime assagie.
Si l'on n'y veille, elle ira jusqu'où?

O qui dira les torts de la Rime?
Quel enfant sourd ou quel négre fou
Nous a forgé ce bijou d'un sou
Qui sonne creux et faux sous la lime?

De la musique encore et toujours!
Que ton vers soit la chose envolée
Qu'on sent qui fuit d'une âme en allée
Vers d'autres cieux à d'autres amours.

Que ton vers soit la bonne aventure
Eparse au vent crispé du matin
Qui va fleurant le menthe et le thym . . .
Et tout le reste est littérature.

[For translation, see p. 305]

Le son du cor s'afflige vers les bois
D'une douleur on veut croire orpheline
Qui vient mourir au bas de la colline
Parmi la bise errant en courts abois.

L'âme du loup pleure dans cette voix
Qui monte avec le soleil qui décline
D'une agonie on veut croire câline
Et qui ravit et qui navre à la fois.

Pour faire mieux cette plainte assoupie,
La neige tombe à longs traits de charpie
A travers le couchant sanguinolent,

Et l'air a l'air d'être un soupir d'automne,
Tant il fait doux per ce soir monotone
Où se dorlote un paysage lent.

[For translation, see p. 306]

De la musique avant toute chose,
Et pour cela préfère l'Impair[5]

In the opening lines of the *Art poétique* Verlaine indicates his preference for the asymmetrical, the unbalanced. In place of the twelve-syllable alexandrine Verlaine counsels the use of lines with an uneven syllable count—5, 7, 9, 11. In place of the regular caesuras of the alexandrine, Verlaine calls for a poetry whose cadences remain unpredictable. Verlaine also advises the frequent use of enjambment to preserve the fluidity of the verse. We can see the contrast between Verlaine's style of versification and that of his predecessors by comparing his *Le Son du cor* with *La Mort du loup* by Alfred de Vigny. Vigny, writing nearly half a century before Verlaine, exemplifies the Romantic tradition which the *Art poétique* disavows.

[5] See Alain Baudot, "Poésie et Musique chez Verlaine, Forme et Signification," *Etudes Françaises* 4 (1968):31–56; René Chalupt, "Verlaine, ou: de la Musique en Toute Chose," *Contrepoints* 6 (1949):62–73; Maurice Got, " 'Art Poétique': Verlaine et la Technique Impressioniste," *Table Ronde* 159 (March 1961):128–136; Albert Schneider, "L'Art Poétique de Paul Verlaine," *Academie de Metz, Memoires* 146 / sér.5, t.10 1967 (1964–1965):107–116; Alfred Wright, "Verlaine's 'Art Poétique' Re-Examined," *Modern Language Association Publications* 74 / 3 (June 1959):268–275.

Les Nuages couraient / sur la lune enflammée,
Comme sur l'incendie / on voit fuir la fumée,
Et les bois étaient noirs / jusques à l'horizon.
Nous marchions, sans parler, / dans l'humide gazon.
[Vigny]

Les son du cor s'afflige / vers les bois
D'une douleur / on veut croire / orpheline
Qui vient mourir / au bas de la colline
Parmi la bise / errant en courts abois.
[Verlaine]

The beginning of *La Mort du loup* is written in conventional alexandrines with a caesura in the middle of each line and a punctuation mark at the end. Although there is a measure of freedom in the poem, as Vigny imitates the trackless wandering of memory, the rhythm is clear throughout. The meter of *Le Son du cor,* while not "uneven," is a little "odd." Decasyllabic verse was out of fashion in Verlaine's time. Moreover, Verlaine departs from the conventional decasyllables by eliminating the usual caesura after the fourth syllable. The dotted lines in our example indicate only brief pauses. There are neither strong interruptions within the line nor punctuation marks at the ends of lines.

A musical equivalent to the asymmetrical rhythm which Verlaine prefers is triple meter. The "even" time signatures representing duple meter (2/4, 4/4, 6/8, 6/4, 12/8) have an inherent regularity due to the constant alternation of accented and unaccented beats. This regularity is less strong in the "uneven" time signatures of triple meter (3/8, 3/4, 9/8) where an accented beat is followed by two unaccented beats. Debussy apparently prefers the *Impair* to set the poetry of Verlaine, since he uses triple meter twice as often as duple meter. By comparison, two-thirds of the poems of other poets are set to "even" time signatures.[6]

Debussy sets *Le Son du cor* in an "uneven" meter of 9/8. He generally avoids the regularity of four-measure phrases and eight-measure periods without excluding them altogether. He obscures the phrase structure by elision and by overlapping the changing patterns of the accompaniment. The tempo also remains fluid, with four changes written into the score in addition to the subtle *tempo rubato* that a sensitive performer will introduce (see accompanying figure).

[6] See Appendix C.

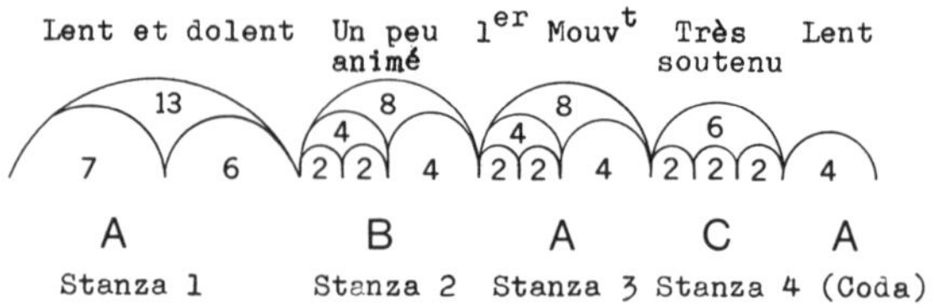

Il faut aussi que tu n'ailles point
Choisir tes mots sans quelque méprise:

The word *méprise* has roughly the same set of meanings as the English word *mistake*: a misunderstanding; taking something the wrong way; mis-taking one thing for another. Verlaine's poetry contains a variety of different *méprises.*

A *méprise* of semantics occurs in the line, "Le son du cor s'afflige." How can a sound be afflicted? The unusual combination of words produces a sensation which goes beyond ordinary logical restrictions.

A *méprise* of lexicon appears in the line "Où se dorlote un paysage lent." What is a "paysage lent" and how does it coddle itself? The answer lies not in logical explication but in the idea which this unorthodox combination of words evokes. "Choisir tes mots," Verlaine advises, selecting not the expected but the surprising.

The line "D'une douleur on veut croire orpheline" contains a *méprise* of syntax. Verlaine has left out the punctuation which might make this phrase look more familiar: "D'une douleur (on veut croire) orpheline."

Elsewhere in the poem Verlaine commits a *méprise* of fiction by making us think we see something which is not really there: we hear the cry of a wolf coming to die at the base of a hill, but there is no wolf; we hear the short barks of the dogs, but it is only the wind.

In each of these examples Verlaine has combined words in a way which seems slightly off but which, when we think about it, makes sense. The first line of *Le son du cor,* for example, gives us pause, forces us to stop and make an unfamiliar association between the sound of a horn—which might be called mournful—and the cause which provokes such a mournful sound. Verlaine uses an unorthodox combination of words to reorder our experience and to jar our ordinary perception of the world.

Debussy shared Verlaine's preference for avoiding the *mot juste* of the Parnassians. In advising Toulet in his adaptation of *As You Like It,* Debussy writes: "Toutes les fois que vous pourrez remplacer le mot exact par son correspondent lyrique n'hésitez pas." [7] As early as 1885 Debussy describes his difficulties in finding a text congenial to his musical sympathies, and complains of heaviness and "correctness" in poetry:

> Ces grands imbéciles de vers qui ne sont grands que par sa longueur, m'assomment, et ma musique serait dans le cas de tomber sous le poids—puis autre chose de plus sérieux, c'est que je crois que jamais je ne pourrais enfermer ma musique dans un moule trop correct. Je me dépêche de vous dire que je ne parle pas de la forme musicale, c'est simplement à un point de vue littéraire.[8]

Already we see Debussy's taste for a verse "sans rien en lui qui pése ou qui pose." Twenty years later Debussy reaffirms his dissatisfaction with the strictness of traditional form:

> Par ailleurs, je me persuade, de plus en plus, que la musique n'est pas, par son essence, une chose qui puisse se couler dans une forme rigoureuse et traditionnelle. Elle est de couleurs et de temps rythmés. . . .[9]

Debussy employs several varieties of *méprise* in his use of harmony. The deceptive cadence, which we discussed earlier, is like a *méprise* of semantics. An unfamiliar resolution forces us to reconsider the relationship between two chords. Such a *méprise* occurs on a grand scale in *Le Son du cor,* in which the opening chords turn out not to be the key of the piece after all, but the subdominant of the true key, revealed only later.

Elsewhere in Debussy's music a *méprise* of lexicon occurs in the intrusion of unexpected, "foreign" elements, what Lavauden calls "L'humour dans l'oeuvre de Debussy." [10] One thinks of the interruptions of *Le Sérénade interrompue*, the "wrong" notes in the first Etude, the appearance of the *Sehnsucht* motive from *Tristan und Isolde* in the *Golliwogg's Cakewalk.*

Sometimes Debussy suspends the traditional rules of harmonic progression altogether in a *méprise* of musical syntax. The logic of a succession of chords is then governed by melody instead of by harmony as, for example, the setting of "La neige tombe . . ." in measure 26.

[7] *Correspondance de Claude Debussy et P.-J. Toulet* (Paris: Le Divan, 1929), p. 15.

[8] Henry Prunières, "A la Villa Médicis," *Revue Musicale* 7 (1926):125(29).

[9] *Lettres de Claude Debussy à son Éditeur* (Paris: A. Durand et Fils, 1927), p. 55.

[10] Thérèse Lavauden, "L'Humour dans l'Oeuvre de Debussy," *Revue Musicale* 11 (1930):97–105.

Debussy, like Verlaine, is a master of making us think we hear something which is not really there. The tonal structure of *Le Son du cor* is quite convincing even though there is not a single perfect cadence in the piece. The harmonic basis of the song consists of a number of progressions of the form iv . . . V, concluding with iv . . . I (Example 1).

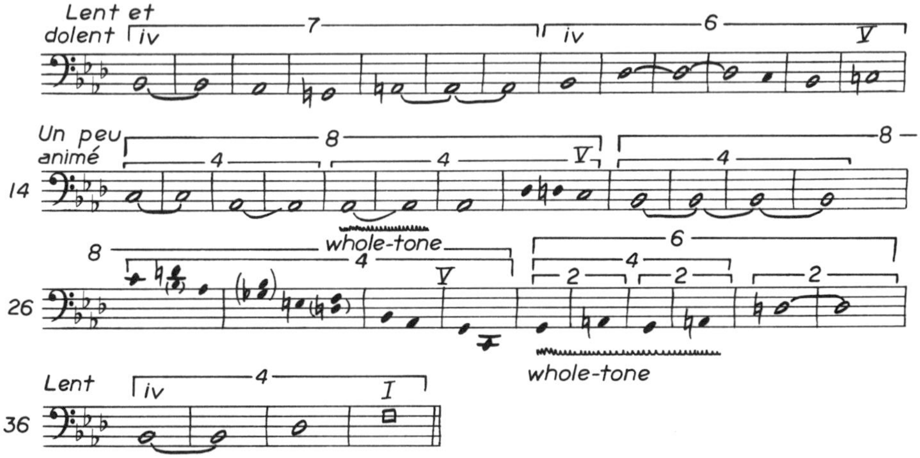

Example 1

Debussy employs a similar fiction by letting a mere fragment evoke our memory of the whole melody. In music as in poetry the *méprise* makes us ask "Why?", and in answering the question we come to see things differently.

> Rien de plus cher que la chanson grise
> Où l'Indécis au Précis se joint.

Just as rhythm is to be made more supple through the avoidance of regularity, so the tone of the poetic language is to remain imprecise through the use of gray backgrounds and music *en sourdine.* Verlaine's *méprises* contribute substantially toward joining "L'Indécis au Précis." The absence of assertiveness in phrases like "une agonie on veut croire câline" or "l'air a l'air d'être un soupir d'automne" prepares us for the peculiar imprecision in the "narrative." The traditional elements of the hunt seem to be present—we think we hear the hunting horn, the baying hounds, the wounded wolf dying at sunset—but when we try to pin them down they disappear into the background. In so far as the poem is "about" anything, it seems to be about a special kind of *paysage* in which sorrow and agony can become one with the sound of the horn and the wind, where the soul of a wolf can become one with the sigh of autumn, and where the snow reduces all sounds, colors, and feelings to a *monotone.*

Debussy succeeds in composing for this poem a "gray" music "qui ravit et qui navre à la fois." Certainly the whole-tone scale, with its complete lack of differentiation among its pitches, is one element of a "chanson grise." Likewise the prolongation of minor seventh and minor ninth chords contributes to a background that is both gray and sonorous. The extension of a single harmony comes to have the incantatory effect of an extended rhythmic pattern. In *Le Son du cor* Debussy uses both static harmonies and rhythms to evoke a background which may be called *monotone.*

So well did Debussy learn the lesson of precision joined to vagueness that it pervaded his everyday speech. Pasteur Vallery-Radot writes: "Sa phrase est souvent embuée d'imprécision pour rendre l'incertitude d'une idée ou d'une impression, avec un mot qui éclate tout à coup, vibrant." [11]

Car nous voulons la Nuance encor,
Pas la Couleur, rien que la nuance!

Color in *La Mort du loup* begins with the first line: "Les nuages couraient sur la lune *enflammée.*" The woods are *noirs,* the eyes of the wolf *flamboyaient.* The wolf dies "tout baigné dans son sang." In Verlaine's poem, on the other hand, the only color appears in the description of the sun, "le couchant sanguinolent." Even this color sounds mild in comparison to the dying sun in Baudelaire's *Harmonie du soir:* "Le soleil s'est noyé dans son sang qui se fige. . . ."

In a setting where color has been subdued, slight variations in shading assume greater importance. In the absence of color, subtle nuances can be conveyed through different shades of gray. Debussy's concern for nuance is well known. His music is filled with instructions to find for each phrase the proper shading of expression. In *Le Son du cor* we find the indications *lent et dolent; doux et expressif; murmuré; en mourant; très soutenu; lent.* All of these instructions fall within a rather narrow range. In such music the mere change of a semitone can be used to color the sound,

[11] *Lettres de Claude Debussy à sa Femme Emma*, ed. Pasteur Vallery-Radot (Paris: Flammarion, 1957), p. 35.

and the end of a phrase can be indicated by the gradual reduction of the musical texture as the left-hand of the piano part releases its notes one at a time (Example 2).

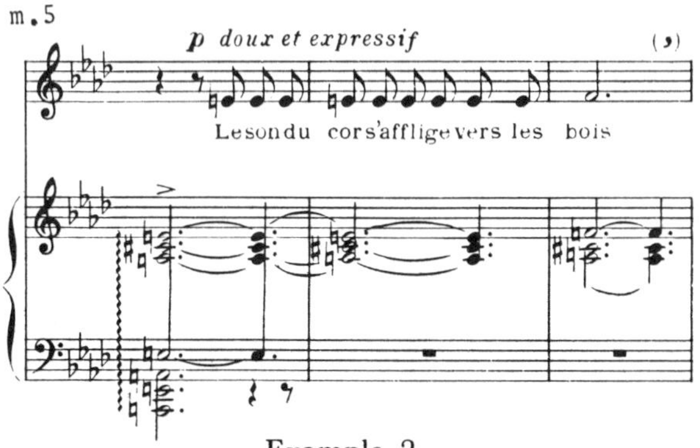

Example 2

Debussy displays the same sense of *nuance* in the care he gives to the spacing of notes within a chord and of chords on the staff. The harmony of a chord remains unchanged by spacing, but its expressive effect may vary considerably with the relative position of its notes. In *Le Son du cor* the piano part remains rather high for the first two-thirds of the song. At the words "La neige tombe" the chords of the accompaniment descend, *en mourant.* This downward transfer of the tessitura gives a darker color to the sound appropriate to the death of the day and of the wolf (see Example 1).[12]

Debussy demanded of his collaborators this same attentiveness to shading. Debussy's inability to find a librettist who could write with the subtlety of a Verlaine for the length of an entire play explains in part his failure to produce a successor to *Pelléas et Mélisande.* Debussy's marginal notes on *Orphée-Roi,* a proposed collaboration with Segalen, witness his preoccupation with *la Nuance:*

> changer atteindre; sonorité trop dure
> trop tôt, trop clair. A venir plus tard.
> pas lyrique
> trop lourde

[12] We shall discuss this aspect of musical texture in greater detail in chapter 10.

trop précoce, trop explicatif
trop balancé, trop opéra
trop littérature
moins grandiloquent, moins boursouflé. Plus intime.
Le son ne me plaît pas. Idée peut rester.[13]

Oh! la nuance seule fiance
Le rêve au rêve et la flûte au cor!

The sounds of different musical instruments carry powerful associations which can be evoked—almost conjured up—by reference to their names. The naming of a musical instrument brings to mind both the characteristic sound of that instrument and the circumstances with which we associate it. Such musical references occur frequently in Verlaine's poetry. Consider these examples from the poems which Debussy set to music:

Et la mandoline jase
Parmi les frissons de brise.

[Mandoline]

Tournez, tournez au son des hautbois
. . . Tournez au son joyeux des tambours, tournez.

[Chevaux de bois]

L'onde roulée en volutes
De cloches comme des flûtes
Dans le ciel comme du lait.

[L'Échelonnement des haies]

masques et bergamasques
Jouant du luth et dansant.

[Clair de lune]

Jusqu'á cette heure dont la fuite
Tournoie au son des tambourins.

[Le Faune]

The mandolin in Verlaine's poem evokes in many minds an image of serenaders which complements the description in the text. The example from *L'Échelonnement des haies* illustrates the joining of two sounds: the tintinnabulation of bells produces a clangorous arabesque of sound

[13] Published in *Segalen et Debussy*, ed. Annie Joly-Segalen and André Schaeffner (Monaco: Editions du Rocher, 1961).

which resembles the convolution of a typical flute line. The tambourine in *Le Faune* establishes the rhythm of the dance which becomes the central metaphor of the poem.

The composer also has the evocative power of these associations at his command. The English horn, for example, has been used so often in pieces with titles like *Pastorale* that the mere sound of the instrument is enough to produce idyllic visions in some listeners. The actual instrument need not even be present if the composer can produce its characteristic musical patterns on some other instrument. The horn calls in the second movement of Debussy's *En blanc et noir,* for example, sound no less vivid for being played on two pianos rather than on a horn. In this case it is not the timbre of the horn but the reproduction of its idiomatic triadic figures, associated with military signals, which contributes to the musical portrayal of a battle scene.

In Verlaine's *Le Son du cor*, on the other hand, it is the particular timbre of the horn—dark, mellow, almost mournful—which enters the "paysage lent" and blends into "ce soir monotone." In the course of the poem Verlaine extends, clarifies, specifies this basic image of the horn so that the reader puts from his mind the military associations of the horn and preserves only those which suit the poet's purpose:

> Le son du cor
> s'afflige
> vers les bois
> d'une douleur
> (on veut croire) orpheline.

Debussy's imitation of other musical instruments in his piano pieces seems almost literary. The carillon and organ in *La Cathédrale engloutie,* the *quasi tambouro* in *Minstrels*, the bells of *Cloches à travers les feuilles*, the flute in *The Little Shepherd*, the castanets of *Pour la danseuse aux crotales*: they are not simply evidence that Debussy thought in orchestral terms. Rather they call forth all the associations which these instruments bear, and contribute to an evocative quality in Debussy's music which one may regard as analogous to the metaphors of symbolism.

Prends l'éloquence et tords-lui son cou!

By *éloquence* Verlaine means the rhetorical devices which an orator employs in addressing an audience. Verlaine makes fun of this inflated style in the melodramatic image of strangulation. In this sense *La Mort du loup* is an "eloquent" poem. It begins with a narrative in the first person plural, describing the scene as the group of hunters perceive it. Then the narrative changes to the first person singular as the speaker relates his own experience of seeing the wolf. The death of the wolf is described in the first person plural, then back to the singular for the reflection on the escape of the other wolves. Then the speaker addresses the dead wolf: "Ah! je t'ai bien compris, sauvage voyageur." The wolf dies "sans parler," but the poem ends with a speech in which the speaker assumes the role of the wolf—the rhetorical device of *prosopopeia*—to express a philosophy of stoical resignation:

> Gémir, pleurer, prier, est également lâche.
> Fais énergiquement ta longue et lourde tâche,
> Dans la voie où le Sort a voulu t'appeler,
> Puis, après, comme moi, souffre et meurs sans parler.

By contrast, *Le Son du cor* ends with the evocation of a landscape. While we do feel the presence of a voice in the poem, there is no *je* present. In contrast to the forthright metaphors of *La Mort du loup*—"comme sur l'incendie on voit fuir la fumée"—Verlaine's sonnet contains only tentative comparisons: "Et l'air a l'air d'être un soupir d'automne."

In music, *éloquence* in the sense that Verlaine uses the word might be described as bombast, pomposity, showiness. We can all think of places in the orchestral literature of the nineteenth century where there is a great deal of noise and furious activity but actually very little happening. We find few such spots in Debussy's music. In the whole of the *Prélude à l'après-midi d'un faune,* for example, there are but six measures where the orchestra plays *forte,* and there is only one *fortissimo.* The dynamics of *Le Son du cor* are even more severely restricted: four measures are *mezzoforte,* all the rest *pianissimo*, with only an occasional *sforzando* or *forte-piano* interruption.

When we imagine the rhetorical declamation of a text we think not only of an elevated dynamic level but also of exaggerated inflections. Such is the case in grand opera, where the difficulty of a role is frequently measured in terms of the vocal range which it demands. By contrast, in Debussy's mature songs we find few dramatic leaps. The normal range of Debussy's songs is an octave and a half, but the later songs show an increasing tendency toward a recitative-like style, with careful preparation for extremes of tessitura. Several songs have a far more constricted range. Debussy's setting of Verlaine's *Le Faune*, like his setting of Louÿs' *La Flûte de Pan*, contains the entire vocal line within a single octave. In *Le Son du cor* there are several measures in which the voice remains on a single note or moves about within the range of a minor third. Both in dynamics and in vocal range Debussy prefers subdued statement.

Yet another manifestation of *éloquence* is length: the eloquent statement, in the sense we have been using, is rarely brief. Vigny's *La Mort du loup*, at eighty-eight lines, is the shortest poem but one in *Les Destinées*. Verlaine's *Le Son du cor*, on the other hand, has only fourteen lines. His *Art poétique*, with thirty-six lines, is one of his longest poems.

The catalogue of Debussy's music contains few really long works. His best-known works, of course, are the longer orchestral pieces: *Trois Nocturnes*, *La Mer*, *Images*, *Jeux*. Most of the abandoned projects were also of a larger scale: incidental music, cantatas, operas. But among the published works—the successful products of Debussy's musical aesthetic—these are outweighed by the preponderance of relatively brief piano pieces and songs. Moreover, Debussy displays a notable economy in his use of musical material. Rather than spin out a long melodic line, Debussy will frequently repeat one- or two-measure groups. Often he will repeat a measure after the intervention of another measure to form the pattern a b a c. The extended repetition of a rhythm leads to ostinato; the extended repetition of a single note or melodic pattern produces a pedal-point; both are characteristic features of the composer's style.

Debussy's aversion to eloquence goes deeper still, as Xavier Leroux, one of the composer's confreres at the Villa des Medicis, recalls:

> Il avait en horreur la grandiloquence dans tous les arts. Il était surtout touché par les sensations intimes. Les productions humaines à grandes dimensions l'étonnaient, mais sans l'émerveiller ni l'enthousiasmer. . . .[14]

Heroic posturing, titanic struggle, climactic statement, grand design—in short, everything that tended to make music into prose—was alien to Debussy's philosophy. He had no patience for traditional forms which

[14] Quoted by Léon Vallas in *Claude Debussy et son Temps* (Paris: Editions Albin Michel, 1958), pp. 74–75.

present music as a logical discourse. About the symphony he wrote, "Il me semble que, depuis Beethoven, la preuve de l'inutilité de la symphonie était faite." [15] Nor had he any sympathy with the obvious craft which draws variations from a theme:

> Il se trouve que je n'ai jamais aimé les "variations." Ce n'est qu'un procédé facile pour tirer *beaucoup* de *très peu*: quelquefois, c'est une vengeance; plus rarement le pauvre théme se fâche et semble repousser avec dégoût les transvestissements qu'une ingéniosité obstinée lui impose.[16]

Debussy's craft disguises itself in a cloak of apparent improvisation and yet the proportions of his music are no less carefully measured than the balanced periods of a more "eloquent" composer:

> Il est curieux que deux mesures "parasites" puissent démolir l'édifice le plus solidement construit! C'est ce qui vient exactement de m'arriver. . . . Et rien ne vous en prévient, pas plus la "vieille expérience" que le "plus beau don"! C'est encore l'instinct—vieux comme le monde—qui, seul, peut vous sauver! [17]

Debussy's music aspires to the state of poetry just as Verlaine's poetry aspires to the state of music. When Debussy says "Tout chez moi est instinctif, irraisonné," [18] he acknowledges the source of his music in dream, in the subconscious. The working out of that music must depend not on eloquence but on nuance, which alone "fiance/Le rêve au rêve et la flûte au cor!"

> Tu feras bien, en train d'énergie,
> De rendre un peu la Rime assagie.

In a broader sense, the word *éloquence* may be understood to include rhyme as well as the devices of oratory. Verlaine's complaint against the misuse of rhyme is in some respects a reaction to Banville's *Petit traité de poésie française* of 1872. As we have seen, Banville was a versatile poet who could write with facility in any of the classical poetic forms. Banville maintained that these existing forms were so diverse that poets should not attempt to create new ones. A brilliant versifier, Banville firmly

[15] Debussy, *Monsieur Croche*, p. 25.
[16] *Lettres á Deux Amis* (Paris: Librairie José Corti, 1942), p. 165.
[17] *Lettres de Claude Debussy á son Éditeur*, p. 176.
[18] Quote from conversation, *Segalen et Debussy*, p. 71.

defended a strict construction of the rules of rhyme. "On n'entend dans un vers que le mot qui est à la rime, et ce mot est le seul qui travaille à produire l'effet voulu par le poète." [19] Elsewhere he writes that there is no rhyme without a *consonne d'appui*, in other words, that nothing but *rimes riches* will do. On the subject of poetic license he wrote, "Il n'y en a pas."

Verlaine found these ideas too restrictive for his taste and sought to make rhyme a bit more obedient. It was not rhyme that Verlaine opposed—he was no *vers libre* poet—but the virtuosity which placed too much emphasis on rhyme. In order to diminish the importance of sounds at the ends of lines Verlaine emphasized sounds within lines by alliteration ("qui pèse ou qui pose") and by interior rhyme (*Indécis*, *Précis*; *nuance*, *fiance*). Other factors also served to deemphasize rhyme: enjambment; use of nonrhyming lines; use of unstressed words at the rhyme; use of a single word to rhyme with itself.

The abuse which Verlaine attacks is comparable to the "tyranny of the barline" in music, with its insistence on regularly recurring accents. Debussy employs a number of devices to weaken these downbeat accents in *Le Son du cor:*

(a) The suppression of the downbeat by tying notes across the barline;

(b) The establishment of a melodic pattern which cuts across the barline;

(c) The addition of dynamic stresses which cut across the barline (Example 3). Debussy freely alters the length of the measure when it suits his purpose, using a single 6/8 measure to separate the third and fourth stanzas, both in 9/8.

Verlaine did not always follow the directions given in his *Art poétique*, which apply better to his *Fêtes galantes* than to the later poetry. Still, the ideas which that poem contains joined the sentiments of other writers who also preferred suggestion to declamation, evocation to oratory. One observes the concern for *la Nuance* in these words of Mallarmé from 1891:

> Le contemplation des objets, l'image s'envolant des rêveries suscitées par eux, sont le chant. . . . *Nommer* un objet, c'est supprimer les trois quarts de le jouissance du poème qui est faite de deviner peu à peu: le *suggérer*, voilà le rêve.[20]

[19] Théodore de Banville, *Petit Traité de Poésie Française* (Paris: G. Charpentier, 1887), p.48.

[20] Stéphane Mallarmé, *Oeuvres Complètes*, ed. Henri Mondor and G. Jean-Aubry (Paris: Bibliothèque de la Pléiade, 1965), p.869.

Example 3

There was a certain time-lag before these ideas found their musical counterparts. When Verlaine wrote his *Art poétique* in 1874 the music in the air was that of Gounod and Berlioz and Bizet, music which paralleled the poetry of Vigny. It was nearly twenty years later that Debussy composed *Le Son du cor*. By then Debussy was not the only composer who preferred suggestion to statement. Fauré had already composed his *Requiem* (1887) and the six Verlaine songs which we discussed earlier. These works, like Debussy's, avoid any display of virtuosity or grandiloquence. Debussy seems to have derived his musical style not so much from the older Fauré, however, or from any other musician, as from the ideas expressed by the poets.

> Oh! la nuance seule fiance
> Le rêve au rêve et la flûte au cor!

Viewed against Debussy's career, Verlaine's lines sound almost prophetic, for it is indeed *la nuance* which connects the dreamy landscape of Verlaine's *Le Son du cor* to the dreamworld of the faun in Mallarmé's eclogue. Only a year after evoking the sound of the horn, Debussy was to capture the nuances of *L'après-midi d'un faune* in the arabesques of a flute.

7

MALLARMÉ I: *L'Apres-midi d'un Faune*

In 1894 Mallarmé was the acknowledged master of French poets. Although never a favorite with the public during his lifetime, Mallarmé exerted considerable influence over writers and painters toward the end of the nineteenth century. Debussy set only four of Mallarmé's poems to music: the early *Apparition* (1882–1884) written while Debussy was still at the Conservatoire, and the *Trois Poèmes de Stéphane Mallarmé*, composed in 1913, fifteen years after Mallarmé's death. Debussy's *Prélude à l'après-midi d'un faune* was composed during a period when Debussy knew Mallarmé quite well, and the history of the work gives an unusually vivid insight into Debussy's association with the poet.

Mallarmé, like other poets of his time, sought to create a certain musicality in his verse, but was somewhat reluctant to have anyone else set his poetry to music. When Mallarmé first heard of Debussy's intention to write music for his poem *L'Après-midi d'un faune*, perhaps in 1893, he is reported to have remarked, "Je croyais l'avoir mis moi-même en musique." [1] When Debussy played the score for him on the piano in 1894, however, Mallarmé discovered that this music was not what he had anticipated. Debussy describes the scene:

> Mallarmé vint chez moi, fatidique et orné d'un plaid écossais. Après avoir écouté, il resta silencieux pendant un long moment, et me dit: "Je ne m'attendais pas à quelque chose de pareil! Cette musique prolonge l'émotion de mon poème et en situe le décor plus passionnement que la couleur.[2]

Debussy invited Mallarmé to the premiere performance, 22 December 1894, with this brief note, written in an imitation of Mallarmé's prose style:

> Ai-je besoin de vous dire la joie que j'aurais si vous voulez bien encourager de votre présence les arabesques qu'un peut-être coupable orgueil m'a fait croire d'être dictées par la flûte de votre Faune?[3]

Mallarmé was favorably impressed with the first performance of Debussy's orchestral poem. He wrote the composer:

> Votre illustration de *l'Après-midi d'un faune*, qui ne présenterait de dissonance avec mon texte, sinon qu'aller plus loin, vraiment, dans la nostalgie et dans la lumière, avec finesse, avec malaise, avec richesse.[4]

Mallarmé had neglected to send Debussy the copy of the poem he had promised, and when Debussy inquired about it, Mallarmé wrote:

> Je n'ai pas mis de côte *le Faune* que, bien sûr, vous avez envoyé chercher: et soudain hier, en regardant l'eau couler, j'y songeai, pourquoi? . . .[5]

Shortly thereafter Debussy received the copy, illustrated by Manet, on which Mallarmé had penned the following dedication:

> Sylvain d'haleine première
> Si ta flûte a réussi
> Ouïs toute la lumière
> Qu'y soufflera Debussy.

[1] Henri Mondor, "Stéphane Mallarmé et Claude Debussy," *Journal Musical Français* 1 (25 September 1951):8.

[2] *Lettres à deux amis* (Paris: José Corti, 1942), p. 121.

[3] Mondor, "Stéphane Mallarmé et Claude Debussy."

[4] Stéphane Mallarmé, *Oeuvres complètes* ed. Henri Mondor and G. Jean-Aubrey, (Paris: Bibliothèque de la Pléiade, 1965), p. 1465.

[5] *Ibid.*

Once again Mallarmé describes Debussy's *Prélude* in terms of light, recalling the letter quoted earlier in which he said that Debussy had extended his text "dans la lumière."

Both Mallarmé's eclogue and Debussy's *Prélude* went through several metamorphoses before achieving their final forms. The first mention of the poem comes in a letter from Mallarmé to his intimate friend Henri Cazalis, June 1865. Mallarmé was only 23 at the time.

> Je rime un intermède héroïque, dont le héros est un Faune. Ce poëme renferme une très haute et belle idée, mais les vers sont terriblement difficiles à faire, car je le fais absolument scénique, non possible au théâtre, mais exigeant le théâtre. Et cependant je veux conserver toute la poésie de mes oeuvres lyriques, mon vers même, que j'adapte au drame. Quand tu viendras, je crois que tu seras heureux: l'idée de la dernière scène me fait sangloter, la conception en est vaste, et le vers très travaillé. . . . J'ajoute que je compte le présenter en août au Théâtre-Français.[6]

In July Mallarmé described the difficulty of fulfilling his vision:

> Tu ne saurais croire comme il est difficile de s'archarner au vers que je veux très neuf et très beau, bien que dramatique (surtout plus rythmé encore que le vers lyrique parce qu'il doit ravir l'oreille au théâtre). . . . Mais si tu savais que de nuits désespérées et de jours de rêverie il faut sacrifier pour arriver à faire des vers originaux (ce que je n'avais jamais fait jusqu'ici) et dignes, dans leurs suprêmes mystères, de réjouir l'âme d'un poëte.[7]

Mallarmé read this first version, *Monologue d'un faune*, to Constant Coquelin and Théodore de Banville, in September 1865. While the verse may have delighted their ears, the *Monologue* lacked the dramatic interest required for a successful stage production. Mallarmé writes:

> Les vers de mon *Faune* ont plu infiniment, mais de Banville et Coquelin n'y ont pas rencontré l'anecdote nécessaire que demande le public et m'ont affirmé que cela n'intéresserait que les poëtes. J'abandonne mon sujet pendant quelques mois dans un tiroir pour le refaire plus librement plus tard.[8]

After a silence of nearly ten years, the *Faune* turned up again, this time under the title *Improvisation d'un Faune.* It was supposed to be published in the third series of the *Parnasse Contemporain* in 1875. Despite Banville's

[6] *Ibid.*, p. 1449.
[7] *Ibid.*
[8] *Ibid.*, p. 1450.

support for this revised version, however, the editorial board rejected the work, which was published in its final form in 1876. Mallarmé's description of the rejection sheds light on his previously quoted remark, that he thought he had set the poem to music himself:

> Plus tard, vers 1875, mon *Après-midi d'un Faune,* à part quelques amis, . . . fit hurler le Parnasse tout entier, et le morceau fut refusé avec un grand ensemble. J'y essayais, en effet, de mettre, à côté de l'alexandrin dans toute sa tenue, une sorte de jeu courant pianoté autour, comme qui dirait d'un accompagnement musical fait par le poëte lui-même et ne permettant au vers official de sortir que dans les grandes occasions.[9]

In contrast to the well-documented history of Mallarmé's *Faune* the information on Debussy's *Prélude* is rather sparse.[10] The date on the manuscript attests that it was begun in 1892 but we do not know what shape the first sketches took. The score of *La Damoiselle élue*, published in 1893, announced a forthcoming *Prélude, interludes et paraphrase finale pour l'Après-midi d'un faune.* This title also appeared on a program of Debussy's music performed in Brussels on 1 March 1894 but the piece was not performed on that occasion. The final form of the *Prélude*, without *interludes* or *paraphrase finale*, must have been completed by 23 October 1894 for on that date Debussy assigned all rights for the composition to G. Hartmann, the publisher.

Many of Debussy's biographers have insisted that his *Prélude à l'après-midi d'un faune* is not closely related to the poem. Debussy's remarks, as usual, are ambiguous. In a letter to the critic Willy (Henry Gautier-Villars), dated 10 October 1895, Debussy describes his music as a general impression of the poem.

> Le *Prélude à "l'Après-midi d'un faune,"* cher Monsieur, c'est peut-être ce qui est resté de rêve au fond de la flûte du faune? Plus précisement, c'est l'impression générale du poème, car à le suivre de plus près, la musique s'essoufflerait ainsi qu'un cheval de fiacre concourant pour le Grand Prix avec un pur sang.

[9] *Ibid.,* p. 870.

[10] I have relied on Edward Lockspeiser, *Debussy, His Life and Mind* (London: Cassell, 1965); Léon Vallas, *Claude Debussy et son temps* (Paris: Editions Albin Michel, 1958). Additional material may be found in William Austin, *Debussy: Prelude to "The Afternoon of a Faun* (New York: W. W. Norton, 1970).

The music attempts to contain all the shadings of the text, while following the "rising movement" of the poem.

> C'est aussi le dédain de cette "science de castors" qui alourdit nos plus fiers cerveaux, puis, c'est sans respect pour le ton! et plutôt dans un mode qui essaye de contenir toutes les nuances, ce qui est très logiquement démontrable. Maintenant, cela suit tout de même le mouvement ascendant du poème, et c'est le décor merveilleusement décrit au texte, avec, en plus, l'humanité qu'apportent trente-deux violonistes levés de trop bonne heure! La fin, c'est le dernier vers prolongé: "Couple, adieu! Je vais voir l'ombre que tu devins." [11]

In another note, apparently drafted by Debussy, we read:

> La musique de ce Prélude est un illustration très libre du beau poème de Mallarmé. Elle ne prétend nullement à une synthèse de celui-ci. Ce sont plutôt les décors successifs à travers lesquels se meuvent les désirs et les rêves du faune dans la chaleur de cet après-midi. Puis, las de poursuivre la fuite peureuse des nymphes et des naïades, il se laisse aller au sommeil enivrant, rempli de songes enfin realisés, de possession totale dans l'universelle nature.[12]

According to the distinguished critic Charles Mauron, Debussy is said to have declared that he followed the poem verse by verse in composing his music.[13] Whether this information is accurate or not, it seems more than coincidental that the number of lines of the poem is identical to the number of measures of music.

With this much to go on, certainly we are justified in examining the poem and the music more closely, to determine in what manner the music evokes "les décors successifs à travers lesquels se meuvent les désirs et les rêves du faune dans le chaleur de cet après-midi." In short, we shall see whether Debussy's *Prélude* is anything more than "one of the best guides to the *mood* of the poem." [14]

Our investigation will be based on a comparison of the structure of the poem with that of the music. Neither Mallarmé's eclogue nor

[11] Vallas, *Debussy*, pp. 181–182.

[12] *Ibid.*, p. 181.

[13] Stéphane Mallarmé, *Poems*, translated by Roger Fry with commentaries by Charles Mauron (New York: Oxford University Press, 1965), p. 124.

[14] Robert Greer Cohn, *Toward the Poems of Mallarmé* (Berkeley: University of California Press, 1965), p. 13; emphasis added.

Debussy's *Prélude* breaks apart into discrete sections. Both poet and composer minimize the internal divisions of their work so that one idea flows into the next. In order to clarify the overall "arch-form" which characterizes both works we shall label the subsections in a manner that emphasizes their distinctness. When the poem is read—or the music performed, however, these distinctions fade into an overall continuity whose dreamlike, improvisatory quality obscures the underlying organization.

The most prominent element of form in Mallarmé's poem is the variation in typography.[15] Some thirty lines of the text, in three sections, are set off from the rest by italic type and quotation marks. These lines are written in the past tense and relate, with a good deal of clarity, what has taken place during the afternoon as the faun remembers it. The rest of the poem, for the most part, is a gloss on the memory of these events. The narrative itself is clear; it is the spreading out of the narrative among the meditations that weakens the distinction between reality and fantasy.

L'Après-midi d'un Faune

Ces nymphes, je les veux perpétuer.
Si clair,
Leur incarnat léger, qu'il voltige dans l'air
Assoupi de sommeils touffus.

Aimai-je un rêve?
Mon doute, amas de nuit ancienne, s'achève
En maint rameau subtil, qui, demeuré les vrais
Bois mêmes, prouve, hélas! que bien seul je m'offrais
Pour triomphe la faute idéale de roses.
Réfléchissons . . .

ou si les femmes dont tu gloses
Figurent, un souhait de tes sens fabuleux!
Faune, l'illusion s'échappe des yeux bleus

[15] The account that follows deals primarily with the structure of the poem. For a full exegesis the reader is directed to Bernard Weinberg, *The Limits of Symbolism* (Chicago: University of Chicago Press, 1966), and Cohn, *Toward the Poems of Mallarmé*, to which the present study owes much. See also Wallace Fowlie, *Mallarmé* (Chicago: University of Illinois Press, 1953), and A. R. Chisholm, *Mallarmé's L'Après-midi d'un Faune, An Exegetical and Critical Study* (Carlton: Melbourne University Press, 1958).

Et froids, comme une source en pleurs, de la plus chaste:
Mais, l'autre tout soupirs, dis-tu qu'elle contraste
Comme brise du jour chaude dans ta toison?
Que non! par l'immobile et lasse pâmoison
Suffoquant de chaleurs le matin frais s'il lutte,
Ne murmure point d'eau que ne verse ma flûte
Au bosquet arrosé d'accords; et le seul vent
Hors des deux tuyaux prompt à s'exhaler avant
Qu'il disperse le son dans une pluie aride,
C'est, à l'horizon pas remué d'une ride,
Le visible et serein souffle artificiel
De l'inspiration, qui regagne le ciel.

O bords siciliens d'un calme marécage
Qu'à l'envi de soleils ma vanité saccage,
Tacite sous les fleurs d'étincelles, CONTEZ
"Que je coupais ici les creux roseaux domptés
"Par le talent; quand, sur l'or glauque de lointaines
"Verdures dédiant leur vigne à des fontaines,
"Ondoie une blancheur animale au repos:
"Et qu'au prélude lent où naissant les pipeaux
"Ce vol de cygnes, non! de naïades se sauve
"Ou plonge . . ."

Inerte, tout brûle dans l'heure fauve
Sans marquer par quel art ensemble détala
Trop d'hymen souhaité de qui cherche le *la*:
Alors m'éveillerai-je à la ferveur première,
Droit et seul, sous un flot antique de lumière,
Lys! et l'un de vous tous pour l'ingénuité.

Autre que ce doux rien par leur lèvre ébruité,
Le baiser, qui tout bas des perfides assure,
Mon sein, vierge de preuve, atteste une morsure
Mystérieuse, due à quelque auguste dent;
Mais, bast! arcane tel élut pour confident
Le jonc vaste et jumeau dont sous l'azur on joue:
Qui, détournant à soi le trouble de la joue,
Rêve, dans un solo long, que nous amusions
La beauté d'alentour par des confusions
Fausses entre elle-même et notre chant crédule;
Et de faire aussi haut que l'amour se module
Evanouir du songe ordinaire de dos

Ou de flanc pur suivis avec mes regards clos,
Une sonore, vaine et monotone ligne.

Tâche donc, instrument des fuites, ô maligne
Syrinx, de refleurir aux lacs où tu m'attends!
Moi, de ma rumeur fier, je vais parler longtemps
Des déesses; et par d'idolâtres peintures,
A leur ombre enlever encore des ceintures:
Ainsi, quand des raisins j'ai sucé la clarté,
Pour bannir un regret par ma feinte écarté,
Rieur, j'élève au ciel d'été la grappe vide
Et, soufflant dans ses peaux lumineuses, avide
D'ivresse, jusqu'au soir je regarde au travers.

O nymphes, regonflons des SOUVENIRS divers.
"Mon oeil, trouant les joncs, dardait chaque encolure
"Immortelle, qui noie en l'onde sa brûlure
"Avec un cri de rage au ciel de la forêt;
"Et le splendide bain de cheveux disparaît
"Dans les clartés et les frissons, ô pierreries!
"J'accours; quand, à mes pieds, s'entrejoignent (meurtries
"De la langueur goûtée à ce mal d'être deux)
"Des dormeuses parmi leurs seuls bras hasardeux;
"Je les ravis, sans les désenlacer, et vole
"A ce massif, haï par l'ombrage frivole,
"De roses tarissant tout parfum au soleil,
"Où notre ébat au jour consumé soit pareil."
Je t'adore, courroux des vierges, ô délice
Farouche du sacré fardeau nu qui se glisse
Pour fuir ma lèvre en feu buvant, comme un éclair
Tressaille! la frayeur secrète de la chair:
Des pieds de l'inhumaine au coeur de la timide
Que délaisse à la fois une innocence, humide
De larmes folles ou de moins tristes vapeurs.
"Mon crime, c'est d'avoir, gai de vaincre ces peurs
"Traîtresses, divisé la touffe échevelée
"De baisers que les dieux gardaient si bien mêlée:
"Car, à peine j'allais cacher un rire ardent
"Sous les replis heureux d'une seule (gardant
"Par un doigt simple, afin que sa candeur de plume
"Se teignît à l'émoi de sa soeur qui s'allume,
"La petite, naïve et ne rougissant pas:)
"Que de mes bras, défaits par de vagues trépas,

"Cette proie, à jamais ingrate se délivre
"Sans pitié du sanglot dont j'étais encore ivre."

Tant pis! vers le bonheur d'autres m'entraîneront
Par leur tresse nouée aux cornes de mon front:
Tu sais, ma passion, que, pourpre et déjà mûre,
Chaque grenade éclate et d'abeilles murmure;
Et notre sang, épris de qui le va saisir,
Coule pour tout l'essaim éternel du désir.
A l'heure où ce bois d'or et de cendres se teinte
Une fête s'exalte en la feuillée éteinte:
Etna! c'est parmi toi visité de Vénus
Sur ta lave posant ses talons ingénus,
Quand tonne un somme triste ou s'épuise la flamme.
Je tiens la reine!

O sûr châtiment . . .

Non, mais l'âme
De paroles vacante et ce corps alourdi
Tard succombent au fier silence de midi:
Sans plus il faut dormir en l'oubli du blasphème,
Sur le sable altéré gisant et comme j'aime
Ouvrir ma bouche à l'astre efficace des vins!

Couple, adieu; je vais voir l'ombre que tu devins.

[For translation, see p. 307]

INTRODUCTION (lines 1–3)

"Ces nymphes, je les veux perpétuer." The opening line states the theme of the work, yet it seems not to be a beginning. Rather, we enter in the middle of something. What nymphs is the faun talking about? They are, of course, the nymphs described in italics later on, but when we read the poem in its proper order we do not know that. The word *perpétuer* is ambiguous: if the nymphs are real, then it suggests prolonging their existence in some fashion; if they are not, it implies giving them an existence which they do not really have. In either case, the word *veux* tells us that an act of will is required. Just how the faun will go about "perpetuating" the nymphs will become more apparent later on in the poem.

FIRST SECTION (lines 4–41)

"Aimai-je un rêve?" Mallarmé adopts the device of stichomythia to set off this key question. The first line of the poem implies that the faun has already been thinking about the nymphs. The second half of the third line raises a doubt about their existence. The faun attempts to deal with this question in four conjectures which comprise the first large section of the poem and which take the faun from his original drowsy state to one of wakefulness.

Lines 4–7

The form of the nymphs ("leur incarnat léger") still shimmers in the shadows of the trees, but as the faun emerges from sleep, these illusions vanish while only the trees remain. His sensual conquest was only a dream.

Lines 8–22

The faun considers a second hypothesis, that the nymphs were but the creation of his own desire ("un souhait de tes sens fabuleus"). This hallucination might have been shaped by the faun's impressions as he slept. The chaster of the two nymphs had cold, blue eyes—like the murmuring of a spring. The other, all sighs, formed a contrast like the breeze of a warm day. But no! Everything is still in this fresh morning—the heat would stifle any movement of the air. The only murmuring of water is that which the faun's flute pours out, and the only wind, outside of the exhalation of his pipes, is the artificial breath of inspiration. Hence, there was nothing but the faun's dream. Or, since there was no water or breeze, perhaps the nymphs were real. The faun remains confused.[16]

Lines 23–37

So far the faun has been unable to elicit any assistance from his surroundings. The trees under which he awoke were confused with the shadows of the nymphs; the illusion of water and wind failed to answer his question; indeed, these Sicilian shores seem to confound his vanity

[16] Cohn, *Toward the Poems of Mallarmé*, p. 18.

just as much as the stifling sun does. In spite of the apparent unwillingness of nature to aid the investigation, the faun calls on the "calme marécage" to relate what has happened during the afternoon. While cutting the hollow reeds, the faun saw an animal whiteness rippling in the distance. Then, as his first breath gave birth to the pipes—now become a musical instrument—there was a flight of swans, no! of naiads.

The faun, meditating on this memory, speaks of his excessive desire ("trop d'hymen") as he tunes his instrument. The afternoon and the landscape remain inert, "sans marquer par quel art" the naiads had fled. If the adventure was but an illusion, then the faun will awake alone, as he has recently awakened. Neither his memory nor his musing has brought him to an answer.

Lines 38–41

The faun's last conjecture deals with two ambiguous bits of evidence. He remembers the kiss of the nymphs, "qui tout bas des perfides assure." But the kiss is also described as "ce doux rien"—did it really happen? The nymphs are "perfides" not to have given stronger proof of their existence. There is the "morsure mystérieuse," however, which "attests"—a stronger verb than "assures"—the presence of some august tooth. But the faun's chest is "vierge de preuve"—how can this be? Various critics, attempting to reconcile "une morsure" with "vierge de preuve," have contrived a number of ingenious explanations, all of which seem to depend on explaining away one phrase or the other. Perhaps the least cumbersome reading is a literal one—there is a "morsure mystérieuse" and yet the faun's chest is "vierge de preuve" because he cannot be sure what produced the bite. This seems to be the line which the faun himself takes, for he rejects this futile ratiocination with an impatient "Mais, bast!" Only his flute seems to know the answer to this mystery.

This division, between lines 41 and 42, presents certain difficulties, since it does not coincide with any break in typography as all the other divisions do. A break does occur at this point in the *Monologue d'un faune*; in both versions the faun has clearly rejected as unsatisfying his attempts to answer the question "Aimai-je un rêve?"

MIDDLE SECTION (lines 42–61)

LINES 42–51

The doubt cannot be resolved one way or the other. The faun looks instead to music as a conscious means of evocation which can turn the curve of an ordinary dream into "une sonore, vaine et monotone ligne." These three adjectives depart somewhat from their usual meanings and here suggest a solitary line which is music and nothing else. It is *sonore*—only sound, although inspired by a vision which has been transformed "aussi haut que l'amour se module." It is *vaine*—both in the sense of "empty," without objective reference, and "unreal," since it is a transformation of the ordinary. At the same time it is "futile," since art cannot really influence nature. The faun can turn the curve of his dream into music but he cannot thereby turn the dream into reality. It is *monotone*—not monotonous in the sense of being boring, but literally "one-toned." It is a single line, since the flute plays only one note at a time, and because the other curves of back and flank have disappeared. This line of melody has been drawn out—"faire . . . évanouir"—from the others.

LINES 52–61

The faun throws down the flute and tells it to become a reed again. He will perpetuate the nymphs in speech, elevating their status to that of goddesses, evoking their presence "par d'idolâtres peintures." The ecstatic state which the faun has produced by blowing into hollow reeds and turning them into a syrinx is compared to the delight of blowing into empty grapeskins and seeing the light shine through them. The music can almost make him forget his regret at not having the nymphs. But the illusion cannot be sustained, hence the frustrated "Tâche donc, . . . Syrinx, de refleurir aux lacs." In the first line of the next section, the faun calls on the nymphs once again to refill the empty memories. Four successively cloudier images mark the faun's return to slumber.

FINAL SECTION (lines 62–109)

Lines 62–81

The first image, set in italics to indicate the memory of past experience, is the clearest of the four. The faun, running to investigate the white shapes which his flute had aroused (lines 30–32) comes across two nymphs interlaced in languid embrace ("meurtries / De la langueur goûtée à ce mal d'être deux"). Without disengaging the pair, the faun seizes them and flies to a thicket.

In the gloss which follows (lines 75–81) the faun delights in his memory of the anger of the virgins, and, as earlier in the poem, distinguishes between the two nymphs, one "inhumaine," the other "timide."

Lines 82–92

The second image, like the first, is in italics, but is less clear. Although there are a number of erotic expressions ("divisé la touffe," "replis heureux," "s'allume") the language has been "recomposed" in such a way that there is no clear description of a licentious act. In fact, the faun tells us that his prey escaped before he could consummate his desire ("à jamais ingrate se délivre / Sans pitié du sanglot dont j'étais encore ivre.") His only "crime" was his separation of the pair.

Lines 93–104

The faun dismisses the memory of the nymphs and imagines that he will find happiness in some "others" who will not escape so easily. They will be attracted to his desire just as bees swarm about a freshly burst pomegranate. The faun then contemplates an autumn feast in which the image of the bursting pomegranate is replaced by the eruption of a volcano and the swarm of bees by Venus, the queen of love. To imagine taking so exalted a prize must certainly invite the punishment of the gods ("O sûr châtiment").

Lines 105–109

The faun must succumb at last to the heat of midday which he has put off during an afternoon of meditation. He drifts to sleep, opening his mouth to the grape-ripening sun ("à l'astre efficace des vins"), his desire still unfulfilled.

CONCLUSION (line 110)

"Couple, adieu; je vais voir l'ombre que tu devins." The faun recognizes that the nymphs never existed, and abandons hope of reanimating them through his playing. Rather, in sleep the faun will see the shade, or shadow, of the nymphs that he had desired to perpetuate.

The overall form of the poem may be represented as follows (Example 1). The arch form is suggested by the symmetry of the first and

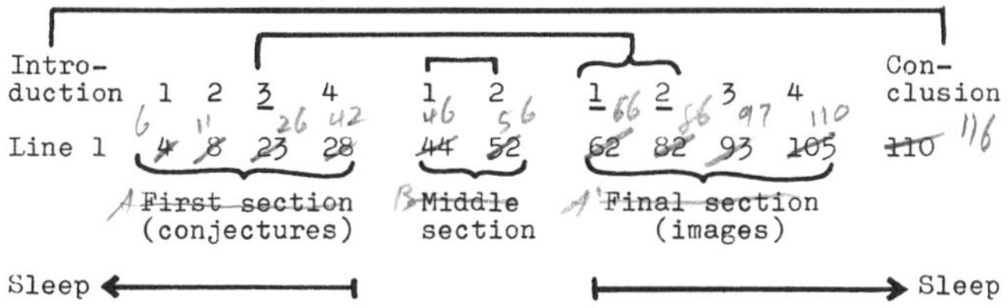

Example 1

last lines of the poem, and by the balancing of the four parts of the first section—moving from drowsiness to lucidity—against the four parts of the final section, moving from lucidity to drowsiness and sleep. The sections in italics are underlined.

This representation of the form of the poem is very similar to the way one may represent the form of Debussy's orchestral *Prélude.* The musical form is based on a number of variations on an opening theme. The presence of this theme in the outer sections and its absence in the central section divides the work into an A B A′ form. The structure is further subdivided by minute differences in the successive presentations of the theme. (Example 2).[17]

The identification of the subtle correspondences between these presentations requires further supporting evidence:

[17] This outline is based on the analysis by D. Dille, "Inleiding tot het vormbegrip bij Debussy," in *Hommage à Charles van den Borren Mélanges* (Anvers: N. V. de Nederlandsche Boekhandel, 1945), pp. 175–196. For a different analysis of the structure see Jean Barraqué, *Debussy* (Paris, Editions du Seuil, 1967). Austin, *Debussy*, discusses both these analyses and compares them with several others.

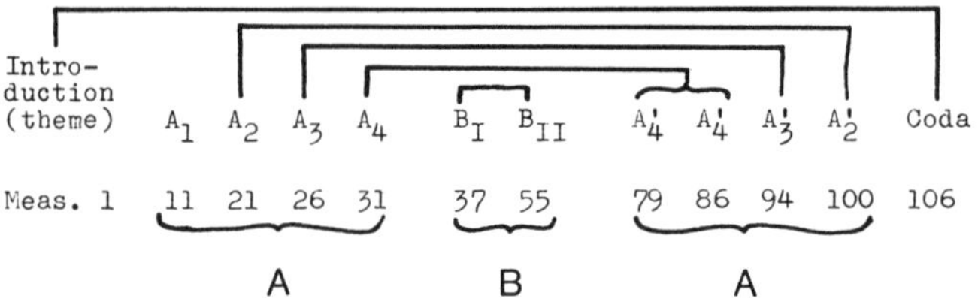

Example 2

1. A_4 and A'_4

a. These are the only statements of the theme by instruments other than the flute. The clarinet presents the theme at measure 31; the oboe presents it at measure 86. Debussy describes the care with which he selects instrumental timbres in a letter to Segalen: "Je m'efforce d'employer chaque timbre à l'état de pureté, . . . de le mettre *à sa vraie place.*" [18]

b. These are the only appearances of the theme which do not begin on C♯. A_4 begins on G; A'_4 begins on E and E♭ in its two presentations.

c. The motives which accompany these statements of the theme are chromatic—the cellos in measures 31–34 and the oboe in measures 83–84.

d. A_4 and A'_4 are essentially double statements. A_4 is in two parts, the second a literal transposition of the first. A'_4 is stated twice, the second statement a transposition of the first.

e. A_4 and A'_4 are the only statements of the theme in which the initial descent is completely chromatic, beginning with a half-step instead of a whole-step.

2. A_3 and A'_3

a. These are the only presentations of the theme which include the cascades of triplets.

b. There is a trill in the accompaniment of each of these statements—the only places in the piece where such trills occur—the bassoons in measure 28 and the strings in measure 94.

3. A_2 and A'_2

a. These statements are vaguely connected by motives built on a

[18] *Segalen et Debussy*, ed. Annie Joly-Segalen and André Schaeffner (Monaco: Editions du Rocher, 1961), p. 107; emphases added.

perfect fourth and a segment of the chromatic scale, played by the strings in measures 23–24 and by the flute in measure 102.

b. These are the only presentations which, beginning on C♯, move to C♮ in the course of their development—A_2 in measure 25; A_2' in measure 103.

The themes of the middle section are also derived from the opening theme, but they are heard as basically new material (Example 3).

Example 3

Mallarmé's poem may be regarded as a series of digressions upon the opening line, "Ces nymphes, je les veux perpétuer," which carry the faun through memory, imagination, supposition, artistic transformation, and finally resignation to dream. Debussy's *Prélude* likewise emanates entirely from the opening flute solo, which is varied in the versions we have labeled A and transformed in the versions labeled B. Debussy rejects the notion of development through repetition, for each appearance of a motive, or bit of musical material, has for him a different emotional value.

> Déjà pour Beethoven l'art de développer consiste en des redites, d'incessantes reprises de motifs identiques. . . . Pensez-vous que dans une composition une même émotion puisse être exprimée deux fois? Il faut qu'on n'ai pas réfléchi, ou c'est un effet de la paresse. Ne vous laissez pas duper au changement du rythme ou du ton: c'est renchérir tout uniment sur la tromperie.

Rather Debussy seeks a music which either does away with motives entirely, or, as here, which draws all its material from a single, uninterrupted motive.

> Je voudrais qu'on arrive, j'arriverai à une musique vraiment dégagée de motifs, ou formée d'un seul motif continu, que rien n'interrompt et qui jamais ne revienne sur lui-même. Alors il y aura développement logique, serré, déductif; il n'y aura pas, entre deux reprises du même motif, caractéristique et topique de l'oeuvre, un remplissage hâtif et superflu. Le développement ne sera plus cette amplification matérielle . . . mais on le prendra dans une acception plus universelle et enfin psychique.[19]

The thematic unity of Debussy's *Prélude* is only part of a higher unity of melody, harmony, and tonality which pervades the work. The beginning of the basic theme, expressed in skeletal form, outlines a tritone from C♯ to G and back to C♯. The tritone is tonally ambiguous—the key of the piece remains undefined. The continuation of the theme, however, outlines an E major triad before ending on A♯ (= B♭). The relationship E–B♭ outlines another tritone a minor third above the first, and combined with it forms a diminished seventh chord which stands at the root of the entire piece (Example 4). The tritone C♯–G, of course,

Example 4

appears in successive presentations of the theme: A_1, A_2, A_3. At A_4 (measure 31) the theme is altered to eliminate the tritone in the melody. Instead of beginning on C♯ it begins on G, but is accompanied by C♯ in the bass. In the following measure the bass line repeats this tritone C♯–G. At measure 34 the entire texture is transposed up a minor third so that now the theme begins on B♭ and the bass has E and B♭ as its structural notes—the other tritone of the piece.

The long middle section in D♭ (measure 55) is, of course, enharmonically in C♯, and the opening measures of this section are supported by the tritone D♭ (= C♯)–G.

[19] André Fontinas, *Mes Souvenirs du Symbolisme* (Paris: Editions de la Nouvelle Revue Critique, 1928), pp. 92–93.

One harmonic relationship also occurs with enough frequency to merit attention (Example 5). This progression occurs clearly in A_2

Example 5

(measure 21) and in a harmonically enriched form at A_3 (measure 26) (Example 6).

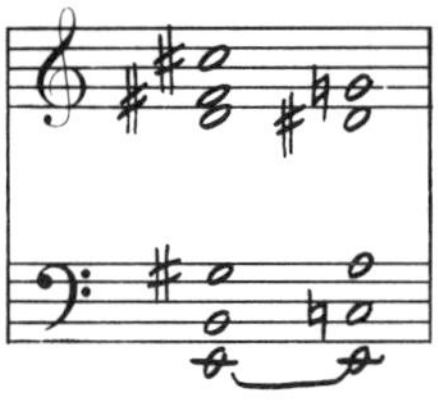

Example 6

The progression E^{+6}–C_6 reappears in an expanded form at A_4' (measure 79). Measures 79–80 are a prolongation of E major, measure 81 introduces the C♯ added sixth, measure 82 adds the F♯ which completes a pentatonic scale on E, then measures 83–85 prolong the C_6 chord (Example 7).

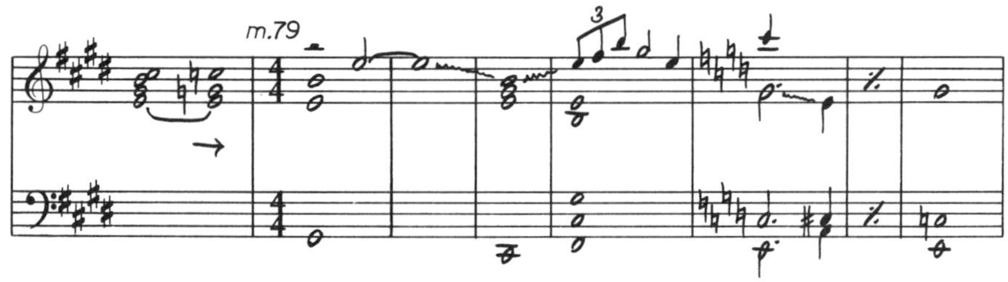

Example 7

This relationship is summarized briefly in the Coda (measure 107) (Example 8).

The whole-tone scale is used sparingly in this work, but it is part of the basic musical fabric. The tritone which forms the skeleton of the opening theme belongs to the whole-tone scale, and one may look upon

Example 8

the intervening chromatic notes as passing notes in an essentially whole-tone melodic progression.

There are, of course, two whole-tone hexachords, one of which contains C♯, the other of which does not. A tetrachord of the latter whole-tone scale—A♭, B♭, C, D—appears divided up among several instruments in measures 8–10. Both whole-tone scales appear in the A_4 section: one in measures 32–33, the other in measures 35–36. A whole-tone melodic segment appears in measures 57–59, accompanied in measure 58 by a whole-tone chord.

The similarity in formal structure between the poem and the music tends to confirm certain correspondences between the works which might occur to any sensitive reader-listener, even if he were unaware of the formal symmetry. The opening flute theme, like the first line of the poem, seems not to have a definite beginning, but is simply there. The harp glissando in measures 4 and 7 seems aptly to represent "leur incarnat léger," just as the questioning dominant seventh chord at the end of the musical introduction fits the question at the end of the poem's introduction: "Aimai-je un rêve?"

The four variations of the opening theme each have a different harmonization, almost as if the changing key centers symbolized the "décors successifs" of the faun's hypotheses. The third of the faun's four conjectures contains a section in italics, the narrative recalling the events preceding. The corresponding section of Debussy's score, A_3, prepares a very strong cadence on the dominant, in fact, the strongest perfect cadence in the entire work. The association of tonality and reality, which we shall pursue at greater length in our discussion of *Autre éventail*, acts here to affirm the distinction between what "actually" happened to the faun, according to his recollection, and what may or may not have happened, according to his reflections.

In the last line of the poem the faun resigns himself to seeing only the "ombre" of the nymphs that he had desired to perpetuate. The last line thus answers the first. The *Coda* of Debussy's *Prélude* recalls the E^{+6}–C_6 progression in the chords of the horns and violins. The melodic line presents the mere "ombre" of the opening melody. In Example 9, the "missing" notes are indicated in parentheses. (Example 9).

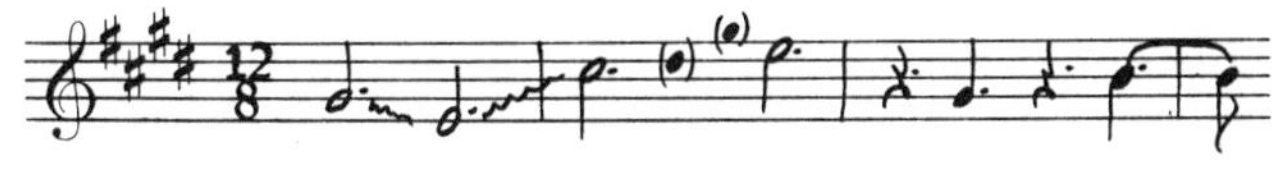

Example 9

These correspondences must not be pressed too far. In asserting a structural similarity between poem and *Prélude* we are mainly concerned with relationships within the two works, not between them. Within this symmetry of form, however, the question of proportion is revealing. What we have called the middle section of Mallarmé's poem comprises a mere twenty lines (42–61). The middle section of Debussy's *Prélude* extends for forty-two measures (37–78). Keeping in mind that the number of lines in the poem is the same as the number of measures in the *Prélude*, we see that Debussy has increased the importance of this section considerably. He has expanded the lines which deal with the faun playing on his pipes into a rapturous melody which escapes for a few moments the vagueness of rhythm and tonal sense which accompanies the faun's earlier, troubled musings.

Debussy thus emphasizes the idea of music as a means of perpetuating experience. The faun's sexual desire is thwarted by the escape of the nymphs, and his only compensation is the conjuring forth of images of bursting pomegranate and erupting volcano. The middle section of the poem is a temporary fulfillment, between the frustrated questioning of the first section and the sublimation of desire in the images of the final section. As Mallarmé said, "cette musique prolonge l'émotion de mon poème et en situe le décor plus passionément que la couleur." While it is difficult to be sure what Mallarmé intended by these words, our discussion suggests that Debussy was indeed more attentive to articulating changing settings than to painting in music the faun's colorful dreams.

The theme of the flute runs through the first half of Mallarme's poem like a countermelody:

> Ne murmure point d'eau que ne verse *ma flûte*
> *Au bosquet arrosé d'accords; et le seul vent*
> *Hors des deux tuyaux* prompt à s'exhaler avant
> Qu'il disperse le son dans une pluie aride,
> C'est . . . le . . . souffle artificiel
> De l'inspiration.
>
> [lines 6–22]
>
> "Et qu'au prélude lent où naissant *les pipeaux*
> Ce vol de cygnes, non! de naïades se sauve
> Ou plonge. . . .
>
> [lines 30–33]
>
> Mais, bast! arcane tel élut pour confident
> Le jonc vaste et jumeau dont sous l'azur on joue.
>
> [lines 42–43]
>
> Tâche donc, *instrument* des fuites, ô maligne
> *Syrinx*, de refleurir aux lacs où tu m'attends!
>
> [lines 52–53]

This flute motif fails to reappear after the middle section of the poem. Debussy's *Prélude*, on the other hand, is completely permeated by the sound of the flute, and all of the musical material may be derived from the opening flute solo.

The correspondences between word and music in the *Prélude* relate to broader symmetries between poet and composer. Mallarmé makes the less-than-clear statement by "designating only a part or an aspect of the object instead of the whole of it; by using allusions to objects that have not been identified, or by using unclear allusions."[20] Debussy creates a language in which he can allude to harmonies rather than stating them, and in which harmonies are no longer closely tied to functional references.

Mallarmé disturbs the normal word order or the normal meaning of words, through the use of etymological or metaphorical senses; he collapses constructions in a way to make a single word or formula have several kinds of reference simultaneously.[21] Debussy weakens the tonic-

[20] Weinberg, *The Limits of Symbolism*, pp. 167–168.
[21] *Ibid.*

dominant relationship through the repeated use of unresolved dominant seventh chords; he extends the diatonic orbit to include additional functions, thereby obscuring the boundaries between tonalities; he condenses traditional harmonic progressions so that only the initial and final chords remain, the intermediate explanatory steps having been suppressed.

Debussy expresses his concern that the overuse of certain chords may lead not only to banality but also to the loss of their value as symbols:

> Comme il me parlait de certains mots de la langue française dont l'or s'était terni à trop fréquenter du vilain monde, je pensais en moi-même qu'il en était de même pour certains accords dont la sonorité s'était banalisée dans des musiques d'exportation, cette réflexion n'est pas d'un nouveauté poignante, si je n'ajoute qu'ils ont perdu en même temps leur essence symbolique.[22]

His suggestion that "la musique aurait dû être une science hermétique" obviously derives from his understanding of Mallarmé's philosophy, though characteristically he goes on to propose "la fondation d'une 'Société d'ésotérisme Musical' " which might help discourage those who serve music "avec la désinvolture que l'on met à servir d'un mouchoir de poche!" [23]

Debussy returns to the same theme in another letter to Chausson:

> D'ailleurs, je ne sais pourquoi je dis cela n'ayant nullement l'intention de régner sur l'esprit de mes contemporains, mais c'est égal ça serait gentil, de fonder une école de Néomusiciens, où l'on s'efforcerait de garder intact les symboles admirables de la musique.[24]

Mallarmé substitutes nuance for clear ideas or well-outlined emotions.[25] Debussy reduces the overall dynamic range so that nuances of tone color largely replace dynamic variation; he creates melodies whose ambiguous harmonic implications permit an extended equivocation in

[22] "Claude Debussy et Ernest Chausson," *Revue Musicale* 7 / (1926):118.

[23] *Ibid.*

[24] *Ibid.*, p. 120–121. This notion of a society of artists appears again in the theater-piece *F.E.A.* which Debussy wrote in collaboration with René Peter. See Edward Lockspeiser, "Frères en Art: Pièce de théâtre inédite de Debussy," *Revue de Musicologie* 56 / (1970):165–176.

[25] Weinberg, *The Limits of Symbolism*, pp. 167–168.

setting the tonal center of the piece. He creates a musical language which suggests rather than states, and which casts doubt upon the separations between reality, memory, and fantasy.

This harmony between poetry and music was not lost on Debussy's poet friend Pierre Louÿs. After hearing the first public performance of the *Prélude* Louÿs went home and wrote Debussy:

> Ton prélude est admirable. Il n'était pas possible de faire une paraphrase plus délicieuse aux vers que nous aimons tous deux. . . .[26]

In October 1895 Debussy sent Louÿs a copy of the orchestral score to the *Prélude* with this dedication: "Quelques airs de flûte pour charmer Bilitis."[27] The titles of the three Bilitis poems which Debussy was to set to music in 1897 contain some of the same poetic elements as Mallarmé's eclogue: *Le Faune*; *Le Chevelure* (one recalls "le splendide bain de cheveux" and "la touffe échevelée" from Mallarmé's poem); and *Le Tombeau des naïades.* The music for these poems is based on the same vocabulary as that of the *Prélude*: sinuous melody which resembles an arabesque; chromatic harmony which refuses to accept the restrictions of a single key; scales which go beyond the conventional limits of major and minor. The basic materials are the same; the musical distance between the *Prélude* and the *Chansons de Bilitis* is as great as the poetic distance between Mallarmé and Louÿs.

[26] *Correspondance de Claude Debussy et Pierre Louÿs*, ed. Henri Borgeaud (Paris: Librairie José Corti, 1945), p. 63.

[27] *Ibid.*

8

LOUŸS: *Chansons de Bilitis*

For nearly a decade beginning around 1893 Debussy's closest friend was Pierre Louÿs. Like Debussy, Louÿs was little known to the public at that time, having published only *Astarté*, a small volume of poems, in a private printing of seventy-five copies. In 1893 Louÿs produced *Léda*, *Chrysis* (the first chapter of *Aphrodite*), and some translations, *Poésies de Méléagre*, always in the most strictly limited editions. The completion of *Aphrodite* in 1896 drew attention to this "apologist and apostle of the antique modes of life" and the popularity of this novel of courtesan life in ancient Alexandria led to a wider publication of the poet's works.[1] The novels that followed, *La Femme et le Pantin* in 1898 and *Les Aventures du Roi Pausole* in 1900, further increased Louÿs' reputation, but the poet, preferring his former seclusion to the burdens attending popular acclaim, determined to withdraw from the public eye, and published nothing from 1900 until his death twenty-five years later.

Debussy and Louÿs may well have encountered each other *chez*

[1] Vance Thompson, *French Portraits* (Boston: Richard G. Badger, 1900), p. 131.

Bailley, at the *Librairie de l'Art Indépendent*, which published Debussy's Baudelaire songs as well as the first works of Louÿs. Perhaps more likely, they met at the *Auberge du Clou*, where Satie was pianist. For nearly a dozen years the two men were inseparable companions: Louÿs, living comfortably on inherited wealth, passionately interested in music; Debussy, preferring the company of literary men, always hovering on the brink of financial disaster. Although their friendship was based on more than money alone, Debussy depended heavily on Louÿs' generosity, and enjoyed the symbolism of his friend's last name, as evidenced in a letter from around 1895:

> On est dans la purée noire, comme qui dirait en fa dièze mineur! verte, multicolore et jusqu'au cou! Claude vient demander à son petit ami le service d'un LOUIS! ! ! pour lequel il lui adresse un merci reconnaissant, pour Pierre, qu'il reçoive son amitié dévouée.[2]

Debussy occasionally sent Louÿs copies of his compositions inscribed with some bit of verse, while Louÿs, who at one point had seriously contemplated a career in music, responded with humorous songs of his own composition, including one bearing the remark, "On est prié de ne pas se rappeler la 3e étude de Chopin."[3]

Louÿs announced his engagement to the daughter of the poet José-Maria de Hérédia in the spring of 1899: "Par un amour de la rime riche qui lui vient sans doute de son père, Mlle. Louise de Hérédia échange son nom contre celui de Louise Louÿs qui est plus symétrique et plus équilibré." [4] Louÿs asked Debussy's assistance in making musical arrangements for the wedding, requesting in particular that he compose a march for the occasion.

> Le mariage aura lieu à Saint-Philippe dans six semaines. Connais-tu l'organiste de ce curieux monument? J'ai intention de lui suggérer un petit programme sébastienbachique quel on pourrait donner pour introduction la célèbre et inédite *Hochzeitsmarsch* de Debussy. Es-tu disposé à calligraphier deux cents mesures pour deux claviers et pédale, dans le rythme bizarre de la marche à quatre temps,—morceau d'un caractère pompeux, lascif et jaculatoire comme il sied aux cortèges nuptiaux? [5]

[2] *Correspondance de Claude Debussy et Pierre Louÿs*, ed. Henri Borgeaud (Paris: Librairie José Corti, 1945), p. 82.

[3] *Ibid.*, p. 89. [4] *Ibid.*, p. 129. [5] *Ibid.*

Debussy agreed to supply the requested music, apparently not suspecting that his own marriage would follow closely on the heels of that of his friend.

> Je n'ai pas l'honneur de connaître l'organiste qui dispense l'harmonie aux fidèles de Saint-Philippe, mais je me ferais un devoir d'écrire les deux cents mesures que tu me demandes. Si ça n'est très beau, ça sera au moins très fraternel, avec en plus, l'émotion inséparable d'un début dans l'expression de sentiments inexplorés par moi jusqu'ici. J'ai peur que ça soit d'ailleurs, une fois pour toutes, mon vieux collage avec la Musique empêchant que je devienne nuptial! [6]

A month later Louÿs expressed concern that the organist, a professor of bassoon at the Conservatoire, would be able to learn the music in time for the ceremony. Debussy implied that the music still remained uncomposed.

> Ça n'a d'ailleurs pas d'importance . . . les 15,000 personnes qui assisteront à ton mariage auront bien autre chose à faire qu'à peser la valeur amicale de mes harmonies.—L'encrier est sur ma table et n'en a plus bougé que ma tendresse pour toi.[7]

The wedding march, if it was in fact ever composed, remains undiscovered. Vallas speculates that Debussy may have fulfilled his obligation with a brief improvisation at the organ.[8] Debussy himself was married a few months later, an event which he described to Robert Godet in terms similar to those of Louÿs: "Mademoiselle Lilly Texier a changé son nom inharmonique pour celui de Lilly Debussy, bien plus euphonique." [9]

The intimacy of the association between poet and musician could not be sustained after their respective marriages. Debussy seems to admit the fact of their alienation even while trying to deny it in a letter dated 19 June 1903:

> Une situation de jeune marié ne pouvait ni ne vouler changer quoi que ce soit à nos relations. Tu étais mon ami beaucoup trop

[6] *Ibid.*, p. 130. [7] *Ibid.*, p. 132.

[8] Léon Vallas, *Claude Debussy et son temps* (Paris: Editions Albin Michel, 1958), p. 199.

[9] *Lettres à deux amis*, ed. Robert Godet and G. Jean-Aubry (Paris: Librairie José Corti, 1942), p. 101.

> solidement, pour que personne au monde, même *une femme*, puisse songer à toucher à cela.[10]

A few days earlier Debussy had written Louÿs after nearly a year's separation:

> Tu es celui de mes amis que j'ai certainement le mieux aimé, et je ne me console du manque de ta présence qu'en imaginant ta figure dans un décor tellement lointain que tout espoir de communiquer avec toi est impossible.[11]

By 1904 the relationship had been entirely severed.

One of Louÿs' few literary compositions after his withdrawal from public life was a brief *Poétique*. Like Verlaine before him, Louÿs employed the vocabulary of music to discuss literary style, comparing the poet's choice of the exact word to express his idea with the composer's choice of the exact sound to express his musical conception.

> Dans la conception artistique de l'écrivain le style doit dominer. L'harmonie d'une phrase est aussi importante que l'expression de cette phrase. Qu'est-ce que le thème choisi par le musicien, avant qu'il soit distribué à différents instruments? Le style correspond au choix des timbres orchestraux. Penser n'est pas tout pour l'artiste-écrivain. Il lui faut savoir exprimer, colorer sa pensée avec des mots exacts dont chacun d'eux garde une existence individuelle dans la phrase.[12]

Sometime after Debussy's death Louÿs' secretary recorded this remark: "Je ne lui enverrai pas ma *Poétique*, me dit-il avec malice, car dans son désir de m'être agréable, il ne manquerait pas de la mettre en musique!" [13]

The poet's words may reflect a certain bitterness over the unsuccessful attempts of the two men to collaborate on a theater piece. Around 1895 Debussy and Louÿs had discussed a ballet on the subject *Daphnis et Chloé*. In 1896 Louÿs, at Debussy's request, had incorporated four sonnets

[10] *Revue de Musicologie* 57 / (1971):35.

[11] *Correspondance de Claude Debussy et Pierre Louÿs*, p. 173.

[12] Robert Cardinne-Petit, *Pierre Louÿs intime, le solitaire du Hameau* (Paris: Jean-Renard, 1942), pp. 52–53.

[13] *Ibid.*, p. 40.

of Dante-Gabriel Rossetti into a text entitled *La Saulelaie.* Dcbussy planned a symphonic suite on Louÿs' *Le Roi Pausole* and contemplated a musical adaptation of his *Aphrodite.* None of these projects ever came to fruition.

Perhaps the most disappointing episode concerned *Cendrelune*, a Christmas story by Louÿs which went through several titles—*Geneviève*; *Psyché*; *Kundrynette*—in the course of successive versions. The interminable demands for revisions from Debussy and the publisher Hartmann must have been frustrating for the poet who wrote "Choisir le mot, il n'en est qu'un, ensorceler une page blanche." [14] Finally Louÿs wrote to his friend: "Ecris TOI-MEME *Cendrelune.* Tu en es parfaitement capable. A force de faire des changements à ce petit livret, il m'est devenu complètement étranger." [15]

The only music to emerge from the decade of friendship is that associated with the *Chansons de Bilitis*, one of the most celebrated literary hoaxes of the nineteenth century. Early in 1895 Louÿs published what purported to be a French translation of an ancient Greek poetess named Bilitis. The volume of bucolics, elegies, and epigrams was prefaced by a somewhat fanciful story of the poetess's life, including her early defloration at Pamphylia, her sojourn on the island of Lesbos, her later career as a courtesan in Kypros, and the discovery of her tomb, whose walls were covered with the poems included in the collection. The affair is described by Robert Cardinne-Petit, who served as private secretary to Louÿs from 1917 until his death:

> After the appearance of the *Chansons de Bilitis* an impassioned debate ensued among all the noted archeologists who supported Louÿs' hoax with all the force of their erudition. The discovery of the tomb of Bilitis was especially remarked. . . . Pierre Louÿs had sent the translation of Meleager (genuine, that) and of the *Chansons de Bilitis* to a M. X, professor of Greek archeology at one of the leading universities. M. X, in a letter of thanks, declared that Meleager and Bilitis were not unknown to him, and that he had for a long time considered them personal friends.[16]

Louÿs pursued the spoof by publishing *Notes sur les sources des Chansons de Bilitis.* In 1917 Louÿs was still laughing at the ridicule of a whole

[14] *Ibid.*, pp. 30–31.

[15] *Correspondance de Claude Debussy et Pierre Louÿs*, p. 54.

[16] Cardinne-Petit, *Pierre Louÿs intime*, pp. 146–147, my translation.

generation of literary critics "qui avaient affirmé avoir déjà lu *ça* dans le texte grec!" [17] Still he maintained a kind of ambivalence as to the effect of the poems on his reputation:

> Bilitis fut à la fois mon succès et ma perte. Comme poète, elle me valut, je le reconnais, quelques joies. Mais comme historien littéraire, elle attira sur moi, plus tard les foudres des pontifes. L'homme est d'un commerce supportable jusqu'au moment où il commence à se prendre au sérieux. Pour les critiques je devins un mystificateur, et ils me reprirent leur confiance. L'histoire de Bilitis les avait chagrinés.[18]

Debussy naturally read the poems upon their publication. "*Bilitis* est dans toutes les mains," he wrote Louÿs in January 1895. At that time he was preoccupied with the first revisions of his opera. "Pelléas et Mélisande sont mes seuls petits amis en ce moment." [19] Not until December 1897 did Debussy have occasion to return to the poems. "Maintenant, l'*Image* (le revue de Floury) me demande de la musique. J'ai très envie d'en faire sur une des *Chansons de Bilitis*, entre autres celle qui porte le n° 20. Cela te plaît-il et n'y a-t-il aucun inconvénient?" [20] This was *La Flûte de Pan*, the first of three poems which Debussy set to music from the Bilitis collection. The choice of this poem reflects Debussy's attraction to the flute as an instrument of pure melody. Other "flute" pieces include *Le Faune*, a setting of Verlaine; *The Little Shepherd* from *The Children's Corner*; *Syrinx* for flute solo; and best known, the *Prélude à l'après-midi d'un faune*.

The second poem in the set, *La Chevelure*, did not appear in the first edition of Louÿs' poems early in 1895, but was published along with several others, in the *Mercure de France* in August 1897. Louÿs sent Debussy an advance copy in May with the words "Voici la chanson." [21] By the beginning of July Debussy had completed the musical settings of *La Flûte de Pan* and *La Chevelure*, which he referred to in a brief note: "Bilitis et moi sommes à tes pieds." [22] Louÿs responded a few days later: "Ce que tu as fait sur mes *Bilitis* est adorablement bien; tu ne peux

[17] *Ibid.*, p. 58. [18] *Ibid.*, p. 145.

[19] *Correspondance de Claude Debussy et Pierre Louÿs*, pp. 41–42.

[20] *Ibid.*, p. 94. [21] *Ibid.*, p. 95.

[22] *Ibid.*, p. 97. [23] *Ibid.*

pas sentir le plaisir que j'en ai. Apporte le cahier samedi, vcux-tu?" [23] Debussy rejoined the next day: "Tu es trop gentil pour Bilitis et pour moi; seulement je t'en remercie tout de même car cela me fait plaisir." [24] Debussy's setting of *La Chevelure* appeared in l'*Image* in October 1897 under the title *Chanson de Bilitis*. Debussy finished the third song of the set, *Le Tombeau des Naïades*, and sent word to Louÿs on the day before Christmas 1897: "La *Troisième Chanson de Bilitis* s'orne de toute la musique dont je suis redevable à ma nature bien organisée; je pense te la soumettre à ton retour." [25]

The songs did not appear in proof until September 1898, when Debussy left a set for Louÿs with a visiting card: "Voilà les *Chansons de Bilitis*, vaut mieux tard que jamais." [26] Louÿs wrote to Debussy in October proposing that he accompany a singer in a performance of the Bilitis songs in the course of a public lecture on Bilitis. Debussy demurred, arguing that his music would add nothing and might distract the listeners from the pure sounds of Louÿs' words:

> Donc, Mr. A. Segard va faire une conférence sur les *Chansons de Bilitis*, qui contiennent, dans une merveilleuse langue, tout ce qu'il y a d'ardemment tendre et cruel dans le fait d'être passionné, tellement, que les gens les plus subtilement voluptueux sont obligés de reconnaître l'enfantillage de leurs jeux vis-à-vis de cette terrible et charmeuse Bilitis.
>
> Veux-tu me dire, maintenant, ce que viendraient ajouter mes trois petites musiques à l'audition pure et simple de ton texte? Rien du tout, mon vieux; je dirais même que cela disperserait maladroitement l'émotion des auditeurs.

Debussy comes close to explaining his purpose in setting the poems to music, but backs off coyly at the last moment:

> A quoi bon, vraiment, accorder la voix de Bilitis soit en majeur, soit en mineur puisqu'elle a la voix la plus persuasive du monde?—Tu me diras, "pourquoi as-tu fait de la musique?" Ça, vieux loup, c'est autre chose. . . . C'est pour d'autres décors; mais crois-moi, quand Bilitis est là, laissons-la parler toute seule.[27]

Debussy expressed his hope of finding a suitable interpreter for the songs, which finally received their first public performance on 17 March 1900, with the composer accompanying Blanche Marot.

[24] *Ibid.*, p. 98. [25] *Ibid.*, p. 105.
[26] *Ibid.*, p. 115. [27] *Ibid.*, p. 118.

> Je ne te parlerais pas d'autres difficultés, toutes matérielles, comme par exemple de trouver une jeune personne, qui pour nos esthétiques et pâles figures, se consumerait dans l'étude de ces trois chansons, en se contentant de l'assurance de notre parfaite considération. Puis, il y a moi, qui suis pris de la fâcheuse manie de semer les fausses notes à pleines mains, quand je joue devant plus de deux personnes. J'ai tout dit, et j'espère que tu me comprendras. Je veux te servir et non me dérober. . . .[28]

Six months after the first performance of the songs, Louÿs prevailed upon Debussy to write some incidental music for a recitation and pantomime of twelve other poems from the collection.

> As-tu l'esprit assez libre pour écrire huit pages de violons, de silences et d'accords cuivrés qui donnent ce qu'on peut appeler "une impression d'art" aux Variétés—sans faire hurler d'avance ce pauvre directeur juif qui, au fond, aimerait mieux Serpette.
>
> Je te demande cela, parce que, *à ta place je le ferais*; et je suis convaincu que tu peux écrire ainsi des pages "absolument de toi" tout en entretenant le public des Variétés dans l'espèce d'agitation qui lui est nécessaire.—Et puis, ça t'empêcherait de penser au terme de janvier, mon vieux.[29]

The music, prepared in haste, consisted of a hundred and fifty or so measures, scored for two flutes, two harps, and celeste. Debussy himself performed at the celeste, apparently improvising his part. Although there was only one performance, at the Salle des Fêtes of *Le Journal* on 7 February 1901 (not, as planned, *aux Variétés*), it must have been a memorable experience, judging from Louÿs' account of the rehearsals:

> Je passe cette semaine toutes mes après-midi avec des femmes nues. C'est du joli. Il s'agit de modèles qui vont représenter onze *Chansons de Bilitis* sur la scène du Journal, tantôt avec des voiles drapés, tantôt en robes de kôs, tantôt sans rien du tout que leurs deux mains ou leur position, de trois-quarts en arrière.[30]

In 1914, in response to an entreaty from his publisher, Debussy drew on some of this incidental music as the source of the *Six épigraphes antiques*, "Pièces assez courtes pour piano à 4 mains."

[28] *Ibid.* [29] *Ibid.*, p. 151. [30] *Ibid.*, p. 157.

The *Chansons de bilitis* which inspired Debussy's songs, incidental music, and four-hand piano music, appear at first to be prose translations. Louÿs, as part of his *mystification*, claimed that they were "traduites de grec," and included in the table of contents a list of the poems that had been left untranslated.

> Each song consists of four prose stanzas, suggesting the probable length of a prose version of a Sapphic or Alcaic stanza—a correspondence which unquestionably aided in winning credence for the hoax. The verse comes to a full stop at the end of each stanza. Beyond this restriction, the poems have a complete freedom, and the infinite changes of rhythm possible in such lyric prose defy analysis.[31]

Louÿs' prose verges on poetry, a particularly sinuous poetry that may help us better to understand Debussy's use of melody.

La Flûte de Pan

Pour le jour des Hyacinthies, il m'a donné une syrinx faite de roseaux bien taillés, unis avec la blanche cire qui est douce à mes lèvres comme du miel.

Il m'apprend à jouer, assise sur ses genoux; mais je suis un peu tremblante. Il en joue après mois; si doucement que je l'entends à peine.

Nous n'avons rien à nous dire, tant nous sommes près l'un de l'autre; mais nos chansons veulent se répondre, et tour à tour nos bouches s'unissent sur la oûte.

Il est tard; voici le chant des grenouilles vertes, qui commence avec la nuit. Ma mère ne croira jamais que je suis restée si longtemps à chercher ma ceinture perdue.

[For translation, see p. 310]

Louÿs evokes the image of the sinuous melody of a syrinx. Both the image and the language recall the flute in Mallarmé's *L'Après-midi d'un faune*, which dreams "dans un solo long . . . une sonore, vaine et monotone ligne." In the first stanza the initial syntactical impetus comes with the subject, verb and object: ". . . il m'a donné une syrinx." The phrases that follow roll along with the volute grace of an ornamented line:

[31] D'Elbert Ernest Keenan, "Pierre Louÿs," Dissertation, Ithaca, New York, 1927, p. 51.

une syrinx
/
faite de roseaux bien taillés
/
unis avec la blanche cire
/
qui est douce à mes lèvres
/
comme du miel.

The serpentine line contunually turns back upon itself, as in the spiraling reflexives of the third stanza:

> *Nous* n'avons rien *à nous* dire,
> tant nous sommes près *l'un de l'autre*,
> mais nos chansons veulent *se répondre*,
> et *tour à tour* nos bouches *s'unissent* sur la oûte.

Gestures of curved lines play throughout the poem, with the contour of "mes lèvres" repeated in "nos bouches," and the circle of their posture, "assise sur ses genoux" (one assumes they sit *vis-à-vis*) reiterated in the circumference of the lost waistband. Even the jaggedness of conversational (as opposed to poetical) speech is replaced by the musical curves of "nos chansons" and "le chant des grenouilles."

The mythological associations of the text preserve the metaphor of the closed circle. Syrinx was a nymph pursued by Pan who, to escape, was changed by Diana into a reed from which Pan made a flute. The festival of Hyacinthus was a ceremonial in honor of a vegetation-deity.[32] The narrative of Louÿs' text clearly reflects the erotic implications of the myth, in which Pan literally plays upon Syrinx, like Mallarmé's faun, employing the flute—a highly suggestive instrument for the purpose—to transform sexual frustration into art.

In the contours of this prose poem Louÿs has captured the sinuosity of the Art Nouveau, whose linear motifs find a musical counterpart in Debussy's melodies.[33] For Debussy, melody was the supreme element in music—"ma musique n'aspire qu'à être mélodie," he is reported to have

[32] H. J. Rose, *A Handbook of Greek Mythology* (New York: E. P. Dutton, 1928, 1965), pp. 142, 168.

[33] See chapter 9 below.

said—and the curves of his melodic lines reappeared in his very gestures:[34]

> Ses gestes sont tout en courbes, comme un dessin de Vinci. On est séduit: il est bien l'homme de ses oeuvres; pendant qu'on le regarde et qu'on l'écoute, elles vous enveloppent de leur mélodieux souvenir.[35]

Debussy employed the word *arabesque* to describe melodies of particular beauty. In a review of Ysaÿe's performance of the Bach Violin Concerto in G, Debussy writes:

> Pourtant, ce concerto est une chose admirable parmi tant d'autres déjà inscrites dans les cahiers du grand Bach; on y retrouve presque intact cette "arabesque musicale" ou plutôt ce principe de "l'ornement" qui est la base de tous les modes d'art. (Le mot "ornement" n'a rien à voir ici avec la signification qu'on lui donne dans les grammaires musicales.)[36]

There is no Violin Concerto in G listed as such among Bach's works. Debussy had special praise for the *Andante* movement of the concerto in question, and Jarocinski assumes he is referring to the fourth Brandenburg Concerto (BWV 1049) which is in G, does have an *Andante* movement, and in nineteenth-century editions was titled: "Brandenburg Concerto No. 4 in G major for Solo Violin with accompaniment of 2 Flutes. . . ." The *Andante* contains a fine example of arabesque (Example 1). Charles Cushing suggests instead the Violin Concerto in G *minor*,

Example 1

[34] Quoted by Vallas, *Claude Debussy,* p. 291.

[35] *Lettres de Claude Debussy à sa femme Emma*, ed. Pasteur Valléry-Radot (Paris: Flammarion, 1957), pp. 35–36.

[36] *Monsieur Croche et autres écrits*, ed. François Lesure (Paris: Gallimard, 1971), p. 34.

a transcription of the clavier concerto in F minor (BWV 1056) whose middle movement is one long arabesque (Example 2). We may also get

Example 2

an idea of what Debussy means by the word *arabesque* by examining the early piano pieces which he entitled *Deux Arabesques* (Example 3). The

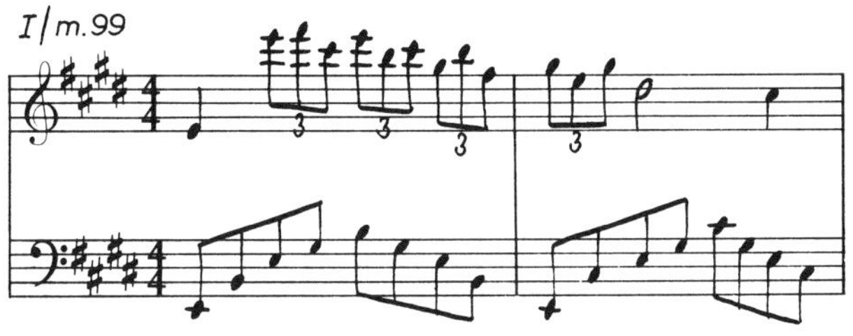

Example 3

idea of the arabesque, then, is essentially one of line, and in particular, ornamented line.

Françoise Gervais, in an important article on Debussy's melodic practice, distinguishes three elements of arabesque.[37] First, Debussy's melodies tend to be relatively conjunct, composed either of adjacent scale

Example 4

[37] Françoise Gervais, "La notion d'arabesque chez Debussy," *Revue Musicale* 241 (1958) *Carnet Critique.*

Example 5

degrees, as in the opening of the piano accompaniment to *La Flûte de Pan* (Example 4), or of small intervals, often with the recitative-like repeated notes that sometimes distinguish Debussy's vocal lines (Example 5).

Second, Debussy's melodies tend to be free from definite harmonic implications.

> Dès les premières oeuvres de Debussy, on voit la mélodie *se distancer* du fond harmonique comme si elle en était relativement indépendante, c'est-à-dire comme si elle avait reconquis son autonomie et qu'elle ait une existence en soi préablement au fond harmonique sur lequel elle se présente.[38]

The melody may be completely unaccompanied, as in the flute solo

[38] Ernest Ansermet, "Le langage de Debussy," in *Debussy et l'évolution de la musique au XXe siècle*, ed. Edith Weber (Paris: Editions du centre national de la recherche scientifique, 1965), p. 38.

which opens the *Prélude à l'après-midi d'un faune.* In music of the common practice period even melodies written for a solo instrument carry with them an implied harmony, as in Bach's Gigue from Partita in d for Violin, BWV 1004 (Example 6). Debussy's solo melodies, on the other

Example 6

hand, while they generally gravitate toward some tonal center, often give no clue as to harmonic implications, as in this example from *Syrinx* (Example 7).

Example 7

Debussy occasionally uses the term *arabesque* to describe the delicate embroidery which Renaissance composers wove above the supporting *cantus firmus*:

> Les primitifs, Palestrina, Vittoria, Orlando di Lasso, etc., se servirent de cette divine "arabesque." Ils en trouvèrent le principe dans le chant grégorien et en étayèrent les frêles entrelacs par de résistants contrepoints. Bach en reprenant l'arabesque la rendit plus souple, plus fluide, et, malgré la sévère discipline qu'imposait ce grand maître à la Beauté, elle put se mouvoir avec cette libre fantaisie toujours renouvelée qui étonne encore à notre époque.[39]

In Debussy's own music this principle may take the form of a single chord with a melodic line evolving freely above it, as in the opening of *La Flûte de Pan* (see Example 4), or a melody which asserts its independence

[39] *Monsieur Croche*, p. 34.

from the supporting harmony by employing nonchordal tones, as in the third measure (see Example 5).

The avoidance of common harmonic progressions also strengthens the sense of melodic independence.

> Le vieux Bach, qui contient toute la musique, se moquait, croyez-le bien, des formules harmoniques. Il leur préférait le jeu libre des sonorités, dont les courbes, parallèles ou contrepriées, préparaient l'épanouissement inespéré qui orne d'impérissable beauté le moindre de ses innombrable cahiers.
>
> C'était l'époque où fleurissait "l'adorable arabesque," et la musique participait ainsi à des lois de beauté inscrites dans le mouvement total de la nature. Notre époque serait plutôt le triomphe du "style plaqué"—je parle au général et n'oublie pas le génie particulier de certains de mes confrères.[40]

In Debussy's music the use of chromatic harmonies and chords of the ninth and eleventh increases the number of chords which can accompany a melody and thus makes the harmony less predictable. On hearing this melody from *La Flûte de Pan* (Example 8), one would not necessarily

Example 8

expect the accompanying harmony which Debussy employs, a harmony into which the opening flute theme fits almost casually (Example 9).

Finally, Debussy's melodies are frequently ornate, a quality he esteems in the counterpoint of Lasso and Palestrina.

> Puis je considère comme un véritable tour de force les effets qu'ils tirent simplement d'une science énorme du contrepoint. Vous ne vous doutez probablement pas que le contrepoint est la chose la plus rébarbative qui soit en musique.
>
> Or, avec eux, il devient admirable; soulignant le sentiment des mots avec une profondeur inouïe et parfois, il y a des enroulements de

[40] *Ibid.* pp. 66–67.

Example 9

> dessins mélodiques qui vous font l'effet d'enluminures de très vieux missels.[41]

In Debussy's melodies the decoration may take the form of a single repeated note with ornaments (Example 10), or a small interval, as in measures 7–8, or more extended scale passages embroidered with triplets and involutions, as in these examples drawn from the incidental music for the *Chansons de Bilitis* (Example 11).

Melody is more than just one element of Debussy's music; it is the organizing force which coordinates all the musical elements. In particular, melody exerts a profound influence on harmony, as Debussy observes in describing a mass of Palestrina:

> Cette musique qui pourtant est d'une écriture très sévère, paraît toute blanche, et l'émotion n'est pas traduite (comme cela s'est fait

[41] Letter to Vasnier, quoted in Henry Prunières, "A la Villa Médicis," *Revue Musicale* 7 (1926):33.

Example 10

> depuis) par de cris, mais par des arabesques mélodiques. Cela vaut en quelque sorte par le contour, et par ses arabesques s'entre-croisant pour produire cette chose qui semble être devenue unique: des harmonies mélodiques![42]

Each of Mlle Gervais's observations about Debussy's melodic practice has a counterpart in describing a harmonic practice which comes to depend on melody.

The superposition of several melodic lines produces chords, again a practice for which Debussy finds a precedent in Bach:

> Dans la musique de Bach, ce n'est pas le caractère de la mélodie qui émeut, c'est sa courbe; plus souvent même, c'est le mouvement

Example 11

[42] Letter to Poniatowski, *Rassegna Musicale* 21 (1951):59.

> parallèle de plusieurs lignes dont la rencontre, soit fortuite, soit unanime, sollicite l'émotion. A cette conception ornementale, la musique qu'acquiert la sûreté d'un mécanisme à impressionner le public et qui fait surgir les images.[43]

If the several melodic lines follow scale patterns, parallel chords result, an effect which becomes idiomatic in Debussy's later music. The counterpart of Debussy's melody of repeated notes is a static harmony in which the rhythmic activity is but the elaboration of a single stationary chord.

The decorative aspect of the melodic arabesque also has its counterpart in harmony. In place of direct movement from one tonal position to another, the harmonic line is embroidered with retrogressions, repeated patterns, and nontonal chords, as the harmonic line of *La Flûte de Pan* illustrates (Example 12). In measures 1–5 we see the prolongation

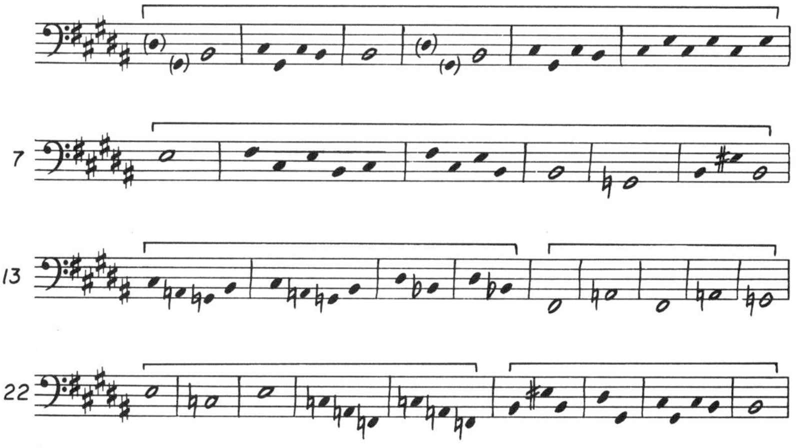

Example 12

of a single harmony, B, with decorating chords. In measure 6 the undulation of the two chords is not functional in the traditional sense, but serves as the harmonic equivalent of a trill. The chords in measures 17–21, which close in on G from both sides, also illustrate a harmonic procedure derived from melodic decoration.

Debussy's habit of retrogression—going back to repeat a measure

[43] *Monsieur Croche*, p. 34.

before going on—avoids a direct movement from one harmony to the next. The sense of holding back, the avoidance of direct expression, may be what Debussy finally finds most appealing in the arabesque.

> Enfin, cela donne du courage pour continuer à vivre dans son rêve, et à chercher sans lassitude l'inexprimable qui est l'Idéal de tout art.[44]

La Chevelure

Il m'a dit: "Cette nuit, j'ai rêvé. J'avais
ta chevelure autour de mon cou. J'avais tes cheveux
comme un collier noir autour de ma nuque et sur ma
poitrine.

"Je les caressais; et c'étaient les miens; et
nous étions liés pour toujours ainsi, par la même
chevelure, la bouche sur la bouche, ainsi que deux
lauriers n'ont souvent qu'une racine.

"Et peu à peu, il m'a semblé, tant nos membres
étaient confondus, que je devenais toi-même ou que
tu entrais en moi comme mon songe."

Quand il eut achevé, il mit doucement ses mains
sur mes épaules, et il me regarda d'un regard si
tendre, que je baissai les yeux avec un frisson.

[For translation, see p. 310]

La Chevelure purports to be prose but might almost be a sonnet in disguise. The arrangement of lines into quatrains and tercets and the suggestion of rhyme in "poitrine . . . racine" and "songe . . . frisson" tie the sentences together. Each new stanza increases the feeling of entwinement. In the first stanza the girl's hair surrounds his neck like a collar, falling on either side until it reaches his breast. In the second stanza the couple are metaphorically joined; their hair comes from the same root, "ainsi que deux lauriers n'ont souvent qu'une racine." He caresses her hair only to find that it is his own. Not only do their locks entwine but their very mouths are joined.

In the third stanza they become physically united, "tant nos membres étaient confondus," so that he "becomes" her, or she enters into him like his dream. Then the dream is over. He puts his hands upon her

[44] Letter to Poniatowski, *Rassegna Musicale*, p. 59.

shoulders in a simple physical gesture which embodies the basic image of the poem: her two shoulders extend from her body like two trees growing from the same root, like the cascade of hair falling on both sides of the neck, the collar which fits on the shoulders like a yoke, the extension of the legs from the torso.

Debussy lets this image infuse the very substance of his song, whose two halves emerge from the center like branches. In this central moment the vocal line descends by whole steps from C to D, then ascends again by scale degrees to high E. At the same time the piano melody replicates this motion in reverse, ascending from C to D in measures 10–11, and descending from E to the octave E in measure 12 (Example 13). The contrary motion of voice and piano produces unisons at the words *miens* (F♯ = G♭), *ainsi*, the third syllable of *chevelure*, and the end of *bouche.*

From this dramatic central event the rest of the song extends on both sides (see accompanying figure). The vocal melody in measures 7–9

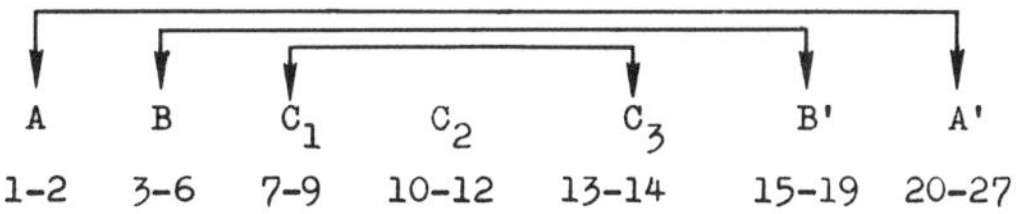

appears in variation in measures 13–14. A similar melody appears in the piano accompaniment in measures 3–6, and in measures 15–18. The opening measures of the piece introduce the chromatic lines whose semitonal movement represents the intimacy in which hair is intertwined, lips are united, and finally two bodies become as one (Example 14).[45] These two measures which introduce the dream at the opening of the song are repeated, then expanded, at the end when the dream has been concluded. They appear in augmentation in the final two measures. The basic gesture of movement outward from a single center appears once more in the piano accompaniment at the very end of the song, where starting in measure 24 the upper line goes by scale degrees B♭-C♭-D♭-D-E♭-F-G♭ while the lower line moves G♭-F♭-E♭-D-D♭-C♭-B♭♭, which then resolves to B♭ to end the song in major (Example 15).

[45] See chapter 4 for a discussion of Debussy's use of the chromatic scale to express intimacy.

m. 9
- - - ne.
p
3
Je les ca-ressais, et c'étaient les miens;
3
(,)
et nous é - tions li - és pour toujours ain-si,
en pressant
mf
cresc.
3
(,)
f
par la mê-me che - ve-lu - re la bouche sur la bou - - - che,
mf
5
cresc.
f

Example 13

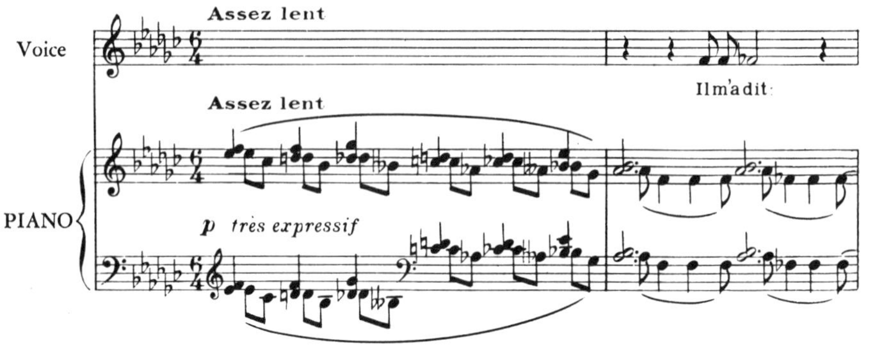

Example 14

Example 15

Le Tombeau des naïades

Le long du bois couvert de givre, je marchais; mes cheveux devant ma bouche se fleurissaient de petits glaçons, et mes sandales étaient lourdes de neige fangeuse et tassée.

Il me dit: "Que cherches-tu?"—Je suis la trace du satyre. Ses petits pas fourchus alternent comme des trous dans un manteau blanc. Il me dit: "Les satyres sont morts.

"Les satyres et les nymphes aussi. Depuis trente ans il n'a pas fait un hiver aussi terrible. La trace que tu vois est celle d'un bouc. Mais restons ici, où est leur tombeau."

Et avec le fer de sa houe il casse la glace de la source où jadis riaient des naïades. Il prenait des grands morceaux froids, et les soulevant vers le ciel pâle, il regardait au travers.

[For translation, see p. 310]

The satyrs and the nymphs are dead. Like Verlaine's *Colloque sentimentale*, which Debussy also selected to close a cycle, the poem is set in winter, the season of death, an association which appears explicitly in the third stanza. Again, as in *Colloque sentimentale,* the woman speaks of happier times now past: "jadis riaient des naïades." Only a trace of that past remains, the spring where the nymphs used to laugh. *La source*, both "spring" and "origin," the source of water which once flowed like laughter, now is frozen. Images of frozen water abound in the poem—*givre*, *glaçons*, *neige*, *glace*, *morceaux froids*—and represent death as the cessation of motion in this season of entombment. Only the melting of ice, the return of solid to liquid, can produce the icicles which flower like harbingers of spring upon the girl's hair.

Footsteps in the snow appear like holes in a white cloak, a worn-out garment that has seen better days. The mantle of snow keeps one from seeing what lies beneath; the footsteps allow one to glimpse what has passed, both literally and figuratively. The girl has mistaken the hoofprints of a goat for those of a satyr. The only genuine vestiges of the nymphs are their tomb—once again, a hole in the ground—and the hole that her companion makes in the ice. He takes the blade of his hoe—a tool one associates with spring rather than winter—and breaking the ice, lifts great chunks into the air. Louÿs has transformed the estival image of

L'Après-midi d'un faune—"J'élève au ciel d'été la grappe vide / Et . . . je regarde au travers"—into this wintry setting.[46] The hole in the ice, like the holes in the white mantle of snow, opens a way through to the past, a frozen once-present that the man lifts toward the ideal and looks through.

Debussy employs the Lydian mode as an alternative to major or minor in setting off the two openings into the past, for as he wrote Louÿs, "A quoi bon, vraiment, accorder la voix de Bilitis soit en majeur, soit en mineur puisqu'elle a la voix la plus persuasive du monde." This mode colors the entire first section and the conclusion of *La Flûte de Pan.* It occurs briefly in *La Chevelure* at the words "par la même chevelure, la bouche sur la bouche." In *Le Tombeau des Naïades* the Lydian mode first appears at the words "Je suis la trace du satyre," the footprints in the snow. The tonal center of this section is G, not the key of the piece, F♯, for these are not really the hoofprints of a satyr but only of a billy goat. The trail of hoofprints in fact wanders directly away from F♯: F♯-A-C♯-G-E-C (Example 16).

This refrainlike music returns at the evocation of the naiads in the fourth stanza. The voice soars to its highest pitch, F♯, after having fallen to a low C for "Les satyres sont morts." This time the section in the Lydian mode is approached by a tonal wedge, centering first on E ("leur tombeau") then on A♭ ("la source") and finally on F♯.

The harmonic rhythm of the music expresses the polarity between the absence of motion in the frozen present and the movement associated with the fluid past. The first stanza, which portrays the icy winter landscape, has only one chord to a measure. The harmonic rhythm flows with three or four chords to a measure at the description of the footprints, but only a single chord supports "Les satyres sont morts" (see Example 16).

The sixteenth note motion of the accompaniment remains constant throughout the song, suggesting perhaps the continuity of past and present, life and death, water and ice, which infuses the poem. As the man lifts the ice to the sky the opening music returns, joining the ice of the winter landscape with the ice which embodies a frozen vision of the past.

[46] I am grateful to Professor Robert G. Cohn for this observation.

Example 16

Debussy's use of modes in the *Six épigraphes antiques* illustrates how they were derived from the earlier incidental music. Plainly, the expansion of one hundred fifty-odd measures of incidental music into two hundred seventy-two measures of four-hand piano music was more than just a matter of padding. In fact, only about half of the original incidental music was retained in the *Epigraphes*: the rest was new. The juxtaposition of old and new material was cleverly done, and in listening to the *Epigraphes* one is not conscious of the connecting links. If one investigates Debussy's use of modes, however, the divisions become clearer: the "old" material in the *Epigraphes* is highly modal; the new material generally is not. This is somewhat surprising, since Debussy was using modes freely in his piano preludes, written around the same time as the *Epigraphes.*

Debussy's use of modes in the *Chansons de Bilitis* and elsewhere demonstrates the extent to which considerations of melody dominate his musical thought. The altered chords which appear in modal harmony follow naturally from the melodic differences between the modes and the major and minor scales on which tonal harmony is based.

The use of chords that depend on the chromatic scale for the logic of their succession takes harmony even further from its traditional course and, if carried far enough, leads eventually to the breakdown of tonality. Tonal relations in the second series of *Fêtes galantes* and in the *Trois poèmes de Stéphane Mallarmé* reveal how far Debussy went in this direction, to what extent he was willing to follow the line of what he called the *adorable arabesque.*

Before moving on to these twentieth-century songs, having surveyed the spectrum of poets whose influence on Debussy was greatest, let us turn to the cycle of songs in which Debussy acted as his own poet, the *Proses Lyriques.*

9

THE COMPOSER AS POET: *Proses Lyriques*

Debussy rarely discussed his work publicly, and seldom disclosed his thoughts on poetry, although he was greatly influenced by poets. His only extended discourse on poetry and music is an interview which appeared in *Musica* in March 1911. At first Debussy tried to dismiss his questioner with a tongue-in-check remark:

> Les rapports du vers et de la musique? Je n'y ai pas pensé. Je m'occupe très peu de musique. Les musiciens et les poètes qui parlent toujours musique et poésie me semblent aussi insupportables que les gens de sport qui parlent toujours de sport.

But the subject was one to which the composer had clearly devoted considerable thought, and here was an opportunity to air some of his pet views:

> Et d'abord, la vérité, on ne peut pas la dire. Vous voulez la savoir? Eh bien! c'est qu'en effet les musiciens qui ne comprennent rien aux vers ne devraient pas en mettre en musique. Ils ne peuvent que les gâcher.

As we have seen, the rhythm of poetry does not always correspond to the rhythm of a musical idea:

> Les vrais vers ont un rythme propre qui est plutôt gênant pour nous. . . . C'est très difficile de suivre bien, de "plaquer" les rythmes tout en gardant une inspiration.

Free verse puts fewer restrictions on the composer; Debussy goes on to suggest that the composer might well write his own text:

> Avec la prose rythmée, on est plus à son aise, on peut mieux se retourner dans tous les sens. Si le musicien devrait faire lui-même sa prose rythmée? Pourquoi pas? Qu'est-ce qu'il attend? [1]

Although Debussy does not mention it in the interview, his *Proses Lyriques* constitute just such an endeavor.

Around 1892 Debussy brought four poems that he had written to Henri de Régnier for his opinion. Régnier was sufficiently impressed to recommend the poems to Francis Vielé-Griffin, who subsequently published the first two, *De rêve* and *De grève*, in his journal, *Entretiens politiques et littéraires*, in December 1892. Debussy set the poems to music in 1893, under the title *Proses Lyriques*, and performed two of the pieces, *De fleurs* and *De soir*, in 1894, accompanying Thérèse Rogers, his fiancée at that time. Debussy had hoped to write another set of songs on his own poetry. The early appearance of this cycle, entitled *Nuits blanches*, was announced by Debussy's publisher, Fromont, in 1900, but in fact the composer never completed more than a few of the poems and apparently none of the music.[2]

In the *Proses Lyriques* we find a direct expression of Debussy's relation to poetry and to the artistic movements with which he was involved at the *fin de siècle.*

De rêve

La nuit a des douceurs de femmes!
Et les vieux arbres sous la lune d'or, songent
A celle qui vient de passer la tête emperlée,

[1] Reprinted in *Correspondance de Claude Debussy et Pierre Louÿs*, ed. Henri Borgeaud (Paris: Librairie José Corti, 1945), pp. 197–198.

[2] A sketch of one poem from *Nuits blanches* appears in Edward Lockspeiser, *Debussy: His Life and Mind* (New York: Macmillan, 1962), vol. I, p. 131.

Maintenant navrée!
A jamais navrée!
Ils n'ont pas su lui faire signe. . . .

Toutes! Elles ont passé
Les Frêles,
Les Folles,
Semant leur rire au gazon grêle,

Aux brises frôleuses
La caresse charmeuse
Des hanches fleurissantes!
Hélas! de tout ceci, plus rien qu'un blanc frisson

Les vieux arbres sous la lune d'or, pleurent
Leurs belles feuilles d'or
Nul ne leur dédiera plus la fierté des casques d'or
Maintenant ternis!
A jamais ternis!
Les chevaliers sont morts sur le chemin du Grâal!

La nuit a des douceurs de femmes!
Des mains semblent frôler les âmes
Mains si folles!
Mains si frêles!

Au temps où les épées chantaient pour Elles! . . .
D'étranges soupirs s'élèvent sous les arbres
Mon âme! c'est du rêve ancien qui t'étreint!

[For translation, see p. 311]

European music at the end of the nineteenth century had reached the end of a tradition which had unified some five hundred years of common practice. After Mahler the symphony could scarcely become longer; after Strauss the orchestra could scarcely grow larger. After the *Gesamtkunstwerk* the heroic gesture could only become a self-parody, and *Das Kunstwerk der Zukunft* turned out not to have a future after all—Debussy described it as "a beautiful sunset that was mistaken for a dawn."[3] The old tonal principle of departure and return had been stretched so far by chromatic harmony that the ear might despair of ever

[3] Léon Vallas, *The Theories of Claude Debussy* (New York: Dover Publications, 1967), p. 126.

returning, and wander aimlessly amid an endless succession of departures.

Yet this picture of musical decadence more accurately describes the German style than that of Debussy. As we have seen, Debussy had little sympathy for rhetoric, bombast, or heroic grandeur. In his own way Debussy contributed to the dissolution of tonality, but except for the Baudelaire songs one does not find an excess of chromatic harmony in his music. Rather we can best approach the *fin de siècle* quality of Debussy's music by way of the literary state of mind which prevailed in certain circles between 1880 and 1890, a spirit of overwhelming *langueur,* futility, and nostalgia which Jules Laforgue described as *L'esprit décadent.*[4]

Characteristics of decadence which occur in Debussy's *Proses Lyriques* include a preoccupation with inner feelings; a sense of ennui; obscurity arising from private imagery and from the obvious reluctance to *name* an object; "an overwhelming aura of something lost—a nostalgic, semimysticism without clear direction or spiritual commitment, but with frequent reference to exotic religions . . . or to such mysterious substitutes as . . ." (in *De rêve*) the pursuit of the Holy Grail.[5] Debussy's poem may be usefully compared with Régnier's *Songe de la Forêt*, which it resembles both in subject and in style.

Régnier, like Debussy, sets his poem in the magic of a moonlit forest:

> En l'aurore où par la lune de nuit stellaire
> [Régnier]
> Les vieux arbres, sous la lune d'or.
> [Debussy]

Both poets describe an enchanted lady of the forest:

> La Dame merveilleuse, là, prélève
> Les lauriers dont se laure sa natte hautaine,
> En couronne. . . .
> [Régnier]
> A celle qui vient de passer la tête emperlée.
> [Debussy]

[4] Paraphrased from the article "L'esprit décadent" in Harvey and Heseltine, *The Oxford Companion to French Literature* (Oxford: At the Clarendon Press, 1969), pp. 254–255.

[5] Article on "Decadence" in *Princeton Encyclopedia of Poetry & Poetics*, ed. Alex Preminger (Princeton, N.J.: Princeton University Press, 1965), p. 185.

Both poets occasionally use a word to rhyme with itself, either internally or at the end of the line:

> roses la colline
> plaines des collines!
>
> chantaient la Dame merveilleuse,
> jouaient la Dame merveilleuse.
> [Régnier]
>
> Maintenant navrée,
> A jamais navrée
>
> Maintenant ternis!
> A jamais ternis!
> [Debussy]

Like Debussy, Régnier unfolds a dream:

> Un songe m'a roulé par des ans et des mondes
> A travers l'ombre étrange et la mort des soleils.

Régnier treats his dream far more expansively than Debussy, and uses an entire page to say essentially what Debussy expresses in the single line: "Mon âme, c'est du rêve ancien qui t'étreint." Taking his lesson from Mallarmé, Debussy evokes where Régnier describes. Régnier goes on for stanzas to elaborate on the armored knights and their struggles, a scene which Debussy suggests in a few words:

> Nul ne leur dédiera plus la fierté des casques d'or
> Maintenant ternis!
> A jamais ternis!
> Les chevaliers sont morts sur le chemin du Grâal!

Where Régnier proceeds with a fairly matter-of-fact narrative, Debussy allows images and impressions to come and go in the manner of a dreamlike stream of consciousness. Several lines flow from a single color:

> Les vieux arbres sous la lune d'or, pleurent
> Leurs belles feuilles d'or
> Nul ne leur dédiera plus la fierté des casques d'or.

Lines return as an echo of a previous thought: "Maintenant navrée, / A jamais navrée" becomes "Maintenant ternis, / A jamais ternis." "Les Frêles, / Les Folles" returns as "Mains si folles, / Mains si frêles."

The poem appears as an unbroken line of thought, whose main points of articulation are the recurrences of the first two lines of the poem, in reverse order, later in the body of the poem. "Mon âme c'est du rêve ancien." The poem has no future, only a past. The end has been reached; the helmets now tarnished shall never shine again. The woman who has just gone by shall remain forever broken-hearted. The days of laughter and of struggle are over, never to return; no purpose worthy of sacrifice can be found. "Les chevaliers sont morts sur le chemin du Grâal." Life in the present has no substance; it seems only to be part of an ancient dream. Debussy's poem captures the general feeling of malaise and decadence of the *fin de siècle,* a feeling which also appears in his musical setting of the text.

The principal theme conveys a feeling of purposelessness through the absence of either clearly defined goal or unifying tonal center. The theme suggests no definite harmonic context, and takes on a different accompaniment at each appearance. The chords which support the

Example 1

theme, moreover, give no sense of logical progression, but rather move in ambiguous successions of seconds and thirds (Example 1).

The theme which introduces the song carries a suggestion of the whole-tone scale, which appears in full at the word *d'or.* Gold, the characteristic color of the *fin de siècle,* becomes a unifying element in the middle of the poem, which Debussy again sets in the whole-tone scale (Example 2).

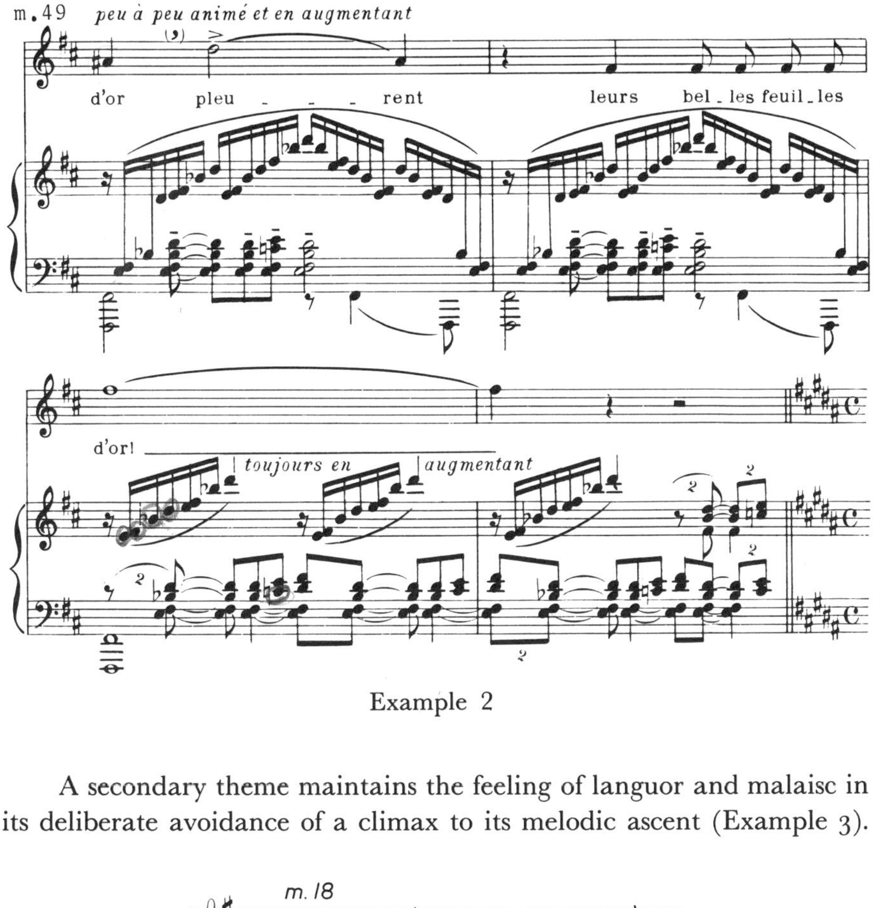

Example 2

A secondary theme maintains the feeling of languor and malaisc in its deliberate avoidance of a climax to its melodic ascent (Example 3).

Example 3

In this context of musical decadence Debussy is able to employ occasional passages of harmonic stability as a nostalgic evocation of the past. At the mention of golden helmets the music becomes suddenly louder, *dans un rythme plus accusé,* and the harmony settles on a B major chord in second inversion, the position of greatest harmonic tension

Example 4

(Example 4). In addition Debussy employs a fanfare based on triadic harmonies at the points in the text which most directly evoke the days of knighthood: "la fierté des casques d'or," "sur le chemin du Grâal," "les épées," with an echo of the fanfare, *en se perdant,* at the close of the song (Example 5).

Example 5

These observations do not apply to all of Debussy's music, of course. In other songs Debussy also avoids heroic gesture but still writes vigorous melodies based on the elemental strength of the pentatonic scale. In other songs Debussy also avoids rhetoric but still organizes the harmony in clear, if nontraditional, patterns. But in the *Proses Lyriques*, especially *De rêve* and *De fleurs,* Debussy indulges in a melodic and harmonic malaise to create a musical expression of *l'esprit décadent.*

De grève

Sur la mer les crépuscules tombent
Soie blanche éffilée!
Les vagues comme de petites folles
Jasent, petites filles sortant de l'école,
Parmi les frous-frous de leur robe
Soie verte irisée!

Les nuages, graves voyageurs
Se concertent sur le prochain orage
Et, c'est un fond vraiment trop grave
A cette anglaise aquarelle . . .
Les vagues, les petites vagues
Ne savent plus où se mettre
Car voici la méchante averse
Frous-frous de jupes envolées
Soie verte affolée!

Mais la lune, compatissante à tous!
Vient apaiser ce gris conflit
Et caresse lentement ses petites amies
Qui s'offrent comme lèvres aimantes
A ce tiède et blanc baiser . . .

Puis plus rien! . . .
Plus que les cloches attardées
Des flottantes églises
Angelus des vagues! . . .
Soie blanche apaisée! . . .

[For translation, see p. 312]

Shortly before the composition of the *Proses Lyriques* Debussy became acquainted with the work of J. M. W. Turner, the English forerunner of Impressionism. Instinctively he was drawn to an artist who wrote "Indistinctness is my forte," a painter whom Debussy later proclaimed as the greater creator of mystery in art.[6] Color reproductions of Whistler and Turner decorated the walls of Debussy's home at 24 Square Bois de Bologne, where he moved in 1905.

No doubt Debussy also felt an affinity to Turner's treatment of the sea and, as with the French Impressionists, his close attention to the effects of color. Debussy's love of the sea can be observed in his choice of musical subjects, not only in the large tone poem *La Mer* and the *Sirènes* movement of the *Nocturnes*, but also in the piano pieces *(Ce qu'a vu le vent d'Ouest; Voiles; L'Isle joyeuse; La Cathédrale engloutie)* and the songs *(La Mer est plus belle; De grève)*. The sea even permeates works whose title alone gives no indication of this influence: according to Debussy, the twelfth piano Etude "emprunte la forme d'une Barcarolle sur une mer un peu italienne." [7]

Debussy's fastidious concern for color is a recurring theme in his letters to his publisher, which deal with every detail of design and layout, including the tint of paper and ink used in printing his compositions.[8] In the case of *The Children's Corner* Debussy himself painted the whimsical cover design.

The kinship which Debussy perceived between color and sound is suggested in a letter of 1908. Referring to a Rondel of Charles d'Orléans he writes, "Je trouve cette pièce si pleine de douce musique intérieure que naturellement je ne peux me retenir de 'L'extériorser.' " Asking his friend Laloy for the exact meaning of several words in the poem, Debussy continues, "J'aime mieux vous dire tout de suite que j'attends votre réponse pour fixer mes couleurs." [9]

While we do not know which of Turner's paintings Debussy actually knew, descriptions of Turner's work seem appropriate both to the text of *De grève* and to the musical setting of the poem.[10] Gardner mentions "the investment of the commonplace with imaginative coloring" and goes on to suggest that "later Turner paintings are almost abstract visualizations

[6] Quoted in Edward Lockspeiser, *Music and Painting* (London: Cassell, 1973), p. 9.

[7] Jacques Durand, ed., *Lettres de Claude Debussy à son éditeur* (Paris: A. Durand, 1927), p. 144.

[8] *Ibid.* contains numerous examples, e.g., pp. 10–11.

[9] Letter to Laloy published in Special Issue of *Revue de Musicologie* 1962: 29–30.

[10] There is some evidence that Debussy's first exposure to Turner's work came through forgeries. Edward Lockspeiser discusses the question in *Music and Painting*.

of space and light."[11] Canaday writes, "In his art, the English love of nature is expanded to grander dimensions; fields, clouds, streams, and sunlight are transmuted into abstract symbols of earth, air, fire, and water."[12]

Debussy, in his watercolor poem, invests the commonplace pictorial subject of young maidens walking on the beach before a storm with the white of foamy waves and moonlight and the green of silk dresses, while describing the background of the storm—"un fond vraiment trop grave à cette anglaise aquarelle"—as a gray struggle. The silk of the girls' rustling dresses, compared metaphorically with the raveling of waves, comes to stand apart and serve as punctuation for this prose poem: "soie blanche éffilée"—the waves chatter like schoolgirls; "soie verte irisée"—the rainbow of color formed by light on water or shining silk; "soie verte affolée"—the flight of rustling skirts and waves; "soie blanche apaisée"—the sea at rest, calmed by the "blanc baiser" of white moon and white waves. Edmund Wilson describes this use of symbols as "metaphors detached from their subjects."[13] As in a Turner painting, the inessential elements are stripped away and transmuted into abstract symbols.

These same metaphors return years later in Debussy's remarks on the sea. In 1904 he writes to his publisher, "La mer a été bien pour moi, elle m'a montré toutes ses robes," and in 1915 describes "la mer qui s'agite, veut empiéter sur la terre, mord les rochers et a des colères de petite fille."[14]

In 1906 Debussy wrote in a letter to his stepson Raoul Bardac: "Music has this over painting—it can bring together all manner of variations of color and light—a point not often observed though it is quite obvious."[15] Debussy's observations can be illustrated by examining a single motive from *De grève* as it appears in various colors. The motive initially appears in measure 3, the first disturbance of the tranquillity of the perfect triad which opens the song. The motive outlines a diminished triad above the rocking motion of the accompaniment (Example 6). At its second occurrence the motive appears in diminution. In contrast with

[11] Helen Gardner, *Art Through the Ages* (London; G. Bell, 1959), pp. 679–680.

[12] John Canaday, *Metropolitan Seminars in Art: The War of Illusions* (New York: The Metropolitan Museum of Art, 1959), p. 24.

[13] Edmund Wilson, *Axel's Castle* (New York: Scribner's, 1931), p. 21.

[14] Jacques Durand, *Lettres de Claude Debussy*, pp. 19, 144.

[15] Quoted in Edward Lockspeiser, *Debussy* (New York: Collier Books, 1962), p. 270.

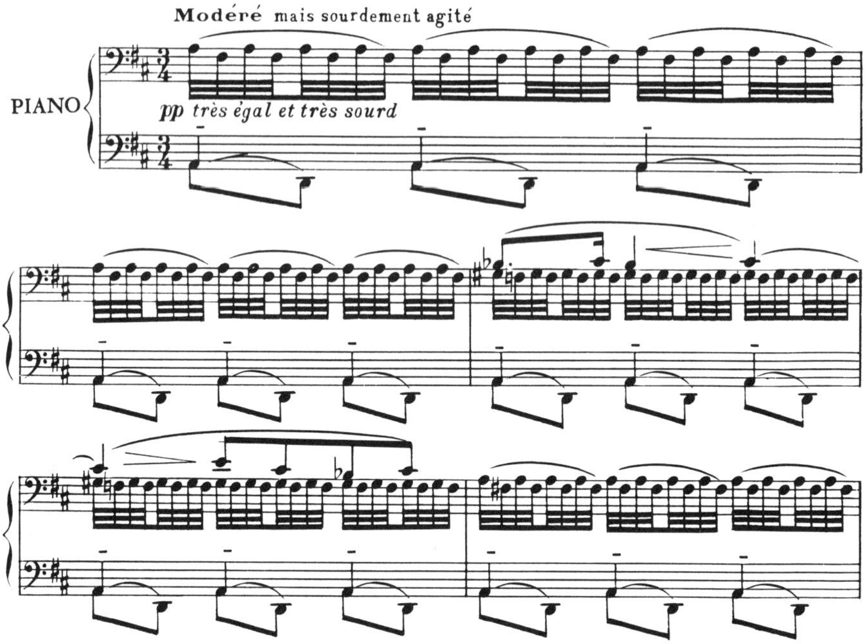

Example 6

the example given above, in which the motive is superimposed upon a rocking accompanimental figure in the bass, the motive in its second appearance interrupts this prevailing figure with deep, sustained chords to set off the line "Soie blanche éffilée." The third appearance of the motive, an octave higher than before, has a lighter color and texture. In place of a rocking accompaniment or deep chords, a succession of darting arpeggios in the bass suggests the iridescent reflections of the text: "soie verte irisée!" The harmony contributes to the effect with the sharp dissonance of a chord of the minor ninth (Example 7). The motive returns to portray "cette anglaise aquarelle" in the vague shades of the whole-tone scale, a scale that lacks the definite center of gravity which accompanies the motive in its first appearance. The whole texture has been transposed upward, producing a much lighter color of sound than before. The displacement of the beat creates a tension which seems appropriate to little waves who know not where to go (Example 8).

At the approaching storm the tessitura rises still higher, the dynamic level increases to *forte* and *fortissimo,* the rhythm of the motive merges with

Example 7

Example 8

Example 9

a constant, frantic thirty-second-note motion, the rustling of fleeing skirts (Example 9). The moon brings peace to troubled waters; the music proceeds *en se calmant.* The motive appears in its original rhythm and pitch values, but unlike the softly agitated quality of the opening of the song, this final section has a strange air of solitude produced by the enormous distance separating the right and left hands of the piano part. The nearly three-octave gap leaves space for sounds to resonate, a space which Debussy then gradually fills in, first with the two-note accompanying figure, then with an arpeggiated diminished seventh chord.[16]

Debussy accomplishes these changes of light and color by his choice of texture—how thick or thin the music should sound; of tessitura—where the notes should be placed; of accompaniment—what kind of rhythm, harmony and figuration should support the main motive. Such music, like the later Turner paintings, borders on an abstract visualization of space and light.

> J'essaie du faire "autre chose"—en quelque sorte, des *réalités*—ce que les imbéciles appellent "impressionisme," term aussi mal employé que possible, surtout par les critiques d'art qui n'hésitent pas à en affubler Turner, le plus beau créateur de mystère qui soit en art! [17]

De fleurs

Dans l'ennui si désolément vert de la serre de douleur,
Les fleurs enlacent mon coeur de leurs tiges méchantes.
Ah! quand reviendront autour de ma tête
Les chères mains si tendrement désenlaceuses?
Les grands Iris violets
Violèrent méchamment tes yeux
En semblant les refléter,
Eux, qui furent l'eau du songe où plongèrent mes rêves
Si doucement enclos en leur couleur;
Et les lys, blancs jets d'eau de pistils embaumés,
Ont perdu leur grâce blanche
Et ne sont plus que pauvres malades sans soleil!

[16] For a further discussion of "resonance" in Debussy see André Schaeffner, "Le Timbre," in *La Résonance dans les Echelles Musicales*, ed. Edith Weber (Paris: Editions du Centre National de la Recherche Scientifique, 1963), pp. 215–220.

[17] Durand, *Lettres de Claude Debussy*, p. 58.

Soleil! ami des fleurs mauvaises,
Tueur de rêves! Tueur d'illusions!
Ce pain béni des âmes misérables!
Venez! Venez! Les mains salvatrices!
Brisez les vitres de mensonge,
Brisez les vitres de maléfice,
Mon âme meurt de trop de soleil!
Mirages! Plus ne refleurira la joie de mes yeux
Et mes mains sont lasses de prier,
Mes yeux sont las de pleurer!
Eternellement ce bruit fou des pétales noirs de l'ennui
Tombant goutte à goutte sur ma tête
Dans le vert de la serre de douleur!

[For translation, see p. 312]

Les grands Iris violet
Violèrent méchamment tes yeux
En semblant les refléter.

The word-play by which *violèrent* becomes a violation of *violets* serves as the central metaphor for this poem of evil flowers, literally "les fleurs du mal." Straight stems are perverted into spiteful tendrils which entwine about the poet's heart and hold him captive in the hothouse of sorrow. The irises have ravished his lover's eyes while seeming to reflect them. The lilies have lost their white grace for lack of sun and now display a sickly pallor. Death hovers nearby, both in the fall from grace ("ont perdu leur grâce") and in the poor invalids, for whom the funeral flowers, "de pistils embaumés," have already been arranged. One recalls Baudelaire's *La Mort des amants*: "Nous aurons des lits pleins d'odeurs légères, / Des divans profonds comme des tombeaux; / Et d'étranges fleurs sur des étagères," and Verlaine's *Spleen.*

The sun, friend of the spiteful flowers, breeds evil and delusion while destroying dream, destroying the holy mysteries which surround the consecrated bread, destroying the creative illusion which constitutes art. Elsewhere Debussy writes:

> L'art est le plus beau des mensonges. Et quoiqu'on essaie d'y incorporer la vie dans son décor quotidien, il faut désirer qu'il reste un mensonge, sous peine de devenir une chose utilitaire triste comme une usine. Le peuple aussi bien que l'élite ne viennent-ils pas y chercher l'oubli, ce qui est encore une forme du mensonge? . . . Ne

> désillusionnons donc personne en ramenant le rêve à de trop précises réalités. Contentons-nous de transpositions plus consolantes par ce qu'elles peuvent contenir d'une expression de beauté qui ne mourra pas.[18]

The soul perishes from too much sun. The spiteful flowers, nurtured in the concentrated sunlight of the hothouse, will not permit "la joie de mes yeux" to bloom again. Eyes weary of weeping have no tears left for mourning. Instead, the falling of black petals anoints the head in a perverted baptism.

The elaborate floral imagery of *De fleurs* reflects Debussy's preoccupation with the aesthetic theories of the Art Nouveau movement. Lockspeiser concludes several instructive paragraphs on Debussy's relationship with the Art Nouveau painters with the words:

> His finely shaped handwriting, his monogram consisting of mysteriously entwined initials, his preoccupation with the decorative features of his publications, particularly the colors and spacing of the title page, the furnishings of his humble home in the rue Cardinet ("your Art Nouveau den," as Pierre Louÿs described it)—all this indicates that Debussy was deeply affected by specific trends in the visual arts.[19]

Let us examine what Debussy refers to as "des courbes que décrit la musique à travers le textes." [20] The song opens with simple major and minor triads, the building blocks of tonal harmony. This static succession of chords, constantly returning to the same point, suggests the unrelieved ennui of "la serre de douleur." Debussy uses a pattern of unresolved dominant seventh chords to represent the "bruit fou" at the end of the song. A similar alternating succession of chords to set the question "When will those dear . . . hands reappear?" anticipates the answer which comes later: Nevermore. Having established the melancholy major-minor succession to represent the ennui of the hothouse, Debussy employs alterations of these chords to suggest the perversion of the spiteful flowers. The succession in measures 19–20 ends not in a major triad but in an augmented triad, and the repetition in measure 21 leads

[18] Claude Debussy, *Monsieur Croche et autres écrits* (Paris: Gallimard, 1971), p. 67.
[19] Lockspeiser, *Debussy: His Life and Mind*, vol. I, p. 119.
[20] *Lettres inédites à André Caplet* (Monaco: Editions du Rocher, 1957), p. 67.

to a new key altogether, at the text "Les grands Iris violets. . . ." The continuation of the text—"Violèrent méchamment tes yeux, en semblant les refléter"—is set to two phrases, the second a near, but not a true, imitation of the first. The next phrase, the sinking of dream into dream, is set to an extended deceptive cadence—V^7-vi. The fresh whiteness of lilies has turned into the sick pallor of invalids. Debussy sets these lines to a prolonged diminished triad, whose constricted sound contrasts with the fullness of the major and minor triads at the beginning of the song. The tonal centers after the opening section in C have gradually moved up the whole-tone scale: E-F♯-G♯-B♭. In the section beginning "Tueur de rêves!" this whole-tone progression—a "violation" of traditional tonality—is repeated with whole-tone harmonies. Just as the pallor produced by too little sun finds musical expression in diminished triads, so the despair which follows the line "mon âme meurt de *trop* de soleil!" is accompanied by augmented triads. After a brief return of the opening chords at the words "Venez! Les mains salvatrices," the augmented chords return to reflect hands tired from too much praying, eyes tired from too much crying—a harmony of chords "too big" to be major triads. Black petals fall drop by drop in a crazy noise of unresolved dominant seventh chords. The song ends as it began with the oppressive verdure of the hothouse of sorrow.

De soir

Dimanche sur les villes,
Dimanche dans les coeurs!
Dimanche chez les petites filles
Chantant d'une voix informée
Des rondes obstinées où de bonnes Tours
N'en ont plus que pour quelques jours!
Dimanche, les gares sont folles!
Tout le monde appareille pour des banlieux d'aventure
En se disant adieu avec des gestes éperdus!
Dimanches, les trains vont vite,
Dévorés par d'insatiables tunnels;
Et les bons signaux des routes
Echangent d'un oeil unique
Des impressions toutes mécaniques
Dimanche, dans le bleu de mes rêves,
Où mes pensées tristes de feux d'artifice manqués

Ne veulent plus quitter le deuil
De vieux Dimanches trépassés.
Et la nuit, à pas de velours,
Vient endormir le beau ciel fatigué,
Et c'est Dimanche dans les avenues d'étoiles;
La Vierge or sur argent
Laisse tomber les fleurs de sommeil!
Vite, les petites anges, dépassez les hirondelles
Afin de vous coucher, forts d'absolution!
Prenez pitié des villes,
Prenez pitié des coeurs,
Vous, la Vierge or sur argent!

[For translation, see p. 313]

Jules Laforgue (1860–1888) was among the most innovative poets of his time. Laforgue was one of the first in France to experiment with *vers libre*, making frequent use of alliteration and internal rhyme to replace the regular structure of strict verse. Laforgue loved to amuse himself with words, coining new expressions like "vendanges sexiproques," "céleste éternullité," "crucifiger," "sangsuelles." He shared with Baudelaire the themes of ennui and the force of evil in the world; like Verlaine, his vocabulary closely approached that of spoken language.

Two words which occur frequently in criticism of Laforgue's work are *ennui* and *irony*. One writer describes the poet as "un prince de l'ennui." [21] Another speaks of "Melancholy mingled with urbane irony." [22] Still another finds in Laforgue "a newer kind of adolescent, promenading his bitterness through the twilight surburban Sundays to the plaintive accompaniment of pianos played by forever inaccessible *jeunes filles*." [23] Both themes, irony and ennui, come together in a succession of poems, each titled *Dimanches*, in which Laforgue mocks the platitudes of ordinary life, the mediocrity of mankind.[24] Sunday morning one joins the faithful congregation:

[21] Léon Guichard, *Jules Laforgue et ses poésies* (Paris: Presses Universitaires de France, 1950), p. 78.

[22] Leo Weinstein, "Laforgue and His Time" in *Jules Laforgue, Essays on a Poet's Life and Work*, ed. Warren Ramsey (Carbondale: Southern Illinois University Press, 1969), p. 58.

[23] Robert Greer Cohn, "Laforgue and Mallarmé" *in Jules Laforgue*, ed. Warren Ramsey.

[24] Antoine Adam, *et al.*, *Littérature Française* (Paris: Larousse, 1968), p. 191.

> Les Jeunes Filles inviolables et frêles
> Descendent vers la petite chapelle
> Dont les chimériques cloches
> Du joli joli dimanche,
> Hygiéniquement et élégamment les appellent.
> *[Dimanches]*

Sunday afternoon one makes an excursion with the family:

> Mais l'Infinis est là, gare de trains ratés,
> Où les gens, aveuglés de signaux, s'apitoient
> Sur le sanglot des convois, et vont se hâter
> Tout à l'heure! et crever en travers de la voie.
> *[Gare au bord de la mer]*

Whether the crowd be gathered for sacred purposes or profane, Laforgue "felt the vulgarity of people massed together, inevitably drawn toward what is most garish, ignoring or striking down what is less so." [25]

Michael Collie finds in Laforgue an "ambiguous feeling: on the one side a miserable, adolescent sense of inferiority and incompatibility; on the other, an assurance of superiority amounting almost to arrogance." [26] Collie points out the importance of visual elements in Laforgue's poetry, and comments that Laforgue "was vitally interested in poets, but learnt from painters." [27] Laforgue learned from musicians, too, and occasionally wrote poems "inspired by music mingled with street songs—what we should nowadays call *musique concrète.* The subjects of these poems include the monotonous strumming at the piano of a 'Chopin waltz threadbare and stale as love' heard in the course of an afternoon stroll." [28] The influence of Laforgue is evident in Debussy's Sunday poem, *De soir.*

The poem falls into two unequal sections, the first depicting the hurly-burly of Sunday afternoon, the second invoking "la Vierge or sur argent" as protectress of the night. We meet once again the "jeunes filles" of *De grève* and Laforgue's *Dimanches.* On Sundays the little girls play a circle game in which one girl represents the tower and the others

[25] Warren Ramsey, *Jules Laforgue and the Ironic Inheritance* (New York: Oxford University Press, 1953), p. 29.

[26] Michael Collie, *Laforgue* (London: Oliver and Boyd, 1963), p. 2.

[27] *Ibid.*, p. 23.

[28] Lockspeiser, *Music and Painting*, p. 102.

turn around her, singing "des rondes obstinées," which Bernac quotes as follows (Example 10).[29] Even good towers will last only a few days in this

la tour prends gar-de la tour prends gar-de de
te lais-ser a - bat-tre

Example 10

children's game, roughly akin to the English "London bridge is falling down." Debussy has no more sympathy for massed crowds than Laforgue does. His people are reduced to feed for voracious tunnels, objectified so that, ironically, the signals along the way regard the passengers, comparing notes among themselves, rather than the other way around.

Debussy's distaste for the grosser manifestations of turn-of-the-century technology can be found both in his letters and in his music criticism. Writing on "futuristic" music Debussy comments:

> Elle prétend rassembler les bruits divers des modernes capitales dans une totale symphonie, depuis les pistons des locomotives jusqu'à la clarine des raccommodeurs de porcelaine. C'est très pratique quant au recrutement de l'orchestre; seulement ça atteindra-t-il jamais à la sonorité, déjà satisfaisante, d'une usine métallurgique en pleine travail?

(One thinks of Debussy's fondness for the phrase "usines du Néant," quoted from "notre Jules.") He concludes: "Prenons garde à la mécanique qui a déjà dévoré tant de belles choses." [30] The all-devouring locomotive appears again in a letter to Jean-Aubrey:

> J'ai passé l'été à l'ombre du chemin de fer de ceinture qui borde ma maison, pénétré de l'idée qu'il n'est pas nécessaire d'entendre le

[29] Pierre Bernac, *The Interpretation of French Song* (London: Cassell, 1970), p. 194.

[30] Claude Debussy, *Monsieur Croche*, p. 234. The Laforgue quote appears in Claude Debussy, *Lettres à deux amis* (Paris: Librairie José Corti, 1942), p. 160, and elsewhere. Lockspeiser gives other examples in *Debussy: His Life and Mind*, vol. 2, p. 220.

> chant du rossignol, celui des locomotives répondant bien mieux aux préoccupations modernes de l'art.[31]

For Debussy, then, the secular side of Sunday is mechanistic, insensitive, mad, directionless, transitory (Towers which will not last.)

In the second half of the poem the tone becomes more personal and sentimental, as night comes to put the sky to sleep. Terms of religious connotation appear: *deuil*, *trépassés*, *anges*, *vierge*, *forts d'absolution*. The crowds of people have disappeared, since for Debussy religion takes place not among the company of the faithful but alone, in the "temple de piliers vivants" of nature. The elements of his pantheistic philosophy take the form of stars, swallows, and flowers of sleep. Such a religion is not corporate but personal, individual. ("mes rêves," "mes pensées.")

This pantheistic philosophy resembles the natural religion of Baudelaire in *Harmonie du soir*, *La Mort des amants*, and especially *Correspondences*, which begins, "La nature est un temple." Similar themes may be found in Verlaine's poetry of church bells heard across a field *(L'Échelonnement des haies)*, a cathedral of the sea *(La Mer est plus belle)*, and a funeral knell ending a day of revelry *(Chevaux de bois)*. Debussy saw no need for the official sanction of the institutional church.

> Je ne pratique pas selon les rites consacrés. Je me suis fait une religion de la mystérieuse nature. Je ne pense pas qu'un homme revêtu d'une robe abbatiale soit plus près de Dieu, ni qu'un lieu dans la ville soit plus favorable à la méditation.[32]

For Debussy the vastness of nature surpasses any edifice that man could erect, and the contemplation and adoration of the natural firmament constitutes for Debussy a form of prayer.

> Devant un ciel mouvant, en contemplant, de longues heures, ses beautés magnifiques et incessamment renouvelées, une incomparable émotion m'étreint. La vaste nature se reflète en mon âme véridique et chétive. Voici les arbres aux branches remontées vers le firmament, voici les fleurs parfumées qui sourient dans la prairie, voici la terre douce tapissée d'herbes folles. Et, insensiblement, les mains prennent des poses d'adoration. Sentir à quels spectacles troublants et souver-

[31] *Lettres à deux amis*, p. 118.
[32] *Monsieur Croche*, p. 302.

> ains la nature convie ses éphémères et tremblants passagers, voilà ce que j'appelle *prier*.[33]

Debussy's occasional impatience with those who fail to appreciate the glory of nature betrays a Laforguian irony.

> Il y a en face de l'hôtel une jeune fille que je ne connais pas, et à laquelle je vous jure que je n'ai jamais fait le moindre mal, qui joue du Franck pendant une bonne partie de l'après-midi. Seigneur! quand il y a la mer, et des couchers de soleil à pleurer! Si j'étais le soleil, j'irais me coucher ailleurs! [34]

Each half of *De soir* has its own dominant motive based on the pentatonic scale, Debussy's favorite scale for evoking nature:[35] the first half a variation of the children's game, the second half a bell motive. The opening chords are based on the perfect fifths G♯–D♯ and C♯–G♯. The voice enters on a melody which employs only three pitches—G♯–D♯–C♯—an unusual effect. These pitches also compose the bell motive later in the song. The children's melody appears shortly thereafter in the piano (Example 11). The ostinato eighth-note pattern of the accompaniment conveys the mechanistic nature of the activity in the first half of the poem. The weak root movement, generally by thirds with practically no cadential movement by fourths and fifths, expresses the poet's feeling of of *de trop* with the frenetic activity of the crowds.

The bell motive first appears in measure 33 and dominates the second half of the piece (Example 12). Debussy transforms the motive into a lullaby as the night is put to sleep; the tempo becomes *moins vite*, the rhythm changes from duple meter to a rocking compound meter. Throughout the second half, strong root movement by fourths and fifths predominates. The conclusion of the song recapitulates the rhythmic motive of the opening, but now the tempo has become much slower, and

[33] *Ibid.*

[34] *Lettres à deux amis*, p. 160. Lockspeiser also finds echoes of Laforgue in *F.E.A.*, a theater-piece which Debussy wrote in collaboration with René Peter. See Edward Lockspeiser, "Frères en Art: Pièce de théâtre inèdite de Debussy," *Revue de Musicologie* 56 (1970):165–176.

[35] For an exhaustive study of Debussy's use of the pentatonic scale see Constantin Brailoiu, "Pentatony in Debussy's Music," in *Studia Memoriae Belae Bartók Sacra* (Budapest: Publishing House of the Hungarian Academy of Sciences, 1959), pp. 377–417.

Modérément animé
Voice
PIANO
mf
Di_man - che sur les
vil - les, Di - man_che dans les cœurs!
Diman_che chez les pe_ti_tes fil - les chantant d'u_ne voix in_for_
children's
song
p
_mée des rondes obsti - né - es ou de bonnes Tours n'en ont

Example 11

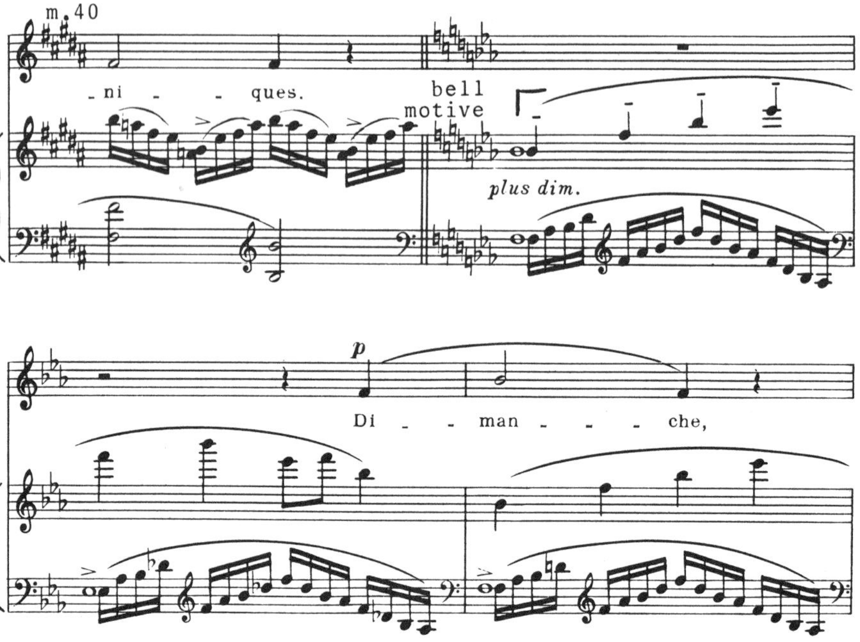

Example 12

the chains of frenetic motion have been broken. A pause occurs after each appearance of the motive as Debussy invokes the pardon of "La Vierge or sur argent" on behalf of the people of the cities.

The *Proses Lyriques* belong to a world that was coming to an end. Elements of literary decadence appear throughout the poems: an emphasis on personal experience, a preoccupation with corruption and morbidity, "scorn of contemporary society and mores," "nostalgia for a better world now lost." [36] The musical settings also suggest the end of a line: melodies that lack direction or deliberately avoid a natural climax; harmonies based on an ever-richer piling of triad upon triad; tonality weakened through chromaticism, the whole-tone scale, and avoidance of strong progressions. But Debussy was not simply a late nineteenth-century composer. Like Josquin des Près, Monteverdi, Handel, and Beethoven, Debussy stands as a watershed between two eras of music

[36] Preminger, *Princeton Encyclopedia.*

history. The Mallarmé songs, like the twentieth-century orchestral and chamber works, contain ideas which contemporary composers continue to explore. Before concluding our study with these twentieth-century songs, let us survey the development of Debussy's style as a composer of songs by examining his settings of Verlaine's *Fêtes galantes.*

10

VERLAINE IV: *Fetes galantes*

During the course of his career, Debussy set to music eight poems from Verlaine's collection of *Fêtes galantes.* Six of the titles appear in Debussy's two cycles called *Fêtes galantes*, series one and two, published in 1892 and 1904, respectively. Of these, *En sourdine, Fantoches*, and *Clair de lune* were initially set around 1882. The "revisions" in this first series of *Fêtes galantes* amount to new settings. The second series includes *Les Ingénus, Le Faune*, and *Colloque sentimental.* Two other poems, *Mandoline* and *Pantomime*, appear among Debussy's earliest works.

In 1912 Debussy, Charles Morice, and the publisher Jacques Durand signed a contract for *Crimen amoris,* "conte lyrique en trois actes d'après Paul Verlaine." Debussy found the scenario that Morice wrote unsatisfactory, as we see in a letter to Laloy dated 30 November 1913;

> Il suffisait, ainsi que vous le démontrez, d'avoir du goût et de la sensibilité—bannir surtout les tours de force par lesquels Moriceoblat semble arracher les vers de ce pauvre Verlaine, comme de mauvaises dents! [1]

[1] Special Issue, *Revue de Musicologie* 1962, p. 39.

Debussy requested that Laloy revise the scenario for him. A new contract was concluded on 27 January 1914 for a *Fêtes galantes* which Debussy described in an interview a few days later:

> Quant aux *Fêtes galantes* que Charles Morice et moi avons tirées des poèmes de Verlaine, ce sera un ballet, un "opéra ballet." Ce n'est pas terminé, loin de là! [2]

Neither work was ever completed, but as late as 1915 Debussy still had hopes of writing a theater piece drawn from Verlaine's works.

The eight poems which Debussy did set to music span more than two decades of his creative life. In previous chapters we have considered three of the poems: *Mandoline*, *Clair de lune*, and *En sourdine.* In the present chapter we shall study the remaining five as an index to the development of Debussy's style as a composer of songs.

Pantomime

Pierrot, qui n'a rien d'un Clitandre,
Vide un flacon sans plus attendre,
Et, pratique, entame un pâté.

Cassandre, au fond de l'avenue,
Verse une larme méconnue
Sur son neveu déshérité.

Ce faquin d'Arlequin combine
L'enlèvement de Colombine
Et pirouette quatre fois.

Colombine rêve, surprise
De sentir un coeur dans la brise
Et d'entendre en son coeur des voix.

[For translation, see p. 314]

Verlaine's *Fêtes galantes* show a master of words playing—sometimes seriously, sometimes facetiously—with literary traditions. In *Mandoline*, discussed earlier, we encountered characters from the classic pastorale—"C'est Tircis et c'est Aminte, / Et c'est l'éternel Clitandre, / Et c'est Damis . . ."—the diversion of an aristocratic society which distracts the mind and body in an amorous commerce ruled by a delicate "usage." [3]

[2] Claude Debussy, *Monsieur Croche et autres écrits* (Paris: Gallimard, 1971), p. 308.

The cast of *Pantomime* come of rather more common lineage: the company of players known in Italy as the *commedia dell'arte.*

The Gelosi company brought to the Paris of 1570 a new style that was to remain popular for over two hundred years.

> During these many years in Paris, the Italian comedy fell so completely under French influence that the actors performed plays written in French by French authors. The Italian theatre thus became a French theatre except that it retained the licentiousness, buffoonery, and satire, the pantomime, drollery, canzonettes and dances, in fact, all the spirit of Italian impromptu comedy.[4]

Robert Hall describes the action of the *commedia:*

> The structure of the typical improvised comedy was quite simple, usually revolving around a love intrigue, comic but vulgar. The actors made little or no effort to indicate psychological niceties, and put all their efforts into enlivening, through their clever improvisation of dialogue and "gags," a trite plot whose elements were already known to the audience.[5]

In *Pantomime* we recognize familiar personnages from the *commedia dell'arte,* along with a few names borrowed from the pastorale: there are Pierrot and Harlequin, the buffoons; Clitander, the young lover; Cassandre, an old dupe; Colombine, the heroine, Pierrot's wife. These performers offer us four vignettes acted out in the silence of pantomime.

At first sight the episodes seem unconnected. Pierrot, who is quite unlike the languorous Clitander, waits for his lover no longer but empties a flask and, in a businesslike manner, cuts into a pie. Meanwhile Cassandre, down at the end of the street—already the stage takes on a quality of depth—sheds an unnoticed tear for her disinherited nephew. The strange juxtaposition of words in the phrase "larme méconnue" emphasizes the dissociation among the vignettes. No one notices Cassandre's tear, or if they notice they fail to understand.

In the third stanza we see the rascal Harlequin pirouette four times as he plots the seduction of Colombine. In the fourth stanza we meet

[3] René Bray, *La Préciosité et les Précieux* (Paris: Librairie Nizet, 1945), p. 298.

[4] Joseph Spencer Kennard, *Masks and Marionettes* (Port Washington, N.Y.: Kenniket Press, 1935, 1967), p. 32.

[5] Robert A. Hall, Jr., *A Short History of Italian Literature* (Ithaca, N.Y.: Linguistica, 1951), p. 285.

Colombine herself, whose daydreaming is interrupted by the sensation of someone's heart in the breeze and the sound of voices in her own heart.

This repetition of the word *coeur* in the fourth stanza, and its appearance in the unusual phrase "un coeur dans la brise," signals the endpoint of a movement through the poem from outward gestures to inner feelings. In the first stanza Pierrot's earthy gestures of eating and drinking are readily apparent. In the second stanza Cassandre can mime the shedding of a tear but the poet must tell us the object of her weeping. Harlequin's pirouettes—literally the only real action that takes place on the stage—are but the outward expression of his inner design. By the time we reach the fourth stanza the movement has been completed—there is no action at all, only a description of Colombine's feelings as she synaesthetically combines the sensation of rushing air and the sounds of voices within her reverie.

If there is so little action, why do we suppose in reading the poem that we have been witness to a drama? In the absence of dialogue one might expect even greater emphasis on gesture, the essence of pantomime. Verlaine creates the effect of drama through the use of explicit stage directions. Harlequin pirouettes exactly four times—no more, no less. Pierrot cuts into a pie in a businesslike manner. The entire poem, set in four sentences written in the present tense, reads like the stage directions to a play. Verlaine has taken the characters of a literary tradition and treated them in the same manner that a playwright would treat real actors on a real stage. The resulting illusion of drama breathes life into the inanimate stock characters.

> We shall be in error, therefore, if we dismiss the commedia characters as "types." That they are types in one sense is true, but by their repetition in different circumstances they create the illusion that they are living beings.[6]

Debussy alters the text somewhat in his setting of this poem. He replaces the regular three-line stanzas by repeating certain lines:

Verlaine	a b c	d e f	g h i	j k l
Debussy	a b c a b	d e f	g h i i	j k l l

[6] Allardyce Nicoll, *The World of Harlequin* (Cambridge: At the University Press, 1963), p. 22.

Debussy ends the song with an eighteen-measure coda on the syllable "ah."

The piano prelude introduces the principal motive for the song and establishes an air of buffoonery for the mime which follows (Example 1).

Example 1

Each episode has a separate musical treatment. To Pierrot belongs the rhythmic pattern of the introduction, performed *détaché.* A sudden change of key, elevated pitch, and change in accompaniment isolate the single word *pratique* and suggest a rather broader gesture than one might

Example 2

imagine in simply reading the word (Example 2). Debussy expresses Cassandre's tears in a descending chromatic scale of staccato sixteenth notes. The obviousness of the musical gesture, the bald statement of a chromatic scale, makes a caricature of the tears. This is boffo humor, the way a circus clown cries, with exaggerated motions and much to-do. (Example 3). The pirouettes of Harlequin are accompanied by broken

Verse u-ne lar-me mé-con-nue

Example 3

chords and an accent on the offbeat. For the final stanza, Colombine's dream, the character of the song undergoes a marked change. The *allegro moderato* of the opening turns to *andante* and the piquant rhythms yield to uninterrupted arpeggios. The song does not end with the dreamlike mood of this final stanza; the accompaniment returns to the material of the first stanza while the vocal line sustains a long, melismatic "ah" in an extremely high tessitura.

Debussy portrays the external action of Verlaine's poem with a quality of caricature that borders on burlesque. The episodes seem to remain unconnected, perhaps because Debussy has not yet found a way to express the inner feelings that accompany the outer gestures. The movement from external to internal in Verlaine's poem helps to give a depth to the pantomime which is absent in Debussy's musical setting. For Debussy the characters remain types, and the song remains charming but somewhat naive.

Fantoches

Scaramouche et Pulcinella
Qu'un mauvais dessein rassembla
Gesticulent, noirs sur la lune.

Cependant l'excellent docteur
Bolonais cueille avec lenteur
Des simples parmi l'herbe brune.

Lors sa fille, piquant minois,
Sous la charmille, en tapinois,
Se glisse, demi-nue, en quête

De son beau pirate espagnol,
Dont un langoureux rossignol
Clame la détresse à tue-tête.
[For translation, see p. 314]

Once again Verlaine offers stage directions for a troupe of *commedia dell'arte* players, performing their wordless drama on the "paysage choisi" of your soul. This time the cast of characters includes Scaramouche, characteristically a mute figure who performs in pantomime; Pulcinella, a gross and vulgar fellow of crude wit; Dottoro Graziano, the "docteur bolonais" who usually appears as a lawyer, occasionally as a physician (Verlaine may have had in mind Pantalon, the father of Colombine.)[7] The worthy doctor tends, like Polonius, to express the obvious in circumlocutions, a triumph of verbiage over thought. The young maiden and the pirate complete the roll.[8]

The poet conveys the grotesque quality of the scene in a few phrases: two figures silhouetted against the moon, a man gathering herbs in the moonlight, a scantily clad maiden stealing under the arbor; Verlaine merely outlines the stage.

The language of the poem draws not on the vulgarity of the Italian comedy but on the sophistication of the French *précieux* style.[9] Rather than a broad reference to oversexed sailors Verlaine modestly uses the word *détresse* to indicate the pirate's urgency, and entrusts the message not to the pirate himself but to a conveniently sympathetic nightingale. But this is not the Romantic nightingale of *En sourdine* ("voix de notre désespoir, le rossignol chantera"). Instead, as the word *clame* indicates, this is a stage prop nightingale, indiscreetly bawling the pirate's predicament at the top of his lungs.

Verlaine again echoes the *précieux* tradition, which delighted in the use of exaggerated statement, in the expression "à tue-tête" in place of the more literal "à voix haute." "A tue-tête" is a commonplace expression in modern French, but etymologically it is cousin to such

[7] Jacques-Henry Bornecque, *Lumières sur les* Fêtes galantes" *de Paul Verlaine* (Paris: Librairie Nizet, 1959), p. 163.

[8] For a detailed description of the *commedia dell'arte* personages, see Nicoll, *The World of Harlequin*, pp. 40–94.

[9] See Bray, *La Préciosité et les Précieux*, for a full exposition of the *précieux* tradition.

favorite *précieux* usages as "furieusement," "fortement," "terriblement," "effroyablement." Likewise, "avec lenteur" in the second stanza, while unremarkable in itself, in this context exemplifies the kind of word order used in *précieux* periphrasis.

The *précieux* goal of elevating the banal and commonplace to the level of art through the use of conceits—oxymoron, periphrasis, synecdoche—which take one by surprise, finds musical expression in Debussy's setting of the poem. The various figures of the accompaniment are no more than stock devices which have been used for chase music from before Schumann's *Knecht Ruprecht* to the piano improvisations accompanying silent film melodramas (Example 4). The vocal melody, when

Example 4

not imitating the chromatic scurrying of the accompaniment, consists mostly of major and minor triads, the most elemental building blocks of tonal music.

Debussy's "conceits" come in his departures from the expected. Having begun a fairly ordinary accompanimental formula in measures 8–9, he startles us with an unexpected continuation in measures 10–11, only to thumb his nose at our surprise with an utterly banal phrase, set to "la la la" in measures 12–13. Thus the "mauvais dessein" of the first stanza appears as a "bad" harmonic plan.

Debussy paints the character of the doctor's daughter in some detail. At the words "piquant minois" the basic motive breaks off and the accompaniment presents a surprising chord. The melody makes a coquettish leap of a ninth at "sous la charmille," a crescendo to a *subito piano* at "se glisse," and an almost mocking "la la la" after the word

Example 5

"demi-nue" (Example 5). The nightingale cries out in the chromatic twistings of the basic motive, and the singer must carry "à tue-tête" to a high A while the piano trills in distress, then almost disappears in a two-and-a-half-octave glissando (Example 6). One could argue that the basic motive incorporates most of the action of the poem: the staccato steps of the maiden "en tapinois," the chromaticism of the nightingale's cry, the deviousness of the gesticulating pair.

In contrast to the early songs, in which a new accompanimental pattern appears for each change of stanza or character or idea, *Fantoches* uses variations on a constant sixteenth-note rhythm and a single chromatic motive to connect the several episodes of the poem. Harmonically the song appears a transition between the functional use of chords in the early songs and the coloristic use of chords in later works. The free use of chords a semitone on either side of the main chord eventually obscures the distinction between main chords and decorative chords until either some other device, such as Debussy's use of pedal points, comes to define tonality, or else the sense of tonality itself is weakened to the vanishing point.

Example 6

Les Ingénus

Les hauts talons luttaient avec les longues jupes,
En sorte que, selon le terrain et le vent,
Parfois luisaient des bas de jambes, trop souvent
Interceptés!—et nous aimions ce jeu de dupes.

Parfois aussi le dard d'un insecte jaloux
Inquiétait le col des belles sous les branches,
Et c'étaient des éclairs soudains de nuques blanches,
Et ce régal comblait nos jeunes yeux de fous.

Le soir tombait, un soir équivoque d'automne:
Les belles, se pendant rêveuses à nos bras,
Dirent alors des mots si spécieux, tout bas,
Que notre âme, depuis ce temps, tremble et s'étonne.

[For translation, see p. 315]

Verlaine tells his recollection of youth in an artless, unsophisticated style. The narrative, set in the conversational *imparfait* rather than the more literary *passé simple*, includes colloquial or informal usages such as "en sorte que," the word *et* to begin a clause ("et nous aimions,"), "parfois aussi," "alors." The story has a naive charm, with girls dressed up in fancy clothes to which they are unaccustomed, the astonishment at a glimpse of neck or leg, the dreaming maidens leaning on gentlemen's arms at day's end. The scene might have come directly from Watteau, whose *L'Assemblée dans un parc* depicts a couple at twilight, the lady taking the gentleman's arm, holding up her long gown with the other hand.

The form of the poem displays an appropriate simplicity: consistent *a b b a* rhyme scheme, alternation of twelve- and thirteen-syllable lines. Yet beneath the apparent ingenuousness of the tale Verlaine plays again on a theme that we encountered earlier in *En sourdine*, also a member of the *Fêtes galantes*. Bornecque refers to it as "le thème de la connivence entre la nature et l'amour." [10] In the first stanza the terrain or the wind is responsible for revealing a glimpse of leg. In the second stanza a bothersome insect produces a sudden flash of white neck. In the third stanza "un soir équivoque" favors "des mots si spécieux."

Littré insists on the Latin sense, "qui est le sens propre" for the word

[10] Bornecque, *Lumières sur les* "Fêtes galantes," p. 161.

spécieux: "qui a une belle appearance," and derives the etymology from *speciosus,* beautiful, from *species,* beauty, and from *specio,* to see. The original meaning serves the poet well, for "ce jeu de dupes" is a game of seeing, not of doing. The young men rejoice at a glimpse of leg or flash of neck. When night falls the girls amaze them with unrealized visions. The magic of these innocent moments endures to the present since, lying outside the realm of action, the specious words cannot be contradicted by later sophistication, a sophistication which brings participation and responsibility in a life which "les ingénus" perceive only in glimpses, flashes, and fair-seeming appearances.

In setting *Les Ingénus* Debussy uses a tone of voice which brings a remarkable depth to Verlaine's text. The musical material of the song has a deceptive simplicity. If we examine the first thirteen measures in detail, for example, we find an accompaniment based on repeated major thirds, the chromatic ascent of a major second, and the harmonic statement of a major second: nothing more. The right hand has but two six-note patterns, which alternate in a symmetrical structure. The left hand is no more complex, while the vocal line assimilates elements from both hands of the accompaniment. Looking to the second section of the song, measures 16–26, we find that the right hand of the accompaniment repeats a single pattern for ten measures, with but the slightest alteration in the eleventh. The left hand shows almost as much consistency.

From these elemental materials and simple patterns Debussy evokes not the straightforward, artless narrative that one might have expected, but rather a strange tone of mystery. The enchained thirds of the first measure define a special scale which borrows elements from pentatonic and harmonic minor: A♭-B♭-C-E♭-F♭-G-A♭. The A♭-C-E♭ triad clearly establishes the scale as major, yet the F♭-G-A♭, with the characteristic augmented second, speaks just as strongly for minor. The scale sets the tone for "un soir équivoque d'automne." The second section of the song is set almost entirely in the whole-tone scale, whose utter undifferentiation of tones complements the somewhat exotic mystery of the first section with a mystery of obscurity. The two scales mingle together in the recapitulation, where Debussy sets the third stanza of the poem *le double moins vite.* The accompaniment of the opening measures now reappears in fuller harmonies which alternate between the two hexachords of the whole-tone scale.

In the midst of this atmosphere of mystery and obscurity come occasional glimpses of clarity. At the words "trop souvent interceptés" the harmony suddenly turns to ordinary major triads. For "des éclairs soudains de nuques blanches" Debussy writes a firmly diatonic passage in major, followed immediately by a rich dominant harmony in a different key whose opulent chords of the 13th provide a musical feast for "ce régal." The expectancy generated by this prolonged dominant harmony finds no resolution in the music which immediately follows, but is echoed in measures 46–47 in the setting of "des mots si spécieux, tout bas." Once again a glimpse, a promise of something to come, but again, no resolution. The vocal melody for "notre âme . . . tremble et s'étonne" makes a dissonance against the minor triad of the accompaniment, and the piece ends on an ambiguous augmented triad.

In so treating Verlaine's text Debussy presents the world of the unsophisticate as one of obscurity and ignorance, not the blissful ignorance of sunshine but the mysterious ignorance of twilight, with only an occasional glimpse into the adult world beyond. Debussy's interpretation of the poem may well have been influenced by his direct experience with the work of Watteau. He dwelled for several weeks in 1885 at the home of Count Giuseppe Primoli, who owned the largest private collection of Watteau's paintings. Georges Jean-Aubry goes so far as to speculate that "Watteau inspira le Debussy des Fétes galantes plus encore qu'il n'inspira leur Verlaine, et peut-être plus que ce poète n'eût inspiré ce musicien sans le secours de ce peintre." [11]

Debussy's depth of poetic interpretation seems to parallel the maturing musical vocabulary with which he expresses his musical thoughts. *Les Ingénus*, the first song in the second series of *Fêtes galantes*, goes several steps beyond *Fantoches*, the last song in the first series, written twelve years earlier. Debussy's early habit of repeating words of text and adding wordless melismas has disappeared, while his later habit of repeating motives, figures, or entire measures appears prevalently. Functional harmony has been substantially supplanted by parallel chords and special scales, and while the song remains strongly tonal, it is the tonality of pedal points rather than of cadences.

This economy of means, this paring away of all inessential

[11] Claude Debussy, *Lettres à deux amis* (Paris: Librairie José Corti, 1942), p. 39.

material—analogous to Mallarmé's insistence on artistic purity—characterizes Debussy's twentieth-century style, as Dukas observes in recalling his last talks with the composer:

> Au cours des derniers entretiens . . . qui j'ai eus avec lui, il m'a marqué bien souvent le besoin qu'il éprouvait de se simplifier, d'épurer son art, d'en faire disparaître toute apparance de virtuosité professionnelle. . . . Sa nature, au fond, tendait à s'exprimer par des moyens sans complication.[12]

One of Debussy's most endearing qualities as a composer is this ability, similar to that of Verlaine, to conceal his consummate artistry behind an apparent ingenuousness, so that the glimpse of leg or flash of neck in *Les Ingénus* may be taken as metaphors for our occasional successes in penetrating Debussy's craft.

Le Faune

Un vieux faune de terre cuite
Rit au centre des boulingrins,
Présageant sans doute une suite
Mauvaise à ces instants sereins

Qui m'ont conduit et t'ont conduite,
—Mélancoliques pèlerins,—
Jusqu'à cette heure dont la fuite
Tournoie au son des tambourins.

[For translation, see p. 315]

In commenting on his *Fêtes galantes* Verlaine followed the remarks on the Italian comedy and Watteau, quoted earlier, with these words: "On peut trouver aussi là quelques tons savoureux d'aigreur veloutée et de câline méchanceté," after which Verlaine quotes the first few lines of *Pantomime*, *Les Ingénus*, and *Le Faune*.[13]

Certainly one tastes the bittersweet flavor of mischievous caress in the half-serious, half-playful game of time that Verlaine sets spinning in *Le Faune*. Time, as portrayed by Verlaine, has none of the fixity that

[12] Quoted by Brussel in "Claude Debussy et Paul Dukas," *Revue Musicale* 7 (1926):105.

[13] Paul Verlaine, *Oeuvres Posthumes*, Volume III (Paris: Albert Messein, 1929), p. 167.

characterizes most of man's artifice: neither the unchanging mold of the terra-cotta faun (malleable earth baked into permanence) nor the perfect consistency of the bowling green (irregular growth manicured into a surface). Time, as reflected here, follows not the monotonous order of a straight-line continuum, but rather the sinuous spiraling of a whirling dance.

Expressions of time hover about the poem, refusing to submit to the rigid order of past-present-future. The "vieux faune" has evidently been there for some time, looking toward the future in the expressions "présageant" and "suite mauvaise." The "instants sereins" of the melancholy pilgrims refuse to be pinned down in time, as *ces* refers to "these moments" in the first stanza but suddenly becomes "those moments" as one crosses into the second stanza. "Cette heure" presumably means the present moment, but a few words later the instant vanishes.

The poem itself bears the imprint of the spiral, a single sentence coiling in toward the center as surely as the pilgrims are attracted toward the faun, then the identification of the pilgrims (whose gender Verlaine establishes in an elegant conceit), and the reversal of direction outwards, as time flees to the sound of the drums.

We have probably identified the woodland deity with Pan, and supply in our minds his traditional pipe. The "tambourin" is a small drum, attached at the waist and played with a stick, while the other hand fingers the pipe. Verlaine's use of the plural may intend a two-headed drum, whose monotonous alternation of sounds, reflected in Verlaine's use of but two rhymes, accompanied the old Provençal dance known as a "tambourin."

The monotonous rhythm of the drum accompanies the "monomanie" of the pilgrims, while the spiraling dance is the only outward reflection of their melancholy, that "délire roulant exclusivement sur une série d'idées tristes" (Littré). While we need not pursue the "inhibition of motor and psychomotor functions" which accompanies the state of melancholy, we note that no verbs are associated with the human figures, that the subject of the poem remains the dance of time.

Debussy's setting opens with a brilliant solo line in the piano, to be played *ainsi qu'une flûte,* followed by the soft, insistent beat of the drum, *très lointain, sans nuances, mais pourtant bien rythmé.* The flutelike melody joins the drum ostinato at measure 7, *avec une expression sourde.* The dynamic level of this lightfooted *tambour* remains quiet throughout, from the opening *piano* to the closing *pianissimo e perdendosi . . . plus rien.*

Reflecting the relatively subordinate position of the human figures in the poem, the voice appears in fewer than half the measures of the song, and the vocal melody, when it does appear, plays within the confines of a single octave, the natural range of the flute. Debussy's harmonies, freed from strict progression like time freed from continuum, whirl in a spiral to the accompaniment of the underlying perfect fifth. The right hand builds first chords of the ninth then chords of the eleventh. The first real sense of harmonic progression comes in measures 23–25, where V^7 / IV resolves to IV at the text "qui m'ont conduit," but the repetition of V^7 / IV in measure 26 remains unresolved, as the harmonies continue their "delirium" traveling along a series of seventh chords. As the voice concludes, the piano accompaniment sustains a dominant harmony which resolves to the same complex tonic harmony which opened the piece.

Debussy's depth of penetration in Verlaine's poem contrasts with the delightful but relatively monochromatic treatment of *Mandoline*, another poem from the *Fêtes galantes* in which a musical instrument serves as a unifying element. The delicate reserve of Debussy's setting of *Le Faune*, his attentiveness to "orchestrating" the piano accompaniment, and the subtle interaction of complex harmonies over the constant drum ostinato seem to provide for Verlaine's text "quelques tons savoureux d'aigreur veloutée et de câline méchanceté."

Colloque sentimental

Dans le vieux parc solitaire et glacé,
Deux formes ont tout à l'heure passé.

Leurs yeux sont morts et leurs lèvres sont molles,
Et l'on entend à peine leurs paroles.

Dans le vieux parc solitaire et glacé,
Deux spectres ont évoqué le passé.

—Te souvient-il de notre extase ancienne?
—Pourquoi voulez-vous donc qu'il m'en souvienne?

—Ton coeur bat-il toujours à mon seul nom?
Toujours vois-tu mon âme en rêve?—Non.

—Ah! les beaux jours de bonheur indicible
Où nous joignions nos bouches!—C'est possible.

—Qu'il était bleu, le ciel, et grand, l'espoir!
—L'espoir a fui, vaincu, vers le ciel noir.

Tels ils marchaient dans les avoines folles,
Et la nuit seule entendit leurs paroles.

[For translation, see p. 315]

The *fêtes galantes* are over, the old park is deserted and ice-covered on an evening in winter. Two figures have just gone by. Who are they? Verlaine tells us nothing, using words like *formes* and *spectres* to cloak the two characters in the anonymity of death.

The structure of the poem, the only poem of the collection in rhymed couplets, represents the colloquy. The repetition of rhymes at the beginning and end of the poem sets off the dialogue: a b a (dialogue) b. The repetition of details describing the setting in the third couplet only makes us more aware of how little we know about the two characters. Their words appear without explanatory remarks; even their respective genders remain unstated, although one supposes that the woman speaks familiarly to the man while he uses the more respectful *vous.* Two specters have just come to evoke the past.

The speeches of the dialogue are rather elevated in tone, as if the characters were speaking lines, or exchanging vows. The language seems appropriate to a certain solemnity or nobility of occasion, as reflected in the use of the *passé simple* in the last line of the poem. She calls on him to recall their former life; he wonders why she is trying to resurrect something which has ended. More persistantly she recalls sentiments that he might have spoken at the beginning of their romance, but which he can no longer avow. Finally she evokes her memory of the past in rapturous phrases, to which he responds first with an ambivalent "c'est possible," then, picking up her last word, *espoir,* he declares that hope has fled, defeated, that the blue sky of her ecstatic vision has grown dark. *L'espoir*—the future which had once been anticipated—has been defeated by the passage of time; there is no longer a future, only an immutable past. The dialogue ends, and one hears an ironic echo of the words "Deux spectres ont évoqué le passé" since the past seems not to have had a single identity for the two figures, and because the dialogue has served as much to exorcise the past as to evoke it.

The poem ends and we know little more about the characters than we did at the outset. The kind of language Verlaine uses here suggests that the words exchanged in the colloquy have a heightened significance —in fact, the words which end the poem, which remain in our ears, are "leurs paroles"—but characteristically Verlaine, having made the suggestion, goes no further.

Debussy's setting of *Colloque sentimental* goes beyond most of his songs in exploring the use of musical texture. The systematic investigation of texture has occurred relatively recently in Western music. A concern for organizing the number of notes sounding at any one point, their relative density or separation from one another, the tessitura of the musical fabric, as well as variations of texture—for example, the dropping out of several voices to expose a single held note—all these possibilities have come under closer examination in the twentieth century than ever before. Debussy anticipates and initiates these developments in his late piano music (as well as in his orchestrations), but such considerations also play a part in *Colloque sentimental*, in which attention to texture appears not only as decoration but as an element of structure.

In *Colloque sentimental* the texture varies from a single vocal or piano line to a ten-note piano chord accompanying the voice; the vocal range extends an octave and a sixth while the piano part ranges over nearly six octaves. The song opens with two interweaving whole-tone melodies in the piano, the upper voice containing a motive which appears throughout the opening section setting the first three couplets, and which recurs in measures 49–50 at the end of the colloquy. The first entrance of the voice is accompanied by the evanescent sound of a sustained piano chord, then by silence at "parc solitaire et glacé." The two piano lines return briefly at "deux formes." The repetition of the line "Dans le vieux parc solitaire" is sung over a piano chord whose disposition of open fifths conveys a feeling of emptiness.

The middle section of the song, the dialogue proper, contains perhaps the longest pedal tone to be found in Debussy's music, a repeated A which continues without interruption for thirty-two measures.[14] The suppression of main beats in this monotone produces a

[14] Cf. the long, but interrupted, pedal point in *Soirée dans Grenade.*

syncopation whose tension is much like the tension we feel in listening to two people who are not quite speaking to the same subject. In fact, Debussy increases the syncopation at the point where the woman tries to insist upon their one-time unanimity: "où nous joignions nos bouches!"

During the dialogue we hear rolled diminished seventh chords, *très expressif, mélancolique et lointain,* going high into the piano range. From time to time the "nightingale" motive from *En sourdine* ("voix de notre désespoir") returns as if to link *Colloque sentimental* with the first song in the first series of *Fêtes galantes.*[15] Throughout this section the piano part remains elevated above the pedal tone during the woman's speeches, rising to an extreme at the sixth couplet. The vocal melody reaches its highest point on the word *indicible,* as if to suggest that the voice is incapable of expressing the magnitude of that one-time (or imagined) joy.

The man's first response centers around the pitch a tritone from the pedal point, creating a dissonance which remains unresolved. The second response, a monosyllable, is accompanied by a root position chord followed by a dominant ninth chord, *très expressif et soutenu,* unresolved in measure 42, but picked up and expanded during the woman's final speech, then shattered in an unrelated diminished seventh chord which accompanies the man's final speech. The vocal melody drops to its lowest point on the word *noir.* The chords never resolve, but only vanish, leaving only the pedal tone.

The final couplet returns to the original key, accompanied by piano chords of irregular rhythms, as if to convey the motion of the word

[15] Bornecque suggests a poetic connection between the two poems, observing that essential words of lines 5–6 in *En sourdine*

Fondons nos *âmes,* nos *coeurs*
Et nos *sens extasiés* . . .

appear transposed in lines 7–10 of *Colloque sentimental*:

Te souvient-il de notre *extase ancienne?*
. . . .
Ton coeur bat-il toujours à mon seul nom?
Toujours voix-tu *mon âme* en rêve?—Non.
Ah! les beaux jours de bonheur indicible
Où nous *joignions* nos bouches. . . .

The elements of fusion in the former poem have become dissociated in the latter. *Lumières sur les* "Fêtes galantes," p. 177.

marcher, putting one foot in front of the other. The "nightingale" motive of the middle section returns, now without the rolled chords, in a widely spaced texture—as the night swallows up the words—which dies away to a single descending line, *plus rien.* The song ends with a staccato octave in the bass, whose disappearance leaves an unstable chord in the right hand.

Debussy was aware that his concern for musical texture was ahead of his time.

> Car nous en sommes encore à la "marche d'harmonie," et rares sont ceux-là à qui suffit la beauté du son! J'ose vous parler de cela à vous qui êtes sensibles plus que les "musiciens" à cette émotion qui commence à cette *frontière* qu'ils ne peuvent franchir! [16]

Debussy's word *frontière* aptly describes the new territory into which he ventured in exploring "la beauté du son" in the last set of *Fêtes galantes.* The explorations carried him even further in the *Trois Poèmes de Stéphane Mallarmé.*

[16] "Trois Lettres de Claude Debussy à Bernardino Molinari," *Suisse Romande,* Sér, 3 (1939):55.

11

MALLARMÉ II: *Trois Poemes*

In 1891 Mallarmé was interviewed by Jules Huret, representing the *Echo de Paris.* Mallarmé's responses were published under the title *L'Évolution littéraire.*

> Perhaps more accurately than any other of his works, *The Evolution of Literature* evokes Mallarmé's style on those Tuesday evenings when he stood chain-smoking and whispering literary theories in front of the white porcelaine stove at 89 Rue de Rome, *au troisième.* One of the superb conversationalists (or monologuists) of his time (quiet of speech and manner and possessed of a delicate sense of humor), he drew some of the greatest minds to these *causeries:* André Gide, Paul Valéry, Paul Claudel, Paul Verlaine, Paul Gauguin and Claude Debussy. But no lesson was taught and none of the disciples recorded the master's sayings. Hence the value of *Evolution.*[1]

[1] Bradford Cook, *Mallarmé: Selected Prose Poems, Essays and Letters* (Baltimore: Johns Hopkins Press, 1956), p. 118.

Between 1901 and 1914 Debussy wrote music criticism for several Paris journals. His occasional observations on the nature of music, some of which were collected in his book *Monsieur Croche antidilettante*, were obviously influenced by his attendance at those *mardis chez Mallarmé*. The selections given below, drawn from Mallarmé's *Evolution* and Debussy's critical writings, indicate the overlapping of thought between poet and musician.

Mallarmé opposes the direct presentation of objects in poetry as practiced, for example, by the Parnassians. Such directness destroys the sense of mystery which Mallarmé feels is essential to poetry:

> La contemplation des objets, l'image s'envolant des rêveries suscitées par eux, sont le chant: les Parnassiens, eux, prennent la chose entièrement et la montrent: par là ils manquent de mystère; ils retirent aux esprits cette joie délicieuse de croire qu'ils créent.[2]

Debussy opposes the direct imitation of natural objects in music as practiced, for example, by Beethoven in his Pastoral Symphony. The imitation of the nightingale and the cuckoo belong to the craft of the watchmaker more than to nature. The mystery of nature cannot be captured by precise measurement but must be evoked. Debussy prefers those pages in Beethoven's music which have this quality of evocation:

> Combien certaines pages du vieux maître contiennent d'expression plus profonde de la beauté d'un paysage, cela simplement parce qu'il n'y a plus imitation directe mais transposition sentimentale de ce qui est "invisible" dans la nature. Rend-on le mystère d'une forêt en mesurant la hauteur de ses arbres? Et n'est-ce pas plutôt sa profondeur insondable qui déclanche l'imagination.[3]

The image of the forest appears in Mallarmé's *Crise de vers* where the poet renounces slavish description in favor of sensitivity to feeling:

> Abolie, la prétention, esthétiquement une erreur, quoiqu'elle régît les chefs-d'oeuvre, d'inclure au papier subtil du volume autre chose que par exemple l'horreur de la forêt, ou le tonnerre muet épars au feuillage; non le bois intrinsèque et dense des arbres.[4]

[2] Stéphane Mallarmé, *Oeuvres Complètes*, ed. Henri Mondor and G. Jean-Aubry (Paris: Bibliothèque de la Pléiade, 1965), p. 869.

[3] Claude Debussy, *Monsieur Croche et autres écrits*, ed. François Lesure (Paris: Gallimard, 1970), p. 94.

[4] Mallarmé, *Oeuvres Complètes*, pp. 365–366.

Mallarmé prefers a poetry of allusion, a poetry of suggestion rather than statement. Instead of presenting an object directly, the poet should evoke it little by little:

> *Nommer* un objet, c'est supprimer les trois quarts de la jouissance du poème qui est faite de definer peu à peu: le *suggérer,* voilà le rêve. C'est le parfait usage de ce mystère qui constitute le symbole: évoquer petit à petit un objet pour montrer un état de l'âme, ou, inversement choisir un objet et en dégager un état d'âme, par une série de déchiffrements.[5]

Debussy asserts that music can best accomplish this kind of evocation because it is not fixed in time or space. The painter can depict a scene only in one particular instant but the musician can evoke nature even while it moves and capture the "immense palpitation" of the universe:

> Or, la musique est précisement l'art qui est le plus près de la nature, celui qui tend le piège le plus subtil. Malgré leurs prétentions de traducteurs-assermentés, les peintres et les sculpteurs ne peuvent nous donner de la beauté de l'univers qu'une interprétation assez libre et toujours fragmentaire. Ils ne saisissent et ne fixent qu'un seul de ses aspects, un seul de ses instants: seuls, les musiciens ont le privilège de capter toute la poésie de la nuit et du jour, de la terre et du ciel, d'en reconstituer l'atmosphère et d'en rythmer l'immense palpitation.[6]

Poetry of allusion does not create things but seizes on the relationships between them. Such a poetry approaches the condition of music.

> . . . les choses existent, nous n'avons pas à les créer; nous n'avons qu'à en saisir les rapports; et ce sont les fils de ces rapports qui forment les vers et les orchestres.[7]

Debussy likewise believes that music should seize the relationships between nature and the imagination:

> Je voulais à la musique une liberté qu'elle contient peut-être plus que n'importe quel art, n'étant pas bornée à une reproduction

[5] *Ibid.,* p. 869.

[6] Debussy, *Monsieur Croche*, pp. 239–240.

[7] Mallarmé, *Oeuvres Complètes*, p. 871.

> plus ou moins exacte de la nature, maix aux correspondances mystérieuses entre la Nature et l'Imagination.[8]

Debussy was perhaps thinking of Mallarmé—perhaps the Mallarmé who advised Henri Cazalis to omit the beginning and end of what he wrote—when he wrote this plea for greater purity and simplicity in music:

> Epurons notre musique. Appliquons-nous à la décongestionner. Cherchons à obtenir une musique plus nue. Gardons-nous de laisser étouffer l'émotion sous l'amoncellement des motifs et des dessins superposés: comment en rendrions-nous la fleur ou la force en conservant la préoccupation de tous ces détails d'écriture, en maintenant une impossible discipline dans la meute grouillante des petits thèmes qui se bousculent et se chevauchent pour mordre aux jambes le pauvre sentiment qui cherche bientôt son salut dans la fuite! En règle générale, toutes les fois, qu'en art, on pense à compliquer une forme ou un sentiment, c'est qu'on ne sait pas ce qu'on veut dire.[9]

Certainly Debussy's twentieth-century settings of Mallarmé are written in a purer, more "uncongested" style than, say, the Baudelaire songs of a quarter of a century earlier.

Debussy anticipates his treatment of Mallarmé's texts in this undated letter to Chausson, praising Mallarmé's ability to draw a work of art from a single idea.

> Trop souvent nous songeons au cadre avant d'avoir le tableau, et quelquefois la richesse de celui-ci nous fait passer sur l'indigence de l'idée. . . . On gagnerait, il me semble, à prendre le parti contraire, c'est-à-dire à trouver le dessin parfait d'une idée et de n'y mettre alors que juste ce qu'il faudrait d'ornements. . . . Regardez la pauvreté de symbole cachée dans plusieurs des derniers sonnets de Mallarmé, où pourtant le métier d'ouvrier d'art est porté à ses dernière limites.[10]

We think of Debussy's desire, quoted earlier, to write music in which a single motive would serve for the entire composition.

The *mardis chez Mallarmé* continued almost up to the poet's death. In

[8] Debussy, *Monsieur Croche*, p. 61.

[9] *Ibid.*, pp. 241–242.

[10] "Correspondance inédite de Claude Debussy et Ernest Chausson," *Revue Musicale* 7 (1926):122.

1913, fifteen years later, his complete collected poems were published for the first time. In that same year Debussy set three of these poems, and dedicated them "à la mémoire de Stéphane Mallarmé et en très respectueux hommage à Madame E. Bonniot (Née G. Mallarmé.)"

Soupir

Mon âme vers ton front où rêve, ô calme soeur,
Un automne jonché de taches de rousseur,
Et vers le ciel errant de ton oeil angélique
Monte, comme dans un jardin mélancolique,
Fidèle, un blanc jet d'eau soupire vers l'Azur!
—Vers l'Azure attendri d'Octobre pâle et pur
Qui mire aux grands bassins sa langueur infinie
Et laisse, sur l'eau morte où la fauve agonie
Des feuilles erre au vent et creuse un froid sillon,
Se traîner le soleil jaune d'un long rayon.

[For translation, see p. 316]

Like some of Verlaine's shorter poems, *Soupir* consists of a single sentence, but unlike, say, *Le Faune*, Mallarmé's sentence departs considerably from the word order of ordinary speech. Although the poetic sentence begins properly enough with a subject—"mon âme"—we have to wait until the fourth line for the verb—"monte." The independent clause which "comme" introduces does not appear until the following line, after the adverb "fidèle" and the adverbial phrase "dans un jardin mélancolique." In the second half of the poem the verb "laisse" has to wait several lines for its infinitive complement, "se traîner." If we pare away all the relative clauses, appositive phrases, and secondary modifiers, we are left with the proposition:

Mon âme monte vers ton front comme un blanc jet d'eau soupire vers l'Azur.

In the actual poem, in place of "mon âme monte," Mallarmé gives us "mon âme *vers*." The unusual position of the preposition calls attention to the fourfold appearance of the word in the space of ten lines:

vers ton front
vers le ciel
vers l'Azur!
—Vers l'Azur.

The repetition of the word *Azur*, which Mallarmé frequently uses as a symbol for the ideal, reinforces the upward direction suggested by these four prepositional phrases: "vers ton front," then higher, "vers le ciel," and finally "vers l'Azur," toward the ideal. "L'Azur," at the very center of the poem, represents the culmination of an upward movement expressed both in the phrases beginning with "vers" and in the verbs *monter* and *soupirer.*

The ideal, however, by definition can never be attained. It is not

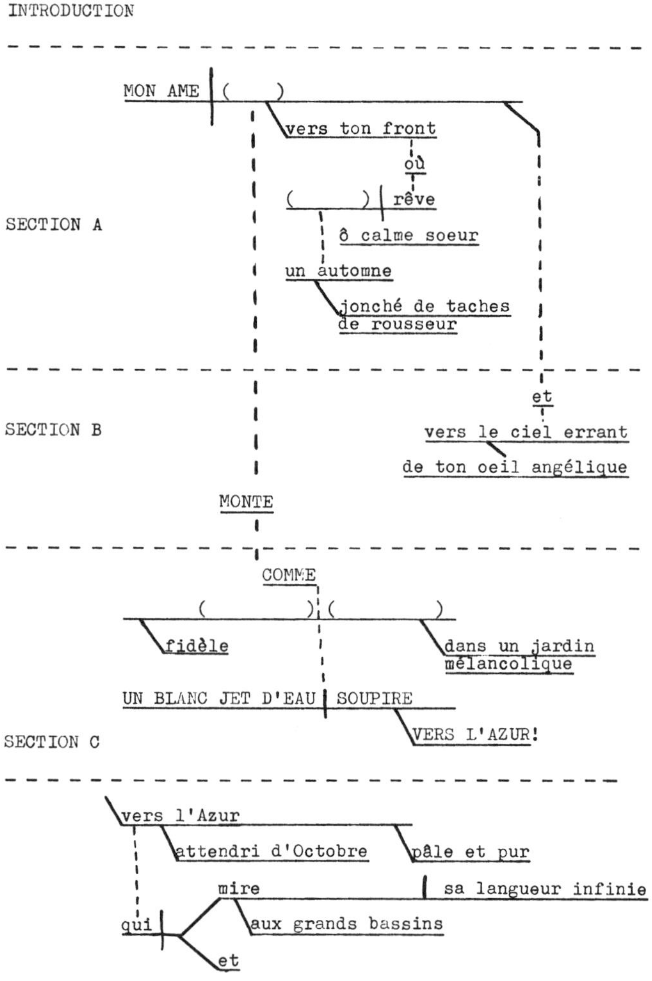

Example 1

Example 1 *(continued)*

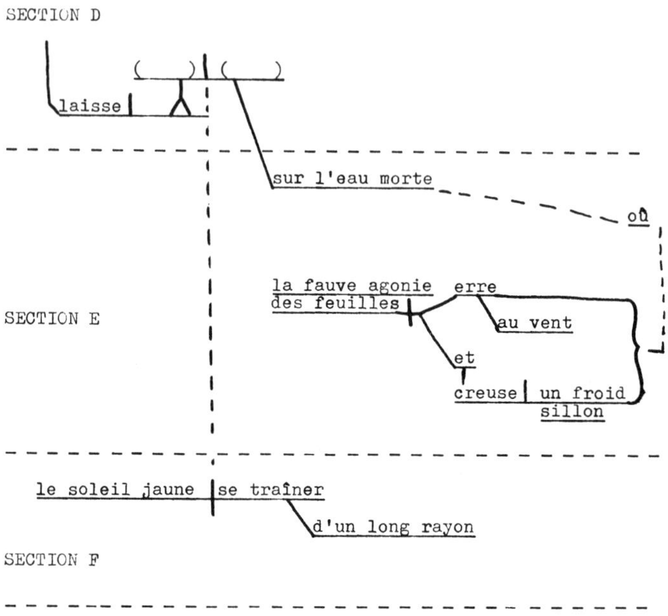

"mon âme" which ascends toward "L'Azur," after all, but "un blanc jet d'eau," in which water comes down as well as going up. Moreover, the verb associated with the fountain is not *monter* but *soupirer,* an ambiguous word which includes both sighs of aspiration and sighs of resignation. The Azure reflects its infinite languor in great pools of still water. Poetically, "l'Azur . . . qui mire" in the second half of the poem reflects "le ciel" from the first half, just as "errant" in line 3 is mirrored by "erre" in line 9. Like water falling into a fountain, so the leaves of "un automne jonché de taches de rousseur" die and fall, in a "fauve agonie." As the leaves wander windward they plow a cold furrow, reflected above by the last rays of the sun.

This mirror effect can also be found in the syntactical structure of the poem. The first half contains all the forward movement—the subject and the verb. The second half is only an extended prepositional phrase, a release of the tension built up in the first half. "Vers l'Azur" is the center of symmetry for this reflection, just as it is the apex of the up-and-down motion.

Debussy's setting of this poem may be regarded as an attempt to sort out the various phrases and clauses that complicate its grammatical structure. The poem itself can be divided syntactically into six sections, three on each half of the central phrase, "vers l'Azur." In the diagrammatic representation of the poem which follows, empty parentheses stand for the "normal" positions of the displaced words, with dotted lines leading to their actual positions in the text (Example 1).

Variations in the density of the musical texture and in the tessitura of melody and accompaniment divide Debussy's song into six sections, corresponding to the divisions in the poem:

Section	*Text*	*Measure*	*Description*
Introduction		1–6	piano alone
A	Mon âme . . . rousseur	7–10	voice with a few chords
B	Et vers . . . Monte	11–12	voice alone
C	comme . . . vers l'Azur!	13–17	high tessitura of accompaniment
D	Vers l'Azur . . . Et laisse	18–22	wide range of accompaniment
E	sur l'eau . . . sillon	23–26	low tessitura of voice and accompaniment
F	Se traîner . . . rayon	27–31	high tessitura of accompaniment

The midpoint of the song, between sections C and D, is the same as that of the poem, the repeated phrase "vers l'Azur." Section C sets off the essential simile of the poem, the comparison of "mon âme" to "un blanc jet d'eau." Section E isolates that part of the text which separates "laisse" from its infinitive complement "se traîner."

Debussy further distinguishes the sections by a kind of word-painting. Making use of a device known to composers since the fourteenth century, Debussy chooses from each section some word or phrase and gives it a musical depiction. The introduction presents the striving "Soupir" motive which returns at the end of the song (Example 2). The accompaniment of section A, broken chords followed by

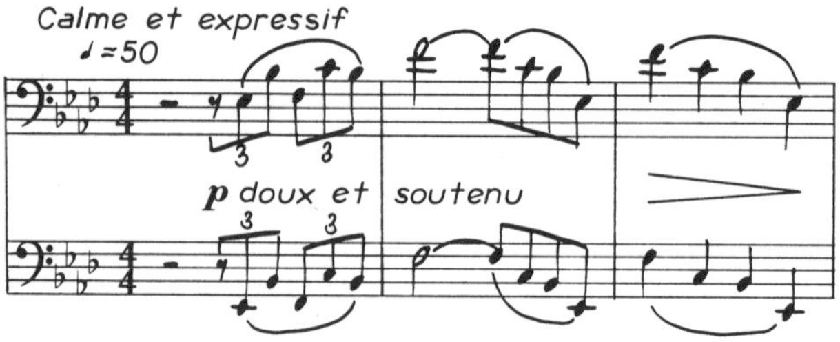

Example 2

pianissimo staccato notes, seems to be an illustration of the phrase "jonché de taches de rousseur" (Example 3). In section B the piano remains

Example 3

silent. In section C the repeated octaves represent the rising and falling pattern of the fountain, and resemble the figure which Debussy used in setting *Le Jet d'eau.* In section D the accompaniment contains several figures which may be intended as the musical representation of a languorous sigh. The use of a descending second for this purpose has become a musical convention for expressing melancholy.[11] The idea of reflection—"L'Azur . . . qui mire"—is suggested by the inversion of a semitone, ascending in measure 20, descending in measure 21 (Example 4). The accompaniment of section E, marked *murmurando,* suggests dead

[11] Deryck Cook, *The Language of Music* (London: Oxford University Press, 1959), p. 76.

Example 4

leaves in stagnant water through the use of static harmonies and the dark low notes of the piano. The pulsating rhythm in the accompaniment of section F seems to be a representation of "se traîner." The idea of "dragging" is enhanced by the slower overall tempo of this section.

In addition to these accompanimental figures, derived from images in the text, each section also contains some reference to the "Soupir" motive, some suggestion of aspiration toward the Ideal. In the introduction it is the "Soupir" motive itself. In section A the staccato notes rise in octaves. In section C this octave motion becomes the upwards and downwards cycle of the fountain. In section D, which corresponds to the beginning of the second half of the poem, the transposition of major and minor seconds conveys this effect. The difference between the accompaniment to this section and that of the preceding sections should be noted: just as the first half of the poem implies an upward striving, while the second half suggests a falling, dying motion, so the accompanimental motives of the song rise (section A), are bent into the rising and falling of the fountain (section C), then become essentially falling figures (section D). The octave transpositions at the end of section E suggest the "Soupir" image, while the motive itself returns at the end of section F.

A distinction between longer and shorter note durations separates certain key words of the song. Since the prevailing note value is the eighth note, with a few connecting quarter notes, we are interested in the cases where there are half notes, or several quarter notes, or notes set off by rests. The following examples show how Debussy has used rhythmic values to emphasize important words (Example 5).

Example 5

Variations of pitch also serve the composer who would use music to punctuate a poem. In previous examples we have seen the care with which Debussy chooses which words should fall at the extremes of the vocal range. In *Soupir*, however, it may be more interesting to see how Debussy shapes the overall melodic curve in each section. Just as a series of octaves can stand for a fountain in particular or for cyclical motion in general, so a repeated oscillation of the melodic curve can suggest periodicity. Naturally one cannot compose melodies which are perfectly regular, for they would be dull. The curves in the illustrations below, then, are meant to indicate the general contour of the melody, not to represent graphs of the actual pitches (Example 6).

The melodic curve in section C, which remains almost on a straight line until the eruption of *Fidèle*, reinforces the emphasis on this word which we observed in our discussion of note values. The pitches of the word *Fidèle* are incorporated into the oscillation of "un blanc jet d'eau": the pitches E-C-A♭ are prolonged as E-G-A♭-C-A♭-G-C-G-A♭-C. In section E the generally low tessitura acts like a recitation, spoken *sotto voce*, in isolating the clause which separates "laisse" from "se traîner."

Debussy uses tonality in *Soupir* to translate into musical terms the up-and-down motion on which the structure of the poem is based. If the key center of the piece, A♭, stands for the earthbound, the "jardin mélancolique," then the aspiration toward the ideal can be represented by an "escape" from this tonality, and the resignation of the sigh represented by a return to the original key. In the introduction, for example, the "Soupir" motive, although in the A♭ pentatonic scale, contains no A♭, and it is only in the fourth measure that we find the perfect fifth A♭–E♭ which ties the music down to earth. The tonal progression of the song is summarized below:

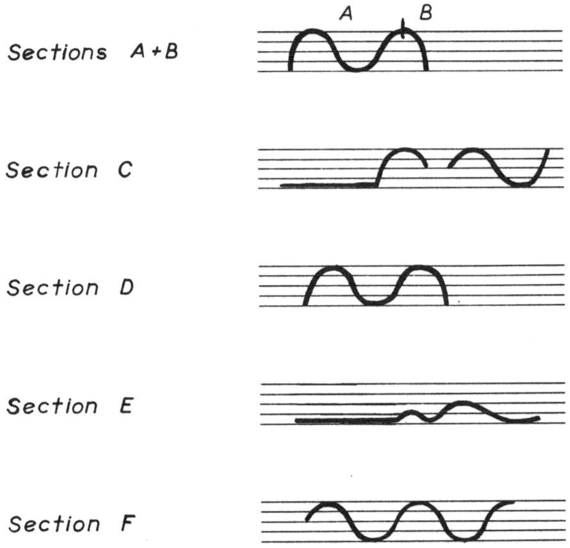

Example 6

Introduction A♭ pentatonic
Section A A♭ pentatonic melody over enriched diminished seventh chords

Section B	E pentatonic melody ending G♯ (= A♭)–E
Section C	E pedal, enriched A♭ chords, then C–A♭; the section may be seen as an ornamentation of the augmented triad A♭–C–E
Section D	A♭ pedal, variety of chords
Section E	Whole-tone (D pedal)—D♭–C
Section F	C–B♭–A♭ (ending A♭ pentatonic)

The first three sections of the song depart frequently from A♭. While section A has a melody based on the A♭ pentatonic scale, section B, "Et vers le ciel errant de ton oeil angélique," is in E pentatonic, ending with G♯(= A♭)–E on the word *Monte.* Section C has a pedal on E throughout, with chords on C and A♭. The word *Fidèle*, already isolated rhythmically, is set to the pitches E–C–A♭, the three primary tonal centers of the song. It is this section which introduces the images of the fountain. The last three sections of the piece, corresponding to the second half of the poem, draw progressively closer to A♭. Section D has a variety of chords which fit no single key, with A♭ as a pedal. Section E begins in the whole-tone scale, with D as a pedal, then moves to D♭ and C. Section F continues this downward progression of centers, going from C through B♭ back to A♭.

Now the idea of departing from a key and returning to it is no novelty of Debussy's invention. This principle has been the basis of nearly all Western music written between the seventeenth and twentieth centuries. The tonal movement in *Soupir*, however, does not conform to traditional rules of harmonic progression. The root movement leaps from A♭ to E then subsides by whole-step to A♭ like the rising and falling of a fountain or a sigh.

The tonal scheme of *Soupir* organizes all the elements that punctuate the poem: distinctive accompanimental motives, carefully chosen note durations and melodic contours. The punctuation of a poem is one of the most basic functions of a song setting; in a poem with the grammatical complexity of *Soupir* it is also one of the most important.

Placet futile

Princesse! à jalouser le destin d'une Hébé
Qui poind sur cette tasse au baiser de vos lèvres,

J'use mes feux mais n'ai rang discret que d'abbé
Et ne figurerai même nu sur le Sèvres.

Comme je ne suis pas ton bichon embarbé,
Ni la pastille ni du rouge, ni jeux mièvres
Et que sur moi je sais ton regard clos tombé,
Blonde dont les coiffeurs divins sont des orfèvres!

Nommez-nous . . . toi de qui tant de ris framboisés
Se joignent en troupeau d'agneaux apprivoisés
Chez tous broutant les voeux et bêlant aux délires,

Nommez-nous . . . pour qu'Amour ailé d'un éventail
M'y peigne flûte aux doigts endormant ce bercail,
Princesse, nommez-nous berger de vos sourires.

[For translation, see p. 316]

If Debussy chose from Banville "des poèmes en avance verlainiens" one could say that from Mallarmé he drew texts "d'après Verlaine," for *Placet futile* stands in the literary tradition of the *Fêtes galantes.* "C'est le même ton, à mi-chemin de l'ironie et du sentiment, le même appareil mythologique et pastoral, le même mélange de figures conventionnelles et d'impressions vécues, de saisissante réalité et de libre imagination, le même rococo." [12]

Mallarmé skillfully weaves his themes together: elements of mythology—Hebe, cupbearer of the gods; an oblique reference to her brother Hephaestos, one of "les coiffeurs divins"; Eros, the god of love—combined with elements of eighteenth-century galanterie. "Amor" appears winged with a fan, of which Mallarmé later wrote in *La Dernière Mode*:

> Rien ne vaudra jamais un éventail, riche tant qu'on voudra par sa monture, ou même très simple, mais présentant, avant tout, une valeur idéale. Laquelle? celle d'une peinture: ancienne, de l'école de Boucher, de Watteau, et peut-être par ces maîtres.[13]

In fact, the last tercet of the poem originally read:

Nommez-nous . . . et Boucher sur un rose éventail
Me peindra . . .

[12] René Bray, *La Préciosité et les Précieux* (Paris: Editions Albin Michel, 1948), p. 324.

[13] Stéphane Mallarmé, *La Dernière Mode* (New York: Publications of the Institute of French Studies, 1933), p. 28.

The standard props of eighteenth-century art are all to be found here: bearded lapdogs, pastilles, and assumed appearances. One thinks of Madame de Pompadour, under whose patronage artists like Boucher painted cupids, flutes, and fans, and the great porcelain makers of Sèvres decorated their cups with portraits of Hebe.

For Mallarmé conceived art as a game. He writes in *La Musique et les Lettres*: "A quoi sert cela—A un jeu," [14] and in a letter to Verlaine speaks of the "jeu littéraire." Such games with words, such "jeux mièvres," are the essence of *préciosité*, which Bray describes as "l'art qui joue. . . . Pure construction de l'imagination, il établit sa loi dans l'artifice, son oeuvre ne répond à rien, qu'à elle-même." [15]

The comparison of the lady's laughter to a flock of tame lambs becomes a "métaphore prolongée: le poéte prend une métaphore rebattue et l'interprète à la fois comme métaphore et comme réalité; il en tire une conséquence inattendue." [16] No sooner does the poet evoke the image of lambs than they begin to wander about, "chez tous broutant les voeux et bêlant aux délires." In the first version of the poem the line reads "Qui vont, broutant les coeurs et bêlant aux délires." The poet implies that the lady has been too free with her smiles, feeding on the ardor of those about her. He would become the shepherd—and in pastoral poetry one naturally reads *berger* as *amant*—who would keep the flock under control, "flûte aux doigts endormant ce bercail."

The threefold appearance of the phrase "Nommez-nous" brings to our attention the incantatory power of words to create by naming, reflected in the bit of magic whereby an image can dawn at the touch of a lip, or Cupid can paint a scene on the very fan which provides his wings. "Nommez-nous": the original poem, entitled simply *Placet*, suggests that the wish might be granted. The first quatrain ends, "Et n'ai point, *jusqu'ici*, figuré sur le Sèvres," and the second quatrain contains the more conclusive line "Et qu'avec moi pourtant vous avez succombé." The revisions of the definitive version in line 4 and especially in line 7, however, make the poem clearly a "placet futile."

Bray finds additional examples of *préciosité* in the periphrasis of *Soupir*—"le ciel errant de ton oeil angélique" and "la fauve agonie des

[14] Mallarmé, *Oeuvres complètes*, p. 647.
[15] Bray, *La Préciosité et les Précieux*, p. 396.
[16] *Ibid.*, p. 201.

feuilles"—and the last stanza of *Eventail*, which we shall examine presently. He concludes: "Mallarmé est un précieux: il en a la politesse, le dégoût du banal, la volonté de purisme, l'amour de l'artifice et de l'ornement, le sens du jeu poétique." [17]

As Edward Cone has observed, "It is often the case . . . that the important developments of a composition can be shown to be expansions of striking events in the opening measures." [18] In Debussy's *Placet futile* both the integrity of the work as a whole and the relation of the music to the text develop from the beginning of the song (Example 7).

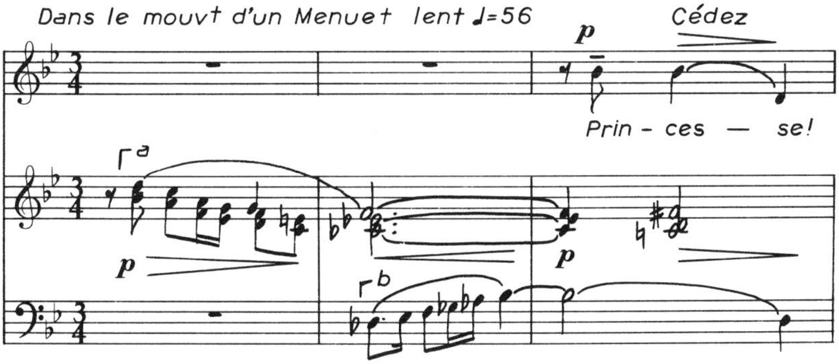

Example 7

Example 8

[17] *Ibid.*, p. 333.

[18] Edward T. Cone, "On the Structure of *Ich folge dir*," *College Music Symposium* 5 (1965):79.

1. The opening measures form the basis for the melodic material of the piece. Motive *a*, in the first measure of the accompaniment, returns in various forms throughout the work (Example 8). Motive *b*, from the

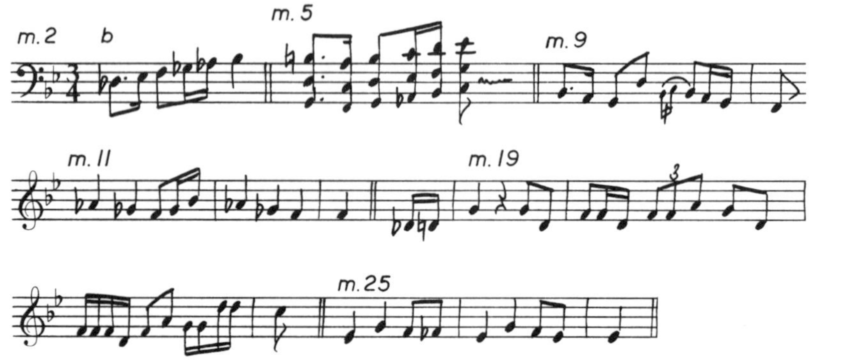

Example 9

second measure of the accompaniment, has the same rhythm as a similar figure in the fifth measure, and combines subtly with motive *a* to generate another set of melodic fragments (Example 9).

Example 10

The motive of a descending sixth appears in the first two notes sung by the voice and recurs twice more during the song (Example 10). The sixth also appears as part of a triad in measure 6, the first of a class of triadic figures (Example 11). When the notes of the triad are sounded

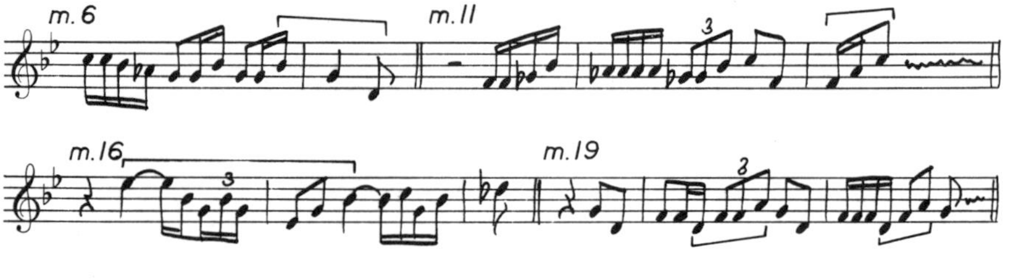

Example 11

together, they produce a chord which serves as the basis for several chordal patterns (Example 12).

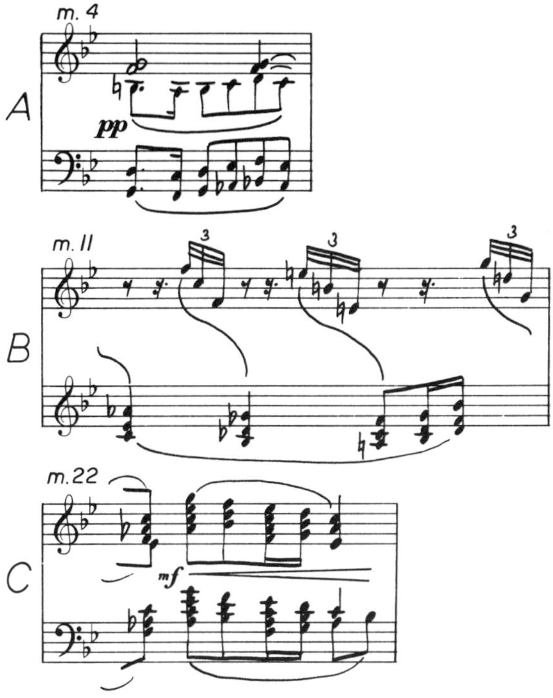

Example 12

2. The opening measures also contain references to two special scales: the pentatonic scale and the whole-tone scale. The melody of motive *a* is pentatonic on F; this motive appears in pentatonic form throughout the piece. There is only one brief passage in which the entire musical texture is drawn from a single pentatonic scale. This occurs at measures 27–28, which are pentatonic on G♭ (Example 13). Motives drawn from the pentatonic scale, however, appear frequently (Example 14).

The chord on the downbeat of measure 2 contains four notes of the whole-tone scale: C♭, D♭, E♭, F. This same chord is found in transposition in measures 14–15, where it is enriched to include the

Example 13

Example 14

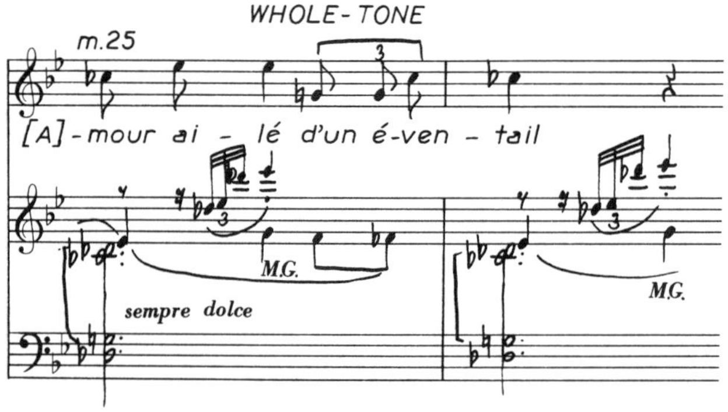

Example 15

entire hexachord. The other hexachord of the whole-tone scale appears in measures 25–26 (Example 15).

3. The opening measures establish the prevailing intervals of the song. The interval of the sixth, which separates the first two notes of the vocal line, is anticipated by motive *a*, which has a range of a sixth. But that interval may also be viewed as a fifth plus a second, as its rhythmic treatment in the first two measures suggests (Example 16). This idea is

Example 16

Example 17

supported by the appearance of motive *a* in measure 6, where it is compressed within the interval of a fifth (Example 17). The interval of a fifth recurs thereafter at various points in the song (Example 18).

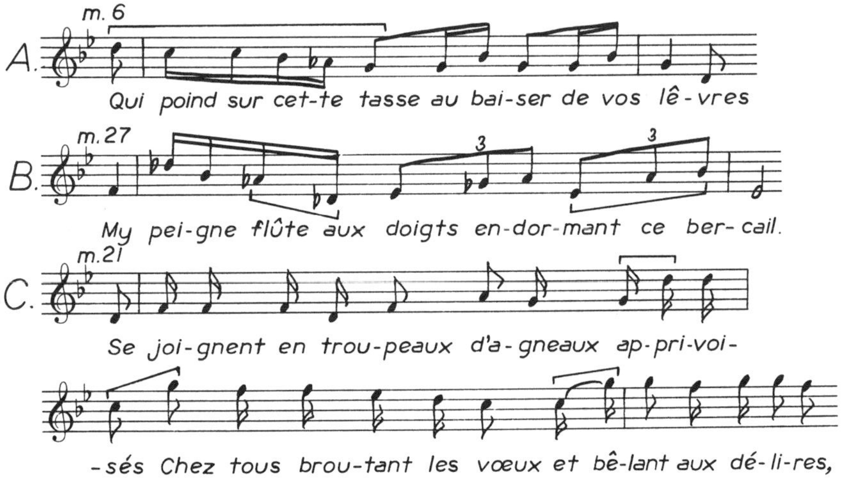

Example 18

Pursuing this line of reasoning, we see that the first three measures of the song contain all the elements of the overall tonal scheme, if the major sixth of motive *a* is regarded as a perfect fifth, D–G, plus a major second, G–F, and if the F♯ at the end of motive *a* is taken to be the enharmonic equivalent of G♭ (Example 19)—after brief references to G

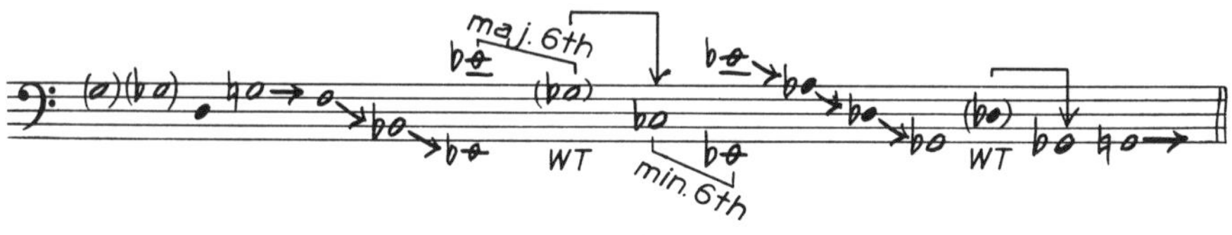

Example 19

and G♭(= F♯) there is a movement from G to F, followed by a descent by perfect fifth: F–B♭–E♭. This pattern is interrupted by the descent of a major sixth; E♭–G♭. (The G♭ section, although written in the whole-tone scale, does function as the dominant of C♭.) After a descent of a minor sixth, C♭–E♭, the downward movement by fifth is resumed: E♭–A♭–D♭–G♭. A second whole-tone section functions as the dominant of G♭, which then leads to G natural, reversing the progression which began the song. The descending fifths and descending major and minor sixths form a close link between this tonal scheme and the material of the opening measure.

At the close of the piece some of the relations are reversed. Motive *a* is altered to outline a *minor* sixth, while the motive of the vocal line is expanded to a *major* sixth (Example 20). The song begins with a melody pentatonic in F but harmonized in such a way as to suggest G minor; the

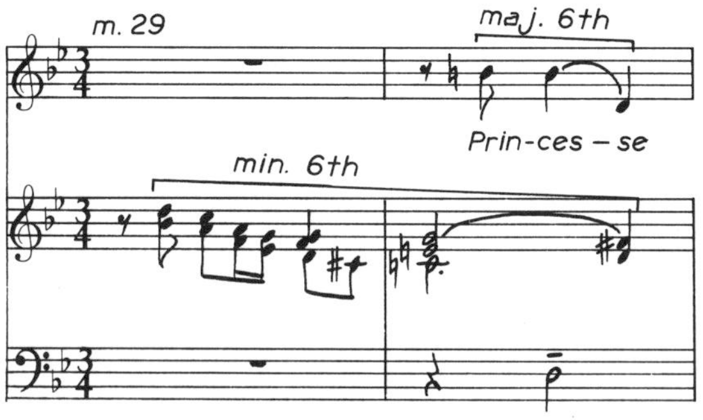

Example 20

song closes with a pentatonic scale on G with the addition of an F natural. The interpolation of this F natural forms a tetrachord—F, G, A, B—which evokes the whole-tone scale. Melodically, harmonically, and tonally, then, the development and conclusion of the song are seen to be expansions of events in the opening measures.

The pentatonic scale appears in melodic fragments throughout the song, and governs the entire texture at the point at which the pastoral images appear most strongly, in measures 27–28, at the words "M'y peigne flûte aux doigts endormant ce bercail." The actual petition, the pleading "Princesse," is set to a descending major sixth. It seems not unreasonable to identify motive *a*—drawn from the pentatonic scale, extending the range of a major sixth—with the "placet."

The whole-tone scale governs the entire musical texture in measures 14–15, at the words "Et que sur moi je sais ton regard clos tombé," the point which most clearly expresses the futility of the entreaty. The pentatonic "placet" and the whole-tone "futile" are joined in the opening of the song and summarized in its ending. The final melody and the grace notes of the accompaniment outline both the desire (G pentatonic scale) and the single note (F natural) which represents its frustration (Example 21).

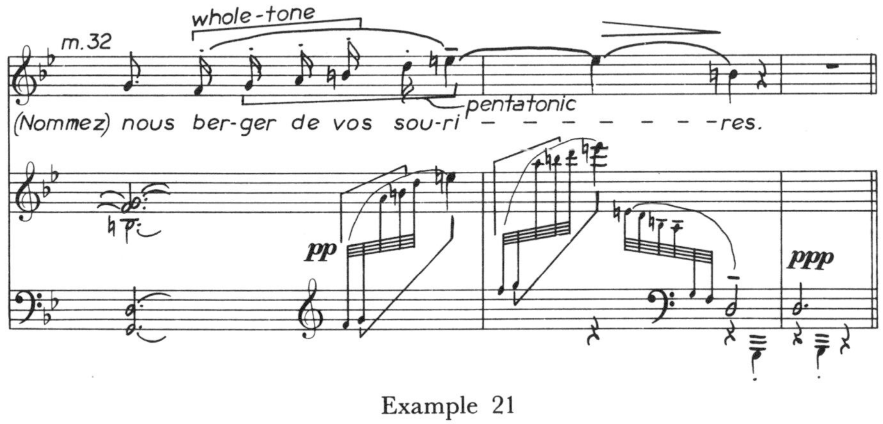

Example 21

In analyzing *Placet futile* we have treated the music in some detail before seeking out textual associations. We have proceeded in this manner partly to overcome two misconceptions that may have crept into the reader's mind as he has followed the discussion up to this point. The first is the notion that a song is but a succession of expressive devices, that all a composer need do to interpret a poem is to place harmonic changes at appropriate places and be discreet in his use of the whole-tone scale. A second possible misconception is the idea that music with a text is easier to write than music without since the unity of the poem will compensate for shortcomings in the music. Both ideas are mistaken, and if we have not troubled to challenge them until now it has been in order to unseat the more persistent misconception that a song can be adequately analyzed without more than a passing reference to the relationship between music and text. By now it should be clear that in Debussy's songs, at least, such an analysis would be incomplete.

A song setting is not simply an interpretation of a poem, although it must bear an intelligible relationship to its text. A song exists alongside the poem as an independent entity whose relation to the text is ultimately unresolvable. It is pointless to ask what the music tells us about the poem that we could not have discovered alone; rather we should ask how the juxtaposition of musical meaning and poetic meaning may lead us to look at each in turn more closely.[19]

Eventail [20]

O rêveuse, pour que je plonge
Au pur délice sans chemin,
Sache, par un subtil mensonge,
Garder mon aile dans ta main.

Une fraîcheur de crépuscule
Te vient à chaque battement
Dont le coup prisonnier recule
L'horizon délicatement.

[19] For a further development of this idea see Edward T. Cone, "Words into Music: The Composer's Approach to the Text," in *Sound and Poetry*, ed. Northrop Frye (New York: Columbia University Press, 1956), pp. 3–15.

[20] Debussy's title; Mallarmé entitled the poem *Autre éventail*. This discussion is based in part on Robert Greer Cohn, *Toward the Poems of Mallarmé* (Berkeley: University of California Press, 1965), pp. 113–116; and Jean-Pierre Richard, *L'Univers imaginaire de Mallarmé* (Paris: Editions du Seuil, 1961), pp. 309–313.

Vertige! voici que frissonne
L'espace comme un grand baiser
Qui, fou de naître pour personne,
Ne peut jaillir ni s'apaiser.

Sens-tu le paradis farouche
Ainsi qu'un rire enseveli
Se couler du coin de ta bouche
Au fond de l'unanime pli!

Le sceptre des rivages roses
Stagnant sur les soirs d'or, ce l'est,
Ce blanc vol fermé que tu poses
Contre le feu d'un bracelet.

[For translation, see p. 317]

Mallarmé was, among other things, an exceptionally gifted occasional poet. He took delight in composing a quatrain which would include the name of a friend or benefactor in a brilliant rhyme. He wrote sixteen *Offrandes à divers du faune* to accompany copies of *L'Après-midi d'un faune*, one of which he sent to Debussy. Among Mallarmé's favorite presents were poems written on a fan—"on" both in the sense that they were about a fan, and that they were actually copied onto the surface of a fan. In addition to these brief *vers de circonstance* Mallarmé composed three *Poésies* on fans, including this *Eventail* for his nineteen-year-old daughter, Geneviève.

It is the fan who speaks, addressing the girl as "Rêveuse." The fan beckons her to hold it in such a way that it may dive into pure, trackless delight. This can be accomplished "par un subtil mensonge." Mallarmé liked to refer to the fan as the wing of a bird (*aile*) which in open position it resembles. The wing gives the illusion of flight, but it is actually held fast in the girl's hand. The lines "Sache . . . main" establish a tension, preserved throughout the poem, between the free and fixed, between the fictive and the real.

With each stroke comes the coolness of twilight, that hour which is neither night nor day, as the fan pushes back the horizon, the line of separation between earth and sky, between reality and imagination. The similarity between the curve of the fan and the curve of the horizon weakens the distinction between the real and the fictive.

"Vertige!" The oscillation of the fan and of reality produces a dizziness in the mind of the dreaming girl. The space between the horizon of the earth and the horizon of the fan trembles uncertainly: belonging to neither the real nor the imaginary it can neither spring up nor subside but remains suspended like a kiss, "fou de naître pour personne."

The girl experiences this fierce paradise as she rests the fan, now closed, at the corner of her mouth. The bird has alighted; the wing has closed into a unanimous fold. The laugh which had been stifled flows to the very depths of the closed fan. The tension is released; that which had been restrained—literally, entombed—is set free. The tension between the real and fictive is likewise resolved as the dreaming girl becomes the sovereign of the world which the fan has revealed. The symbol for a potential other-world has become the scepter which rules the rosy shores colored by the setting sun.

Mallarmé's fan crosses freely between the world of imagination and the world of reality. In the first stanza the fan, securely held in the girl's hand, is also a wing which can fly into pure delight. In the last stanza the scepter is simply this, the "vol fermé" placed against the sun-reflecting bracelet. The two worlds are separated by a narrow boundary, expressed in words like *horizon, crépuscule, rivage,* and *paradis* (etymologically a "place walled in"). We can gain entrance to the other world not by crossing the boundary but by dissolving it in imagination. The passage is "sans chemin"; it is achieved "par un subtil mensonge" which draws back the horizon delicately.

Debussy uses tonality to convey in music this idea of a virtual world, parallel to the real world, which can be entered by dissolving the boundary which ordinarily separates them. The tonal movement in his song setting is from G♭ to F to E. According to the circle of fifths, the classical "chemin" which connects one key to another, these keys are very remote from one another, but if there were some way to dissolve the usual tonal boundaries, they would be very close, only a semitone apart. Debussy produces just this effect through the use of the whole-tone and chromatic scales, both of which—as we have seen in previous examples—have the power to weaken our sense of tonality.

Just as Mallarmé's poem hovers between the real and the virtual, so a good deal of Debussy's song hangs poised between key centers, not part of any harmonic progression but "sans chemin," suspended in the trembling space of atonality. In the third stanza, for example, the dizziness of vertigo is suggested musically by a flurry of sixteenth notes moving by semitone. The chromatic scale combines with the whole-tone scale to express the lack of direction of the void, "fou de naître pour personne." The fourth stanza, by comparison, comes both as a moment of repose after the chromaticism of the "Vertige!" section, and as a point of arrival. From a dreaming perception of the "real" world the girl has come, through the agency of the fan, to the world of imagination. The accompaniment contains the first clear tonic chords which we have heard up to this point. Debussy here uses not a major scale but a pentatonic scale, which he frequently employs to evoke a deliberately archaic atmosphere or something "not from here." [21]

Both a sense of the other-worldly and the archaic are to be found in the fourth stanza of *Eventail.* The word *paradis* has overtones of the mythical Garden of Eden which man formerly inhabited, while *enseveli* can refer to an entombment of long duration. This interpretation is supported by the second of the fan poems in Mallarmé's *Vers de Circonstance*:

> Jadis frôlant avec émoi
> Ton dos de licorne ou de fée,
> Aile ancienne, donne-moi
> L'horizon dans une bouffée.

The only other point of clearly defined tonality comes at the end of the song, which presents a melody in e minor pentatonic over an accompaniment which is first e melodic minor then e harmonic minor. The associations of the pentatonic scale with something "not from here" cause us to reflect back upon the preceding stanzas, and remind us that this fan, now lying in repose against the bracelet, is more than it appears.

The question of tonality in the remainder of the piece is sufficiently complex that it may be well to consider the melody separately from the accompaniment.

[21] Brailoiu cites as examples the oriental quality of *Pagodes*, the mysteriousness of *La Fille aux cheveux de lin,* the pastoral atmosphere of *Placet futile,* and the middle section of the *Prélude à l'après-midi d'un faune* in "Pentatony in Debussy's Music," *Studia Memoriae Belae Bartók Sacra* (Budapest: Publishing House of the Hungarian Academy of Sciences, 1959), pp. 378, 380, 414.

Stanza 1 The melody is chromatic and lacks any consistent tonal center—it is "sans chemin." The presence of the major third in each stanza (circled in the examples) serves as a unifying element (Example 22).

Stanza 2 A suggestion of F major in the first two lines anticipates the "paradis" of the fourth stanza. The moving back of the horizon is set in the whole-tone scale (Example 23).

Example 22

Example 23

Example 24

Sens-tu le pa-ra-dis fa-rou-che Ain-si qu'un rire en-se-ve-li Se cou-
- ler du coin de ta bou-che Au fond de l'u-na-ni-me pli!

Example 25

Le scep-tre des ri-va-ges ro-ses Stag-nants sur les soirs d'or,
ce l'est, Ce blanc vol fer-mé que tu po-ses Con-tre le feu d'un
bra-ce-let.

Example 26

Stanza 3 An F♯ octave on *Vertige!* is followed by major thirds—moving by semitone—which are then inverted to minor sixths (Example 24).

Stanza 4 The entire melody is centered on F, mostly F pentatonic (Example 25).

Stanza 5 The melody is rather chromatic, centering mostly on B then resolving on e minor pentatonic (Example 26).

The accompaniment opens with a rather striking motive which begins in G♭ pentatonic then moves beyond the control of any key center (Example 27). This motive occurs before the words "O rêveuse," after the line "Garder mon aile dans ta main," and in between the words "l'unanime pli!" and "Le sceptre." It seems not unreasonable to identify this motive with the spreading and closing of a fan.

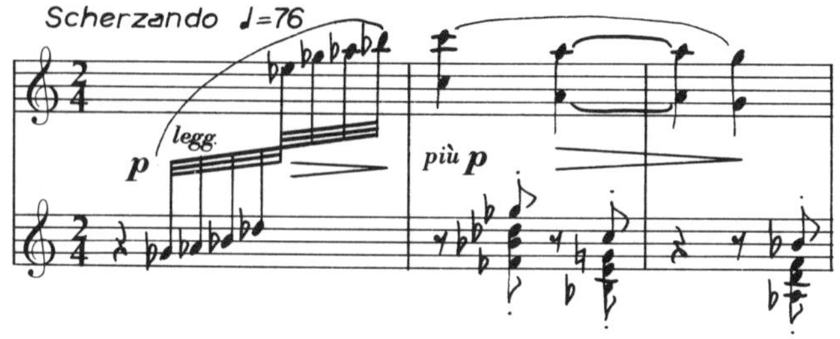

Example 27

Stanza 1 In between occurrences of the fan motive the accompaniment gradually builds up a whole-tone hexachord, with chromatic notes as decoration, by successively emphasizing the pitches F♯–D–G♯–E–C. Only the absence of A♯ prevents it from being a complete hexachord.

Stanza 2 The first half of the stanza prolongs the dominant seventh chords at the end of the fan motive. In the second half of the stanza, whole-tone chords resolve to dominant seventh chords on E.

Stanza 3 Whole-tone elements and chromatic elements combine and the two whole-tone hexachords alternate at a dizzying speed.

Stanza 4 A chromatic succession of dominant seventh chords leads to the extended section in F pentatonic; followed by the recurrence of the fan motive.

Stanza 5 The accompaniment begins with whole-tone chords moving chromatically and ends in e minor with grace notes composed of major thirds moving chromatically.

The tonal scheme which emerges from these details of melody and accompaniment is a twice-repeated movement from G♭(= F♯) to F to E, with the whole-tone and chromatic scales acting in combination to dissolve ordinary harmonic progression between these key centers and to permit direct semitonal movement (Example 28).

The piece as a whole, then, moves over three key centers which are spatially close but tonally rather distant. If our identification of tonality with reality has any validity, the tonal scheme supports Mallarmé's suggestion that the world of imagination is very close to the world of reality in that in certain respects it resembles it closely, but that getting

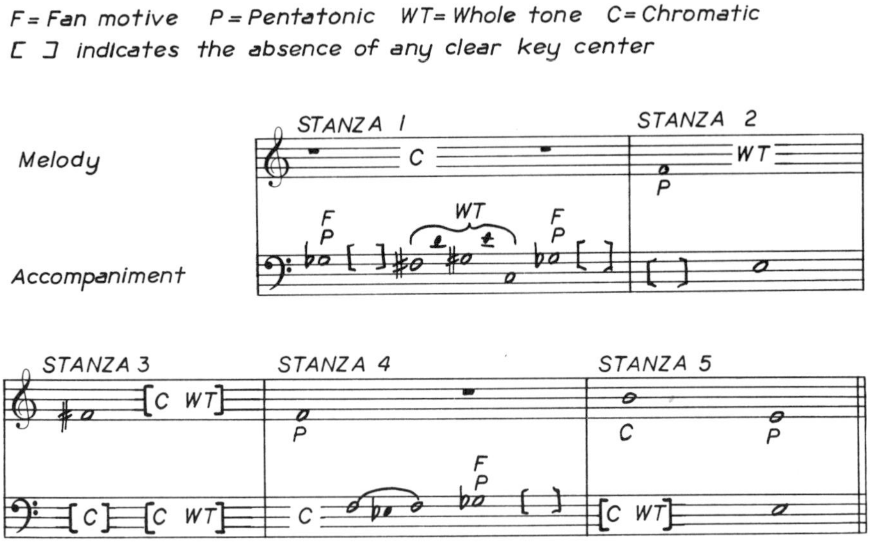

Example 28

there is accomplished by dissolving the ordinary boundaries which separate them. The suggestion of E as a center just before the dizzying plunge into the trackless realm is recapitulated in the conclusion of the piece and reminds us once again of the potency which lies closed within the fan.

The Mallarmé songs were the last which Debussy was to set to music before his death in 1918. Except for a Christmas song on his own text in 1915 they are also his last complete work with a text, for the *Ode à la France*, a cantata on words of Louis Laloy, was never finished. The *Trois poèmes de Stéphane Mallarmé* form a culmination of Debussy's art, both chronologically and artistically, which we shall trace by way of conclusion to this essay.

12

CONCLUSION

"La plus forte influence qu'ait subie Debussy est celle des littérateurs. Non pas celle des musiciens." Debussy learned much from the poets, who helped him to discover his own musical language. Such a strong influence inevitably led to a certain dependence. For Debussy the failure to find suitable words frequently arrested the flow of music, as we observed in the chapter on Banville. What kind of poet could furnish the text Debussy desired?

> Celui qui, disant des choses à demi, me permettra de greffer mon rêve sur le sien; qui concevra des personnages dont l'histoire et la demeure ne seront d'aucun temps, d'aucun lieu; qui ne m'imposera pas, despotiquement, la "scène à faire" et me laissera libre, ici ou là, d'avoir plus d'art que lui, et de parachever son ouvrage.[1]

Debussy found such a poet only once: the Maeterlinck of *Pelléas et Mélisande*. The last two decades of Debussy's life witnessed an unsuccessful attempt to compose a worthy successor to his only opera.

Debussy's most consistent achievements in uniting music and word

[1] Maurice Emmanuel, *Pelléas et Mélisande de Debussy* (Paris: Editions Mellottée, 1933), p. 35.

came in his songs. Toulet accurately remarked, "Vous avez un goût très-pur en littérature," and the generally high level of literary value in the texts Debussy chose elicited some of his finest work as a composer.[2] Werner Danckert observes that Debussy's field of experimentation was the song, and we have seen in Debussy's songs the development of music as a language. Debussy's *Trois poèmes de Stéphane Mallarmé*, considered individually, represent the culmination of three lines of development within Debussy's expressive vocabulary. Considered together they form a compendium of the musical devices which Debussy uses to relate poetry to music. Each of our examples, whether from Banville, Verlaine, Baudelaire, Louÿs, or Debussy himself, can be placed, with some overlapping, into the three categories represented by these Mallarmé songs.

SOUPIR

One of the most basic functions of a song setting is the punctuation of a poem, the sorting out and identifying of contrasting elements within the poem. The most direct method of punctuation is the association of a single melody with two different lines of text, either in the vocal line or the accompaniment. In theory, a composer could use practically any identifiable bit of melody for this purpose, but in practice he will try to invent a melody that sounds somehow appropriate to the text. The vagueness of this formulation reflects the great latitude of expression which we find among composers setting the same kind of poetic idea. No one can prescribe the way a composer should express sorrow, for example; one judges only whether a particular expression seems musically appropriate to sorrow.

In our discussion of Banville, in our analyses of Verlaine's *En sourdine* and *C'est l'extase,* Baudelaire's *La Mort des amants* and Louÿs' *La Flûte de Pan*, the common element is this idea of punctuation through the use of musically appropriate materials. Sometimes punctuation will take the form of word-painting, finding an appropriate expression for each section of a poem, as in *Pantomime* or *Fantoches*. Other poems may require the composer to distinguish contrasting elements by use of contrasting melodies, as in *De soir,* or contrasting scales, as in *De rêve.* The idea

[2] *Correspondance de Claude Debussy et P.-J. Toulet* (Paris: Le Divan, 1929), p. 43.

appears in its most abstract form in our discussion of the *Prélude à l'après-midi d'un faune*, in which we did not try to identify the poem line by line with the music but observed that the underlying structures of the poem and the prelude seem to be similar.

PLACET FUTILE

A second order of musical expression, exemplified by *Placet futile*, goes beyond the first by not only identifying certain segments of music with certain segments of text but also transforming that musical material in a way which may influence our reading of the text. In *Il pleure dans mon coeur*, for example, having identified an accompanimental melody with the song of the rain, and the harmonic progression of the music with the mental state of the speaker, Debussy makes a musical commentary on the poem when he alters or arrests the accompanimental activity or when he varies the logic of the harmony. In *Mandoline* and in *Clair de lune* the accompaniment is more than simply appropriate to the text: it suggests a tone of voice in which the text might be read, and has the same influence on our understanding of the poem as the tone of a speaking voice has. This function may also be filled by harmony, as in *Green, Spleen,* and *Chevaux de bois*, by motives, as in *De grève*, by choice of triads, as in *De fleurs*, or by texture, as in *Colloque sentimental.* The transformation of musical material appears in rather abstract form in *Harmonie du soir*, where two musical motives in the song become one, just as two trains of thought in the text become one.

EVENTAIL

The highest order of musical expression is to create a personal expressive idiom based on established musical conventions. Traditionally certain kinds of music have been associated with certain emotions, moods, ideas, situations. Generally these associations are unspecific, and are best understood by observing the correspondences between music and poetry in a wide range of examples.

One of the strongest such traditions in Western music in general is the difference between major and minor modes. In Debussy's music in particular we find one example of a personal expressive idiom in his use of other scales and modes. In *Green*, *Le Jet d'eau*, *Recueillement*, *La Chevelure*, and *Le Tombeau des naïades* we encounter certain recurring usages that often seem to be significant to our understanding of the text: the whole-tone, chromatic and pentatonic scales, the ancient modes, occasionally a special scale. In no case can we say that the pentatonic scale means a pastoral scene or that the whole-tone scale means an escape into another world. Rather we observe a certain pattern in the situations in which Debussy employs these musical idioms, and the awareness of this pattern causes us to look for its significance at each new encounter. A composer's invention of a personal idiom goes beyond the notion of appropriateness. In judging the aptness of a musical figure, its capacity to punctuate a poem, we measure that musical figure against its immediate poetic context. The progressive elaboration of a personal musical idiom, on the other hand, leads the composer to associate certain musical idioms with certain classes of ideas regardless of their specific poetic context.

Frequently Debussy employs conventional procedures to express the central metaphor of a poem, as witness the circle of fifths in *L'Échelonnement des haies,* the "evaporating" harmonies in *Harmonie du soir*, the tritone mirrors of *L'Ombre des arbres*, the "dissolving" harmonies of *Eventail.*

Naturally these categories overlap. Debussy's setting of *Le Balcon* enhances the separation of stanzas which punctuate the poem, transforms musical material to depict suns "rejuvenated," and employs a personal language of special scales. Our categories serve to suggest the number of ways in which Debussy treats a text, often employing more than one procedure for a single poem.

The element which underlies all three orders of musical expression is melody. To document the determining effect of melody on Debussy's musical thought would require another book, but even in our brief discussion of Debussy's style we see that all of his expressive resources derive ultimately from melody. Moreover, Debussy's most important innovations in harmonic and tonal practice result from placing these elements under the rule of melody. But the original, inexhaustible source of melody is song, the association of music with word. Although the setting of preexisting text to music forms an essentially artificial union, the sovereignty of melody returns music to an earlier state where music and poetry were one.

The relation of poetry to music or the influences of poetry and poets on Debussy's music are not the kinds of subjects about which one can make final statements. We have, however, learned enough from Debussy and the poets to be able to ask better questions. The first question which comes to mind concerns Debussy's works which have no direct association with a text. If we have become sensitive to the appearance of certain musical idioms in Debussy's songs, we are likely to wonder what the recurrence of these idioms might mean in his piano pieces. Moreover, the hints by which Debussy from time to time reveals a private musical language make us wonder whether any of his music is truly abstract. We have not only the suggestive titles of his piano pieces but also the occasional cryptic remarks in his letters:

> Pendant très longtemps, l'emploi continu de sixtes me faisait l'effet de demoiselles prétentieuses, assises dans un salon, faisant maussadement, tapisserie, en enviant le rire scandaleux des folles neuvièmes.[3]

This consideration of works without a text brings us face to face with a question which this essay has carefully skirted but which every musician who has thought at all about the philosophy of music has pondered: What does music mean? This is a frightening question which has led many to assert that music simply has no meaning.[4] After having examined levels of meaning in Debussy's relation to poetry can we easily accept their dismissal of the problem? Perhaps the question can best be approached by remembering that in the history of man's culture the association of music with poetry has been the normal and not the exceptional case. Such associations belong to the province of dream, for Debussy the wellspring of artistic inspiration.

[3] *Lettres de Claude Debussy à son éditeur* (Paris: A. Durand et fils, 1927), p. 147. Elsewhere in these letters to Durand Debussy drops fascinating hints concerning his piano Etudes.

[4] Meyer summarizes several philosophical positions in the first chapter of *Emotion and Meaning in Music* (Chicago: University of Chicago Press, 1956). See also John Hospers, *Meaning and Truth in the Arts* (Chapel Hill: University of North Carolina Press, 1946); Sidney Finkelstein, *How Music Expresses Ideas* (New York: International Publishers, 1952), and of course Eduard Hanslick's classic essay, *The Beautiful in Music* (New York: Bobbs Merrill, 1957). Stanley Burnshaw discusses the common origin of music and poetry in *The Seamless Web* (New York: George Braziller, 1971).

> Mais, sapristi, la musique, c'est du rêve dont on écarte les voiles! Ce n'est même pas l'expression d'un sentiment, c'est le sentiment lui-même.[5]

In the course of this study we have attempted to draw back a few of the veils the better to understand the literary side of Debussy's art. But the relationship between poetry and music remains ultimately a mystery, and it is probably best that it remain so.

> Soutenons que la beauté d'une oeuvre d'art restera toujours mystérieuse, c'est-à-dire qu'on ne pourra jamais exactement vérifier "comment cela est fait." Conservons, à tout prix, cette magie particulière à la musique. Par son essence, elle est plus susceptible d'en contenir que tout autre art.[6]

[5] From a letter to Poniatowski, published in *Rassegna Musicale* 22 (1951):59.

[6] Claude Debussy, *Monsieur Croche et autres écrits*, ed. François Lesure (Paris: Gallimard, 1971), p. 224.

Appendix A

Catalogue of Debussy's Published, Completed, or Projected Works

Debussy's association with the poets pervades his work to a degree that statistics alone inadequately represent. If we include projected and unfinished works with the usual catalogue the extent of the literary influence is even more apparent. In the following catalogue, extracted from biographies and articles on Debussy, published works are listed by date of completion, projected works by the date at which they were considered or abandoned. Works with text are songs unless otherwise indicated. Songs published in a group are listed together even though they may have been composed in different years.

?	*Intermezzo* for cello and piano
?c.1878	*Madrid, princesse des Espagnes* (Musset) unpublished
	Ballade à la lune (Musset) unpublished
1878	*Rapsodie* (piano)
?c.1879	*Fleur des eaux* (Maurice Bouchor) unpublished
	L'Archet (Charles Cros) unpublished
	Nuit d'étoiles (Banville)

1879	*Florise* (Banville) unfinished
?c.1880	*Fleur des blés* (André Girod)
	Egloque, duet for soprano and tenor (Leconte de Lisle) unpublished
	La Fille aux cheveux de lin (Leconte de Lisle) unpublished
1880	*Jane* (Leconte de Lisle)
	Caprice (Banville)
	Hymnis (Banville) unfinished cantata
	Scherzo for violin and piano, unpublished
	Trio in G major for piano, violin, and cello, unpublished
	Nocturno for violin and piano, unpublished
	Danse bohémienne (piano)
	Andante for two pianos, unpublished
	Symphonie en si, piano duet version only
?c.1881	*Aimons-nous* (Banville)
	Souhait (Banville) unpublished
1881	*Zéphyr* (Banville)
?1882	*Sérénade* (Banville) unpublished
1882	*Pierrot* (Banville)
	Les Lilas (*O Floraison divine . . .*) (Banville) unpublished
	Les Roses (Banville) unpublished
	Fête galante (Banville) unpublished
	Rondel chinois (?) unpublished
	Flots, palmes, sables (Armand Renaud) unpublished
	Tragédie (Heine, trans. Léon Valade) unpublished
	Rondeau: fut-il jamais (Musset)
	La Belle au bois dormant (Hypsa)
	Beau soir (Paul Bourget)
	Pantomime (Verlaine)
	En sourdine (Verlaine)
	Mandoline (Verlaine)
	Clair de lune (Verlaine)
	Fantoches (Verlaine)
	Triomphe de Bacchus, orchestral interlude (only piano duet version completed) based on Banville's poem *Le Triomphe de Bacchos à son retour des Indes*
	Intermezzo for orchestra, based on Heine's *Lyrisches Intermezzo* from the collection *Poèmes et Légendes*, translated by Gérard de Nerval, unpublished
	Scherzo for cello and piano, unpublished

	Il dort encore, from Banville's *Hymnis*, unpublished
	Salut printemps (Comte de Ségur) chorus
1883	*Coquetterie posthume* (Gautier) unpublished
	Chanson espagnole, duet for soprano and tenor (Gautier)
	Romance: silence ineffable (Bourget) unpublished
	Musique (Bourget) unpublished
	Paysage sentimental (Bourget)
	Romance: voici que le printemps (Bourget)
	Invocation (Lamartine) chorus for male voices, piano-vocal score only
	Le Gladiateur (Emile Moreau) unpublished cantata
1884	*Regret: devant le ciel d'été* (Bourget) unpublished
	Séguédille (J.-L. Vauthier) unpublished
	Apparition (Mallarmé)
	Rondel chinois, unpublished
	Daniel (Emile Cécile) unpublished cantata
	Suite d'orchestre, unpublished
	L'Enfant prodigue (Edouard Guinand) cantata
	Printemps (Jules Barbier) unpublished work for orchestra and small choir singing with closed lips
1885	*Salammbô* (Flaubert) unpublished sketches
c.1886	*Diane au bois* (Banville) unfinished cantata
	Zuleima (Heine, *Almansor*) music has disappeared,
	Accepts offer to write music for Maurice Vaucaire's adaptation of *As You Like It*
1887	*Printemps* for orchestra
1888	*Ariettes, Paysages belges et Aquarelles* (Paul Verlaine) reissued in 1903 as *Ariettes oubliées*
	C'est l'extase (1887)
	Il pleure dans mon coeur (1887)
	L'Ombre des arbres (1888)
	Chevaux de bois (1885)
	Green (1886)
	Spleen (1888)
	Deux Arabesques for piano
1889	*Cinq poèmes de Charles Baudelaire*
	Le Balcon (1888)
	Harmonie du soir (1889)

Le Jet d'eau (1889)
Recueillement (c.1888)
La Mort des amants (1887)
La Damoiselle élue (Dante-Gabriel Rossetti, translated and arranged by G. Sarrazin) cantata
Fantaisie for piano and orchestra
Petite Suite for piano duet
En bateau (title of poem by Verlaine)
Cortège (title of poem by Verlaine)
Menuet
Ballet
Begins a symphony on Poe's *Fall of the House of Usher*
Axel (Villiers de l'Isle Adam) one scene, unpublished

1890 Several pieces for piano solo
Rêverie
Ballade or *Ballade slave*
Danse (originally *Tarantelle styrienne*)
Valse romantique
Nocturne or *Interlude*
L'Âme évaporée (Bourget)

1891 Requests permission from Maeterlinck to set *La Princesse Maleine*
Deux Romances (Bourget)
Romance
Les Cloches
Les Angélus (G. le Roy)
Dans le jardin (Paul Gravollet)
Trois mélodies (Paul Verlaine)
La Mer est plus belle
Le Son du cor s'afflige
L'Échelonnement des haies
Mazurka (piano solo)
Marche écossaise sur un thème populaire (piano duet)
Score announced of *L'Embarquement pour ailleurs* (Gabriel Mourey)
Project for *Les Noces de Sathan* in cooperation with Jules Bois

1892 *Rodrigue et Chimène* (Catulle Mendès) unfinished opera
Streets (Verlaine) unpublished
Fêtes galantes (Verlaine) first series
En sourdine (second version)

Fantoches (revised)
Clair de lune (second version)

1893 *Proses lyriques* (Claude Debussy)
De rêve
De grève
De fleurs
De soir
String Quartet in g minor, opus 10

1894 *Prélude à l'après-midi d'un faune* for orchestra, based on poem by Stéphane Mallarmé, *L'après-midi d'un faune*
Images for piano, unpublished
Valse for two pianos, possible source of *La Plus que lente*, unpublished
Plans *Amphion* with Paul Valéry
La Danseuse (Pierre Louÿs) projected theater piece

1895 Plans stage work on Balzac's *La Grand Bretèche*
String Quartet, abandoned
Plans *La Tentation de Saint Antoine* (Gilbert de Voisins)
Candrelune (Pierre Louÿs) also entitled *Geneviève*, *Psyché*, and *Kundrynette*, abandoned

1896 Ballet on the subject of *Daphnis and Chloe*; scenario by Pierre Louÿs, derived from Oscar Wilde, abandoned
Work begun on *La Saulaie* (Rossetti's *Willow-Wood*, translated by Louÿs)

1897 *Chansons de Bilitis* (Pierre Louÿs)
La Flûte de Pan
La Chevelure
Le Tombeau des naïades

1898 Contemplates setting *Aphrodite* (Pierre Louÿs)
Berceuse for piano solo

1899 *Nocturnes* for orchestra, originally *Trois scènes au crépuscule* based on *Poèmes anciens et romanesques* by Henri de Régnier
Nuages
Fêtes
Sirènes (with female chorus)
Two projects with René Peter
L'Herbe tendre
L'Utile aventure
Marche nuptiale for organ (disappeared)

1900	*Chansons de Bilitis*, incidental music for a recitation of poems of Pierre Louÿs, scored for two flutes, two harps, and celesta *F. E. A. (Frères en art)* libretto completed *Nuits blanches* (Claude Debussy) unfinished song cycle *Esther et la maison des fous*, text for a dramatic work, unpublished
1901	*Pour le piano* (piano solo) *Prélude* *Sarabande* *Toccata* *Lindaraja* (two pianos) *Les Mille et une nuits* (René Peter) projected theater piece *Le Voyage de Pausole* (Pierre Louÿs) project
1902	*Pelléas et Mélisande* (Maurice Maeterlinck) opera in five acts Plans a version as *As You Like It* with Paul-Jean Toulet
1903	*Le Diable dans le beffroi* (Poe-Debussy) notes for the libretto and sketch for Scene i. *Danse sacrée* and *Danse profane* for harp and strings *Estampes* (piano solo) *Pagodes* *Soirée dans Grenade* *Jardins sous la pluie* *D'un cahier d'esquisses* (piano solo) Project to set Maeterlinck's *Joyselle* *Amphion* (Paul Valéery) projected theater piece *Don Juan*, projected theater piece
1904	*Fêtes galantes* (Verlaine) second series *Les Ingénus* *Le Faune* *Colloque sentimental* *Trois chansons de France* *Rondel: Le temps a laissié son manteau* (Charles d'Orléans) *La Grotte* (Tristan Lhermite) same song as *Auprès de cette grotte sombre* of 1910 *Rondel: Pour ce que Plaisance est morte* (Charles d'Orléans) Incidental music for *King Lear* (Shakespeare) *Fanfare* *Sommeil de Lear* (six further pieces sketched) *Masques* (piano solo) *L'Isle joyeuse* (piano solo) *Dionysos* (J. Gasquet) projected theater piece

1905 *Suite bergamasque* (piano solo)
Prélude
Menuet
Clair de lune (title of poem by Verlaine)
Passepied
Rapsodie for saxophone and piano
La Mer (orchestra)
De l'aube à midi sur la mer, originally titled *Mer belle aux Iles Sanguinaires*, title of a short story by Camille Mauclair
Jeux de vagues
Dialogue du vent et de la mer, originally titled *Le Vent fait danser la mer*
Images (piano solo) first series
Reflets dans l'eau
Hommage à Rameau
Mouvement

1907 *Siddharta* (Victor Segalen) project
Suggests to Victor Segalen a libretto on the subject of Orpheus
Discusses project for *Tristan* with Gabriel Mourey

1908 *Trois chansons de Charles d'Orléans* (unaccompanied chorus)
Dieu! qu'il fait bon regarder!
Quand j'ai ouy le tabourin
Yver, vous n'estes qu'un villain, also appears as title of last movement of *En blanc et noir*
Children's Corner (piano solo)
Doctor Gradus ad Parnassum
Jimbo's Lullaby
Sérénade for the doll
The snow is dancing
The little shepherd
Golliwogg's cake-walk
Images (piano solo) second series
Cloches à travers les feuilles
Et la lune descend sur le temple qui fut
Poissons d'or
Orphée triomphant (Segalen) project
Drame cosmogonique, projected theater piece

1909 *Le Petit Nègre* (piano solo)
Hommage à Haydn or *Sur le nom d'Haydn*
Writes the scenario of *Masques et Bergamasques*

L'Orestie (Aeschylus) projected theater piece
Huon de Bordeaux and *Le Marchand de rèves* (Gabriel Mourey) projected theater pieces

1910 *Première rapsodie* for clarinet and piano
Douze Préludes (piano solo) book I
Danseuses de Delphes
Voiles
Le Vent dans la plaine
Les Sons et les parfums tournent dans l'air du soir (line from Baudelaire's *Harmonie du soir*)
Les Collines d'Anacapri
Des pas sur la neige
Ce qu'a vu le vent d'Ouest
La Fille aux cheveux de lin (title of poem by Leconte de Lisle)
La Sérénade interrompue
La Cathédrale engloutie
La Danse de Puck
Minstrels
La Plus que lente (piano solo)
Le Promenoir des deux amants (Tristan Lhermite)
Auprès de cette grotte sombre
Crois mon conseil
Je tremble en voyant ton visage
Trois ballades de François Villon
Ballade de Villon à s'amye
Ballade que feit Villon à la requeste de sa mème pour prier Nostre-Dame
Ballade des femmes de Paris

1911 *Images* for orchestra
Gigues, originally *Gigues tristes*, derived from Verlaine's *Streets*, set to the tune of *The Keel Row*, under the title *Dansons le gigue*, by Charles Bordes in 1890
Ibéria
Par les rues et par les chemins
Les Parfums de la nuit
Le matin d'un jour de fête
Rondes de Printemps, based on a quotation by Pierre Gauthiez of a French translation of one of the *Canzoni a ballo of* Politian
Le Martyre de Saint-Sébastien (Gabriel d'Annunzio) incidental music for a mystery play

Pygmalion, theater project

1912 *Jeux*, ballet, scenario by Nijinsky
Khamma, ballet, scenario by W. L. Courtney and Maud Allen
Ballet persan (Paul-Jean Toulet) projected theater piece

1913 *Douze Préludes* (piano solo) book II
Brouillards
Feuilles mortes
La Puerta del Vino
Les Fées sont d'exquises danseuses (from *Peter Pan* by James Barrie)
Bruyères
General Lavine—eccentric
La Terrasse des audiences du clair de lune
Ondine
Hommage à S. Pickwick, Esq. P.P.M.P.C. (character from Dickens)
Canope
Les Tierces alternées
Feux d'artifice
Syrinx (flute solo) originally titled *Flûte de Pan*, for the play *Psyché* by Gabriel Mourey
La Boîte à joujoux, children's ballet, scenario by André Hellé
Trois poèmes de Stéphane Mallarmé
Soupir
Placet futile
Eventail

1914 *Poème* for violin and orchestra, project
Six épigraphes antiques (piano duet) arranged from the incidental music to the *Chansons de Bilitis* of 1900
Pour invoquer Pan, dieu du vent d'été
Pour que la nuit soit propice
Pour un tombeau sans nom
Pour l'Egyptienne
Pour la danseuse aux crotales
Pour remercier la pluie au matin
Berceuse héroïque pour rendre hommage à S. M. le Roi Albert I de Belgique et à ses soldats (piano solo)
Le Palais du silence, also called *No-ya-ti* (Louis Laloy) project

1915 *Noël des enfants qui n'ont plus de maison* (Claude Debussy) also for children's choir

Project for opera-ballet on Verlaine's *Fêtes galantes* (also referred to as *Crimen Amoris*) scenario by Louis Laloy
En blanc et noir (two pianos) originally *Caprices en blanc et noir*
Douze études (piano solo)
Book I:
Pour les cinq doigts (d'après Monsieur Czerny)
Pour les tierces
Pour les quartes
Pour les sixtes
Pour les octaves
Pour les huit doigts
Book II:
Pour les degrès chromatiques
Pour les agréments
Pour les notes répétées
Pour les sonorités
Pour les arpèges
Pour les accords
Sonata for cello and piano
Sonata for flute, viola, and harp

1917 *Ode à la France* (Louis Laloy) cantata (completed from sketches by Marius-François Gaillard)
Sonata for violin and piano.
Drame fantastique, project
Sonata for oboe, horn, and harpsichord, abandoned

1918 *La Chute de la maison Usher* (Poe-Debussy) opera, libretto (sketches and final version) and vocal score (incomplete)

Sources

Edward Lockspeiser, *Debussy His Life and Mind*, London: Cassell (1965)
Marcel Dietschy, *La Passion de Claude Debussy*, Neuchatel: A la Baconnière (1962)
John Trevitt, "Debussy Inconnu," *Musical Times* 114 (1973): 881–886, 1001–1005

Appendix B

Changes in Text in Songs of Fauré and Debussy

One of the characteristics of a poem which distinguishes it from prose is that to change a word is to change the poem altogether. As Banville expresses it, "a poem cannot be altered without reducing it. There cannot be a poem in prose, for it is impossible to imagine a prose so perfect that one could not add or subtract something."

For a poet there is no such thing as a synonym. Two words which mean the same thing but which sound different, are different. Thus when a composer alters a poem, even if only by the change of a word, it is no longer the same poem.

In examining composers' alterations of texts, we often do not know whether the composer deliberately changed the text or whether he was simply working from a defective copy of the poem. In the main body of this study we have made only passing reference to alterations of words, since in most cases it is unknown whether or not it was the composer who made the changes. The repetition of words or of verses, or the insertion of textless melismas, of course, is clearly the composer's work, and must be considered part of the act of composition. In the following list of variants, no attention has been paid to the vagaries of punctuation which are to be found in most editions of the composers' songs.

Mandoline

Fauré	Line 8: *fit* in place of *fait*
	First stanza of text repeated at the end of the song
Debussy	Twenty-measure melisma on *la* following the last stanza

Clair de lune

Debussy (earlier version)	Line 8 set twice
	Two-measure melisma on *ah* following the last line, then line 9 repeated

En sourdine

Fauré	Line 5: *mêlons* in place of *fondons*
	Line 16: *des gazons* in place of *de gazon*
Debussy (earlier version)	Line 16: omits *roux*
	Last two lines repeated

C'est l'extase

Fauré	Line 14: *Et* in place of *En*

Il pleure dans mon coeur

Fauré	Adds the title *Spleen*, not to be confused with another Verlaine poem of that title
	Lines 10 and 12: *Mon* in place of *Ce*
Debussy	Line 8: *bruit* in place of *chant*

Fantoches

Debussy	Line 11: *amoureuse* in place of *langoureuse*

Chevaux de bois

Debussy	Line 15: *Rien* in place of *Bien*
	Additional *tournez* added after last word

Le Jet d'eau

In the final version of the poem, the refrain reads:

La gerbe épanouie
En mille fleurs
Où Phoebé réjouie
Met ses couleurs,
Tombe comme une pluie
De larges pleurs.

Debussy adopted the variant that appeared in *La Petite Revue* in 1865:

La gerbe d'eau qui berce
Ses mille fleurs
Que la lune traverse
De ses lueurs
Tombe comme une averse
De larges pleurs.

but with the fourth line altered to "De ses pâleurs."

Appendix C

Debussy's Choice of Meter in His Songs

"Préfère l'Impair," Verlaine recommended in his *Art Poétique*. If we regard duple meter as "even," and triple meter as "uneven," it is evident that Debussy did indeed "prefer the uneven" in setting Verlaine's poetry.

Triple meter

	Verlaine	*Others*
3/4	*En sourdine* (first version)	*Beau soir* (Bourget)
	Il pleure dans mon coeur	*Caprice* (Banville)
	L'Ombre des arbres	*Aimons-nous et dormons* (Banville)
	Spleen	*Jane* (Leconte de Lisle)
	Le Son du cor	*Harmonie du soir* (Baudelaire)
	L'Échelonnement des haies	*Le Jet d'eau* (Baudelaire)
	En sourdine (second version)	*La Mort des amants* (Baudelaire)
	Le Faune	*Les Angélus* (Le Roy)
	Colloque sentimental	*De grève* (Debussy)

		La Grotte (Tristan Lhermite)
		Je tremble en voyant ton visage (Lhermite)
		Placet futile (Mallarmé)
3/8	*Clair de lune* (first version)	*Paysage sentimental* (Bourget)
	C'est l'extase	*Dans le jardin* (Gravollet)
	Les Ingénus	
9/8	*Clair de lune* (second version)	*Apparition* (Mallarmé)
	Duple meter	
2/2		*De soir* (Debussy)
2/4	*Pantomime*	*Voici que le printemps* (Bourget)
	Chevaux de bois	*Pierrot* (Banville)
	Fantoches	*Crois mon conseil* (Tristan Lhermite)
		Ballade des femmes de Paris (Villon)
		Eventail (Mallarmé)
4/4	*La Mer est plus belle*	*Fleur des blés* (Girod)
		Zéphyr (Banville)
		Le Balcon (Baudelaire)
		Recueillement (Baudelaire)
		Romance (Bourget)
		Les Cloches (Bourget)
		De fleurs (Debussy)
		La Flûte de Pan (Louÿs)
		Le Tombeau des naïades (Louÿs)
		Le Temps à laissé son manteau (Charles d'Orléans)
		Pour ce que Plaisance est morte (Charles d'Orléans)
		Ballade de Villon à s'amye (Villon)
		Ballade que Villon feit à la requeste de sa mère pour prier Nostre-Dame (Villon)
		Soupir (Mallarmé)
6/4		*La Chevelure* (Louÿs)
6/8	*Mandoline*	*Nuit d'étoiles* (Banville)
	Green	*Rondeau* (Musset)

12/8 *La Belle au bois dormant* (Hypsa)
De rêve (Debussy)

Tabulation

3/4	9	12
3/8	3	2
9/8	1	1
	—	—
	13 Triple meter	15 Triple meter
2/2	0	1
2/4	3	5
4/4	1	14
6/4	0	1
6/8	2	2
12/8	0	2
	—	—
	6 Duple meter	25 Duple meter

Preference for triple meter for Verlaine, 13 songs out of 19, or a ratio of 2.2/1

Preference for duple meter for other poets, 25 songs out of 40, or a ratio of 1.7/1

Appendix D

Translations of the Poems

Pierrot

The good Pierrot, whom the crowd beholds,
Having witnessed the marriage of Arlequin,
Proceeds, while musing, along the church boulevard;
A young girl of supple body
Teases him in vain with her roguish eye;
While mysterious and smooth,
Shining on him its costliest delight,
The white moon with bull horns
Looks askance
At its friend Jean Gaspard de bureau.

[Debussy]

Moonlight

Your soul is a chosen landscape
Charmed by masquers and bergamasquers,
Playing thc lute and dancing, and almost
Sad beneath their whimsical costumes,

Even as they sing in the minor mode
Of triumphant love, and a life of good fortune,
They don't seem to believe in their happiness,
And their song blends with the moonlight,

With the still moonlight, sad and lovely,
Which sets the birds in the trees to dreaming,
And makes the fountains sob with ecstasy,
The tall slim fountains among the marble statues.
[Verlaine]

Mandolin

The serenaders
And lovely listeners
Exchange bland remarks
Under the singing boughs.

There is Tircis and there is Aminta,
And there is eternal Clitander,
And there is Damis, who for many
A cruel Lady fashions many a fond verse.

Their short silken jackets,
Their long dresses with trains,
Their elegance, their joy
And their soft blue shadows

Whirl madly in the ecstasy
Of a rose gray moon
And the mandolin chatters
Amid the shivering of the breeze.
[Verlaine]

Muted

Calm, in the dusk
Formed by high branches
Let us quite imbue our love
With this deep quiet.

Let us dissolve our souls, our hearts,
And our raptured senses,
Amongst the hazy languors
Of the pines and arbutus.

Half-close your eyes,
Cross your arms on your breast,
And from your lulled heart
Dismiss all purpose, forever.

Let us be convinced
By the soft cradling breath
Which here at your feet ripples
Waves of russet lawn.

And when solemn Evening
Falls from the black oaks
The voice of our despair,
The nightingale, will sing.

[Verlaine]

This Is Ecstasy

It is languorous ecstasy,
It is love's weariness,
It's all the shuddering of the woods
Amid the breezes' embrace.
It is, toward the gray boughs,
The chorus of little voices.

Oh, the frail cool murmur,
There are twitterings and whispers,
It's like the gentle cry
Which ruffled grass breathes out.
You might think it was—under the water which eddies—
The muted rolling of pebbles.

This soul which is lamenting
In this subdued plaint,
It is ours, isn't it?
Mine, you know, and yours,
And from them this humble anthem breathes out
So softly, on this warm evening.

[Verlaine]

Green

Here are fruit, flowers, leaves and branches,
And here, too, is my heart which beats only for you.
Do not tear it apart with your two white hands,
And to your lovely eyes may this humble offering seem sweet.

I come, still covered with dew,
Which the morning wind turns to frost on my brow.
Allow my fatigue, resting at your feet,
To dream of the cherished moments that will refresh it.

On your young bosom let me lay my head,
Still resounding from your last kisses;
Let it be calmed after the good storm,
And let me sleep a little, since you are resting.

[Verlaine]

It Weeps in My Heart

It rains gently on the city.

[Arthur Rimbaud]

It weeps in my heart
As it rains on the city.
What is this languor
That penetrates my heart?

Oh, gentle sound of the rain,
On the ground and on the roofs
For a heart that is weary,
Oh, the song of the rain!

It weeps without reason
In this disheartened heart.
What! No betrayal? . . .
This mourning is without reason.

This is truly the worst pain,
To know not why,
Without love and without hate
My heart feels so much pain.

[Verlaine]

Correspondences

Nature is a temple whose living pillars
Now and then permit confused remarks to pass;
Man goes by through forests of symbols
Which watch him with familiar glances.

Like long echoes which mingle afar
Into a dark and profound unity,

Vast as the night and as the light [of day]
Scents, colors and sounds answer one another.

There are scents fresh as a baby's flesh,
Sweet as oboes, green as meadows,
—And others, corrupted, rich, and triumphant,

With the expansiveness of infinite things,
Like amber, musk, benzoin and incense
Which sing the raptures of the spirit and the senses.
[Baudelaire]

The Balcony

Mother of memories, mistress of mistresses,
O you, my every pleasure! O you, my every duty!
You will recall the beauty of caresses,
The peace of the hearth, and the evenings' spell,
Mother of memories, mistress of mistresses!

Evenings lighted by the coals' glowing heat
And evenings on the balcony, veiled by rosy mist,
How sweet your breast was, how tender your heart!
We often said deathless things
On evenings lighted by the coals' glowing heat.

How beautiful suns are in the warm evenings!
How deep is space! How powerful is the heart!
Bending toward you, queen of those adored,
I thought I breathed in the fragrance of your blood.
How beautiful suns are in the warm evenings!

The night was growing denser, like a wall,
And my eyes, in the darkness, discerned your pupils,
And I drank in your breath, o sweetness, o poison!
And your feet were resting in my brotherly hands;
The night was growing denser, like a wall.

I know the art of evoking happy moments,
And I relive my past, snuggled at your knee.
For what's the good of seeking after your languid graces
Elsewhere than in your beloved body and your gentle heart?
I know the art of evoking happy moments!

Those vows, those perfumes, those endless kisses,
Will they be reborn from a gulf we cannot sound?

As the suns made young again rise into the sky,
Having been washed at the bottom of the deep seas?
O vows! O fragrance! O endless kisses!

[Baudelaire]

Evening Harmony

Here now that hour approaches when, trembling on its stem,
Each flower exhales fragrance like a censer;
Sounds and perfumes whirl in the evening air:
A melancholy waltz, a giddy languor.

Each flower exhales fragrance like a censer,
The violin quivers like an afflicted heart:
A melancholy waltz, a giddy languor!
The sky is sad and fine, like a great altar.

The violin quivers like an afflicted heart,
A tender heart, which abhors the vast, black void!
The sky is sad and fine, like a great altar,
The sun has drowned in its own blood, which is congealing.

A tender heart, which abhors the vast, black void,
Gathers up every vestige of the luminous past.
The sun has drowned in its own blood, which is congealing,—
Your memory shines in me like a monstrance.

[Baudelaire]

The Fountain

Your beautiful eyes are weary, my poor lover!
Stay for a long time, without opening them,
In that nonchalant pose
In which pleasure has taken you by surprise.
In the courtyard, the fountain which chatters
And never falls silent, day or night,
Sweetly sustains the ecstasy
In which love has engulfed me tonight.

The column of water which cradles
Its thousand flowers,
Which the moon crosses
With its pale light,
Falls like a shower
Of full tears.

Just so your soul, set aflame
By the burning flash of sensual delight
Leaps, quick and bold,
Toward the vast, enchanted skies.
Then your soul flowers over, dying
In a wave of sad languor
Which, along an invisible slope,
Descends to the depths of my heart.

The column of water which cradles
Its thousand flowers,
Which the moon crosses
With its pale light,
Falls like a shower
Of full tears.

Oh, you, whom the night makes so beautiful
I find it sweet, leaning toward your breasts,
To listen to the eternal lament
That sobs in the fountains.
Moon, sonorous water, blessed night,
You, trees, trembling all about—
Your pure melancholy
Is the mirror of my love.

The column of water which cradles
Its thousand flowers,
Which the moon crosses
With its pale light,
Falls like a shower
Of full tears.

[Baudelaire]

Meditation

Be good, my Sorrow, and behave more calmly;
You were begging for evening; it is falling, here it is!
A dark haze envelops the city,
Bringing peace to some, to others anxiety.

While the base multitude of mortals,
Under the whip of Pleasure, that merciless executioner,
Goes off to store up remorse at the lowly feast,
My sorrow, give me your hand, come this way,

Far away from them. See the dead years leaning
Over the balconies of heaven in faded dresses,
And smiling Regret emerging from the depths of the waters;

The dying sun going to sleep beneath an arch;
And, like a long shroud trailing toward the East,
Hear, my beloved, hear the gentle night walking.

[Baudelaire]

The Lovers' Death

We shall have beds full of gentle scents,
Couches deep as tombs,
And strange flowers set on shelves,
Which have bloomed for us beneath fairer skies.

Vying with each other in their final flames
Our two hearts will be two vast torches,
And will reflect their double light
In our two spirits, those twin mirrors.

One evening made of rose and mystic blue
We shall exchange a single final flash,
Like a long sob, heavy with leavetaking;

And later an Angel, half-opening the doors,
Faithful and joyous, will restore to life
The tarnished mirrors and the flames that have died.

[Baudelaire]

The Shadow of the Trees

The nightingale who from the top of a branch looks down at his reflection, believes that he has fallen into the stream. He is at the top of an oak and yet he is afraid of drowning.

[Cyrano de Bergerac]

The shadow of the trees in the misty river
Is dying like smoke,
While, in the air, among the real branches
The turtledoves lament.

How pallidly, O traveler, this pallid landscape
Mirrored you,
And how your drowned hopes were weeping sadly
In the high foliage.

[Verlaine]

Wooden Horses

Turn, turn, good wooden horses,
Turn a hundred times, turn a thousand times,
Turn often and turn always,
Turn, turn to the sound of the oboe.

The red-faced child and the pale mother,
The lad in black and the girl in pink,
The one down to earth, the other showing off,
Each to be paid a sou on Sunday.

Turn, turn, beloved horses,
While around all your turning
Squints the eye of a crafty pickpocket,
Turn to the sound of the triumphant cornet!

It's astonishing how it intoxicates you
To move thus in this foolish circus:
Good for your stomach, bad for your head,
Heaps of bad and masses of good.

Turn, hobby-horses, without ever needing
The aid of spurs
To direct your round galloping,
Turn, turn, without hope of hay.

And hurry, fanciful horses:
Already the supper bell is sounded
By night, which falls and disperses the crowd
Of gay drinkers, famished by their thirst.

Turn, turn! The sky slowly dons
A velvet of golden stars,
The church tolls a mournful knell.
Turn to the joyous sound of the drums!

[Verlaine]

Spleen

The roses were all red
And the ivy was all black.

Darling, when you become restless,
All my despair is reborn.

The sky was too blue, too tender,
The sea too green and the air too mild.

I always fear—what a thing to await!—
Some cruel flight of yours.

Of the holly with glazed leaf
And the shiny boxwood I am weary,

And of the endless countryside,
And of everything, save only you, Alas!
[Verlaine]

The Sea Is More Lovely

The sea is more lovely
Than the cathedrals,
Faithful nurse,
Lullaby of death-rattles,
The sea over which
The Virgin Mary prays.

It has all qualities,
Terrible and gentle,
I hear its forgiveness
Rumbling its wrath . . .
This immensity
Knows no resistance

Oh, so patient,
Even when malicious.
A friendly breeze frequents
The wave, and sings to us:
"You without hope,
May you die without suffering!"

And then beneath the skies,
Which laugh more brightly,
It looks blue,
Pink, gray, and green . . .
Lovelier than all,
Better than we!
[Verlaine]

The Spacing-Out of Hedgerows

The spacing-out of hedgerows
Froths unendingly, a sea

Bright in the transparent mist
Fragrant with young berries.

Trees and windmills
Pose lightly on the soft greensward,
Where the agility of colts
Comes to frolic and romp.

Here in this Sunday haze
Are also gamboling
The large sheep as
As meek as their white wool [is soft].

Just now broke
The wave, rolled in curls,
Of flute-like bells
In a milk-white sky.

[Verlaine]

Art of Poetry

(Place) Music above all,
And to that end prefer the Uneven,
More indefinite and more soluble in air,
With nothing in it which is ponderous or pretentious.

And when you go to choose your words
It mustn't be without some misprision:
Nothing dearer (to the poet) than the gray song
In which the vague and the precise meet.

It's beautiful eyes behind veils,
It's the great shimmering of mid-day,
It is, in a tepid, autumn sky,
The blue litter of bright stars!

For we want nuance once more,
No Color, only nuance!
Oh! only nuance joins
Dream to dream and flute to horn!

Flee on sight the murderous witticism,
Cruel Wit and lewd Laughter,
Which causes Azure eyes to weep,
And all this garlic of cheap cooking.

Seize eloquence and wring its neck!
You will do well, while you're about it,
To make Rhyme behave itself.
If you don't keep an eye on it, how far will it go?

Oh, who will recite the abuses of Rhyme?
What mute child or foolish savage
Has forged this gem of a penny
Which sounds hollow and false under the file?

Music again and always!
Let your verse be the soaring thing
Felt by one who flees from a soul on its way
Toward other skies to other loves.

Let your verse be the fortune
Scattered to the crisp wind of morning
Which bears the odor of mint and thyme . . .
And all the rest is rhetoric.

[Verlaine]

The Sound of the Horn

The sound of the horn grieves away towards the woods
With a woe (you'd like to think) like an orphan's;
It comes to the foot of the hill and dies
Amidst the breeze that wanders in quick howls.

The wolf's soul weeps in that voice
Rising with the sun that's sinking
In throes (you'd like to think) like a caress:
They're entrancing, and they break the heart.

Better to make that lulled lament,
The snow falls in long shreds of gauze
Across the sunset tinged with blood

And the air seems to be an autumn sigh,
The air's so mild on this monotonous evening
When a slow landscape is darling to itself.

[Verlaine]

The Afternoon of a Faun

These nymphs, I want to perpetuate.
So clear,
Their light incarnadine, that it lilts in the air
Drowsy with tufted slumbers.

Did I love a dream?
My doubt, accumulation of old night, ends
In many a subtle bough, which, [having] remained the true
Woods themselves proves, alas, that all I offered myself
For triumph was the ideal fault [sin] of roses.
Let us reflect . . .

— or what if the women you expound
Represent a wish of your fabulous senses!
Faun, the illusion escapes from the blue
And cold eyes, like a tear-welling spring, of the chaster [nymph]:
But, the other [nymph], all sighs, do you say she contrasts
Like a hot breeze of the (hot) day in your fleece?
But no! through the motionless and weary fainting [heat effect]
Suffocating with heat the fresh morning, if it struggles [up with a breath of air],
Murmurs no [sound of] water but that which my flute pours
Into the grove sprinkled with chords; and the only wind
[Coming] Out of the two pipes prompt to exhale itself before
It disperses the sound in an arid rain
Is, on the horizon unstirred by so much as a wrinkle,
The visible and serene artificial breath
Of inspiration, which regains heaven.

O Sicilian banks of a calm marsh
That my vanity plunders like the [recurrent] suns,
Tacit [the marsh], under the flowers of sparks, TELL
"That I was cutting here the hollow reeds tamed
By talent; when, on the glaucous gold of distant
Greeneries dedicating [clinging] their vine to wellsprings,
Undulates an animal whiteness in repose:
And [Tell] that at the slow prelude with which the pipes are born [start up]
The flight of swans, no! of naiads flees
Or plunges. . . ."

Inert, all burns in the tawny hour
Without showing by what art [ruse] together ran off [the nymphs]

Too much hymen [with the nymphs] desired by [me] the one who seeks
the *la:*
Then I'll awaken to the first fervor,
Straight and alone, under an ancient flood of light
Lily! [or lilies] and one of you all [lilies] in point of candor.

Other than the sweet nothing [the kiss] rumored by their lips,
The kiss, which quietly assures of the perfidious ones,
My breast, virgin of proof, attests a bite,
Mysterious, due to some august tooth;
But, enough! such a mystery chose for its confident
The vast and twin reed on which one plays under the azure:
Which, turning to itself [the reed-flute] the trouble of
the cheek,
Dreams, in a long solo, that we were beguiling
The surrounding beauty [of nature] by false [fictitious] confusions
Between itself [the beauty] and our credulous song;
And [dreams] to make, as high as love modulates,
Vanish [distill] from the ordinary dream of a back
Or a pure flank followed by my closed looks,
[Distill] A sonorous, vain and monotonous line.

Try then, instrument of flights, O wicked
Syrinx, to reflower [as reeds again] at the lakes where you await me!
I, proud of my rumor [sounds I made], am going to speak at length
Of [these?] goddesses; and by idolatrous portrayals,
Lift still more girdles from their shadow.
Thus, when I have sucked from grapes the brightness,
To banish a regret [which is] by my ruse put aside,
Laughing, I raise to the summer sky the empty cluster
And, blowing in its luminous skins, avid
For drunkeness till evening I look through them.

O nymphs, let us reinflate some diverse MEMORIES.
"My eye, piercing the reeds, darted at each immortal
Neck, which drowns in the water its burning
With [on my part] a cry of rage to the forest roof [or sky];
And the splendid bath of hair disappears
In the brightnesses and the shivers, o jewels!
I run up; when, [whereupon] at my feet, are clasped (bruised
From the languor tasted of this [pain or] evil of being two)

[Two] Sleeping women amid their mere [they are naked] random arms;
I ravish them [snatch them up] without disentangling them, and flee
To this clump, hated by the frivolous shadow,
Of roses yielding up all perfume to the sun, where may our
[Amorous] Sporting be like the consumed day."
I adore you, wrath of virgins, O ferocious delight
Of the sacred naked burden which slides
To flee my lip on fire drinking in, as a lightning thrust
Quivers! the secret terror of the flesh:
From the feet of the inhuman [cold, nymph] to the heart of the timid one
Who is abandoned at once by an [her] innocence, humid
With mad tears or less sad vapors.
"My crime, is to have, gay at vanquishing these treacherous fears,
Divided the dishevelled tuft
Of kisses that the gods kept so well mingled:
For hardly was I about to hide an ardent laugh
Under the happy folds of one [keeping
By a simple finger, so her featherlike candor
Might be colored by the emotion of her sister which is beginning to catch fire,
The little one, naive and not blushing):
When from my arms, undone by vague deaths,
This prey forever ungrateful frees itself
Without pity for the sob with which I still was drunk."

So much the worse! towards happiness others will pull me along
By their tresses knotted to the horns of my forehead:
You know, my passion, that, purple and already ripe,
Each pomegranate bursts and murmurs with bees;
And our blood, smitten with whoever will take it,
Flows for all the eternal swarm of desire.
At the hour when this wood with gold and ashes is tinted
A festival is excited in the extinguished foliage:
Etna! It is amid you visited by Venus
On your lava placing her candid heels,
When a sad slumber thunders or the flame exhausts itself.
I hold the queen!
                    O sure punishment (to come) . . .
                                        No, but the soul

Empty of words and this weighted body
Succumb late to the proud silence of noon:
Without any more ado we must sleep in forgetfulness of the
blasphemy,
Lying in the thirsty sand and as I love 108
To open my mouth to the wine-making star (the sun)!

Couple, adieu; I'll see the shadow you became.

[Mallarmé]

The Flute

For the day of Hyacinthus, he gave me a syrinx made of carefully cut reeds, joined with white wax which is sweet as honey to my lips.

He teaches me to play, seated upon his knees; but I tremble a bit. He plays after me; so softly that I can scarcely hear him.

We have nothing to say to each other, so close are we one to the other; but our songs answer each other and, by turns, our lips join on the flute.

It is late; there is the song of the green frogs which begins with nightfall. My mother will never believe that I have stayed so long searching for my lost waistband.

[Louÿs]

The Hair

He said to me: "Last night I dreamed. I had your hair about my neck. I had your locks like a black collar around my neck and over my breast.

"I caressed them, and they were mine; and we were joined thus forever, by the same locks, mouth upon mouth, as two laurels often have but one root.

"And, little by little, it seemed to me that our limbs were mingled, that I became you or that you entered into me like my dream."

When he had finished, he placed his hands gently on my shoulders, and he looked at me with so tender a regard that I lowered my eyes, trembling.

[Louÿs]

The Tomb of the Naiads

I was walking along the frost-covered wood; my hair flowered with little icicles in front of my mouth, and my sandals were heavy with clumps of muddy snow.

He said to me: "What are you looking for?"—I am following the track of the satyr. His little cloven hoofprints alternate like holes in a white cloak. He said to me: "The satyrs are dead.

"The satyrs and the nymphs as well. In thirty years there has not been such a terrible winter. The hoofprint which you see is that of a billy-goat. But let's stop here, at their tomb."

And with the blade of his hoe he broke the ice of the spring where the naiads used to laugh. He took great frozen pieces, and lifting them up toward the pale sky, he peered through them.

[Louÿs]

Of Dreams

The night has a woman's sweetness,
And the old trees, under the golden moon, dream
Of her who just went by, head empearled,
Now wounded,
Forever wounded,
They weren't able to beckon to her . . .

All of them! They are gone:
The Frail,
The Foolish,
Sowing their laughter on the sparse lawn,

On the grazing breezes,
The fascinating caress
Of swelling hips,
Alas! of all this, nothing is left save a pale tremor.

The old trees under the golden moon weep for
Their lovely golden leaves.
Nonc will evermore dedicate to them the pride
of golden helmets,
Now tarnished,
Forever tarnished,
The knights have died on the road to the Grail!

The night has a woman's sweetness!
Hands seem to graze souls,
Hands so foolish,
So frail,
In the days when swords sang for Them! . . .
Strange sighs rise up from under the trees.
My soul! Something from an ancient dream grips you.

[Debussy]

Of Shore

Over the sea twilights fall
(White raveled silk).
The waves like silly girls
Chatter, little girls leaving school,
Among the rustlings of their dresses,
(Green, iridescent silk).

The clouds, grave travelers,
Plan the next storm
And it is really too grave a background
For such an English watercolor.
The waves, the little waves,
Are embarrassed,
For here comes the wretched downpour,
Rustlings of fleeing skirts,
(Green, panic-stricken silk!)

But the moon, pitiful to all!
Comes by and soothes this gray struggle,
And slowly caresses its little friends
Who offer themselves like loving lips
To this warm and white kiss.

Then, nothing more,
Nothing but the belated bells
Of the floating churches,
Angelus of the waves,
(Soothed white silk!)

[Debussy]

Of Flowers

In the ennui, so desolately verdant, of the hothouse of sorrow,
The flowers entwine my heart in their spiteful stems.
Ah! when will those dear, so tenderly disentwining hands
Come back about my head?
The great violet irises
Spitefully ravished your eyes
While seeming to reflect them,
They that were the water of the dream into which my dreams sank,
So gently enveloped in their color;
And the lilies, white fountains of fragrant pistils,

Have lost their white grace
And are now only poor invalids without sun!
Sun! friend of the evil flowers,
Slayer of dreams! Slayer of illusions!
That blessed bread of unhappy souls!
Come! Come! Hands of salvation!
Shatter the panes of falsehood,
Shatter the panes of evil,
My soul is dying of too much sun!
Mirages! Nevermore will the joy of my eyes bloom again,
And my hands are weary of praying,
My eyes are weary of weeping.
Eternally this crazy sound of the black petals of ennui
Falling drop by drop on my head
In the verdure of the hothouse of sorrow!

[Debussy]

Evening

Sunday in the towns,
Sunday in the hearts!
Sunday with the little girls
Singing in childish voices
Persistent rounds where good Towers
Will last only for a few days!
On Sunday the stations are frantic!
Everyone is setting out for some suburb or other,
Saying goodbye to one another with distracted gestures!
On Sunday the trains go quickly,
Devoured by insatiable tunnels;
And the good signal lights along the way
Exchange with a single eye
Their altogether mechanical impressions.
On Sunday, in the blue of my dreams,
Where my sad thoughts of abortive fireworks
Will not leave off mourning
Old departed Sundays.
And the night with velvet steps
Comes to put the lovely, weary sky to sleep,
And it is Sunday in the avenues of the stars;
The virgin of gold upon silver
Lets fall the flowers of slumber!

Quickly, little angels, overtake the swallows
So that you may go to bed, blessed by absolution.
Take pity on the towns,
Take pity on the hearts,
You, Virgin of gold upon silver!

[Debussy]

Pantomime

Pierrot, who has nothing of Clitander about him,
Empties a flask without further ado,
And, very businesslike, cuts into a pie.

Cassandre, at the end of the street,
Sheds a misunderstood tear
For his disinherited nephew.

Harlequin, that rascal, contrives
The abduction of Colombine
And pirouettes four times.

Colombine dreams, surprised
To feel someone else's heart in the breeze
And to hear voices in her own heart.

[Verlaine]

Marionettes

Scaramouch and Pulcinella,
United by an evil design,
Gesticulate, black figures against the moon.

Meanwhile the worthy doctor
From Bologna, with due deliberation,
Gathers medicinal plants among the brown herbs.

Then his daughter of piquant pretty face
Glides half-naked on tiptoe
Beneath the arbor, in search

Of her handsome Spanish pirate,
Whose distress a languorous nightingale
Clamors at the top of his lungs.

[Verlaine]

The Unsophisticates

High heels struggled with long skirts,
So that, depending on the terrain and the wind,
The bottoms of legs occasionally glistened, too often
Intercepted! How we used to love this foolish game.

Oh and sometimes the sting of a jealous insect
Bothered the neck of the pretty maidens under the branches
And there were sudden flashes of white necks,
And this treat overwhelmed our young foolish eyes.

Night fell, an ambiguous autumn twilight:
The lovely maidens, leaning dreamily on our arms,
Softly murmured then such specious words,
That our souls tremble and marvel ever since.

[Verlaine]

The Faun

An old terra-cotta faun
Laughs in the middle of a bowling green,
Probably foreseeing an unfortunate
Sequel to these tranquil moments

Which have brought you and me—
Melancholy pilgrims—
To this hour, whose flight
Whirls to the sound of the drums.

[Verlaine]

Sentimental Colloquy

In the old park, empty and frozen,
Two figures have just gone by.

Their eyes are lifeless and their lips are limp,
And one can scarcely hear their words.

In the old park, empty and frozen,
Two specters have evoked the past.

—Do you remember our rapture of old?
—Why do you wish me to remember it?

—Does your heart still beat faster just at my name?
Do you still see my soul in your dreams? —No.

O, those beautiful days of unspeakable joy,
When we used to join our lips! —It is possible.

—How blue was the sky, how great our hopes!
—Hope has fled, defeated, towards the black sky.

So they trudged among the wild oats,
And only the night heard their words.

[Verlaine]

Sigh

My soul, toward your forehead (where dreams, o calm sister
An autumn strewn with freckles)
And toward the roaming heaven of your angelic eye
Soars: as in a melancholy garden,
Faithful, a white fountain sighs toward the Azure!
—Toward the soft, kindly October Azure, pale and pure,
Which mirrors in the great fountains its languor without end
And leaves (on the still water where the tawny death
Of leaves roams in the wind and plows a cold furrow)
The yellow sun to trail along in a long, low ray.

[Mallarmé]

Vain Entreaty

Princess, envying the lot of Hebe
(Conjured onto this cup by your lips' kiss)
I spend my ardor, but hold only the modest rank of abbé
And won't be portrayed, even nude, on Sèvres paste.

As I am not your lapdog swathed in beard,
Nor the jujube, nor rouge, nor dainty sports,
And as I know your glance falls on me shut,
Blonde with goldsmiths as divine hairdressers,

Name us . . . you whose raspberry-scented laughter
Becomes a flock of tame lambs
Browsing on everyone's desires, bleating in rapt transports,

Name us . . . so that Love winged with a fan
May paint me, flute in hand, putting that fold to sleep,
Princess, name us shepherd of your smiles.

[Mallarmé]

Fan

O dreamer-girl, if you'd have me plunge
Into pure pathless delight,
Manage, through a subtle lie
To keep my wing in your hand.

A freshness of twilight
Comes to you at each beat
Whose imprisoned stroke thrusts back
The horizon delicately.

Vertigo! see how shivers
Space like a great kiss
Which, mad at being born for no one,
Can neither spurt up nor be calmed.

Do you sense the fierce paradise
Like a buried laugh
Flow from a corner of your mouth
Deep into the unanimous fold!

The scepter of pink shores
Stagnant on golden evenings, this it is,
This closed white wing you place
Against the fire of a bracelet.

[Mallarmé]

Bibliography

A. BIBLIOGRAPHICAL TOOLS

Abravanel, Claude. *Claude Debussy*; *A bibliography*. Detroit: Information Coordinators, 1974.

Austin, L. J. "Etat présent des études sur Baudelaire." *Forum for Modern Language Study* 3 (1967):352–369.

Bibliographie Annuelle de l'Histoire de France. Paris: Centre National de la Recherche Scientifique, 1953–

Bibliography of Critical and Biographical References for the Study of Contemporary French Literature. Publication of the Modern Language Association, 1940–

Cargo, Robert T. *Baudelaire Criticism 1950–1967. A Bibliography with Critical Commentary.* University, Alabama: University of Alabama Press, 1968.

Lesure, François. "Bibliographie Debussyste." In *Claude Debussy. Textes et Documents Inédits.* Edited by Lesure. *Revue de Musicologie* (Special Number) 1962:129–143.

Maurice-Amour, Lila. "Mallarmé." *Musik in Geschichte und Gegenwart*, vol. 8:1552–1553.

———. "Musiques inspirées par les Fleurs du Mal." *Revue des Sciences Humaines* 89 (January–March 1958):167–180.

———. "Verlaine." *Musik in Geschichte und Gegenwart*, vol. 13:1492–1496.

Peyre, Henri. *Connaissance de Baudelaire.* Paris: Corti, 1951.

Revue de Musicologie. Annual index to articles on music in various periodicals.

B. POETRY

1. General

Adam, Antoine, *et al. Littérature Fançaise.* Paris: Larousse, 1968.
Bishop, Morris. *A Survey of French Literature*, vol. 2. New York: Harcourt, Brace & World, 1965.
Bray, René. *La Préciosité et les Précieux.* Paris: Editions Albin Michel, 1948.
Burnshaw, Stanley, ed. *The Poem Itself.* New York: Holt, Rinehart and Winston, 1960.
Charpentier, John. *L'Evolution de la poésie lyrique de Joseph Delorme à Paul Claudel.* Paris: Les Oeuvres Représentatives, 1931.
Cohn, Robert Greer. "The ABC's of Poetry." *Comparative Literature* 14 (1962):187–191.
Delattre, Pierre. *Principes de phonétique française.* Middlebury, Vermont: Ecole Française d'Eté, 1951.
de Lisle, Leconte. *Poésies complètes.* Paris: Poulet-Malassis et DeBroise, 1858.
Eliot, T. S. "From Poe to Valéry." In *To Criticize the Critic.* New York: Farrar, Straus & Giroux, 1965.
Gibson, Robert, ed. *Modern French Poets on Poetry.* Cambridge: At the University Press, 1961.
Gilman, Margaret. *The Idea of Poetry in France.* Cambridge, Massachusetts: Harvard University Press, 1958.
Gleason, H. A., Jr. *An Introduction to Descriptive Linguistics.* New York: Holt, Rinehart and Winston, 1961.
Grammont, Maurice. *Le Vers français. Ses moyens d'expression. Son armonie.* [sic] Paris: E. Champion, 1923.
Hall, Robert A., Jr. *A Short History of Italian Literature.* Ithaca, New York: Linguistica, 1951.
Harvey, Sir Paul, and J. E. Heseltine. *The Oxford Companion to French Literature.* Oxford: At the Clarendon Press, 1959, 1969.
Jones, P. Mansell. *The Background of Modern French Poetry.* Cambridge: At the University Press, 1951.
———. *Modern French Verse. An Anthology.* Manchester: Manchester University Press, 1954.
Kennard, Joseph Spencer. *Masks and Marionettes.* Port Washington, New York: Kennikut Press, 1935, 1967.
Morier, Henri. *La Psychologie des styles.* Genève: Georg éditeurs, 1959.
———. *Dictionnaire de Poétique et de Rhétorique.* Paris: Presses Universitaires de France, 1961.
Moser, Ruth. *L'Impressionnisme Français.* Genève: Librairie Droz, 1952.

Nicoll, Allardyce. *The World of Harlequin.* Cambridge: At the University Press, 1963.

Ogden, C. K., and I. A. Richards. *The Meaning of Meaning.* 8th ed. New York: Harcourt, Brace & World, 1946.

Parmée, Douglas. *Twelve French Poets. 1820–1900.* London: Longmans, Green, 1957.

Picherot, R. "Musiciens et Ecrivains." *Education Nationale* (14 April 1966):25–26.

Poulet, Georges. *La Distance Intérieure.* Paris: Librairie Plon, 1952. Volume 2 of his *Etudes sur le temps humain.*

Preminger, Alex, ed. *Encyclopedia of Poetry and Poetics.* Princeton: Princeton University Press, 1965.

Raymond, Marcel. *From Baudelaire to Surrealism.* New York: Wittenborn, Schultz, 1950.

———. *Vérité et Poésie.* Neuchatel: Editions de la Baconnière, 1964.

Richards, I. A. *How to Read a Page. A Course in Efficient Reading with an Introduction to a Hundred Great Words.* Boston: Beacon Press, 1959, 1942.

———. *Practical Criticism.* New York: Harcourt, Brace & World, 1929.

———. *Principles of Literary Criticism.* New York: Harcourt, Brace & World, 1925.

Rose, H. J. *A Handbook of Greek Mythology.* London: Methuen, 1958.

Spire, André. *Plaisir Poétique et Plaisir Musculaire.* New York: S. F. Vanni, 1949.

Valéry, Paul. *The Art of Poetry.* Translated by Denise Folliot. New York: Random House, Vintage Books, 1961.

Vigny, Alfred de. *Les Destinées.* Edited by Verdun L. Saulnier. Paris: Librairie Droz, 1947.

Weber, Jean-Paul. *Genèse de l'Oeuvre Poétique.* Paris: Librairie Gallimard, 1960.

Weinberg, Bernard. *The Limits of Symbolism.* Chicago: University of Chicago Press, 1966.

Whitehead, Alfred North. *Symbolism, Its Meaning and Effect.* Lectures delivered in 1927. New York: Capricorn Books, 1959.

Wilson, Edmund. *Axel's Castle. A Study in the Imaginative Literature of 1870 to 1930.* New York: Scribner's, 1959.

Woodcock, P. G. *Short Dictionary of Mythology.* New York: Philosophical Library, 1953.

2. Banville

Banville, Théodore de. *Poésies complètes.* Paris: G. Charpentier, 1887.

———. *Petit Traité de Poésie Française.* Paris: G. Charpentier, 1888.

Coeuroy, André. *Appels d'Orphée. Nouvelles études de musique et de littérature comparées.* Paris: La Nouvelle Revue Critique, 1928.

Davies, Gardner. "Note on Banville and Mallarmé." *AUMLA, (Journal of the Australasian Universities Language and Literature Association)* 19 (1963):107–111.

Souffrin, Eileen-Margaret. *Les Stalactites de Théodore de Banville.* Paris: H. Didier, 1942.

———. "Théodore de Banville et la Musique." *French Studies* 9 (1955):238–245.

———. "Debussy Lecteur de Banville." *Revue de Musicologie* 46 (1960):200–222.

———. "Une Pétition en faveur de Baudelaire avec une lettre inédite de Théodore de Banville." *Le Bayou* 25/85–86 (1961):324–327.

———. "Théodore de Banville, Inspirateur des Musiciens." *Le Bayou* 27/95 (1963):469–479.

———. "Le Byronisme de Théodore de Banville." *Revue de Littérature Comparée* 37 (1963):497–512.

———. "Théodore de Banville et le ballet romantique." *Revue des sciences humaines* 109 (1963):59–75.

———. "Banville et la mort de Heine." *Revue de Littérature Comparée* 40 (1966):185–211.

———. "Théodore de Banville." *Encyclopedia Britannica*, Chicago, 1968.

3. Baudelaire

Auerbach, Erich. "The Aesthetic Dignity of the 'Fleurs du Mal.' " In *Scenes from the Drama of European Literature.* New York: Meridian Books, 1959, pp. 201–226.

Austin, Lloyd James. *L'Univers poétique de Baudelaire.* Paris: Mercure de France, 1956.

Bachelard, Gaston. *The Poetics of Space.* Translated by Maria Jolas. New York: Orion Press, 1964.

Bandy, W. T. "Baudelaire's 'Recueillement,' Line 1." *Explicator* 20, Item 51.

Baudelaire, Charles. *Les Fleurs du Mal.* Introduction and notes by Antoine Adam. Paris: Garnier Frères, 1961.

———. *Oeuvres complètes.* Edited by Y.-G. le Dantec. Revised by Claude Pichois. Paris: Bibliothèque de la Pléiade, 1968.

Bertocci, Angelo Philip. *From Symbolism to Baudelaire.* Carbondale: Southern Illinois University Press, 1964.

Bruyr, José. "Baudelaire et ses musiciens. Chant d'Automne, de Gábriel Fauré." *Musica Disques* 41 (1957):33–35.

Butor, Michel. *Histoire Extraordinaire. Essay on a Dream of Baudelaire's.* Translated by Richard Howard. London: Jonathan Cape, 1961, 1969.

Chérix, Robert-Benoît. *L'esthétique symboliste.* Thesis. Fribourg, Suisse: 1922.

———. *Commentaire des "Fleurs du Mal."* Genève: Pierre Cailler, 1949. Librairie E. Droz, 1962.

Doucet, J. "Harmonie du Soir de Charles Baudelaire." *Les Etudes Classiques* 11 (1942):100–107.

Eliot, T. S. "Baudelaire." In *Selected Essays.* New York: Harcourt, Brace, 1950, pp. 371–381.

Ferran, André. "Baudelaire et la musique." In *Mélanges de philosophie et d'histoire littéraire offerts à Edmond Huguet.* Paris: Boivin, 1940, pp. 387–393.

Feuerlicht, Ignace. "Baudelaire's 'Harmonie du Soir.'" *French Review* 33 (1959–1960):17–26.

Gallico, Claudio. "Baudelaire e la musica." *Convivium* 23 (1955):68–81.

Hassan, Ihab H. "Baudelaire's *Correspondances*: The Dialectic of a Poetic Affinity." *French Review* 27 (1954):437–445.

Hubert, Judd D. *L'Esthétique des "Fleurs du Mal."* Genève: Pierre Cailler, 1953.

Huxley, Aldous. "Vulgarity in Literature." *Saturday Review of Literature* 7 (1930–1931):158–159.

Hyslop, Lois B. *Baudelaire as Love Poet and Other Essays.* University Park: Pennsylvania State University Press, 1969.

Johansen, Svend. *Le Symbolisme.* Copenhague: Einar Munksgaard, 1945.

Jones, Percy Mansell. *Baudelaire.* "Studies in Modern European Literature and Thought." London and New Haven: Bowes & Bowes and Yale University Press, 1952.

King, William W. "Baudelaire and Mallarmé: Metaphysics or Aesthetics." *Journal of Aesthetics and Art Criticism* 26 (1967):115–123.

Mary Anthony (la mère) "A Note on Baudelaire's *Correspondances.*" *Romance Notes* 4 (1963):13–14.

Meylan, Pierre. *Les Écrivains et la musique.* Lausanne: Editions la Concorde, 1944.

Oxenhandler, Neal. "The Balcony of Charles Baudelaire." *Yale French Studies* 9–10 (1952):56–62.

Pellegrin, Jean. "Baudelaire et les 'Correspondances.'" *Revue des Sciences Humaines* 121 (January–March 1966):105–120.

Peyre, Henri, ed. *Baudelaire. A Collection of Critical Essays.* Englewood Cliffs, N.J.: Prentice-Hall, 1962.

Remacle, Madeleine. "Analyses de poèmes français." *Revue des langues vivantes* 17 (1951):218–227. (On *Recueillement*)

Roedig, Charles F. "Baudelaire and Synesthesia." *Kentucky Foreign Language Quarterly* 5 (1958):128–135.

Roy, Claude. "Les parfums, les couleurs et les sons se répondent." Chapter 10 of *Baudelaire.* Paris: Hachette, Collection génies et réalités, 1961, pp. 241–258.

Rudich, Norman. "*Harmonie du soir* de Charles Baudelaire. Explication de texte." *Information Littéraire* 17/3 (1965):133–138.

Schaeffner, André. "Corrispondenze baudelairiane." *Quaderni della Rassegna musicale* 4 (1968):97–104.

Stephan, Philip. "Verlaine and Baudelaire: Two Uses of Obscured Lightings." *French Review* 35 (1961):26–35.

Ullman, Stephen. *The Principles of Semantics.* Oxford: Basil Blackwell, 1951.

4. Laforgue

Adam, Antoine, *et al. Littérature Française.* Paris: Larousse, 1968.

Collie, Michael. *Laforgue.* London: Oliver and Boyd, 1963.

Guichard, Léon. *Jules Laforgue et ses poésies.* Paris: Presses Universitaires de France, 1950.

Laforgue, Jules. *Poems.* Translated by Patricia Terry. Foreword by Henri Peyre. Berkeley: University of California Press, 1958.

———. *Jules Laforgue and the Ironic Inheritance.* New York: Oxford University Press, 1953.

Ramsey, Warren, ed. *Jules Laforgue. Essays on a Poet's Life and Work.* Carbondale: Southern Illinois University Press, 1969.

5. Louÿs

Borgeaud, Henri, ed. *Correspondance de Claude Debussy et Pierre Louÿs.* Paris: Librairie José Corti, 1945.

Cardinne-Petit, Robert. *Pierre Louÿs intime, le solitaire du Hameau.* Paris: J. Renard, 1942.

Farrère, Claude. *Mon ami Pierre Louÿs.* Paris: Domat, 1954.

Lestang, Paule de. "Les Chansons de Bilitis." *Revue Musicale de Lyon* 4 (1906):235–239.

Lockspeiser, Edward. "Debussy and Louÿs." B.B.C. Radio Broadcast, 9 November 1965.

Louÿs, Pierre. *Les Chansons de Bilitis. Traduites du Grec.* Paris: Albin Michel, Editeur, 1932.

———. *The Songs of Bilitis. Translated from the Greek.* New York: Privately printed for William Godwin, 1933.

———. *Les Poëmes de Pierre Louÿs.* Edited by Yves-Gérard le Dantec. Paris: Albin Michel, 1945.

Thompson, Vance. *French Portraits.* Boston: Richard G. Badger, 1900.

Vallas, Léon. "Une Renaissance de Bilitis." *Domaine musical* 1/1 (1954):150–152.

6. Mallarmé

Adam, Antoine. "L'Après-midi d'un faune. Essai d'explication." *L'Information Littéraire* 1/4 (July–October 1949):137–140.

Austin, Lloyd James. "Mallarmé on Music and Letters." *Bulletin of The John Ryland Library* 42 (1959–1960): 19–39.

———. " 'L'Après-midi d'un faune' de Stéphane Mallarmé. Lexique comparé des trois états du poème." *Studi in onore di Carlo Pelligrini.* Torino: Società Editrice Internazionale, 1963, pp. 733–738.

———. "L'Après-midi d'un Faune. Essai d'explication." *Synthèses* 258/259 (December 1967/January 1968):24–35.

Beausire, Pierre. *Mallarmé. Poésie et poétique.* Lausanne: Mermod, 1949.

Bernard, Suzanne. *Mallarmé et la Musique.* Paris: Librairie Nizet, 1959.

Böhmer, Helga. "Alchimie der Töne. Die Mallarmé-Vertonungen von Debussy und Ravel." *Musica* 22 (1968):83–85.

Canaday, John. *The World Dividing: The 18th Century.* New York: The Metropolitan Museum of Art, 1959.

Chassé, Charles. *Lueurs sur Mallarmé.* Paris: Editions de la Nouvelle Revue Critique, 1947.

———. *Les Clés de Mallarmé.* Paris: Aubier, 1954.

Chisholm, A. R. *Mallarmé's l'Après-midi d'un Faune. An Exegetical and Critical Study.* Carlton: Melbourne University Press, 1958.

Cohn, Robert Greer. *Toward the Poems of Mallarmé.* Berkeley: University of California Press, 1965.

Cook, Bradford. *Mallarmé: Selected Prose Poems, Essays and Letters.* Translated and with an introduction by Bradford Cook. Baltimore: Johns Hopkins Press, 1956.

Cooperman, Hayse. *The Aesthetics of Stéphane Mallarmé.* New York: Koffern Press, 1933.

Fowlie, Wallace. *Mallarmé.* Chicago: University of Illinois Press, 1953.

———. *Love in Literature. Studies in Symbolic Expression.* Bloomington; Indiana University Press, 1965.

Frye, Northrop. *Anatomy of Criticism.* New York: Atheneum, 1967.

Gill, Austin. "Mallarmé et l'Antiquité: L'Après-midi d'un Faune." *Cahiers de l'Association Internationale des Etudes Françaises* 10 (May 1958):158–173.

Hall, Robert A. *A Short History of Italian Literature.* Ithaca, New York: Linguistica, 1951.

Kesting, Marianne. "Mallarmé und die Musik." *Melos* 35 (1968):45–56.

Mallarmé, Stéphane. *Ouevres Complètes.* Edited by Henri Mondor and G. Jean-Aubry. Paris: Bibliothèque de la Pléiade, 1965.

———. "L'après-midi d'un faune." Translated by Aldous Huxley. In *An Anthology of World Poetry.* Edited by Mark Van Doren. New York: Harcourt, Brace, 1936.

———. *La Dernière Mode.* Introduction by S. A. Rhodes. New York: Publications of the Institute of French Studies, 1933.

Mallarmé Stéphane. *Poems.* Translated by Roger Fry with commentaries by Charles Mauron. New York: Oxford University Press, 1937.

———. *Selected Poems.* Translated and annotated by C. F. MacIntyre. Berkeley: University of California Press, 1965.

Mauron, Charles. *Introduction à la Psychanalyse de Mallarmé.* Neuchatel: A la Baconnière, 1950.

———. *Mallarmé l'obscur.* Paris: Librairie José Corti, 1968.

Michaud, Guy. *Mallarmé l'homme et l'oeuvre.* Paris: Hatier-Boivin, 1953.

———. *Mallarmé.* Translated by Marie Collins and Bertha Humez. New York: New York University Press, 1965.

Michell, Joyce. "Symbolism in Music and Poetry." Dissertation. Philadelphia: 1944.

Mondor, Henri. *Histoire d'un Faune.* Paris: Gallimard, 1948.

———. "Stéphane Mallarmé et Claude Debussy." *Journal Musical Français* 1 (25 September 1951):1,8.

Munro, Thomas. " 'The Afternoon of a Faun' and the Interrelation of the Ars." In *Toward Science in Aesthetics.* New York: Liberal Arts Press, 1956: pp. 342–363.

Noulet, E. *L'Oeuvre poétique de Stéphane Mallarmé.* Paris: Librairie E. Droz, 1940.

———. *Vingt poèmes de Stéphane Mallarmé.* Genève: Librairie Droz, 1967.

Richard, Jean-Pierre. *L'Univers imaginaire de Mallarmé.* Paris: Editions du Seuil, 1961.

St. Aubyn, Frederic Chase. *Stéphane Mallarmé.* New York: Twayne Publishers, 1969.

Schmidt-Garre, Helmut. "Rimbaud-Mallarmé-Debussy. Parallelen zwischen Dichtung und Musik." *Neue Zeitschrift für Musik* 125 (1964):290–297.

———. "Mallarmé und der Wagnérisme." *Neue Zeitschrift für Musik* 130 (1969):512–519.

Terenzio, Vincenzo. "Debussy e Mallarmé." *Rassegna Musicale* 17 (1947):132–136.

Thibaudet, Albert. *La Poésie de Stéphane Mallarmé.* Paris: Editions de la Nouvelle Revue Française, n.d.

Weinberger, Marvin Elmer. "The Linguistic Implications in the Theory and Poetry of Stéphane Mallarmé." Dissertation. Cornell University, 1956.

7. Verlaine

Adam, Antoine. *Verlaine.* Paris: Hatier, 1965.

Baudot, Alain. "Poésie et musique chez Verlaine. Forme et Signification." *Etudes françaises* 4 (1968):31–56.

Bishop, John Peale. "The Infanta's Ribbon." In *The Collected Essays of John Peale Bishop.* New York: Scribner's, 1948, pp. 14–22. *(Clair de Lune)*

Bornecque, Jacques-Henry. *Lumières sur les "Fêtes Galantes" de Paul Verlaine.* Paris: Librairie Nizet, 1959.

———. *Verlaine par lui-même.* Paris: Editions du Seuil, 1966.

Chailley, Jacques. "Les goûts musicaux de Verlaine." *Revue de Musicologie* 35 (1953):167.

Chalupt, René. "A propos des mélodies de Charles Bordes." *Revue Musicale* 12 (1932):101–107.

———. "Verlaine, ou: de la musique en toute chose." *Contrepoints* 6 (1949):62–73.

Cuénot, Claude. "Technique et esthétique du sonnet chez Paul Verlaine: des 'Poèmes saturniens' à 'Jadis et naguère.'" *Studi francesi* 4 (1960):456–471.

———. *Le Style de Paul Verlaine.* Paris: Centre de la Documentation Littéraire, 1963.

Dubu, Jean. "Du *Banc de Pierre* de Gautier au *Colloque sentimental* de Verlaine." *Studi francesi* 11 (1967):486–487.

Fortassier, Pierre. "Rythme verbal et rythme musical: à propos de la prosodie de Gabriel Fauré." *Mélanges d'histoire et d'esthétique musicales offerts à Paul-Marie Masson.* Paris: Richard-Masse-Editeur, 1955, pp. 29–37.

———. "Verlaine, la Musique et les Musiciens." *Cahiers de l'Association Internationale des Etudes Françaises* 12 (1960):143–159.

Got, Maurice. "'Art poétique': Verlaine et la technique impressionniste." *Table Ronde* 159 (March 1961):128–136.

Hilty, Gerald. "'Il' impersonnel; Syntaxe historique et interprétation littéraire." *Français Moderne* 27 (1959):241–251. *(Il pleure dans mon coeur)*

Klingsor, Tristan. "Les Musiciens et les Poètes contemporains." *Mercure de France* 36 (November 1900):430–444.

Leclère, Tristan. "Les Musiciens de Verlaine." *Revue Bleue* 72 (14 November 1903):633–635.

Michaud, Guy. *Connaissance de la littérature. L'Oeuvre et ses techniques.* Paris: Librairie Nizet, 1957.

Nadal, Octave. "L'Impressionisme verlainien." *Mercure de France* (1 May 1952):59–74.

Schaettel, Marcel. "Rythme et structure, images formelles et dynamique dans *Clair de Lune* de Verlaine." *Revue des sciences humaines* 130 (1968):259–266.

Schneider, Albert. "L'Art poétique de Paul Verlaine." *Academie de Metz. Memoires* 146/sér.5, t.10 1967 (1964–1965):107–116.

Shearman, John. *Mannerism.* Middlesex: Penguin Books, 1967.

Verlaine, Paul. *Oeuvres poétiques complètes.* Edited by Y.-G. le Dantec. Revised by Jacques Borel. Paris: Bibliothèque de la Pléiade, 1968.

———. "Confessions." *Oeuvres complètes.* Vol. 2. Paris: Le Club du meilleur livre, 1960, pp. 1095–1218.

Verlaine, Paul. "Notes on England." Oeuvres Posthumes. Vol. 3. Paris: Albert Messein, 1929.
———. *Poésies Choisis avec un commentaire par Antoine Fongaro.* Roma: Angelo Signorelli, 1968.
———. *Sagesse.* Edition critique commentée par Louis Morice. Paris: Librairie Nizet, 1964.
———. *Selected Poems.* Translated and annotated by C. F. MacIntyre. Berkeley and Los Angeles: University of California Press, 1948.
———. *Selected Poems.* Edited by R. C. D. Perman. London: Oxford University Press, 1965.
Wright, Alfred John Jr. "Paul Verlaine and the Musicians." Dissertation. Columbia University, 1950.
———. "Verlaine's 'Art Poétique' Re-Examined." *Modern Language Association Publications* 74/3 (June 1959):268–275.
———. "Verlaine and Debussy: *Fêtes galantes.*" *French Review* 40/5 (April 1967):627–635.
Zimmermann, Eléonore M. *Magies de Verlaine.* Paris: José Corti, 1967.

C. MUSIC

1. General

Apel, Willi. *Harvard Dictionary of Music.* 2d ed. Cambridge, Massachusetts: Harvard University Press, 1969.
Cone, Edward T. "On the Structure of *Ich folge dir.*" *College Music Symposium* 5 (1965):77–87.
Cooper, Martin. *French Music from the Death of Berlioz to the Death of Fauré.* London: Oxford University Press, 1951.
Cox, David. "France." In *A History of Song.* Edited by Denis Stevens. London: Hutchinson, 1960, pp. 194–227.
———. "The World of French Song." *The Listener* 68 (6 September 1962):369.
Danckert, Werner. "Melodische Funktionen." In *Festchrift Max Scheider.* Edited by Walther Vetter. Leipzig: Deutsche Verlag für Musik, 1955, pp. 343–346.
Gray, Walter Bernard. "A Comparison of the Latin and English Sacred Choral Compositions of William Byrd." Dissertation. University of Wisconsin.
Grout, Donald Jay. *A History of Western Music.* New York: Norton, 1960.
Harran, Don. " 'Mannerism' in the Cinquecento Madrigal?" *Musical Quarterly* 55 (1969):521–544.
Hickman, Hans. *45 Siècles de Musique dans l'Egypte ancienne à travers la sculpture, la peinture, l'instrument.* Paris: *La Revue Musicale.* Edition Richard Masse, 1956.
Hollander, Hans. "Franz Schubert's Repeated Settings of the Same Song-Texts." *Musical Quarterly* 14 (1928):563–574.

Jähns, Friedrich Wilhelm. *Carl Maria von Weber in seinen Werken. Chronologisch-thematisches Verzeichniss seiner sämmtlichen Compositionen.* Berlin: Verlag der Schlesinger'schen Buch- und Musikhandlung, 1871.

Jankélévitch, Vladimir. *Gabriel Fauré. Ses mélodies, son esthétique.* Paris: Librairie Plon, 1938.

Koechlin, Charles. "La Mélodie." In *Cinquante Ans de Musique Française.* Edited by L. Rohozinski. Paris: Les Editions Musicales de la Librairie de France, 1926, vol. 2, pp. 1–62.

Longyear, Rey M. *Nineteenth-Century Romanticism in Music.* Englewood Cliffs, N.J.: Prentice-Hall, 1969.

McPhee, Colin. "The Five-Tone Gamelan Music of Bali." *Musical Quarterly* 35 (1949):250–281.

Myers, Rollo. *Modern French Music.* Oxford: Basil Blackwell, 1971.

Noske, Frits Rudolf. *La Mélodie Française de Berloiz à Duparc. Essai de critique historique.* Amsterdam: North-Holland Publishing Company, 1954.

Palmer, Christopher. *Impressionism in Music.* London: Hutchinson University Library, 1973.

Szabolcsi, Bence. *A History of Melody.* Translated by Cynthia Jolly and Sara Karig. London: Barrie and Rockliff. 1965.

2. Debussy

Allard, Maurice. "The Songs of Claude Debussy and Francis Poulenc." Thesis. University of Southern California, 1964.

Almendra, Julia d'. "Debussy e la sua obra." *Brotéria* 76 (1963):175–191.

Altenbernd, Nicholas. "Debussy's Afternoon of a Faun." Unpublished paper.

Ambrière, Francis. "La Vie Romaine de Claude Debussy." *Revue Musicale* 15 (1934):20–26.

Ansermet, Ernest. "An Inner Unity: Conversations with Ernest Ansermet on the Art of Debussy." (With Peter Heyworth) *High Fidelity* 12/9 (September 1962):56–58, 131.

Austin, William W. *Music in the 20th Century.* New York: Norton, 1966.

———. Claude Debussy. *Prelude to "The Afternoon of a Faun."* New York: Norton, 1970.

Baron, Bernard. "La Musique de piano de Fauré, Debussy, Ravel." *Technique, art, science; revue de l'enseignement technique* 189 (1965):38–42.

Barraqué, Jean. "Debussy: ou l'approche d'une organisation autogène de la composition." In *Debussy et l'Evolution.* Edited by Edith Weber, pp. 83–95.

———. *Debussy.* Paris: Editions du Seuil, 1967.

Bathori, Jane. *Sur l'Interpretation des mélodies de Claude Debussy.* Paris: Les Editions Ouvrières, 1953.

Beaussant, Philippe. "Debussy ou la liberté." *Table Ronde* 244 (1968):59–64.

Berman, Laurence D. "The Evolution of Tonal Thinking in the Works of Claude Debussy." Dissertation. Harvard University, 1965.

Bonheur, Raymond. "Souvenirs et impressions d'un compagnon de jeunesse." *Revue Musicale* 7 (1926):3–9.

Borris, Siegfried. "Einfluss und Einbruch primitiver Musik in die Musik des Abendlandes." *Sociologus* 2 (1952):52–72.

———. "Neue Formen der Mehrstimmigkeit." *Musikalische Zeitfragen* 9 (1960):110–112.

Boulez, Pierre. "Debussy" in *Encyclopédie de la Musique*, vol. 1. Paris: Fasquelle, 1958, pp. 629–640.

———. "La Corruption dans les Encensoirs." In *Relevées d'Apprenti.* Paris: Editions du Seuil, 1966, pp. 33–39.

Brailoiu, Constantin. "Pentatony in Debussy's Music." In *Studiae Memoriae Belae Bartók Sacra.* Budapest: Publishing House of the Hungarian Academy of Sciences, 1959: pp. 377–417.

———. "Coup d'oeil historique sur l'oeuvre de Claude Debussy." In *Claude Debussy Textes et Documents Inédits.* Edited by François Lesure. Pp. 121–128.

Brussel, Robert, "Claude Debussy et Paul Dukas." *Revue Musicale* 7 (1926):92–109.

Busser, Henri. "Les envois dc Rome de Claude Debussy." *Revue des deux mondes* 17 (1962):70–75.

Caillard, C. François, and José de Bérys. *Le Cas Debussy.* Paris: Bibliothèque du Temps Présent, 1910.

Capellen, Georg. "Exotische Rhythmik, Melodik und Tonalität als Wegweiser zu einer neuen Kunstentwicklung." *Die Musik* 6 (1907):216–227.

———. "L'Exotisme et la musique de l'avenir." *S.I.M.* 6 (1910):541–547.

Chabaneix, Philippe. "Pour un cinquantenaire. Images de Claude Debussy." *Revue des deux mondes* 11–12 (1968):364–370.

Chailley, Jacques. "Apparences et Réalités dans le langage musical de Debussy." In *Debussy et l'évolution.* Edited by Edith Weber. Pp. 47–82.

Cnattingius, Claes M. "Notes sur les oeuvres de jeunesse de Claude Debussy." *Svensk Tidskrift för Musikforskning* 44 (1962):31–59.

Damon, S. Foster. "American Influence on Modern French Music." *Dial* 65 (1918):93–95.

Danckert, Werner. "Das Wesen des musikalischen Impressionismus." *Deutsche Vierteljahrschrift für Literaturwissenschaft und Geistesgeschite* 7 (1929):137–156.

———. *Claude Debussy.* Berlin: Walter de Gruyter, 1950.

Debussy, Claude. *Monsieur Croche et autres écrits.* Edited by François Lesure. Paris: Gallimard, 1971. This volume supersedes previous editions of *Monsieur Croche* and contains Debussy's complete critical writings.

Debussy, Claude. Letters to:

d'ANNUNZIO, Gabriele. *Correspondance inédite.* Edited by G. Tosi, Paris: 1948.

BARDAC, Raoul. In *Debussy.* By Edward Lockspeiser. New York: Collier Books, 1931, 1962. Appendix E.

BARON, Emile. In "La Vie romaine de Claude Debussy." By Francis Ambrière. *Revue Musicale* 15 (1934):20–26.

CAPLET, André. *Lettres inédites à André Caplet (1908–1914) Recueillies et proésentées par Edward Lockspeiser. Avant-propos d'André Schaeffner.* Monaco: Editions du Rocher, 1957.

CHAUSSON, Ernest. "Correspondance inédite de Claude Debussy et Ernest Chausson." *Revue Musicale* 7 (1925):116–126.

———. "Deux lettres de Debussy à Ernest Chausson." *Revue Musicale* 7 (1926):183–184.

———. "Deux amis. Claude Debussy et Ernest Chausson. Documents inédits." *Mercure de France* 256 (1934):248–269.

DEBUSSY, Emma. *Lettres de Claude Debussy à sa femme Emma présentées par Pasteur Vallery-Radot.* Paris: Flammarion, 1957.

DURAND, Jacques. *Lettres de Claude Debussy à son éditeur publiées par Jacques Durand.* Paris: Durand, 1927.

GODET, Robert. "Le Lyrisme intime de Debussy." *Revue Musicale* (Special Issue 1920):167–190.

———. "En marge de la marge." *Revue Musicale* 7 (1926):51–96.

———. *Lettres à deux amis. 78 Lettres inédites à Robert Godet et G. Jean-Aubry.* Paris: Corti, 1942.

LALOY, Louis. "Correspondance de Claude Debussy et de Louis Laloy, 1902–1914." Edited by F. Lesure. *Revue de Musicologie* 28 (1962):3–40.

LOUŸS, Pierre. *Correspondance de Claude Debussy et Pierre Louÿs (1893–1904) recueillie et annotée par H. Borgeaud avec une introduction de G. Jean-Aubry.* Paris: J. Corti, 1945.

———. "Lettres inédites de Claude Debussy à Pierre Louÿs." *Revue de Musicologie* 57 (1971):29–39.

MESSAGER, André. *La Jeunesse de Pelléas. Lettres de Claude Debussy à André Messager.* Paris: Dorbon, 1938.

MOLINARI, Bernardino. "Trois lettres de Claude Debussy à Bernardino Molinari." *Suisse Romande* 3 (1939):51–56.

PETER, René. In *Claude Debussy.* By René Peter. Paris: Gallimard, 1944.

PONIATOWSKI, André. "Due lettere di Debussy." *Rassegna Musicale* 2 (1951):56–59.

SÉGALEN, Victor. *Ségalen et Debussy. Textes recueillis et présentés par Annie Joly-Segalen et André Schaeffner.* Monaco: Editions du Rocher, 1961.

STRAVINSKY, Igor. *Avec Stravinsky*. Monaco: Editions du Rocher, 1958:199–203.
TOULET, Paul-Jean. *Correspondance de Claude Debussy et P.-J. Toulet*. Paris: Le Divan, 1929.
VALLERY-RADOT, Pasteur. *Tel état Claude Debussy suivi de* [17] *lettres* [de Debussy] *à l'auteur*. Paris: René Julliard, 1958.
VASNIER, Eugène-Henry. In "A la Villa Médicis." By Henri Prunière. *Revue Musicale* 7 (1926):119–138.
YSAŸE, Eugène. "Lettre à Eugène Ysaÿe." *Revue Musicale* 7 (1926):127.
———. In *Ysaÿe. His Life, Work and Influence*. By Antoine Ysaÿe and Bertram Ratcliffe. London: Heinemann, 1947: pp. 189–195.
Various: Gaston Courty. "Dernières années de Debussy. Lettres inédites." *Revue des Deux Mondes* (15 May 1958):311–314.
———. "Lettres inédites de Debussy à divers, réunies par Pasteur Vallery-Radot et James N. B. Hill." *Revue Musicale* 258 (1962):109–115.
———. François Lesure. " 'L'Affaire' Debussy-Ravel: Lettres inédites." In *Festschrift Friedrich Blume*. Edited by Anna Amalie Abert and Wilhelm Pfannkuch. Kassel: Bärenreiter, 1963, pp. 231–234.
———. "Remarques." (Introduction by A. Souris) *Nouvelle Revue Française* 11 (1963):1153–1161.
———. "Trois lettres inédites de Claude Debussy, réunies par Jean Roy." *Revue Musicale* 258 (1962):117–120.

Decsey, Ernest. *Debussys Werke*. Graz: Leykam-Verlag, 1948.

Deliège, Célestin. "La Relation Forme-Contenu dans l'oeuvre de Debussy." *Revue Belge de Musicologie* 16 (1962):71–96.

Dietschy, Marcel. "The Family and Childhood of Debussy." *Musical Quarterly* 46 (1960):301–314.

———. *La Passion de Claude Debussy*. Neuchâtel: A la Baconnière, 1962.

Dille, D. "Inleiding tot het vormbegrip bij Debussy." In *Hommage à Charles van den Borren Mélanges*. Anvers: N.V. de Nederlandsche Boekhandel, 1945, pp. 175–196.

Dionisi, Renato. "Aspetti tecinici e sviluppo storico del sistema 'Esacordale' da Debussy in poi." *Rivista Italiana di Musicologia* 1 (1966):49–67.

Douliez, Paul. *Claude Debussy*. Haarlem: Uitgeverij J. H. Gottmer, 1967.

Dukas, Paul. *Les Écrits de Paul Dukas sur la Musique*. Paris: Société d'Editions Françaises et Internationales, 1948.

Dumesnil, Maurice. "Debussy's Principles in Pianoforte Playing." *Etude* 56 (1928):153–154.

———. *How to Play and Teach Debussy*. New York: Schroeder & Gunther, 1932.

———. "Debussy's Influence on Piano Writing and Playing." *Music Teachers' National Association Proceedings* 34 (1945);39–42.

Dunwell, Wilfrid. *The Evolution of Twentieth-Century Harmony*. London: Novello, 1960.

Emmanuel, Maurice. "Les Ambitions de Claude-Achille." *Revue Musicale* 7 (1926):139–146.
———. "Entretiens inédits d'Ernest Guirard et de Claude Debussy." In *Inédits sur Claude Debussy. Collection Comoedia-Charpentier*, pp. 25–33.
———. *Pelléas et Mélisande de Debussy.* Paris: Editions Mellottée, 1933.
Estrade-Guerra, Oswald d'. "Les manuscripts de Pelléas et Mélisande de Debussy." *Revue Musicale*, Special Number 235 (1957).
Evans, Edwin. "Debussy for Singers." *Sackbut* 2/5 (1921):8–14.
Fábiân, Ladislaus. *Debussy und sein Werk mit besonderer Rücksicht auf den musikalischen Impressionismus.* Munich: Drei Masken Verlag, 1923.
Fait, Luigi. "Claude Debussy 'Prix de Rome.' " *Studi Romani* 10 (1962):562–571.
Fontinas, André. *Mes Souvenirs du Symbolisme.* Paris: Editions de la Nouvelle Revue Critique, 1928.
Gervais, Françoise. *Etude parallèle des langages harmoniques de Fauré et de Debussy. Revue Musicale* 272 (1971) Special Issue.
———. "La Notion d'arabesque chez Debussy." *Revue Musicale* 241 (1958) *Carnet Critique.*
———. "Debussy et la tonalité." In *Debussy et l'Evolution. Edited by Edith Weber. Pp.* 97–106.
———. "Structures Debussystes." *Revue Musicale* 258 (1964):77–88.
Goléa, Antoine. "De Wagner à Debussy." *Revue de la Mediterranée* 14/61 (1954);289–302.
Gourdet, Georges. *Debussy.* Paris: Classiques Hachette, 1970.
Gui, Vittorio. "Le due muse di Claude Debussy." *Ponte* 18 (1962):1488–1495.
Handman, Dorel. "Psychology in Debussy's Music." *Musicology* 2/3 (April 1949):243–254.
Hardeck, Erwin. *Untersuchungen zu den Klavierliedern Claude Debussys.* Regensburg: Gustav Bosse Verlag, 1967.
Hermant, Pierre. "Musique de chambre et piano." In *Cinquante-Ans de Musique Française.* Edited by L. Rohozinski. paris: Les Editions Musicales de la Librairie de France, 1926, pp. 63–136.
Heyer, Hermann. "Claude Debussys musikalische ästhetik." *Deutsche Jahrbuch der Musikwissenschaft* 7 (1963):36–59.
Hodeir, André. "Claude Debussy, Musicien Français." *Hi-Fi / Stereo Review* 9/3 (September 1962):51–55.
Inédits sur Claude Debussy. Collection Comoedia-Charpentier. Paris: Les Publications Techniques, 1942.
Jankélévitch, Vladimir. *Debussy et le mystère.* Neuchâtel: Editions de la Baconnière, 1949.
———. *La Vie et la Mort dans la Musique de Debussy.* Neuchâtel: A la Baconniére, 1968.

Jarocinski, Stefan. *Debussy, Impressionisme et Symbolisme.* Translated by Thérèse Douchy. Paris: Editions du Seuil, 1970.

Kecskeméti, Istvan. "Claude Debussy, Musicien Français. His Last Sonatas." *Revue Belge de Musicologie* 16 (1962):117–149.

Keeton, A. E. "Debussy: His Science and His Music." *Nineteenth Century* 66 (1909):492–502.

Klein, John W. "Debussy as a musical dramatist." *Music Review* 23 (1962):208–214.

Koechlin, Charles. "Quelques anciennes mélodies inédites de Claude Debussy." *Revue Musicale* 7 (1926):115–140.

———. "Le Contrepoint chez Debussy." *Cahiers d'art* 1/9 (1926):244–245.

———. "La Léçon de Claude Debussy." *Revue Musicale* 15 (1934):1–19.

———. "Souvenirs sur Debussy, la Schola et la S.M.I." *Revue Musicale* 15 (1934):241–251.

Kolodin, Irving. "Shoots and Deviations." In *The Continuity of Music.* New York: Knopf, 1969.

Lambert, Constant. *Music Ho! A Study of Music in Decline.* London: Faber & Faber, 1966.

Lavauden, Thérèse. "L'Humour dans l'oeuvre de Debussy." *Revue Musicale* 11 (1930):97–105.

Lesure, François. "Debussy e Stravinski." *Musica d'Oggi* n.s. 2/1 (1959):242–244.

———. Claude Debussy. *Textes et Documents Inédits. Revue de Musicologie* (1962) Special Number.

———. "Debussy et le XVIe siècle." In *Hans Albrecht in Memoriam.* Edited by Wilfried Brennecke and Hans Haase. Kassel: Bärenreiter, 1962, pp. 242–245.

———. "Claude Debussy after his Centenary." *Musical Quarterly* 49 (1963):277–288.

Liess, Andreas. "L'Harmonie dans les oeuvres de Debussy." *Revue Musicale* 12 (1931):37–54.

———. "Die Stimme des Orients." *Musica* 14 (1960):769–774.

———. "Claude Debussy—der wegweisende Klassiker der moderner Musik." *Universitas* 17 (1962):1209–1221.

Lockspeiser, Edward. "Debussy and Wagner." *Monthly Musical Record* 65 (1935):81–82.

———. "Some Projects of Debussy." *Chesterian* 17 (September-October 1935):11–16.

———. "Debussy, Tchaikovsky, and Madame von Meck." *Musical Quarterly* 22 (1936):38–44.

———. "Les Symbolistes et Claude Debussy." *Menestrel* (7 and 14 August 1936):241–242.

———. "Mussorgski and Debussy." *Musical Quarterly* 23 (1937):421–427.

———. "Claude Debussy dans la correspondance de Tchaikovsky et de Mme von Meck." *Revue Musicale* 18 (1937):217–221.
———. "Debussy's Unpublished Songs." *Radio Times* 60 (23 September 1938):15.
———. "New Letters of Debussy." *Musical Times* 97 (1956):404–406.
———. "Debussy and Swinburne." *Monthly Musical Record* (March–April 1959):49–53.
———. *Debussy et Edgar Poe.* Monaco: Editions du Rocher, 1961.
———. *Debussy.* New York: Collier Books, 1962.
———. *Debussy: His Life and Mind.* London: Cassell, 1962, 1965.
———. "Debussy's Concept of the Dream." *Proceedings of the Royal Music Association* 89 (1962–1963):49–62.
———. "Mallarmé and Music." *Musical Times* 107 (1966):212–213.
———. "Frères en Art: Pièce de théâtre inédite de Debussy." *Revue de Musicologie* 56 (1970):165–176.
———. *Music and Painting. A Study in Comparative Ideas from Turner to Schoenberg.* London: Cassell, 1973.
Mellers, Wilfrid. "The Later Work of Claude Debussy or Pierrot Faché avec la Lune." *Studies in Contemporary Music.* London: Denis Dobson, 1947, pp. 43–55.
Mueller, Robert Earl. "The Concept of Tonality in Impressionist Music: Based on the works of Debussy and Ravel." Dissertation. University of Michigan, 1954.
Myers, Rollo H. "Claude Debussy and Russian Music." *Music and Letters* 39 (1958):336–342.
Nichols, Roger. "Debussy's Two Settings of 'Clair de lune.' " *Music and Letters* 48 (1967):229–235.
———. *Debussy.* London: Oxford University Press, 1973.
Paap, Wouter. " 'En Sourdine' van Paul Verlaine. Fauré-Debussy-Diepenbrock." *Mensch en Melodie* 1 (1946):188–192.
Palache, John G. "Debussy as Critic." *Musical Quarterly* 10 (1924):361–368.
Panzéra, Charles. *50 mélodies françaises: leçons de style et d'interpretation.* Bruxelles: Schott, 1964.
Park, Raymond. "The Later Style of Claude Debussy." Dissertation. University of Michigan, 1967.
Patry, A.-J. "Du nouveau sur Debussy." *Schweitzerische Musikzeitung* 97 (1957):291–295, 354–358.
Philipps, C. Henry. "The Symbolists and Debussy." *Music and Letters* 13 (1932):298–311.
Pierné, Gabriel, and Paul Vidal. "Souvenirs d'Achille Debussy." *Revue Musicale* 7 (1926):10–16.
Puig, Michel. "Le Choix de Debussy." *Arc* 27 (1965):22–28.

Raad, Virginia. "Musical Quotations in Claude Debussy." *American Music Teacher* 17 (1968):22–23, 34.

Reinhardt, Kurt. "Exotisme in der abendländischen Gegenwartsmusik." *Melos* 18 (1961):129–133.

Reti, Rudolph. "The Tonality of Debussy" in *Tonality in Modern Music.* New York: Collier Books, 1962, pp. 36–48.

Rinaldi, Mario. "Paul Dukas oltre Debussy." *Chigiana* 22 (1965):95–108.

Robertazzi, Mario. "Musica e parola nell' estetica di Claudio Debussy." *Convegno* 14 (1933):69–127.

Ruppel, K. H. "Claude Debussy und sein Werk für die moderne Musik." *Universitas* 23 (1968):611–615.

Ruschenburg, Peter. "Stilkritische Untersuchungen zu den Liedern Claude Debussy." Dissertation. Hamburg, 1966.

Ruwet, Nicolas. "Note sur les duplications dans l'oeuvre de Claude Debussy." *Revue Belge de Musicologie* 16 (1962):57–70.

Salas Viu, Vincente. "La formación estética de Debussy." *Cuadernos Hispanoamericanos* 155 (1962):411–420.

Samazeuilh, Gustave. "La première version inédite de 'En Sourdine.' " In *Inédits sur Claude Debussy. Collection Comoedia-Charpentier*, pp. 34–38.

Schaeffner, André. "Debussy et ses rapports avec la musique russe." In *Musique Russe.* Edited by Pierre Souvtchinski. Vol. 1 Paris: Presses Universitaires de France, 1953, pp. 95–139.

———. "Claude Debussy." In *Histoire de la musique.* Edited by Roland-Manuel. Vol. 2. Paris: Encyclopédie de la Pléiade, 1963, pp. 909–926.

———. "Le Timbre." In *La Résonance dans les Echelles Musicales.* Edited by Edith Weber. Paris: Editions du Centre National de la Recherche Scientifique, 1963, pp. 215–220.

———. "Claude Debussy et ses projets shakespeariens." *Revue d'histoire du théâtre* 16 (1964):446–453.

Schouten, Hennie. *Drie Franse Liederencomponisten. Duparc, Fauré, Debussy.* Amsterdam: Uitgeversmaatschappij, 1950.

Seroff, Victor I. *Debussy. Musician of France.* New York: Putnam's, 1956.

Storb, Ilse. "Untersuchungen zur Auflösung der funktionalen Harmonik in den Klavierwerken von Claude Debussy." Dissertation. Köln, 1967.

Stuckenschmidt, H. H. "Debussy or Berg? The Mystery of a Chord Progression." *Musical Quarterly* 51 (1965):453–459.

Taylor, Eric. "Words and Music. Debussy: The Early Years." *Month* 215 (1963):30–38.

Thompson, Oscar. *Debussy, Man and Artist.* New York: Dodd, Mead, 1937.

Trevitt, John. "Debussy Inconnu." *Musical Times* 114 (1973):881–886, 1001–1005.

Vallas, Léon. *Claude Debussy et son temps.* Paris: Editions Albin Michel, 1958.

Vallas, Léon. *The Theories of Claude Debussy. Musicien Français.* Translated by Maire O'Brien. New York: Dover Publications, 1967.

———. "Debussy, Poète." *Les Nouvelles Littéraires,* 15 April 1933:10.

Vasnier, Marguerite. "Debussy à dix-huit ans." *Revue Musicale* 7 (1926):113–118.

Vincent, John. *The Diatonic Modes in Modern Music.* Los Angeles: University of California Press, 1951.

Weber, Edith, ed. *Debussy et l'Evolution de la Musique au XXe siècle.* Paris: Editions du Centre National de la Recherche Scientifique, 1965.

Wellesz, Egon. "Der Stil der letzten Werke Debussy." *Anbruch* 3 (1921):50–54.

Wenk, Arthur B. "Les sons et les parfums tournent dans l'air du soir." In "An Analysis of Debussy's Piano Preludes, Book I." Thesis. Cornell University, 1967, pp. 31–39.

———. "Claude Debussy and the Poets." Dissertation. Cornell University, 1970.

Wolff, Hellmuth Christian. "Melodische Urform und Gestaltveriation bei Debussy." *Deutsches Jahbuch der Musikwissenschaft* (1966):95–106.

D. POETRY AND MUSIC

Austin, William W. "Words and Music." In *Words and Music: The Composer's View.* Edited by Elliot Forbes. Cambridge, Massachusetts: Harvard University Press, 1972.

Barzun, Jacques. "Music into Words." *Score* 10 (December 1954):50–66.

Beaufils, Marcel. *Musique du Son, Musique du Verbe.* Paris: Presses Universitaires de France, 1954.

Boulez, Pierre. "Son et Verbe." *Relevés d'Apprenti.* Paris: Editions du Seuil, 1966, pp. 57–62.

Bright, William. "Language and Music: Areas for Cooperation." *Ethnomusicology* 7 (1963):26–32.

Brown, Calvin S. *Music and Literature. A Comparison of the Arts.* Athens: University of Georgia Press, 1948.

———. *Tones into Words. Musical Compositions as Subjects of Poetry.* Athens: University of Georgia Press, 1953.

Burnshaw, Stanley. *The Seamless Web.* New York: George Braziller, 1970.

Castelnuovo-Tedesco, Mario. "Problems of a Song-Writer." In *Reflections on Art.* Edited by Suzanne K. Langer, pp. 301–310.

Coeuroy, André. "La Musique aux Prises avec la Littérature." *Revue Musicale* 210 (January 1952):35–53.

Cohen, Gustave. "Musique et Poésie." *Mélanges d'histoire et d'esthétique musicales offerts à Paul-Marie Masson.* Paris: Richard-Mass-Editeur, 1955, pp. 15–19.

Cone, Edward T. "Words into Music: The Composer's Approach to the Text." In *Sound and Poetry.* Edited by Northrop Frye, pp. 3–15.

Cone, Edward T. *The Composer's Voice.* Berkeley: University of California Press, 1974.

Cooke, Deryck. *The Language of Music.* London: Oxford University Press, 1959.

Eliot, T. S. "The Music of Poetry." *On Poetry and Poets.* New York: Noonday Press, 1961, pp. 17–33.

Epperson, Gordon. *The Musical Symbol.* Ames: Iowa State University Press, 1967.

Finkelstein, Sidney. *How Music Expresses Ideas.* New York: International Publishers, 1952.

Fleming, William. *Arts and Ideas.* New York: Henry Holt, 1955.

Frye, Northrop, ed. *Sound and Poetry.* New York: Columbia University Press, 1956.

Georgiades, Thrasybulos. *Greek Music, Verse and Dance.* New York: Merlin Press, 1956?

———. *Schubert. Musik und Lyrik.* Göttingen: Vandenhoeck & Ruprecht, 1967.

Gostuski, Dragutin. "The Third Dimension of Poetic Expression, or Language and Harmony." *Musical Quarterly* 55 (1969):272–383.

Gray, Walter. "Some Aspects of Word Treatment in the Music of William Byrd." *Musical Quarterly* 55 (1969):45–64.

Hadow, W. H. "A Comparison of Poetry and Music." *Collected Essays.* London: Oxford University Press, 1928, pp. 220–237.

Hanslick, Eduard. *The Beautiful in Music.* Translated by Gustav Cohen. New York: Bobbs-Merrill, 1957.

Hollander, John. "The Music of Poetry." *Journal of Aesthetics and Art Criticism* 15 (1958):232–244.

———. *The Untuning of the Sky. Ideas of Music in English Poetry 1500–1700.* Princeton: Princeton University Press, 1961.

Hospers, John. *Meaning and Truth in the Arts.* Chapel Hill: University of North Carolina Press, 1946.

Huxley, Aldous. "Music at Night." *Music at Night and Other Essays.* London: Chatto and Windus, 1931, pp. 43–52.

Kerman, Joseph. "Why Bother with Words?" *High Fidelity Magazine* 13/7 (July 1963):39–41, 87.

La Motte, Diether de. "Analyse einer Wort-Ton-Komposition." *Musikalische Analyse.* Kassel: Bärenreiter, 1968, pp. 61–71.

Langer, Suzanne K. *Feeling and Form.* New York: Scribner's, 1953.

———. *Philosophy in a New Key.* Cambridge, Massachusetts: Harvard University Press, 1963.

———. *Reflections on Art. A Source Book of Writings by Artists, Critics, and Philosophers.* New York: Oxford University Press, Galaxy Books, 1961.

List, George. "The Boundaries of Speech and Song." *Ethnomusicology* 7 (1963):1–16.

Maag, Otto. "Musik und Sprache: Ein Versuch zur Sinndeutung der Musik." *Festschrift Karl Nef zum 60. Geburtstag.* Zürich: Hug, 1933, pp. 165–173.

Mace, Dean T. "Pietro Bembo and the Literary Origins of the Italian Madrigal." *Musical Quarterly* 55 (1969):65–86.

Magdics, Klára. "From the Melody of Speech to the Melody of Music." *Studia Musicologica* 4 (1963):325–346.

Meyer, Leonard B. *Emotion and Meaning in Music.* Chicago: University of Chicago Press, 1956.

Michel, André. *Psychanalyse de la Musique.* Paris: Presses Universitaires de France, 1951.

Peacock, Ronald. *The Art of Drama.* London: Routledge & Kegan Paul, 1957.

Peckham, Morse. *Man's Rage for Chaos. Biology, Behavior and the Arts.* New York: Schocken Books, 1967.

Petri, Horst. *Literatur und Musik. Form- und Strukturparallelen.* Göttingen: Sachse & Pohl Verlag, 1964.

Ronga, Luigi. *The Meeting of Poetry and Music.* Translated by Ekio Gianturco and Cara Rosanti. New York: Merlin Press, 1956.

Ruwet, Nicolas. "Fonction de la Parole dans la Musique Vocale." *Revue Belge de Musicologie* 15 (1961):8–28.

Sachs, Curt. *The Rise of Music in the Ancient World.* New York: Norton, 1943.

Seeger, Charles. "On the Moods of a Music-Logic." *Journal of the American Musicological Society* 13 (1960):224–261.

———. "On the Formational Apparatus of the Music Compositional Process." *Ethnomusicology* 13 (1969):230–247.

Selincourt, Basil de. "Music and Duration." In *Reflections on Art.* Edited by Suzanne K. Langer, pp. 152–160.

Siebeck, Herman. "Sprechmelodie und Tonmelodie in ihrem ästhetischen Verhältnis." *Riemann-Festschrift. Gesammelt Studien.* Leipzig: M. Hesse, 1909.

Siegmeister, Elie. "Words, Melody and Harmony." *Harmony and Melody*, vol. 1. Belmont, California: Wadsworth Publishing Company, 1965, pp. 410–423.

Springer, George P. "Language and Music: Parallels and Divergencies." *For Roman Jakobson.* The Hague: Mouton, 1956, pp. 504–513.

Staempoi, Edward. "Musik, Wort und Sprache." *Melos* 34:339–343.

Sternfeld, Frederick W. "Poetry and Music—Joyce's Ulysses." In *Sound and Poetry.* Edited by Northrop Frye, pp. 16–54.

Tippett, Michael. "Conclusion." In *A History of Song.* Edited by Denis Stevens. London: Hutchinson, 1960, pp. 461–466.

Van Waesberghe, J. Smits. "Phonetics in its Relation to Musicology." In *Manual of Phonetics.* Edited by L. Kaiser. Amsterdam: North-Holland Publishing Company, 1957, pp. 372–384.

Wellek, Albert. "Ueber das Verhältnis von Musik und Poesie." *Studien zur Musikwissenschaft* 25 (1962):574–585.

Westergaard, Peter. "Sung Language." *American Society of University Composers. Proceedings of the Second Annual Conference* (April 1967):9–36.

E. DEBUSSY'S MANUSCRIPTS

Most, but not all, of the manuscripts of Debussy's songs are located in Paris libraries. The following list is taken from an early edition of Vallas's book, Claude Debussy, *His Life and Works.* Since the publication of that work in English translation in 1933, some of the manuscripts have been transferred to the Annexe Musicale of the Bibliothèque Nationale. There seems to be no recent publication on the state and location of Debussy manuscripts.

Cinq Poèmes de Charles Baudelaire. Ms. Bibliothèque de la Conservatoire, Nos. 21–25 (voice and piano) and No. 3 (orchestration of *Le Jet d'eau*).

C'est l'extase *Chevaux de Bois* *Green* *Spleen*	Ms. chez Legouix
Deux Romances	Ms. Bibl. Cons. No. 46
La Flûte de Pan *La Chevelure*	Ms. Bibl. Cons. Collection Charles Malherbe

Fêtes galantes, second series. Vallas lists Ms. Bibl. Cons. No. 13; now BN Ms. 996.
Trois chansons de France. Vallas lists Ms. Bibl. Cons. No. 6; now BN Ms. 981.
La Promenoir des deux amants. Ms. Bibl. Cons. No. 38.
Trois chansons de Charles d'Orléans. Ms. Bibl. Cons. No. 5.
Trois ballades de François Villon. Ms. Bibl. Cons. No. 1.
Trois Poèmes de Stéphane Mallarmé. Ms. Bibl. Cons. No. 37.
Noël des enfants qui n'ont plus de maison. Ms. Bibl. Cons. No. 35.

Index